T0324209

To Nitza and Ariela

Zohar Manna
Department of Computer Science
Stanford University
Stanford,CA 94305 USA
Computer Science Department
Weizmann Institute of Science
Rehovot, 76100 Israel

Amir Pnueli
Computer Science Department
Weizmann Institute
Rehovot, 76100 Israel

Library of Congress Cataloging-in-Publication Data
Manna, Zohar.
   The temporal logic of reactive and concurrent systems / Zohar
Manna, Amir Pnueli.
      p. cm.
   Includes bibliographical references and index.
   Contents: v. 1. Specification
   ISBN 0-387-97664-7 (v. 1)
   1. Electronic digital computers --Programming. 2. Logic, Symbolic
and mathematical. I. Pnueli, A. II. Title.
   QA76.6.M3564   1991
   005.1 dc20   91-28181

Printed on acid-free paper.

Production managed by Karen Phillips; Manufacturing supervised by Robert Paella.
Camera-ready copy prepared from the authors' TEX file.
Printed and bound by R.R. Donnelley and Sons, Harrisonburg, VA.
Printed in the United States of America.

9 8 7 6 5 4 3 2 1

ISBN 0-387-97664-7 Springer-Verlag New York Berlin Heidelberg
ISBN 3-540-97664-7 Springer-Verlag Berlin Heidelberg New York

Zohar Manna   Amir Pnueli

The Temporal Logic of
Reactive and Concurrent Systems

Specification

With 96 Illustrations

Springer-Verlag

New York Berlin Heidelberg London Paris
Tokyo Hong Kong Barcelona Budapest

The Temporal Logic of
Reactive and Concurrent Systems

Preface

This book is about reactive programs, the systems they control, and a methodology for the formal specification, verification, and development of such programs, using the tool of temporal logic.

A *reactive program* is a program whose role is to maintain an ongoing interaction with its environment rather than to compute some final value on termination. The family of reactive programs includes most of the classes of programs whose correct and reliable construction is considered to be particularly challenging, including concurrent and real-time programs, embedded and process control programs, and operating systems.

A fundamental element in reactive programs is that of concurrency. By definition, a reactive program runs concurrently with its environment. Also most of the sample programs studied in this book are concurrent programs, which consist of several processes executed concurrently. The techniques presented are often used to specify and analyze the interaction between the concurrent components of such programs. We may therefore describe the subject matter of the book as the study and analysis of interaction, either between a program and its environment or between concurrent processes within a program.

As has been amply demonstrated in many case histories, the correct construction of reliable reactive programs is one of the most challenging programming activities. Seemingly innocuous small concurrent programs have been known to exhibit completely unanticipated behaviors that, in some cases, may lead to crashes of critical systems. This is why formal approaches to the development of correct programs, such as the one promoted in this book, are so essential to the area of reactive programs.

A *formal methodology* typically consists of several elements. One element is a specification language in which the anticipated requirements from a program can be formally specified. Another is a repertoire of proof methods by which the correctness of a proposed program, relative to the specification, can be formally verified. The advantages of a formal methodology are obvious. Formal specification forces the designers of a program to make early precise decisions about the major functionalities of the program and to remove ambiguities from the description of its expected behavior. Formal verification of a desired property guarantees that the property holds over all possible executions of the program.

As a specification language, we adopt temporal logic, which is an appropriate and convenient language for specifying the dynamic behavior of reactive programs and describing their properties. The main advantage of the temporal language is that it provides a succinct and natural expression of frequently occurring program properties using a set of special operators.

A considerable part of this volume is devoted to a comprehensive and self-contained introduction to temporal logic and the illustration of its use for specifying properties of reactive systems.

Intended Audience and Prerequisites

The book is intended for people who are interested in the design, construction, and analysis of reactive systems and who wish to learn the language of temporal logic and how to apply it to the specification, verification, and development of reactive systems.

The background assumed of our readers consists, on one hand, of some familiarity and experience with programming and programming languages, in particular, some acquaintance with the basic notions of concurrent execution of programs; and on the other hand, a reasonable understanding of first-order logic and the notions of validity and provability by deductive systems. No prior knowledge of temporal logic is assumed, and no detailed knowledge of any particular programming language is necessary, since these two topics are introduced here.

Contents

The book is partitioned into two volumes. The first volume, subtitled *Specification* and consisting of Chapters 1 to 4, presents a computational model and a programming language for reactive programs and the specification language of temporal logic. The second volume, subtitled *Verification* and consisting of Chapters 5 to 11, is dedicated to the presentation of proof methods for verifying that a given program satisfies its specification.

Chapter 1 introduces the computational model and the programming language. In the programming language, we make a special effort to give a comprehensive representation of the main mechanisms for communication and synchronization between concurrent processes. Consequently, the language allows processes to communicate both by shared variables and by message-passing. Our intention in this book is to present a uniform approach to communication within reactive programs, which is independent of the particular communication mechanisms employed. Consequently, we show how some central paradigms in concurrent programming, such as mutual exclusion or producer-consumer, can be programmed in terms of either shared variables or different versions of message-passing.

Chapter 2 further elaborates the computational model. The computational model used in the book represents concurrency by interleaving of atomic actions chosen, one at a time, from parallel processes. This chapter examines the question of how faithfully this representation corresponds to real concurrent execution of programs, in which several parallel statements execute at the same time. By imposing a syntactical restriction on the programs we study and introducing fairness requirements, we ensure exact correspondence between interleaved and real concurrent execution of a program.

Chapter 3 introduces the language of temporal logic, presenting its syntax and semantics. The temporal language contains two symmetric groups of temporal operators, one dealing with the future and the other with the past. We list and discuss many properties of the temporal operators. Formal means for the derivation of temporal properties are provided by a deductive proof system.

Chapter 4 explores the utility of temporal logic as a language for specifying properties of reactive programs. Program properties are classified into a hierarchy of classes, based on their expression in temporal logic. The most important classes are the classes of safety, response, and reactivity properties. For each class, we provide a comprehensive set of examples of commonly encountered program properties. We also explore the important topic of *modular specification*, where each module (process) of the program is independently specified.

This concludes Volume 1.

Volume 2 is dedicated to the presentation of techniques and heuristics for the verification of program properties expressed by temporal formulas. It is organized in three parts, presenting rules for the verification of properties that belong to the classes of safety, response, and reactivity. Chapters 5 to 7 deal with the verification of safety properties, Chapters 8 to 10 with the verification of response properties, and Chapter 11 with the remaining classes.

Teaching the Book

The material contained in the book can be used as a basis for computer science courses on several levels. Each volume is suitable for a one-semester course. The complete book has been taught in a two-semester course at Stanford University and the Weizmann Institute. Such a course can be given both at a senior undergraduate level and at a graduate level.

The Fast Track

There are several sections of Volume 1 that are not essential or central to the understanding of the main topics of the book. If one is interested in a course that covers less material, then these sections are the first candidates for dropping out altogether or assigning as independent reading.

In Chapter 1 these are Sections 1.2, 1.6, and 1.11. In Chapter 2, Sections 2.9

and 2.10 cover more-advanced and less-essential matters and are candidates for
skipping. In Chapter 4, Sections 4.7, 4.8, and 4.9 are less central than the others.

Problems

Each chapter concludes with a set of problems. Some of the problems are intended
to let the readers test their understanding of the material covered in the chapter.
Other problems introduce material that was not covered in the chapter. There
are problems that explore alternatives to the way some topics were introduced
and developed.

The problems are graded according to their difficulty. Difficult problems are
annotated by *. Research-level problems are annotated by **.

To indicate which problems pertain to a given portion of the text, we annotate
the text with references to the appropriate problems, and we provide a page
reference with each problem. In solving a problem, readers may use any results
that appeared in the text prior to the corresponding page reference. They may also
use the results of any previous problem and previous parts of the same problem.

A booklet containing answers to the problems is available to instructors.
Please contact the publisher directly.

Bibliography

Following each chapter, there is a brief bibliographic discussion mentioning some
of the research contributions relevant to the topics covered in the chapter. In spite
of our sincere effort to refer to all the important relevant works, we may have
missed some. We apologize for that omission and would welcome any corrections
and comments.

A Support System

We recommend to our readers a program, available on the Macintosh, that checks
the validity of propositional temporal formulas. This program can help with
exercises concerning temporal logic. For information about obtaining the system,
write to

Temporal Prover
Box 9215
Stanford, CA 94309

Acknowledgment

We wish to acknowledge the help of many colleagues and students in reading
the manuscript in its (almost infinite) number of versions and for their useful
comments and suggestions. Particularly helpful suggestions were made by Rajeev
Alur, Eddie Chang, Avraham Ginzburg, David Gries, Tom Henzinger, Daphne
Koller, Narciso Marti-Oliet, Roni Rosner, Richard Waldinger and Liz Wolf.

We would like to thank our students at Stanford University and the Weizmann Institute for their detailed comments and helpful criticisms.

For support of the research behind this book, we thank the Air Force Office of Scientific Research, the Defense Advanced Research Projects Agency, the National Science Foundation, and the European Community Esprit project.

Sarah Fliegelman has done a magnificent job of typesetting the book. The detailed technical knowledge and expertise, provided by TEX-wizard Joe Weening, have been invaluable.

Eric Muller spent long hours patiently preparing all the computer-generated diagrams, and Yehuda Barbut provided the hand-drawn sketches.

Rajeev Alur has been of special assistance in the preparation of problems for this volume and has written the booklet of solutions.

Roni Rosner was most helpful in the preparation of the bibliographic remarks.

We are particularly grateful to Carron Kirkwood for the design of the cover of the book.

Stanford University   Z.M.
Weizmann Institute   A.P.

Contents

Part I

Models of Concurrency

Chapter 1
Basic Models

Programs and the systems they control can be conceptually partitioned into transformational and reactive programs and systems.

A *transformational program* is the more conventional type of program, whose role is to produce a final result at the end of a terminating computation. Consequently, the useful view of a transformational program is to consider it as a (possibly multivalued) function from an initial state to a final state or a final result. It follows that transformational programs are appropriately specified by characterizing the relation between initial and final states. For such specifications, ordinary predicate logic provides an adequate formulation and reasoning tool.

The role of a *reactive program*, on the other hand, is not to produce a final result but to maintain some ongoing interaction with its environment. Examples of reactive programs are operating systems and programs controlling mechanical or chemical processes, such as a plane or a nuclear reactor. Some reactive programs are not expected to terminate. They cannot be specified by a relation between initial and final states, but must be specified in terms of their ongoing behavior. It is for the specification and analysis of such programs that the formalism of temporal logic, which is conceptually more complex than ordinary predicate logic, is recommended.

Often, a reactive program is strongly intertwined with the hardware system it controls. Different from the transformational case, where many programs are executed by a common and standard computer, the reactive case often consists of dedicated, sometimes special-purpose, hardware on which a single reactive program is permanently run. These cases are often referred to as "embedded systems," implying that the software component (program) is an integrated part of a complete system. Because of that, we refer to our subject of study as *reactive systems*, and we prefer not to make a sharp distinction between the program and the system it controls. In fact, most of the techniques we propose and discuss are applicable, with very few changes, to pure hardware systems and have been successfully used for the specification and verification of digital circuits.

This book is also about concurrency. The notions of reactivity and concurrency are closely related. For example, a good way to explain the difference between transformational and reactive programs is that, in the transformational case, the program and its environment act sequentially, while in the reactive case they act concurrently.

Indeed, an execution of a *transformational* program can be viewed as consisting of three consecutive activities. First, the environment prepares an input. Then, the program performs its computation until it terminates, with no intervention from the environment. Lastly, the environment uses the output generated by the program. In the *reactive* case, we do not enjoy such an orderly sequence of the program and the environment, each acting in its turn. The environment may present new inputs and attempt to use outputs at the same time the program tries to read and write them. One of the main concerns of reactive programming is that, if the program is not fast enough, it may miss some deadlines or fail to respond to or sense important events. Thus, an important characterization of the reactive case is that it describes the situation in which the program and its environment act concurrently, rather than sequentially.

Another point of correlation between reactivity and concurrency is that in any program containing *parallel processes*, i.e., processes running concurrently, it is essential to study and analyze each process as a reactive program. This is because, from the point of view of each process, the rest of the program can be viewed as an environment that continuously interacts with the process. Thus, we may have a program that in its entirety has a transformational role, i.e., it is expected to terminate with a final result. Yet, because it is constructed from parallel processes, it should be analyzed as a reactive program.

In the literature on the formal development and analysis of reactive systems, we find a rich variety of programming languages, each having its own mechanisms for communication and coordination between the program and its environment, or between concurrent components in the program. Some of the constructs offered for communication are based on shared variables, message passing, or remote procedure calls, and some of the available constructs for coordination are semaphores, critical regions, monitors, handshaking, rendezvous, and asynchronous transmissions.

In this chapter we introduce a generic (abstract) model for reactive systems, which provides an abstract setting that enables a uniform treatment of all these constructs. The theory of specification and verification of reactive systems will be formulated in terms of the generic model. This approach makes the theory applicable to most of the currently existing programming languages and their constructs, and probably to many languages that will be proposed in the future.

We therefore begin by presenting our generic model of basic transition systems. We then show how it can be mapped onto concrete programming languages with specific communication and coordination constructs, as well as other formalisms suggested for representing concurrency, such as Petri nets. Our main vehicle for representing a concrete set of programming, communication, and coordination constructs is a programming language, which we introduce in this chapter. This illustration language, modeled after several existing languages that allow concurrency, offers several different mechanisms for communication and coordination between concurrent processes. In the next chapter, we will augment the basic model by adding requirements of fairness, and we discuss the appropriate fairness requirements that should be associated with the various communication and coordination constructs.

In the following chapters, we will present a general theory of specification and verification of reactive systems. The specification language and proof principles are formulated in terms of the generic model. However, they are illustrated by typical examples expressed in our programming language.

1.1 The Generic Model

The main part of the generic model of reactive systems is given by a basic transition system. This part of the model captures the basic concepts of the state of the system and the elementary actions (transitions) that modify the state in the course of a computation. In the next chapter, we augment the model of basic transition system by the additional concept of fairness to obtain the full model of transition systems.

The Underlying Language

To express the syntax of a basic transition system, we use an underlying first-order language with the following elements:

- $\mathcal{V}$ — Vocabulary.

The *vocabulary* consists of a countable set of typed variables. Some of these variables range over data domains used in programs, such as booleans, integers, or lists. Other variables may be used to indicate progress in the execution of a program; they may range over locations in the program.

The *type* of each variable indicates the *domain* over which the variable ranges, e.g., a data variable may range over the natural numbers, and a control variable that refers to the progress of the program may range over a finite set of locations.

We partition the variables into rigid and flexible variables. A *rigid* variable must have the same value in all states of a computation, while a *flexible* variable may assume different values in different states. All the data and control variables in the program will be flexible. We will use rigid variables mainly for specification purposes in order to compare the values assumed by a flexible variable in different states. The use of rigid variables for specification will be demonstrated in Chapters 3 and 4.

- $\mathcal{E}$ — Expressions.

Expressions are constructed from the variables of $\mathcal{V}$ and constants (such as 0, Λ (empty list), and ϕ (empty set)) to which functions (such as $+$, $\bullet$ (appending an element to a list), and $\cup$) and predicates (such as $>$, *null* (a list is empty), and $\subseteq$) over the appropriate domains (such as integers, lists, and sets) are applied. For example,

$$x + 3y, \qquad hd(u) \bullet tl(v), \qquad \text{and} \qquad A \cup B$$

are expressions. Expressions are also typed according to the domain over which their values range.

Expressions whose values range over the boolean domain $\{\text{F}, \text{T}\}$ are called *boolean expressions*. For example,

$$\neg(x > y) \wedge ((z = 0) \vee (u \subseteq v))$$

is a boolean expression.

- $\mathcal{A}$ — Assertions.

Assertions are constructed out of boolean expressions using boolean connectives and quantification ($\forall, \exists$) over some variables that appear in the expressions. For example,

$$\forall x: \left[(x > 0) \rightarrow \exists y: (x = y \cdot y) \right]$$

is an assertion.

- $\mathcal{I}$ — Interpretations.

An *interpretation* $I \in \mathcal{I}$ of a set of typed variables $V \subseteq \mathcal{V}$ is a mapping that assigns to each variable $y \in V$ a value $I[y]$ in the domain of y. The assignment of values to variables provided by I is uniquely extended to an assignment of values to expressions and assertions in the following way:

For an expression e, denote by $I[e]$ the value obtained by evaluating e, using the value $I[y]$ for each variable y appearing in e. Thus, if I is given by

$$I: \langle x: 1, \ y: 2, \ z: 3 \rangle,$$

then $I[y] = 2$ and $I[x + y \cdot z] = 7$.

In the case that φ is a boolean expression or, more generally, an assertion, then $I[\varphi] \in \{\text{F}, \text{T}\}$. If $I[\varphi] = \text{T}$, we say that I *satisfies* φ and write

$$I \models \varphi.$$

In the case that φ is an assertion that contains quantifiers, interpretation I need only provide values for the free variables of φ in order to determine whether $I \models \varphi$ holds. This is because, for evaluating a quantified formula such as $\exists x : \varphi(x)$, it is immaterial how I interprets the bound variable x or whether it interprets it at all. Thus, working over the domain of natural numbers, we can claim that $\langle x : 9 \rangle \models \exists y : (x = y^2)$ holds and $\langle x : 8 \rangle \models \exists y : (x = y^2)$ does not, even though neither of these interpretations assigns any value to y.

An interpretation I can also be applied to a list of expressions $(e_1, \ldots, e_n)$, yielding a list of values

$$I\big[(e_1, \ldots, e_n)\big] \;=\; \big(I[e_1], \ldots, I[e_n]\big).$$

Basic Transition System

A *basic transition system* $\langle \Pi, \Sigma, \mathcal{T}, \Theta \rangle$, intended to represent a reactive program, is given by the following components:

- $\Pi = \{u_1, \ldots, u_n\} \subseteq \mathcal{V}$ — A finite set of flexible *state variables*.

  Some of these flexible variables represent *data variables*, which are explicitly declared and manipulated by statements in the program. Other variables are *control variables*, which represent progress in the execution of the program by indicating, for example, locations in the program or statements about to be executed.

- Σ — A set of states.

  Each *state* s in Σ is an interpretation of Π, assigning to each variable u in Π a value over its domain, which we denote by $s[u]$. A state s that satisfies an assertion φ, i.e., $s \models \varphi$, is sometimes referred to as a φ-*state*.

- $\mathcal{T}$ — A finite set of transitions.

  Each *transition* τ in $\mathcal{T}$ represents a state-transforming action of the system and is defined as a function $\tau : \Sigma \to 2^\Sigma$ that maps a state s in Σ into the (possibly empty) set of states $\tau(s)$ that can be obtained by applying action τ to state s. Each state s' in $\tau(s)$ is defined to be a τ-*successor* of s. It is required that one of the transitions, τ_I, called the *idling transition*, is an identity transition, i.e., $\tau_I(s) = \{s\}$ for every state s.

- Θ — An *initial condition*.

  This assertion characterizes the states at which execution of the program can begin. A state s satisfying Θ, i.e., $s \models \Theta$, is called an *initial state*.

The Transition Relation ρ_τ

Each transition τ is characterized by an assertion, called the *transition relation*

$$\rho_\tau(\Pi,\ \Pi').$$

This assertion relates the values of the state variables in a state s to their values in a successor state s' obtained by applying τ to s. The assertion refers to the state variables using two copies of the set of variables $\Pi = \{u_1, \ldots, u_n\}$. An occurrence of u refers to the value of u in s, while an occurrence of u' refers to the value of u in s'. We call u' the *primed version* of u and denote the set of primed versions of all the state variables by $\Pi' = \{u'_1, \ldots, u'_n\}$.

While more general forms are possible, we use transition relations of the form

$$\rho_\tau(\Pi,\ \Pi'):\quad C_\tau(\Pi)\ \wedge\ (y'_1 = e_1)\ \wedge\ \cdots\ \wedge\ (y'_k = e_k).$$

Such a transition relation consists of the following elements:

- An *enabling condition* $C_\tau(\Pi)$, which is an assertion, stating the condition under which the state s may have a τ-successor.

- A conjunction of *modification statements*

$$(y'_1 = e_1)\ \wedge\ \cdots\ \wedge\ (y'_k = e_k),$$

  where $y_i \in \Pi$, for $i = 1, \ldots, k$, and each expression e_i refers only to unprimed state variables. The variables $y_1, \ldots, y_k$ are pairwise distinct. Each modification statement $y'_i = e_i$ requires that the value of y_i in s' be equal to the value of e_i in s.

We refer to the set of variables $Y = \{y_1, \ldots, y_k\}$ as the *modifiable variables* of ρ_τ.

As an example, for $\Pi = \{x, y, z\}$, the transition relation

$$\rho_{\widehat{\tau}}:\quad (x > 0)\ \wedge\ (z' = x + y)$$

requires that x be positive in s and that the value of z in s' equal the value of $x + y$ in s.

Let τ be a transition with transition relation ρ_τ. A state s has a τ-successor, i.e., $\tau(s) \neq \phi$, iff $s \vDash C_\tau$, that is, C_τ is true when evaluated over s.

If s has τ-successors, it has at most one successor s', i.e., $\tau(s) = \{s'\}$, which is uniquely determined by requiring

- $s'[y_i] = s[e_i]$, for each $i = 1, \ldots, k$. That is, the value of y_i at s' equals the value of e_i when evaluated over s.

- For each $u \in \Pi - Y$, $s'[u] = s[u]$. That is, unmodifiable state variables have identical values in s and in s'.

Thus, for the form of transition relations considered here, $|\tau(s)| \leq 1$ for all τ, s.

Reconsider the example of the transition $\widehat{\tau}$, where $\Pi = \{x, y, z\}$, and $\rho_{\widehat{\tau}}$: $(x > 0) \wedge (z' = x + y)$. Then the state

$$s': \quad \langle x: 1, \ y: 2, \ z: 3 \rangle$$

is a $\widehat{\tau}$-successor of the state

$$s: \quad \langle x: 1, \ y: 2, \ z: 4 \rangle.$$

On the other hand, the state $\widehat{s}: \langle x: 0, y: 2, z: 3 \rangle$ has no $\widehat{\tau}$-successor, since the enabling condition $x > 0$ fails to hold on $\widehat{s}$.

Different formulas may represent the same transition. For example, the two formulas

$$\rho_1: (x > 0) \ \wedge \ (z' = x + y) \qquad \text{and} \qquad \rho_2: (x > 0) \ \wedge \ (z' = x + y) \ \wedge \ (x' = x)$$

represent the same transition. This is because the explicit information contained in ρ_2 but not in ρ_1 is that the state variable x retains its value from s to s'. However, the preservation of x is implicitly stated in ρ_1 by the fact that ρ_1 does not contain x as a modifiable variable.

In general, let ρ_1 be a transition relation with modifiable variables Y_1 and ρ_2 be a formula obtained from ρ_1 by adding one or more conjuncts of the form $x' = x$ for $x \in \Pi - Y_1$. Then clearly, ρ_1 and ρ_2 define the same transition relation. We observe that Y_2, the set of modifiable variables for ρ_2, contains Y_1 and all the variables appearing in the added conjuncts.

In particular, for every transition relation ρ_τ, there exists an equivalent relation ρ_τ^+ in which the set of modifiable variables is the full set Π of state variables. We refer to ρ_τ^+ as the *full transition relation* of τ.

For example, the full transition relation for the transition $\widehat{\tau}$ considered earlier is

$$(x > 0) \ \wedge \ (x' = x) \ \wedge \ (y' = y) \ \wedge \ (z' = x + y).$$

In general discussions concerning transition relations, we often represent the transition relation ρ_τ as

$$\rho_\tau: \quad C_\tau(\Pi) \ \wedge \ (\overline{y}' = \overline{e}),$$

where $\overline{y}' = (y'_1, \ldots, y'_k)$ is the list of primed modifiable variables, $\overline{e} = (e_1, \ldots, e_k)$ is the list of expressions, and the equation $\overline{y}' = \overline{e}$ represents the conjunction

$$(y'_1 = e_1) \ \wedge \ \cdots \ \wedge \ (y'_k = e_k).$$

Enabled and Disabled Transitions

For a transition τ in T and a state s in Σ, we say that:

- τ is *enabled* on s if $\tau(s) \neq \phi$, that is, s has a τ-successor.

- τ is *disabled* on s if $\tau(s) = \phi$, that is, s has no τ-successors.

Clearly, if τ is associated with the transition relation ρ_τ: $C_\tau \wedge (\overline{y}'_\tau = \overline{e})$, then τ is enabled on s iff $s \vDash C_\tau$.

For a set of transitions $T \subseteq \mathcal{T}$ and a state s in Σ, we say that:

- T is *enabled* on s if some τ in T is enabled on s.

- T is *disabled* on s if all τ in T are disabled on s.

A state s is called *terminal* if the only transition that is enabled on s is the idling transition τ_I.

Idling and Diligent Transitions

The idling transition τ_I is intended to model periods in the behavior of the program in which there is no change. This convention is particularly useful for representing all computations, including terminating ones, as infinite sequences of states, since the idling transition may be indefinitely applied to a terminal state. This convention considerably simplifies the analysis of programs.

The transition relation associated with the idling transition τ_I is given by

$$\rho_{\tau_I}: \text{T}.$$

This is consistent with the requirement that $\tau_I(s) = \{s\}$, that is, under an idling transition, all state variables remain unchanged.

If s' is a τ_I-successor of a state s, we refer to it as an *idling successor* of s.

The transitions other than the idling transition are called *diligent transitions*. We denote the set of diligent transitions by

$$\mathcal{T}_D \;=\; \mathcal{T} - \{\tau_I\}.$$

Computations

A *computation* of a basic transition system $\langle \Pi, \Sigma, \mathcal{T}, \Theta \rangle$ is defined to be an infinite sequence of states

$$\sigma: \quad s_0, \; s_1, \; s_2, \; \ldots$$

satisfying the following requirements:

- *Initiation*:   The first state s_0 is initial, i.e., $s_0 \vDash \Theta$.

- *Consecution*:   For each pair of consecutive states s_i, s_{i+1} in σ, $s_{i+1} \in \tau(s_i)$ for some transition τ in $\mathcal{T}$. That is, s_{i+1} is a τ-successor of s_i. We refer to the pair s_i, s_{i+1} as a *τ-step*. Note that it is possible for a given pair to be both a τ-step and a τ'-step for $\tau \neq \tau'$.

- *Diligence*: Either the sequence contains infinitely many diligent steps (i.e., τ-steps for τ in $\mathcal{T}_\mathrm{D}$) or it contains a terminal state. Clearly, all successors of a terminal state can only be idling successors. This requirement excludes sequences in which, even though some diligent transition τ in $\mathcal{T}_\mathrm{D}$ is enabled, only idling steps are taken beyond some point. A computation that contains a terminal state is called a *terminating computation*.

A *computation prefix* is a finite sequence of states

$$s_0, \; s_1, \; \ldots, \; s_m \; .$$

satisfying the requirements of initiation and consecution but not necessarily that of diligence. Obviously, every finite prefix of a computation is a computation prefix.

We refer to the indices i of states in a computation σ as *positions*. If $\tau(s_i) \neq \phi$ (τ enabled on s_i) we say that transition τ is *enabled* at position i of σ. If $s_{i+1} \in \tau(s_i)$ we say that transition τ is *taken* at position i. Note that several transitions may be considered to be taken at the same position.

A state s is called *reachable* (*accessible*) in the basic transition system if it appears in some computation of the system.

As we have seen, every basic transition system has a built-in initial condition Θ, and all computations must start in a Θ-state. In some cases we want to further restrict the set of considered computations. For an assertion φ and a basic transition system, we define a φ-*computation* of the transition system to be any computation whose initial state also satisfies φ.

We often display computations (and computation prefixes) as a sequence of states connected by arrows that are labeled by the transitions that cause the system to move to the next state. Thus, a presentation of a computation as

$$s_0 \xrightarrow{\;\tau_0\;} s_1 \xrightarrow{\;\tau_1\;} s_2 \longrightarrow \cdots$$

provides, in addition to the fact that $s_0, s_1, \ldots$ is a computation, the identity of the transition $\tau_i \in \mathcal{T}$ leading from s_i to s_{i+1}.

With this notation we can reformulate the definition of a computation by saying that the infinite sequence

$$s_0, \; s_1, \; s_2, \; \ldots$$

is a computation if transitions $\tau_0, \tau_1, \ldots$ exist such that

$$s_0 \xrightarrow{\;\tau_0\;} s_1 \xrightarrow{\;\tau_1\;} s_2 \longrightarrow \cdots \; ,$$

s_0 satisfies Θ, and either infinitely many transitions are different from τ_I or the computation has the form

$$s_0 \xrightarrow{\;\tau_0\;} s_1 \longrightarrow \cdots \longrightarrow s_k \xrightarrow{\;\tau_I\;} s_k \xrightarrow{\;\tau_I\;} s_k \longrightarrow \cdots$$

where s_k is terminal.

Concrete Models

Next we present several concrete models of reactive systems and show the correspondence between the abstract entities defined earlier and their concrete counterparts. Each concrete model is characterized by a programming language consisting of the syntax of programs in the model and a semantics, which explains the meaning of a program by mapping it into a corresponding basic transition system.

We will be mainly using two programming languages, a diagram language and a text language. The *diagram language* is a certain variation of flowchart diagrams, extended to provide a graphical representation of concurrent programs. The *text language* is a structured programming language, borrowing notations and constructs from several existing programming languages, such as Pascal, CSP, and Ada.

There is a degree of independence between the syntax and semantics of a model. Thus, on one hand, the semantic idea of nondeterministic selection between possible actions can be represented by completely different syntax in the diagram and text languages. On the other hand, identical syntax, such as **send**(m, α), implying the sending of message m on channel α, can be given significantly different semantic interpretations in different models.

The mapping of the generic model to a concrete one defines for each concrete program the set of computations that represents its possible executions.

We prefer to base our first presentation of concrete models on the simpler syntax of the diagram language. At a later stage we will consider text languages that provide a more structured representation of programs.

1.2   Model 1: Transition Diagrams

The language of transition diagrams provides a convenient presentation of simple concurrent programs. Transition diagrams resemble flowcharts in having nodes and directed edges connecting them, but differ from flowcharts in having the actions associated with the edges rather than with the nodes.

In the transition-diagram language, a *program* P has the following form:

$$P :: \ [\text{declaration}] \ [P_1 \| \ldots \| P_m]$$

where $P_1, \ldots, P_m$, $m \geq 1$, are *processes*.

The program refers to a set of *data variables* $Y = \{y_1, \ldots, y_n\}$, $n \geq 1$, which are declared at the head of the program and are accessible to all the processes for reference and modification.

Declarations

The *declaration* appearing at the head of the program specifies the modes and the types of the data variables and the initial conditions that they satisfy on initiation.

A declaration consists of several *declaration statements* of the form

mode variable, ..., variable: type **where** φ_i.

The *mode* of each declaration statement may be one of the following

in — Specifies variables that are inputs to the program.

local — Specifies variables that are local to the program. These variables are used in the execution of the program, but are not recognized outside the program.

out — Specifies variables that are outputs of the program.

The program is not allowed to modify (i.e., assign new values to) variables that are declared as **in** variables. The distinction between modes **local** and **out** is mainly intended to help in the understanding of the program and has no particular formal significance.

The list

variable, ..., variable: type,

that appears in each declaration statement, lists several variables that share a common type and identifies their type, i.e., the domain over which the variables range. We use *basic types* such as **integer** and **character**, as well as *structured types* such as **array**, **list**, and **set**.

Declaration statements with no explicit mode specification retain the mode of the preceding statement. Thus, we may have a sequence of declaration statements of mode **in**, only the first of which explicitly contains the **in** specification.

The assertion φ_i, which appears in a declaration statement, imposes constraints on the initial values of some of the variables declared in this statement. For a declaration statement of mode **in**, φ_i may be an arbitrary assertion over the input variables, restricting the set of inputs for which the program is expected to behave correctly. The role of φ_i in declarations of modes **local** and **out** is to specify initial values for the local and output variables. For declarations of these modes, φ_i must be a conjunction of equalities of the form $u = e$, where u is one of the variables declared in this statement and e is an expression that may depend only on the input variables. We allow a conjunction, such as $(x = 5) \land (y = 1)$, to be represented as a list of equalities, such as $x = 5$, $y = 1$.

Assertion φ_i may be omitted from a declaration statement if no constraint is imposed on the variables declared in this statement.

Let $\varphi_1, \ldots, \varphi_n$ be the assertions appearing in the declaration statements of a program. We refer to the conjunction

$$\varphi = \varphi_1 \wedge \cdots \wedge \varphi_n$$

as the *data precondition* of the program.

For example, in the declaration

> **in** k, n : **integer where** $0 \leq k \leq n$
>
> **local** y_1, y_2: **integer where** $y_1 = n \,\wedge\, y_2 = 1$
>
> **out** b : **integer where** $b = 1$

the data precondition is

$$\varphi: \ \ 0 \leq k \leq n \,\wedge\, y_1 = n \,\wedge\, y_2 = 1 \,\wedge\, b = 1.$$

To give an explicit representation to the data precondition φ, we often use

$$P :: \ [\text{declaration } \mathbf{where} \ \varphi] \ [P_1 \| \ldots \| P_m]$$

as a schematic representation of a program.

Processes

Each process P_i, $i = 1, \ldots, m$, is represented by a transition diagram, which is a directed graph.

The nodes in the diagram are referred to as *locations*. The locations of process P_i are usually called $\ell_0^i, \ell_1^i, \ldots, \ell_{t_i}^i$. One of these locations, ℓ_0^i, is designated as the entry location, and another location, $\ell_{t_i}^i$, may be designated as the exit location. Exit locations have no outgoing edges. The sets of locations of the different processes are disjoint. Let L_i denote the set of locations of process P_i.

The edges in the diagram for each process are labeled with (*atomic*) *instructions*, which have the form of a *guarded assignment*

$$c \ \rightarrow \ [\bar{y} := \bar{e}]$$

in which c is a boolean expression called the *guard* of the instruction, $\bar{y} = (y_1, \ldots, y_k)$ is a list of data variables, and $\bar{e} = (e_1, \ldots, e_k)$ a list of expressions. The two lists have equal lengths and the type of each e_i matches the type of y_i. The variables appearing in $\bar{y}$ must be declared at the head of the program as either local or output variables. All the variables appearing in condition c and expressions $e_1, \ldots, e_k$ must be declared at the head of the program. The intended meaning of such an instruction is that if c is true the edge may be traversed while simultaneously assigning the values of $\bar{e} = (e_1, \ldots, e_k)$ to $\bar{y} = (y_1, \ldots, y_k)$. The instructions labeling edges in a process are called the *instructions* of the process.

With this set of instructions, communication between the processes is managed via *shared variables*, i.e., one process writing a value into a variable, which another process later reads.

To describe the full state of a program, we need, in addition to the data variables, control variables $\pi_1, \ldots, \pi_m$. Each variable π_i points to the current location of control within process P_i. This is where P_i looks for the next instruction to be performed. Each π_i ranges over L_i, the set of locations belonging to P_i.

Diagrams as Basic Transition Systems

We now identify the four components of a basic transition system — state variables Π, states Σ, transitions $\mathcal{T}$, and initial condition Θ, for the diagram language.

- *State Variables*

  As the set of state variables we take all the control and data variables, i.e.,

  $$\Pi = \{\pi_1, \ldots, \pi_m, y_1, \ldots, y_n\}.$$

- *States*

  As states we take all possible interpretations that assign to the state variables values over their respective domains. The domain of each control variable π_i is the set of locations L_i, and the domain of each data variable is determined by its type as prescribed in the declaration.

- *Transitions*

  The idling transition τ_I is defined by the transition relation

  $$\rho_I\colon \ \text{T}.$$

The diligent transitions correspond to the labeled edges that appear within the processes. Let α be an edge connecting location ℓ to location $\tilde{\ell}$ in process P_i and labeled by the instruction $c \to [\bar{y} := \bar{e}]$.

$$\underset{\alpha}{\overset{c \,\to\, [\bar{y} \,:=\, \bar{e}]}{\ell \xrightarrow{\hspace{3cm}} \tilde{\ell}}}$$

The transition τ associated with α is defined by

$$\rho_\tau\colon \ \ (\pi_i = \ell) \ \wedge \ c \ \wedge \ (\pi'_i = \tilde{\ell}) \ \wedge \ (\bar{y}' = \bar{e}).$$

Thus, transition τ is enabled in a state s if the current location of P_i in s is ℓ and the value of the boolean expression c is true, that is, $s[\pi_i] = \ell$ and $s[c] = \text{T}$. When performed, τ modifies the state by assigning $\tilde{\ell}$ to π_i and $s[\bar{e}]$ to $\bar{y}$, that is, τ leads to a state s' in which $s'[\pi_i] = \tilde{\ell}$ and $s'[\bar{y}] = s[\bar{e}]$.

• *Initial Condition*

Let the program P have the form

$$[\text{declaration } \textbf{where } \varphi] \ [P_1 \| \ldots \| P_m].$$

The initial condition for this program is given by

$$\Theta: \quad \varphi \wedge \bigwedge_{i=1}^{m} (\pi_i = \ell_0^i).$$

This definition claims that, in each initial state, the data precondition holds, and for each $i = 1, \ldots, m$, the value of π_i, the control variable of process P_i is the entry location of P_i.

If for some edge α belonging to a process P_i the transition associated with α is enabled on a state s, we say that P_i is *enabled* on s. Otherwise P_i is *disabled* on s.

Example (binomial coefficient)

Consider the following concurrent program BINOM (Fig. 1.1) for computing the binomial coefficient $\binom{n}{k}$ for integers n and k, where $0 \leq k \leq n$.

The program has two input variables k, n assumed to satisfy $0 \leq k \leq n$, two local variables y_1 and y_2 assumed to be preset to n and 1, respectively, and one output variable b assumed to be preset to 1. Note that the local initial condition is presented as a list (rather than a conjunction) of equalities.

We have adopted some abbreviations for the case in which an instruction does not have both a guard and an assignment part. Instructions whose lists of expressions and assigned variables are empty, i.e., of the form $c \rightarrow [(\ ) := (\ )]$, are abbreviated to $c?$. Clearly, these instructions only test the value of c, but do not assign values to data variables. Instructions whose guard is always true, i.e., of the form $\textsc{t} \rightarrow [\bar{y} := \bar{e}]$, are abbreviated to $\bar{y} := \bar{e}$.

The computation of the binomial coefficient in this program follows the formula

$$\binom{n}{k} = \frac{n \cdot (n-1) \cdot \ldots \cdot (n-k+1)}{1 \cdot \quad 2 \quad \cdot \ldots \cdot \quad k}.$$

Process P_1 computes the numerator of this formula by successively multiplying into b the factors n, $n-1$, ..., $n-k+1$. These factors are successively computed in variable y_1. Process P_2, responsible for the denominator, successively divides b by the factors 1, 2, ..., k, using the integer-division operator **div**. These factors are successively computed in variable y_2.

We have chosen the **div** operator instead of a general division in order to keep the computation restricted to the domain of the integers. However, for the algorithm to be correct, it is necessary that whenever **div** is applied it yields no

$$\textbf{in} \quad k,\ n \ : \textbf{integer where } 0 \leq k \leq n$$
$$\textbf{local } y_1,\ y_2: \textbf{integer where } y_1 = n,\ y_2 = 1$$
$$\textbf{out} \quad b \qquad : \textbf{integer where } b = 1$$

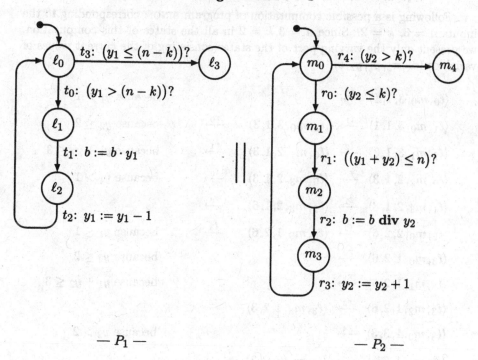

$$- P_1 - \qquad\qquad\qquad\qquad - P_2 -$$

Fig. 1.1.   Program BINOM (binomial coefficient) — transition diagram.

remainder. We rely here on a general property of the integers by which a product of m consecutive integers is evenly divisible by $m!$. Thus, b should be divided by y_2, which completes the stage of dividing b by $y_2!$, only when at least y_2 factors have already been multiplied into b by P_1. Since P_1 multiplies b by n, $n-1$, etc., and y_1 holds the value of the next factor to be multiplied, the number of factors that have been multiplied into b is at least $n - y_1$. Therefore, y_2 divides b as soon as $y_2 \leq n - y_1$, or equivalently, $y_1 + y_2 \leq n$. This condition appearing on edge r_1 ensures that b is divided by y_2 only when it is safe to do so.

To illustrate the concepts of states and computations as they apply to the diagram language, let us consider a computation of program BINOM for particular inputs.

The variables in this program are the control variables π_1, π_2 pointing to locations in P_1 and P_2, and the data variables consisting of inputs n, k, local variables y_1, y_2, and output b. Hence a full representation of a state of the BINOM program is a tuple of seven elements representing the current values of the variables $\langle \pi_1, \pi_2, n, k, y_1, y_2, b \rangle$.

Following is a possible computation of program BINOM corresponding to the inputs $n = 3$, $k = 2$. Since $n = 3, k = 2$ in all the states of this computation, we present only the varying part of the states consisting of the current values of variables $\langle \pi_1, \pi_2, y_1, y_2, b \rangle$.

$\langle \ell_0, m_0, 3, 1, 1 \rangle \xrightarrow{t_0}$ because $y_1 > 1$

$\langle \ell_1, m_0, 3, 1, 1 \rangle \xrightarrow{t_1} \langle \ell_2, m_0, 3, 1, 3 \rangle \xrightarrow{r_0}$ because $y_2 \leq 2$

$\langle \ell_2, m_1, 3, 1, 3 \rangle \xrightarrow{t_2} \langle \ell_0, m_1, 2, 1, 3 \rangle \xrightarrow{r_1}$ because $y_1 + y_2 \leq 3$

$\langle \ell_0, m_2, 2, 1, 3 \rangle \xrightarrow{r_2} \langle \ell_0, m_3, 2, 1, 3 \rangle \xrightarrow{t_0}$ because $y_1 > 1$

$\langle \ell_1, m_3, 2, 1, 3 \rangle \xrightarrow{t_1} \langle \ell_2, m_3, 2, 1, 6 \rangle \xrightarrow{r_3}$

$\langle \ell_2, m_0, 2, 2, 6 \rangle \xrightarrow{t_2} \langle \ell_0, m_0, 1, 2, 6 \rangle \xrightarrow{t_3}$ because $y_1 \leq 1$

$\langle \ell_3, m_0, 1, 2, 6 \rangle \xrightarrow{r_0}$ because $y_2 \leq 2$

$\langle \ell_3, m_1, 1, 2, 6 \rangle \xrightarrow{r_1}$ because $y_1 + y_2 \leq 3$

$\langle \ell_3, m_2, 1, 2, 6 \rangle \xrightarrow{r_2} \langle \ell_3, m_3, 1, 2, 3 \rangle \xrightarrow{r_3}$

$\langle \ell_3, m_0, 1, 3, 3 \rangle \xrightarrow{r_4}$ because $y_2 > 2$

$\langle \ell_3, m_4, 1, 3, 3 \rangle \xrightarrow{\tau_I} \langle \ell_3, m_4, 1, 3, 3 \rangle \xrightarrow{\tau_I} \cdots .$

In this sequence, we labeled the arrows leading from one state to its successor by the names of the transitions that are responsible for the step.

This is only one of the computations that program BINOM can generate. Other computations correspond to different choices of the next transition to be taken. In particular, the computation in which transitions of P_1 are taken before any transition of P_2 is attempted is also possible. A nice feature of program BINOM is that it is *determinate*, i.e., there exists a single terminal state, namely, $\langle \ell_3, m_4, 1, 3, 3 \rangle$, to which all computations eventually converge.

Note that this computation applies idling transition τ_I only after the program terminated by attaining the terminal state $\langle \ell_3, m_4, 1, 3, 3 \rangle$. This is only one possibility, and computations in which idling and nonidling transitions intersperse more liberally are equally acceptable. ∎

A program is defined to be *process-deterministic* if every two guards c_1 and c_2 that label two edges departing from the same location are exclusive, i.e., $c_1 \wedge c_2$ is contradictory (never true). Program BINOM is process-deterministic.

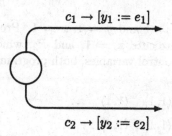

In a process-deterministic program, each process has at most one transition that is enabled on any state. However, the computation is still not uniquely determined since several transitions from different processes may be enabled on a given state.

Representing Concurrency by Interleaving

A most important element of modeling reactive systems by transition systems is that *concurrency* is represented by *interleaving*. Thus, an execution of a program that contains two parallel processes is represented by interleaved execution of the atomic instructions of the participating processes. This approach can be viewed as a reduction of concurrency to nondeterminism, where a given concurrent execution gives rise to many possible corresponding interleaving orders.

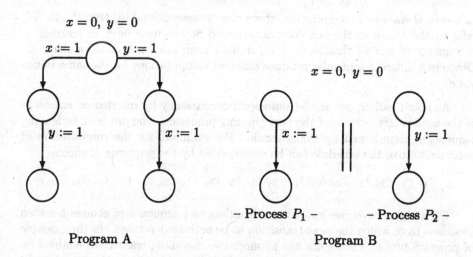

Fig. 1.2. Programs A and B.

Consider, for example, the two programs A and B in Fig. 1.2. Program A consists of a single process that can choose nondeterministically between execution of the sequences $x := 1$, $y := 1$ and $y := 1$, $x := 1$. Program B consists of two processes, P_1, which can execute $x := 1$, and P_2, which can execute $y := 1$. Ignoring the values of the control variables, both programs generate the following two computations:

$$\langle 0,0 \rangle \, , \, \langle 0,1 \rangle \, , \, \langle 1,1 \rangle \, , \, \langle 1,1 \rangle \, , \, \ldots$$

$$\langle 0,0 \rangle \, , \, \langle 1,0 \rangle \, , \, \langle 1,1 \rangle \, , \, \langle 1,1 \rangle \, , \, \ldots \, .$$

Consequently, the transition system model views these two programs as equivalent, despite the fact that program B contains concurrent elements while program A is sequential but nondeterministic.

The question whether the representation of concurrency by interleaving is adequate and acceptable or whether we should treat concurrency as a separate and unique phenomenon that cannot be reduced to nondeterminism, is one of the most debatable issues in the theory of concurrency. The main reason for adopting interleaving as a representation for concurrency in this book is that it leads to a simpler theory of specification and verification of concurrent systems, which is our main topic.

In the next chapter we will reconsider the question of how faithfully interleaving represents concurrency.

Scheduling

In a typical state of a computation, there may be several enabled transitions. We refer to the choice of the enabled transition to be executed next as *scheduling*. A sequence of choices that leads to a complete computation is called a *schedule*. Obviously, different schedules produce different computations for the same initial state.

As noted earlier, our model represents concurrency by *interleaved execution* of the atomic instructions of the participating processes. The precise interleaving sequence is determined by the schedule. For example, for the computation of program BINOM, the schedule can be summarized by the sequence of choices

$$t_0, \, t_1, \, r_0, \, t_2, \, r_1, \, r_2, \, t_0, \, t_1, \, r_3, \, t_2, \, t_3, \, r_0, \, r_1, \, r_2, \, r_3, \, r_4, \, \tau_I, \, \tau_I, \, \ldots \, .$$

On a higher level, we may view scheduling as a sequence of choices between processes from which the next transition to be activated is taken. In the example of program BINOM, each state has at most two nonidling transitions enabled on it, one belonging to P_1 and the other to P_2. Choosing the next process to be activated uniquely identifies the next transition to be taken. Consequently, the transition schedule given earlier corresponds to the process schedule

$$P_1, \, P_1, \, P_2, \, P_1, \, P_2, \, P_2, \, P_1, \, P_1, \, P_2, \, P_1, \, P_1, \, P_2, \, P_2, \, P_2, \, P_2, \, P_2.$$

As long as we stay within the framework of basic transition systems, all schedules are acceptable. For example, a schedule by which P_1 in program BINOM is continuously activated until it terminates at ℓ_3, and only then P_2 is activated, is acceptable. The only restriction a schedule must obey is that as long as some process is enabled, some process must eventually be activated, which is implied by the requirement of diligence.

The requirement of fairness, introduced in the next chapter, imposes additional restrictions on acceptable schedules, leading to the notion of fair transition systems. Typically, it disallows a schedule in which only one process is consistently scheduled while another process is indefinitely delayed.

1.3 Model 2: Shared-Variables Text

The transition diagram representation of shared-variables programs is useful as a framework for definitions and analysis since it has only one type of instruction: a guarded assignment.

However, it is inconvenient as a programming language and does not support structured constructs. Such constructs are considered essential because they allow hierarchical organization and development of programs and lead to better readability, modifiability, and analysis.

Therefore, we next consider a text language that supports parallel statements and communication by shared variables in a structured way. As a first step, we introduce the syntax and semantics of the basic statements of the language. In subsequent sections, we consider additional structuring constructs, called *grouped statements*, that enable the assembly of one or more statements into a single unit that can be performed without interference or interruption. Finally, we introduce a special set of statements that provide for synchronization between concurrent components of the program. The synchronization statements we consider as part of the shared-variables text model are the semaphore and region statements.

To introduce the basic notions of the model, we first define the basic statements of the language. For each statement we present its syntax and an intuitive explanation of its intended meaning. The precise semantics of the statements, in terms of states and transitions, is given in the following section.

Simple Statements

These statements represent the most basic steps in the computation. It is therefore intended that execution of these statements is completed in a single step. Consequently, we also refer to these statements as *atomic*.

- *Skip*

  A trivial do-nothing statement is

  skip.

- *Assignment*

  For $\bar{y}$ a list of variables and $\bar{e}$ a list of expressions of the same length and corresponding types,

  $$\bar{y} := \bar{e}$$

is an *assignment* statement.

- *Await*

  For c a boolean expression,

  await c

is an *await* statement. We refer to the condition c as the *guard* of the statement.

Execution of **await** c changes no variables. Its sole purpose is to wait until c becomes true, at which point it terminates. In a sequential program, an **await** statement is useless, since if c is currently false it will remain so forever. In a process within a concurrent program, however, this statement makes sense, since another process, acting in parallel, may cause c to become true.

The await statement is considered enabled in all states in which c is true (and control is at the statement). In comparison, the skip and assignment statements are always enabled when control reaches them.

Compound Statements

Compound statements consist of a controlling frame applied to one or more simpler statements, to which we refer as the *body* of the compound statement. Typically, execution of a compound statement requires several computational steps which, in our interleaving framework, are often nonconsecutive and may be interleaved with steps of a parallel process. In some cases, the first step in an execution of a compound statement can be attributed to the controlling frame, while the subsequent steps are attributed to the statements of the body. In other cases, all the steps can be attributed to the body, and the controlling frame only controls their selection, which is not considered a separate step.

- *Conditional*

  For S_1 and S_2 statements and c a boolean expression,

  if c **then** S_1 **else** S_2

is a *conditional* statement. Its intended meaning is that the boolean expression c

is evaluated and tested. If the condition evaluates to T, statement S_1 is selected for subsequent execution; otherwise, S_2 is selected. Thus, the first step in an execution of the conditional statement is the evaluation of c and the selection of S_1 or S_2 for further execution. Subsequent steps continue to execute the selected substatement.

When control reaches a conditional statement, the first step in its execution can always be taken. This is because c always evaluates to either T or F and the first step in an execution of the statement is therefore defined for both values of the condition c. In contrast, the first step in an execution of **await** c can be taken only if c evaluates to T.

We refer to S_1 and S_2 as the *children* of **if** c **then** S_1 **else** S_2.

A special case of the conditional statement is the *one-branch-conditional* statement

> **if** c **then** S_1.

Execution of this statement in the case that c is false terminates in one step.

- *Concatenation*

  For S_1 and S_2 statements,

  > $S_1; \ S_2$

  is a *concatenation* statement. Its intended meaning is sequential composition. First S_1 is executed; when it terminates S_2 is executed. Thus, the first step in an execution of $S_1; S_2$ is the first step in an execution of S_1. Subsequent steps continue to execute the rest of S_1, and when S_1 terminates, proceed to execute S_2.

  More than two statements can be combined by concatenation to form a *multiple concatenation* statement S:

  > $S_1; \ S_2; \ \ldots; \ S_n$.

  We refer to S_i, $i = 1, \ldots, n$, as the *children* of S.

  With *concatenation*, we can define the *when* statement

  > **when** c **do** S

  as an abbreviation for the concatenation

  > **await** $c; \ S$.

  We refer to c as the *guard* of the when statement and to S as its *body* or its *child*. The when statement is not atomic. The first step of its execution performs the await statement, while subsequent steps proceed to execute S.

  Note the difference in meaning between the when statement and the similar conditional statement

$$\textbf{if } c \textbf{ then } S.$$

In case that c evaluates to F, the when statement has to wait until c becomes true. The conditional statement, in contrast, simply terminates and skips execution of S.

- *Selection*

  For S_1 and S_2 statements,

$$S_1 \textbf{ or } S_2$$

is a *selection* statement. Its intended meaning is that, as a first step, one of S_1 and S_2, which is currently enabled, is selected and the first step in the selected statement is executed. Subsequent steps proceed to execute the rest of the selected substatement. If both S_1 and S_2 are enabled, the selection is nondeterministic. If both S_1 and S_2 are currently disabled, then so is the selection statement.

Note that all steps in the execution of the selection statement are attributed to its body. This is because the first step in the execution of $S_1 \textbf{ or } S_2$ corresponds to a step in the execution of either S_1 or S_2.

More than two statements can be grouped into a *multiple selection* statement

$$S_1 \textbf{ or } S_2 \textbf{ or } \dots \textbf{ or } S_n,$$

which may be abbreviated to

$$\overset{n}{\underset{i=1}{\textbf{OR}}} \; S_i.$$

We refer to S_i, $i = 1, \dots, n$, as the *children* of the selection statement.

The selection statement is often applied to when statements. This combination leads to *conditional selection*. For example, the general conditional command of the guarded command language (proposed by Dijkstra), of the form

$$\textbf{if } c_1 \rightarrow S_1 \; \Box \; c_2 \rightarrow S_2 \; \Box \; \dots \; \Box \; c_n \rightarrow S_n \; \textbf{fi}$$

can be represented in our language by a multiple selection statement formed out of when statements:

$$[\textbf{when } c_1 \textbf{ do } S_1] \textbf{ or } [\textbf{when } c_2 \textbf{ do } S_2] \textbf{ or } \dots \textbf{ or } [\textbf{when } c_n \textbf{ do } S_n],$$

or in shorter form:

$$\overset{n}{\underset{i=1}{\textbf{OR}}} \; [\textbf{when } c_i \textbf{ do } S_i].$$

The first step in the execution of this multiple selection statement consists of arbitrarily choosing an i such that c_i is currently true, and passing the guard c_i. This implies commitment to execute the selected S_i in subsequent steps. The order in which the alternatives are listed is immaterial and does not imply a higher priority to the alternatives appearing earlier in the list.

Note that we do not require that the c_is be exclusive, i.e., that $c_i \rightarrow (\neg c_j)$ for every $j \neq i$. Nor do we require that the c_is be exhaustive, i.e., that always $\bigvee_{i=1}^n c_i$ is true. Nonexclusivity allows nondeterminism, while nonexhaustiveness allows the possibility of deadlock, e.g., being at a selection statement with all conditions false (which requires waiting until one becomes true).

- *Cooperation*

  For S_1 and S_2 statements,

  $$S_1 \parallel S_2$$

is a *cooperation* statement. It calls for parallel execution of S_1 and S_2. The first step in the execution of a cooperation statement is referred to as the *entry* step. It can be conceived as setting the stage for the parallel execution of S_1 and S_2. Subsequent steps will proceed to perform steps from S_1 and S_2. When both S_1 and S_2 have terminated, there is an additional *exit* step that closes the parallel execution.

Similar to the selection statement, more than two statements can be grouped into a *multiple cooperation* statement

$$S_1 \parallel S_2 \parallel \ldots \parallel S_n \quad \text{or, equivalently,} \quad \parallel_{i=1}^n S_i.$$

We refer to S_i, $i = 1, \ldots, n$, as the *children* of the cooperation statement.

It is important to note that in the combination $[S_1 \| S_2]; S_3$, execution of S_3 will not start until both S_1 and S_2 are terminated.

- *While*

  For c a boolean expression and S a statement,

  while c **do** S

is a *while* statement. Its execution begins by evaluating c. If c is found to be false, execution of the statement terminates. If c is found true, subsequent steps proceed to execute S. If S terminates, c is tested again. Thus, the first step in the execution of a while statement is the evaluation of guard c and either finding it true and committing to execution of at least one more repetition of the body S at subsequent steps, or finding the guard c false and terminating execution of the while statement.

Statement S is called the *body* of the while statement, and is also referred to as its *child*.

The while statement behaves differently from the syntactically similar when statement

when c **do** S.

If c is true, the when statement terminates after S, whereas the while statement returns to test c. On finding c false, the when statement waits until c becomes true, but the while statement terminates.

- **Block**

    A *block* is a statement of the form

    [local declaration; S],

where S is a statement, called the *body* of the block.

A *local declaration* is a list of declaration statements of the form

local variable, ..., variable: type **where** φ.

The local declaration identifies the variables that are local to the block, specifies their type, and optionally specifies their initial values. The assertion φ appearing in the where clause of a declaration statement is of the form $y_1 = e_1, \ldots, y_n = e_n$, where $y_1, \ldots, y_n$ are some of the variables declared in this statement and $e_1, \ldots, e_n$ are expressions that may depend only on the program's input variables. The where clause may be omitted if no initial values are specified for these variables. The intended meaning of the where part is that $e_1, \ldots, e_n$ are the initial values of the variables $y_1, \ldots, y_n$ at the beginning of the computation of the program.

Thus, the initialization associated with the where part of variables that are declared local to a block is *static*. This means that, as is the case with variables declared at the head of the program, they are initialized only once, in the beginning of the computation. If the block may be reexecuted several times during the computation, and the programmer is interested in a *dynamic* initialization, which is performed on each entry to the block, we suggest the use of an explicit assignment. Such an assignment, appearing at the head of the block, will assign the appropriate value to the local variable on each entry to the block.

In principle, we could have adopted the dynamic interpretation of the initialization of local variables, which may appear a more natural choice for block-structured languages. We chose the static interpretation in order to simplify the presentation.

A statement S may refer to a variable only if the variable is declared at the head of the program or at the head of a block containing S.

Programs

A program P has the form

$$P :: \; \Big[\text{declaration}; \; \big[P_1 :: S_1 \, \| \, \cdots \, \| \, P_m :: S_m\big]\Big],$$

where $P_1 :: S_1, \ldots, P_m :: S_m$ are *named processes*. Each S_i is a statement, and P_i is a name for the process. We refer to $S_1, \ldots, S_m$ as the *top-level processes* of the program, and to the statement $[P_1 :: S_1 \| \cdots \| P_m :: S_m]$ as the *body* of the program. The names of the program and of the top-level processes are optional, and any of them may be omitted.

For the sake of uniformity we assume that the body of the program is a cooperation statement, but allow the case $m = 1$.

The syntax of a declaration in the text language is identical to that of declarations in the diagram language. A *declaration* consists of a sequence of *declaration statements* of the form

$$\text{mode variable, } \ldots, \text{ variable: type } \textbf{where } \varphi.$$

The mode of each declaration statement may be **in**, **local**, or **out**. Declaration statements with no explicit mode specification retain the mode of the preceding statement. The assertions φ restrict the initial values of the variables on entry to the program. The assertions may be omitted if the variables declared in that statement are not restricted.

Statements in the body of the program may be labeled. The labels are used as names for the statements in our discussion of the program and later in program specifications. However, no program statements refer to the labels. We will say more about labels in a later discussion.

Example (binomial coefficient)

Program BINOM (Fig. 1.3) is a text representation of the transition diagram (Fig. 1.1) for computing the binomial coefficient $\binom{n}{k}$ for integers n and k, where $0 \le k \le n$.

Note that we adopt several conventions associated with the multiple-line representation of programs. For example, we omit the ";" separating the last statement in a line from its successor in the next line. Some of the statements have been labeled to provide easy reference in our discussion. ◢

Example (greatest common divisor)

As another simple example, consider program GCD for computing the greatest common divisor of two positive integers a and b (Fig. 1.4).

The selection statement within the loop's body branches according to whether $y_1 > y_2$ or $y_1 < y_2$. In the first case y_2 is subtracted from y_1, and in the second case y_1 is subtracted from y_2.

The loop terminates when $y_1 = y_2$, and the value of y_1 is then placed in g as the final result of the program. The correctness of the algorithm is based on the

$$\textbf{in}\quad k,\ n\ :\textbf{integer where } 0 \leq k \leq n$$
$$\textbf{local } y_1,\ y_2:\textbf{integer where } y_1 = n,\ y_2 = 1$$
$$\textbf{out}\quad b\quad :\textbf{integer where } b = 1$$

$$P_1 :: \begin{bmatrix} \ell_0: \textbf{while } y_1 > (n-k)\ \textbf{do} \\ \begin{bmatrix} \ell_1: b := b \cdot y_1 \\ \ell_2: y_1 := y_1 - 1 \end{bmatrix} \end{bmatrix}$$

$$\|$$

$$P_2 :: \begin{bmatrix} m_0: \textbf{while } y_2 \leq k\ \textbf{do} \\ \begin{bmatrix} m_1: \textbf{await } (y_1 + y_2) \leq n \\ m_2: b := b\ \textbf{div } y_2 \\ m_3: y_2 := y_2 + 1 \end{bmatrix} \end{bmatrix}$$

Fig. 1.3. Program BINOM (binomial coefficient)
— text representation.

$$\textbf{in}\quad a,\ b\ :\textbf{integer where } a > 0,\ b > 0$$
$$\textbf{local } y_1,\ y_2:\textbf{integer where } y_1 = a,\ y_2 = b$$
$$\textbf{out}\quad g\quad :\textbf{integer}$$

$\ell_1: \textbf{while } y_1 \neq y_2\ \textbf{do}$

$$\ell_2: \begin{bmatrix} \ell_3: \textbf{when } y_1 > y_2\ \textbf{do } \ell_4: y_1 := y_1 - y_2 \\ \textbf{or} \\ \ell_5: \textbf{when } y_2 > y_1\ \textbf{do } \ell_6: y_2 := y_2 - y_1 \end{bmatrix}$$

$\ell_7: g := y_1$

Fig. 1.4. Program GCD (greatest common divisor).

fact that the two subtractions carried within the loop's body preserve the greatest common divisor of y_1 and y_2. That is,

$$gcd(y_1 - y_2, y_2) = gcd(y_1, y_2) \qquad \text{if } y_1 > y_2$$
$$gcd(y_1, y_2 - y_1) = gcd(y_1, y_2) \qquad \text{if } y_2 > y_1.$$

Initially, $y_1 = a$ and $y_2 = b$, and hence $gcd(y_1, y_2) = gcd(a, b)$. On termination

$y_1 = y_2$, leading to $y_1 = gcd(y_1, y_2)$. Therefore $g = gcd(a, b)$ on termination. ◢

Labels in Text Programs

Each statement in a program may be both pre-labeled and post-labeled. It is required that the labels appearing in the program are distinct. In Fig. 1.5 we present the GCD program whose statements are labeled with the two types of labels.

$$
\begin{aligned}
&\textbf{in} \quad\;\; a,\, b \;\; : \textbf{integer where } a > 0,\; b > 0 \\
&\textbf{local } y_1,\, y_2 \text{: } \textbf{integer where } y_1 = a,\; y_2 = b \\
&\textbf{out} \quad\;\; g \quad\;\; : \textbf{integer}
\end{aligned}
$$

$$
\ell_0 \colon \left[\ell_1 \colon \left[\begin{array}{l} \textbf{while } y_1 \neq y_2 \textbf{ do} \\ \ell_2 \colon \left[\begin{array}{l} \ell_3 \colon \textbf{when } y_1 > y_2 \textbf{ do } [\ell_4 \colon y_1 := y_1 - y_2 : \widehat{\ell_4}] : \widehat{\ell_3} \\ \textbf{or} \\ \ell_5 \colon \textbf{when } y_2 > y_1 \textbf{ do } [\ell_6 \colon y_2 := y_2 - y_1 : \widehat{\ell_6}] : \widehat{\ell_5} \end{array} \right] : \widehat{\ell_2} \\ \ell_7 \colon [g := y_1] : \widehat{\ell_7} \end{array} \right] : \widehat{\ell_1} \right] : \widehat{\ell_0}
$$

Fig. 1.5. A fully labeled GCD program.

In principle, we consider each program to be fully labeled and denote the pre-label and post-label of statement S by $pre(S)$ and $post(S)$, respectively.

We introduce post-labels for statements because we wish to identify, in a state, not only what statements may be executed next, but also what statements have just been executed. Post-labels facilitate this identification.

In actual presentations of programs, such as Fig. 1.4, we often omit many of the labels, particularly the post-labels.

Labels in programs have two important roles. The first is to provide a unique identification and reference to the statements. Thus we may talk about when statement ℓ_3 whose body is assignment ℓ_4.

To illustrate this use, Fig. 1.6 contains a tree, which represents the structural relations and types of statements appearing in Fig. 1.5.

The second important role of the labels is to serve as possible sites of control in a way similar to nodes in a transition diagram. Thus, it is intuitively appealing

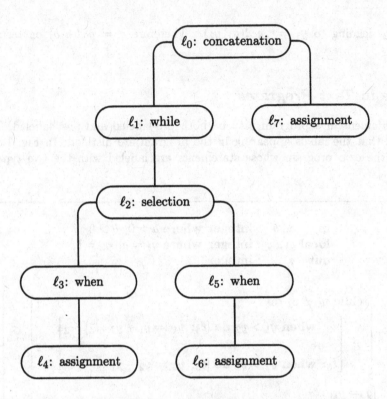

Fig. 1.6   Structure tree of the GCD program.

to envisage control as residing at label ℓ_2 in the program of Fig. 1.5 and, when finding that $y_1 > y_2$, moving to ℓ_4, where it pauses before subtracting y_2 from y_1.

The problem with interpreting labels as unique sites of control is that there are too many of them and we do not necessarily wish to distinguish between them. Consider, for example, post-label $\widehat{\ell_1}$ in Fig. 1.5, which designates the termination of the while statement ℓ_1. Nothing interesting happens between $\widehat{\ell_1}$ and ℓ_7, which is the point just before copying y_1 to g. It seems natural to consider labels $\widehat{\ell_1}$ and ℓ_7 as pointing to the same site of control.

Consider, for comparison, the diagram presentation for the same GCD program given in Fig. 1.7. This diagram has only 6 locations, in comparison to the 16 labels that adorn the program of Fig. 1.5.

To reduce this high redundancy, we introduce an equivalence relation that identifies any two labels ℓ and ℓ' such that we do not wish to distinguish between situations in which control is at ℓ and other situations in which control is at ℓ'.

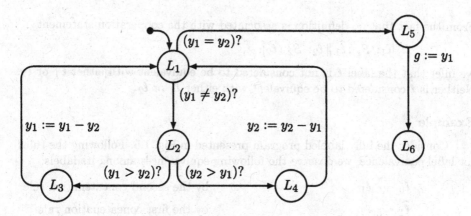

Fig. 1.7. A diagram presentation of the GCD program.

The Label Equivalence Relation

We define a *label equivalence relation* $\sim_L$ by the following rules:

- For a conditional $S = [\textbf{if } c \textbf{ then } S_1 \textbf{ else } S_2]$, we have

$$post(S) \sim_L post(S_1) \sim_L post(S_2).$$

- For a concatenation $S = [\ldots S_i; S_{i+1}\ldots]$, we have

$$post(S_i) \sim_L pre(S_{i+1}).$$

- For a concatenation $S = [S_1; \ldots; S_m]$, we have

$$pre(S) \sim_L pre(S_1)$$

$$post(S) \sim_L post(S_m).$$

- For a when statement $S = [\textbf{when } c \textbf{ do } S']$, we have

$$post(S') \sim_L post(S).$$

- For a selection statement $S = [S_1 \textbf{ or } \ldots \textbf{ or } S_m]$, we have

$$pre(S) \sim_L pre(S_1) \cdots \sim_L pre(S_m)$$

$$post(S) \sim_L post(S_1) \cdots \sim_L post(S_m).$$

- For a while statement $S = [\textbf{while } c \textbf{ do } S']$, we have

$$post(S') \sim_L pre(S).$$

- For a block $S = [declaration;\ S']$, we have

$$pre(S) = pre(S')$$

$$post(S) = post(S').$$

From the fact that no definition is associated with the cooperation statement

$$\ell: \ [\ell_1: \ S_1 : \widehat{\ell_1} \parallel \ell_2: \ S_2 : \widehat{\ell_2}]: \ \widehat{\ell},$$

we infer that the label ℓ is not considered to be equivalent with either ℓ_1 or ℓ_2. Neither is $\widehat{\ell}$ considered to be equivalent with either $\widehat{\ell_1}$ or $\widehat{\ell_2}$.

Example

Consider the fully labeled program presented in Fig. 1.5. Following the rules for label equivalence, we observe the following equivalences among its labels:

$\ell_0 \sim_L \ell_1$	by the second concatenation rule
$\widehat{\ell_1} \sim_L \ell_7$	by the first concatenation rule
$\widehat{\ell_7} \sim_L \widehat{\ell_0}$	by the second concatenation rule
$\ell_1 \sim_L \widehat{\ell_2}$	by the while rule
$\ell_2 \sim_L \ell_3 \sim_L \ell_5$	by the selection rule
$\widehat{\ell_4} \sim_L \widehat{\ell_3} \sim_L \widehat{\ell_6} \sim_L \widehat{\ell_5} \sim_L \widehat{\ell_2}$	by the when and selection rules.

Grouping together equivalent labels, we find that there are only six disjoint equivalence classes

$$\ell_0 \sim_L \ell_1 \sim_L \widehat{\ell_2} \sim_L \widehat{\ell_3} \sim_L \widehat{\ell_4} \sim_L \widehat{\ell_5} \sim_L \widehat{\ell_6}$$
$$\ell_2 \sim_L \ell_3 \sim_L \ell_5$$
$$\ell_4$$
$$\ell_6$$
$$\widehat{\ell_1} \sim_L \ell_7$$
$$\widehat{\ell_7} \sim_L \widehat{\ell_0}.$$

Note that these classes precisely match the six locations appearing in the diagram program of Fig. 1.7. ◢

Locations in the Text Language

We define a *location* in the text language to be an equivalence class of labels with respect to the label equivalence relation $\sim_L$. These are the places where we envisage control to reside before proceeding to perform the next execution step.

For a label ℓ, we denote by $[\ell]$ the equivalence class containing all the labels that are $\sim_L$-equivalent to ℓ:

$$[\ell] \ = \ \{\ell' \mid \ell' \sim_L \ell\}.$$

We call $[\ell]$ the *location corresponding* to the label ℓ.

To illustrate these concepts, we list the six locations defined for the program of Fig. 1.5, relating them to the locations appearing in the transition diagram representation of the same program in Fig. 1.7.

$$L_1 = \{\ell_0, \ell_1, \widehat{\ell_2}, \widehat{\ell_3}, \widehat{\ell_4}, \widehat{\ell_5}, \widehat{\ell_6}\} = [\ell_0]$$
$$L_2 = \{\ell_2, \ell_3, \ell_5\} = [\ell_2]$$
$$L_3 = \{\ell_4\} = [\ell_4]$$
$$L_4 = \{\ell_6\} = [\ell_6]$$
$$L_5 = \{\widehat{\ell_1}, \ell_7\} = [\ell_7]$$
$$L_6 = \{\widehat{\ell_7}, \widehat{\ell_0}\} = [\ell_0].$$

1.4 *Semantics of Shared-Variables Text*

In order to establish the correspondence between text programs and the generic model of basic transition systems, given by $\langle \Pi, \Sigma, \mathcal{T}, \Theta \rangle$, we have to identify the components of a basic transition system in text programs.

State Variables and States

For the text language, the *state variables* Π consist of the data variables $Y = \{y_1, \ldots, y_n\}$ that are explicitly declared and manipulated by the program, and a single control variable π.

The data variables Y include the input, output, and local variables, and range over their respectively declared data domains. Without loss of generality, we assume that there are no name conflicts for variables, i.e., each identifier appears in only one declaration statement.

The control variable π ranges over sets of locations. The value of π in a state denotes all the locations of the program that are currently *active*, i.e., are in front of statements that are candidates for execution.

Note that here we use only one control variable, in comparison to the one variable per process used in the diagram model. However, while the control variables in the diagram model range over single locations, the domain of the single control variable we use here consists of sets of locations.

As states we take all possible interpretations that assign to the state variables values over their respective domains.

For example, consider the program

$$\begin{bmatrix} \qquad\qquad \textbf{out } x\text{: integer where } x = 0 \\ \ell_0\text{: } [\ell_1\text{: } x := x+1;\ \ell_2\text{: } x := 2;\ \ell_3\text{: } x := x+2]\text{: } \widehat{\ell_0} \end{bmatrix}.$$

This program is not fully labeled but it is *adequately labeled*, which means that there exists a representing label for each location of the program. The locations of this program are

$$[\ell_0],\ [\ell_2],\ [\ell_3],\ [\widehat{\ell_0}].$$

The state variables for this program are $\Pi = \{\pi, x\}$. While there are infinitely many states obtainable by assigning to π and x arbitrary values in their respective domains, only four states can ever arise in a computation of this program. These states are given by

$$s_0\text{: } \langle \pi\text{: } \{[\ell_0]\},\ x\text{: } 0 \rangle$$
$$s_1\text{: } \langle \pi\text{: } \{[\ell_2]\},\ x\text{: } 1 \rangle$$
$$s_2\text{: } \langle \pi\text{: } \{[\ell_3]\},\ x\text{: } 2 \rangle$$
$$s_3\text{: } \langle \pi\text{: } \{[\widehat{\ell_0}]\},\ x\text{: } 4 \rangle.$$

To somewhat simplify our notation, we often represent the control value $\{[\ell_1], \ldots, [\ell_m]\}$, consisting of the set of equivalence classes $[\ell_1], \ldots, [\ell_m]$, by the set of representatives $\{\ell_1, \ldots, \ell_m\}$. Thus, the four control values assumed by π in the preceding list of states can be represented, according to the simplifying convention, as $\{\ell_0\}, \{\ell_2\}, \{\ell_3\}, \{\widehat{\ell_0}\}$.

Transitions

The idling transition τ_I is given by the transition relation

$$\rho_I\text{: } \text{T}.$$

We proceed to define the diligent transitions. With each statement S we associate one or more transitions. The set of transitions associated with a statement S is denoted by

$$trans(S).$$

Later we will define the transition relations for the transitions associated with each statement.

To facilitate the presentation of these relations, we employ the notations $+$ and $\dot{-}$ to denote the addition and removal, respectively, of single elements to a set. Let A be some set and a, b, elements from the domain of A. Then:

$A \dot{-} a = A - \{a\}$ — The set obtained by removing the element a from A. If $a \notin A$ then $A \dot{-} a = A$.

$A + b = A \cup \{b\}$ — The set obtained by adding the element b to A. If $b \in A$

then $A + b = A$.

$A \dot{-} a + b = (A - \{a\}) \cup \{b\}$ —   The set obtained by first removing the element a from A and then adding b to the resulting set. If $a \neq b$ then the relative ordering between removal and addition is immaterial, i.e., $(A \dot{-} a) + b = (A + b) \dot{-} a$. But if $a = b$, $(A \dot{-} a) + b$ and $(A + b) \dot{-} a$ may differ.

- *Skip*

  With the statement

  $$\ell: \mathbf{skip} : \widehat{\ell},$$

  we associate a transition τ_ℓ, whose transition relation ρ_ℓ is given by

  $$\rho_\ell: \quad ([\ell] \in \pi) \ \wedge \ (\pi' = (\pi \dot{-} [\ell] + [\widehat{\ell}])).$$

  Relation ρ_ℓ imposes two conditions on the values of π and π' (the value of π in the state s'), in order for state s' to be a τ_ℓ-successor of the state s. The first condition $[\ell] \in \pi$ requires that control is currently at ℓ; that is, the control resides at the statement labeled ℓ. The second condition requires that the value of π in the successor state s' can be obtained by first removing location $[\ell]$ and then adding location $[\widehat{\ell}]$ to π.

- *Assignment*

  With the statement

  $$\ell: \quad \overline{u} := \overline{e} : \widehat{\ell},$$

  we associate a transition τ_ℓ, whose transition relation ρ_ℓ is given by

  $$\rho_\ell: \quad ([\ell] \in \pi) \ (\pi' = \pi \dot{-} [\ell] + [\widehat{\ell}]) \ \wedge \ (\overline{u}' = \overline{e}).$$

- *Await*

  With the statement

  $$\ell: \mathbf{await} \ c : \widehat{\ell},$$

  we associate a transition τ_ℓ, whose transition relation ρ_ℓ is given by

  $$\rho_\ell: \quad ([\ell] \in \pi) \ \wedge \ c \ \wedge \ (\pi' = \pi \dot{-} [\ell] + [\widehat{\ell}]).$$

  The transition τ_ℓ is enabled only when control is at ℓ and the condition c holds. When taken, it moves from ℓ to $\widehat{\ell}$.

- *Conditional*

  With the statement

  $$\ell: \mathbf{if} \ c \ \mathbf{then} \ [\ell_1 : S_1] \ \mathbf{else} \ [\ell_2 : S_2],$$

  we associate two transitions, τ_ℓ^T and τ_ℓ^F. Their transition relations ρ_ℓ^T and ρ_ℓ^F, respectively, are given by

  $$\rho_\ell^T: \quad ([\ell] \in \pi) \ \wedge \ c \ \wedge \ (\pi' = \pi \dot{-} [\ell] + [\ell_1])$$

$$\rho_\ell^F: \quad ([\ell] \in \pi) \,\wedge\, \neg c \,\wedge\, (\pi' = \pi \dotdiv [\ell] + [\ell_2])_.$$

Relation ρ_ℓ^T corresponds to the case that c evaluates to true and execution proceeds to ℓ_1, while ρ_ℓ^F corresponds to the case that c is false and execution proceeds to ℓ_2.

For a *one-branch-conditional*

$$\ell: \big[\textbf{if } c \textbf{ then } [\ell_1:\ S_1]\big]: \widehat{\ell},$$

the two transition relations are

$$\rho_\ell^T: \quad ([\ell] \in \pi) \,\wedge\, c \,\wedge\, (\pi' = \pi \dotdiv [\ell] + [\ell_1])$$

$$\rho_\ell^F: \quad ([\ell] \in \pi) \,\wedge\, \neg c \,\wedge\, (\pi' = \pi \dotdiv [\ell] + [\widehat{\ell}])_.$$

- *When*

  With the statement

  $$\ell: \textbf{ when } c \textbf{ do } [\widetilde{\ell}:\ \widetilde{S}\,]$$

  we associate a transition τ_ℓ, whose transition relation ρ_ℓ is given by

  $$\rho_\ell: \quad ([\ell] \in \pi) \,\wedge\, c \,\wedge\, (\pi' = \pi \dotdiv [\ell] + [\widetilde{\ell}])_.$$

  Note that successful execution of transition τ_ℓ brings the control to location $[\widetilde{\ell}]$, which is at $\widetilde{S}$, the body of the when statement.

- *While*

  With the statement

  $$\ell: \big[\textbf{while } c \textbf{ do } [\widetilde{\ell}: \widetilde{S}\,]\big]: \widehat{\ell},$$

  we associate two transitions, τ_ℓ^T and τ_ℓ^F. Their transition relations ρ_ℓ^T and ρ_ℓ^F, respectively, are given by

  $$\rho_\ell^T: \quad ([\ell] \in \pi) \,\wedge\, c \,\wedge\, (\pi' = \pi \dotdiv [\ell] + [\widetilde{\ell}])$$

  $$\rho_\ell^F: \quad ([\ell] \in \pi) \,\wedge\, \neg c \,\wedge\, (\pi' = \pi \dotdiv [\ell] + [\widehat{\ell}])_.$$

  Note that in the case of a true c control moves, according to ρ_ℓ^T, from ℓ to $\widetilde{\ell}$, while in the case of a false c it moves, according to ρ_ℓ^F, from ℓ to $\widehat{\ell}$.

- *Cooperation*

  Excluding the body of the program, we associate with each *cooperation* statement

  $$\ell: \big[[\ell_1:\ S_1 :\widehat{\ell_1}]\ \|\ \cdots\ \|\ [\ell_m:\ S_m :\widehat{\ell_m}]\big] :\widehat{\ell}$$

  an *entry transition* τ_ℓ^E and an *exit transition* τ_ℓ^X. The corresponding transition relations are given, respectively, by

  $$\rho_\ell^E: \quad ([\ell] \in \pi) \,\wedge\, \Big(\pi' = (\pi \dotdiv [\ell]) \cup \{\ell_1,\ \ldots,\ \ell_m\}\Big)$$

$$\rho_\ell^X: \quad (\{\widehat{\ell_1}, \ldots, \widehat{\ell_m}\} \subseteq \pi) \wedge \left(\pi' = (\pi - \{\widehat{\ell_1}, \ldots, \widehat{\ell_m}\}) + [\widehat{\ell}]\right)$$

The entry transition begins execution of the *cooperation* statement by placing in π the set of locations that are just in front of the parallel statements $S_1, \ldots, S_m$.

The exit transition can be taken only if all the parallel statements have terminated, which is detectable by observing that π contains their terminal locations $[\widehat{\ell_1}], \ldots, [\widehat{\ell_m}]$.

The discerning reader may have observed that we omitted to associate transitions with the concatenation, selection, and block statements. This is because, unlike the preceding statements, each transition associated with one of these three statements is also associated with one of the children of the statement. Consequently, it is not essential to enumerate the transitions associated with these statements.

For completeness, however, we also present the transitions associated with these three types of statements.

- *Concatenation*

  The transitions associated with the concatenation statement

  $$S = [S_1; \ldots; S_m]$$

  are given by

  $$trans(S) = trans(S_1).$$

  Thus, the statement S inherits all of its transitions from its first child.

- *Selection*

  The transitions associated with the selection statement

  $$S = [S_1 \text{ or } \cdots \text{ or } S_m]$$

  are given by

  $$trans(S) = trans(S_1) \cup \cdots \cup trans(S_m).$$

  Thus, the statement S inherits its transitions from all of its children.

- *Block*

  The transitions associated with the block statement

  $$S = [\text{declaration}; \widetilde{S}]$$

  are given by

  $$trans(S) = trans(\widetilde{S}).$$

  Thus, the statement S inherits its transitions from its only child.

The Initial Condition

Consider a program

$$\Big[\text{declaration};\ [P_1 :: [\ell_1:\ S_1] \parallel \cdots \parallel P_m :: [\ell_m:\ S_m]]\Big].$$

Let φ denote the conjunction of all the assertions φ_i that appear in the where clauses of the declarations at the head of the program or at the head of any of the blocks contained in the program. Assertion φ is called the *data precondition* of the program. We define the initial condition Θ for program P as

$$\Theta:\quad \big(\pi = \{\ell_1,\ \ldots,\ \ell_m\}\big) \wedge \varphi.$$

This implies that the first state in an execution of the program begins with the control set to the initial locations of the top-level processes, after all the initialization of the local and output variables has been performed.

For a program P, none of whose declaration statements has a where part, i.e., $\varphi \leftrightarrow \text{T}$, we simply define

$$\Theta:\quad \pi = \{\ell_1,\ \ldots,\ \ell_m\}.$$

Note that this definition is consistent with the fact that no entry or exit transitions are associated with the body of the program.

Computation

Having defined state variables, states, transitions, and an initial condition for the text language, the notion of *computation* follows from the generic definition.

Example (greatest common divisor)

As a simple example, consider program GCD (Fig. 1.5) for computing the greatest common divisor of two positive integers a and b. Let us consider a computation of the program on the set of inputs $(a,\ b) = (4,\ 6)$. Since the values of a and b remain fixed for the computation, we represent the states by listing the current values of the variables π, y_1, y_2, and g, respectively, in the form

$$\langle A,\ d_1,\ d_2,\ d_3 \rangle,$$

where A is a set of labels, representing locations. Since variable g is assigned a value by the program only in the last step, it retains its arbitrary initial value in all the preceding steps. We denote this fact by writing "$-$" for its value.

The computation is described by a sequence of states related by the transitions, as defined earlier.

$$\langle\{\ell_0\},\ 4,\ 6,\ -\rangle \xrightarrow{\ell_1^T} \langle\{\ell_2\},\ 4,\ 6,\ -\rangle \xrightarrow{\ell_5} \langle\{\ell_6\},\ 4,\ 6,\ -\rangle \xrightarrow{\ell_6}$$

$$\langle\{\ell_1\},\ 4,\ 2,\ -\rangle \xrightarrow{\ell_1^T} \langle\{\ell_2\},\ 4,\ 2,\ -\rangle \xrightarrow{\ell_3} \langle\{\ell_4\},\ 4,\ 2,\ -\rangle \xrightarrow{\ell_4}$$

$$\langle\{\ell_1\},\ 2,\ 2,\ -\rangle \xrightarrow{\ell_1^F} \langle\{\ell_7\},\ 2,\ 2,\ -\rangle \xrightarrow{\ell_7} \langle\{\widehat{\ell_0}\},\ 2,\ 2,\ 2\rangle \xrightarrow{\tau_I} \dots$$

Note that we use the simpler notations ℓ_5, ℓ_1^T, etc. as abbreviations for τ_{ℓ_5}, $\tau_{\ell_1}^T$, etc. respectively. ◢

In **Problem 1.1**, we explore some of the implications of the definition of computations.

It is not difficult to see that every sequential text program, i.e., one that has a single main process and does not contain cooperation statements, can be translated into a diagram program consisting of a single process, where the nodes of the graph correspond to locations in front of statements in the program and the edges correspond to the transitions (**Problem 1.2(a)**).

By a simple extension, each text program of the form

$$P :: \quad [\text{declaration } \textbf{where } \varphi;\ [S_1 \| S_2 \| \dots \| S_m]]$$

where each S_i is a sequential statement, i.e., a statement not containing cooperation substatements, can be translated into a general diagram program (**Problem 1.2(b)**). In fact, it can be shown that an arbitrary text program can be translated to an equivalent diagram program (**Problem 1.2(c)**). Translations from diagram representations to text representations also exist. It follows that the two representations are equivalent in expressive power.

Subscripted Variables

In some of our examples, we consider an extension to the programming language that allows the use of subscripted variables of the form $u[e]$ at all places that variables may appear. Variable u must be declared as an array in a declaration that specifies the type and subscript range of the array. Expression e should evaluate to an integer value that is within the declared subscript range of u. We refer to e as a *subscript expression*.

As an example, we allow the use of statements such as

$$u[i] \ := \ v[i] + 1$$

provided u and v are declared as arrays (of integers), and, when evaluated, i yields an integer value within the subscript range of both u and v.

It is straightforward to extend the semantics of the language in order to accommodate subscripted variables.

1.5   Structural Relations Between Statements

In this section, we introduce some structural relations holding between statements in a program. The relations are determined by the syntax of the program.

Substatements

For statements S and S', S is defined to be a *substatement* of S', denoted by

$$S \preccurlyeq S',$$

if either $S = S'$ or S is a substatement of one of the children of S'. Thus, the relation of being a substatement is the reflexive transitive closure of the childhood relation. We also say that S' is an *ancestor* of S and that S is a *descendant* of S'. A statement S is defined to be a *proper substatement* of S', denoted by

$$S \prec S',$$

if $S \preccurlyeq S'$ and $S \neq S'$.

A statement S_1 is said to be *at the front* of a statement S_2 if $S_1 \preccurlyeq S_2$ and $pre(S_1) \sim_L pre(S_2)$. Thus, S_1 is at the front of S_1, $[S_1; S_2]$, and $[[S_1; S_2]$ or $S_3]$, but is not at the front of $S_1 \| S_2$.

The basic definitions, presented in the previous section, identify for each statement S the set of transitions, $trans(S)$, associated with S. Another way to affiliate transitions with a statement S is to accumulate all the transitions associated with substatements of S. We denote this set by $trans\_in(S)$ and define it by

$$trans\_in(S) \;=\; \bigcup_{S' \preccurlyeq S} trans(S').$$

Consider, for example, the statement

$$\ell_0: \; [\ell_1: \; x := 1 \; \| \; \ell_2: \; y := 1].$$

The various possible associations of transitions with this statement are

$$trans(\ell_0) \;=\; \{\tau_{\ell_0}^{\mathrm{E}}, \tau_{\ell_0}^{\mathrm{X}}\}$$

$$trans\_in(\ell_0) \;=\; \{\tau_{\ell_0}^{\mathrm{E}}, \tau_{\ell_0}^{\mathrm{X}}, \tau_{\ell_1}, \tau_{\ell_2}\}.$$

If $\tau \in trans\_in(S)$, we say that the transition τ *belongs* to S.

Least Common Ancestor

A statement S is defined to be a *common ancestor* of statements S_1 and S_2 if $S_1 \preceq S$ and $S_2 \preceq S$. A statement S is the *least common ancestor* (*lca*) of S_1 and S_2 if

a. S is a common ancestor of S_1 and S_2 and

b. For any other common ancestor S' of S_1 and S_2, $S \preceq S'$.

Any two statements in a program have a unique least common ancestor.

For example, consider a program P whose body is

$$[S_1; \ [S_2 \| S_3]; \ S_4] \ \| \ S_5.$$

We observe that

The *lca* of S_2 and S_3 is $[S_2 \| S_3]$,

The *lca* of S_2 and S_4 is $[S_1; \ [S_2 \| S_3]; \ S_4]$,

The *lca* of S_2 and S_5 is $[S_1; \ [S_2 \| S_3]; \ S_4] \ \| \ S_5$, i.e., the body of P.

The State Predicates *at*, *after* and *in*

We introduce several control predicates that identify the current location of control in a state, in terms of labels and statements.

For a label ℓ in the program we define the predicate at_ℓ, whose intended meaning is to test whether control currently resides at the location corresponding to ℓ.

- at_ℓ

  We say that a state s satisfies at_ℓ, and write

  $$s \models at\_\ell,$$

if the assertion $[\ell] \in \pi$ holds in s, i.e., $[\ell] \in s[\pi]$.

Considering, for example, states in the computation of program GCD of Fig. 1.5, it is obvious that at_ℓ_0 holds in the state $\langle \{\ell_0\}, 4, 6, - \rangle$ (due to $[\ell_0] \in \{\ell_0\}$) and in the state $\langle \{\ell_1\}, 4, 2, - \rangle$ (due to $[\ell_0] = [\ell_1] \in \{\ell_1\}$), but does not hold in the state $\langle \{\ell_2\}, 4, 6, - \rangle$ (due to $[\ell_0] \notin \{\ell_2\}$).

- at_S

  The location of control can also be identified in terms of statements. For a statement S, we say that a state s satisfies the predicate at_S, written

  $$s \models at\_S,$$

if the assertion $[pre(S)] \in \pi$ holds in s, i.e., $[pre(S)] \in s[\pi]$. Thus, for the labeled statement $\ell\colon S$, the two predicates at_ℓ and at_S are equivalent.

- $after\_S$, $after\_\ell$

We define the predicate $after\_S$, which holds in a state iff the control in that state is at a location immediately following statement S. Formally, a state s satisfies the predicate $after\_S$, written

$$ s \vDash after\_S, $$

if the assertion $[post(S)] \in \pi$ holds in s, i.e., $[post(S)] \in s[\pi]$. Similarly, for a statement S with pre-label ℓ, we write $after\_\ell$ as an abbreviation for $after\_S$.

For example, in program GCD of Fig. 1.5 we have

$$ \langle \{\ell_7\},\ 2,\ 2,\ - \rangle \ \vDash\ after\_\ell_1 \qquad \text{since} \qquad post(\ell_1) = \widehat{\ell_1} \sim_L \ell_7. $$

Here we denote by $post(\ell)$ the post-label of statement $\ell\colon S$ whose pre-label is ℓ. A slightly unexpected fact is

$$ \langle \{\ell_0\},\ 4,\ 6,\ - \rangle \ \vDash\ after\_\ell_4. $$

This is explained by

$$ post(\ell_4) = \widehat{\ell_4} \in \{\ell_0,\ \ell_1,\ \widehat{\ell_2},\ \widehat{\ell_3},\ \widehat{\ell_4},\ \widehat{\ell_5},\ \widehat{\ell_6}\}. $$

- in_S, in_ℓ

A more comprehensive control predicate is given by

$$ in\_S = \bigvee_{S' \preccurlyeq S} at\_S'. $$

Thus, a state s satisfies in_S if s satisfies at_S' for some substatement S' of S. If ℓ is the pre-label of S, we write in_ℓ as a synonym for in_S.

For example, the state $\langle \{\ell_4\}, 4, 2, - \rangle$ of program GCD satisfies in_ℓ_4, in_ℓ_3, in_ℓ_2, in_ℓ_1, and in_ℓ_0, but not in_ℓ_5. The state $\langle \{\ell_7\}, 2, 2, - \rangle$ satisfies in_ℓ_7 and in_ℓ_0, but not in_ℓ_1.

This points to a certain asymmetry by which at_S always implies in_S, but $after\_S$ does not. In fact, $after\_S$ always implies $\neg in\_S$.

Enabledness of a Statement

A statement S is defined to be *enabled* on a state s if one of the transitions associated with S, i.e., some transition in $trans(S)$, is enabled on s.

For each transition $\tau \in trans(S)$ associated with the statement S, let C_τ be the enabling condition of τ. That is, we assume that the transition relation of τ has the presentation

$$\rho_\tau: \quad C_\tau \wedge (\bar{y}' = \bar{e}).$$

Then, enabledness of the statement S can be expressed by

$$enabled(S): \quad \bigvee_{\tau \in trans(S)} C_\tau.$$

Processes and Parallel Statements

While the notion of processes, which are the parallel components of the program, is self-evident in the simpler diagram language, it needs a more careful definition in the text language. This is because the diagram language allows only one level of parallelism, right at the top, while the text language allows *nested parallelism*, as in the following program:

$$P :: \quad \left[\text{declaration}; \ [[S_1; \ [S_2 \| S_3]; \ S_4] \ \| \ S_5]\right].$$

Let us discuss the corresponding notions for the text language.

For a statement S in a program P, S is defined to be a *process* of P if S is a child of a cooperation statement. Note that this definition also covers the case of the top-level processes, which are children of the body of the program.

Thus, the program P considered earlier contains the following processes:

$$S_1; \ [S_2 \| S_3]; \ S_4 \quad - \quad \text{a top-level process}$$
$$S_5 \quad\quad\quad\quad\quad - \quad \text{a top-level process}$$
$$S_2 \quad\quad\quad\quad\quad - \quad \text{a child of } S_2 \| S_3$$
$$S_3 \quad\quad\quad\quad\quad - \quad \text{a child of } S_2 \| S_3.$$

Two statements S' and S'' in a program P are defined to be (*syntactically*) *parallel* in P if the least common ancestor of S' and S'' is a cooperation statement that is different from both S' and S''.

Thus, in program P, statement S_2 is parallel to S_3 because their *lca* is $S_2 \| S_3$. Statement S_2 is also parallel to S_5 because they belong to different top-level processes. However, S_2 is not parallel to S_4, because their *lca* is $[S_1; \ [S_2 \| S_3]; \ S_4]$, which is a concatenation not a cooperation statement.

Also $S_2 \| S_3$ and S_2 are not parallel even though their least common ancestor is the cooperation statement $S_2 \| S_3$.

Competing Statements

Let S_1 and S_2 be two statements in a program P, and S their least common ancestor. S_1 and S_2 are defined to be *competing* in P if either $S_1 = S_2$ or S is a selection statement, different from both S_1 and S_2, such that both S_1 and S_2 are at the front of S, i.e., $pre(S_1) \sim_L pre(S_2) \sim_L pre(S)$.

Let τ_1 and τ_2 be two transitions associated with statements S_1 and S_2, respectively. We define τ_1 and τ_2 to be *competing* if S_1 and S_2 are competing.

For a statement S, the *competition set* of S, denoted by

$$comp(S),$$

is defined to be the set of all statements that compete with S. Clearly, by definition, S is always a member of $comp(S)$.

Consider, for example, program P given by

$$P :: \quad \Big[\text{declaration; } [S_1; \; [[S_2; S_3] \text{ or } [S_4; S_5]]; \; S_6]\Big].$$

The competition set of S_2 is given by

$$comp(S_2) = \big\{ S_2, \; S_4, \; [S_4; S_5] \big\}.$$

1.6   Behavioral Equivalence

Two very important concepts in the study and analysis of programs are the notions of equivalence between programs and congruence between statements. It is often the case that we wish to explain the meaning of a new statement S by presenting a more familiar statement S' and claiming that the two are *congruent*, i.e., one can be replaced by the other. For example, a major step in the systematic development of programs is the replacement of a statement S by another statement S' that is congruent to S, i.e., performs the same task as S, but may be more efficient.

The questions of equivalence and replaceability are not restricted to the study of text programs and are equally important for other types of basic transition systems. Therefore, we will formulate the appropriate definitions in the more general framework of transition systems, even though most of the applications will be in the area of text programs.

First Approximation

As a first approximation to the concept of equivalence, we may try to define two transition systems P and P' to be *equivalent* if they generate precisely the same sets of computations. However, a closer study shows that this notion of equivalence is too discriminating. There are many cases of programs that we would like to consider as equivalent, but that generate different computations.

For example, we would like to consider the following two programs equivalent:

$$P_1 :: \begin{bmatrix} \textbf{out } x: \textbf{integer where } x = 0 \\ \ell_0: \ x := 1 : \widehat{\ell_0} \end{bmatrix}$$

and

$$P_2 :: \begin{bmatrix} \textbf{out} \quad x: \textbf{integer where } x = 0 \\ \textbf{local } t: \textbf{integer where } t = 0 \\ \ell_0: \ t := 1 : \widehat{\ell_0} \\ \ell_1: \ x := t : \widehat{\ell_1} \end{bmatrix}$$

The reason for wishing to consider P_1 and P_2 equivalent is that they both perform essentially the same task, that of eventually setting the output variable x to 1. The fact that P_2 takes two steps to accomplish this task while P_1 accomplishes it in one step is one of the details we prefer to ignore.

On the other hand, the sets of computations generated by P_1 and P_2 are quite different. Program P_1 generates the computation (listing for each state the values of π and x)

$$\sigma_1: \quad \langle \{\ell_0\}, 0 \rangle \ , \ \langle \{\widehat{\ell_0}\}, 1 \rangle \ , \ \langle \{\widehat{\ell_0}\}, 1 \rangle \ , \ \dots \ .$$

Program P_2 generates the computation (listing the values of π, x, and t)

$$\sigma_2: \quad \langle \{\ell_0\}, 0, 0 \rangle \ , \ \langle \{\ell_1\}, 0, 1 \rangle \ , \ \langle \{\widehat{\ell_1}\}, 1, 1 \rangle \ , \ \langle \{\widehat{\ell_1}\}, 1, 1 \rangle \ , \ \dots \ .$$

This shows that computations contain too much distinguishing information, such as the values of some variables that are irrelevant to the question of whether the program correctly performs its task. For example, both control variable π and local variable t are irrelevant to the correctness of P_2, which can be judged solely by observing the changes to x.

Observable and Reduced Behaviors

Motivated by this, we define a subset of the state variables $\mathcal{O} \subseteq \Pi$ to be the *observable variables*. In the diagram and text languages, these would usually coincide with the variables declared as either input or output variables. There may be exceptions to this rule, and in these cases the observable variables are explicitly specified. Control variables are never observable, e.g., $\pi \notin \mathcal{O}$ in the text language. This is necessary if we wish to consider as equivalent two programs that differ only in the names of the labels (i.e., label renaming).

Given a state s, which has been defined as an interpretation of all the state variables Π, we define the *observable state* corresponding to s, denoted by $s{\restriction}\mathcal{O}$, to be the restriction of s to just the observable variables $\mathcal{O}$. Thus, $s{\restriction}\mathcal{O}$ is an interpretation of $\mathcal{O}$ that coincides with s on all the variables in $\mathcal{O}$.

Given a computation

$$\sigma: \quad s_0, \ s_1, \ \ldots,$$

we define the *observable behavior* corresponding to σ to be the sequence

$$\sigma^{\mathcal{O}}: \quad s_0 {\restriction} \mathcal{O}, \ s_1 {\restriction} \mathcal{O}, \ \ldots.$$

For example, assuming that the observable variables for programs P_1 and P_2 consist of x alone, i.e., $\mathcal{O} = \{x\}$, we obtain the following observable behaviors corresponding to their computations:

$$\sigma_1^{\mathcal{O}}: \quad \langle 0 \rangle, \ \langle 1 \rangle, \ \langle 1 \rangle, \ \ldots$$

$$\sigma_2^{\mathcal{O}}: \quad \langle 0 \rangle, \ \langle 0 \rangle, \ \langle 1 \rangle, \ \langle 1 \rangle, \ \ldots.$$

As we see, these two observable behaviors are not yet identical. They still reflect the fact that it takes P_1 one step to set x to 1, while P_2 needs two steps to accomplish this feat.

Consequently, we define the *reduced behavior* σ^r (relative to $\mathcal{O}$), corresponding to a computation σ, to be the sequence obtained from σ by the following two transformations:

- Replace each state s_i by its observable part $s_i {\restriction} \mathcal{O}$.

- Omit from the sequence each observable state that is identical to its predecessor but not identical to all of its successors.

The qualifying clause of the second transformation ensures that if a computation ends in an infinite repetition of the same state, i.e., $s, s, \ldots$, then this infinite suffix is not deleted.

Applying these transformations to the computations σ_1 and σ_2 (or just the second transformation to $\sigma_2^{\mathcal{O}}$), we obtain

$$\sigma_1^r: \quad \langle 0 \rangle, \ \langle 1 \rangle, \ \langle 1 \rangle, \ \ldots$$

$$\sigma_2^r: \quad \langle 0 \rangle, \ \langle 1 \rangle, \ \langle 1 \rangle, \ \ldots.$$

Note that σ_2^r is obtained from $\sigma_2^{\mathcal{O}}$ by deletion of the second state, which is identical to its predecessor.

Equivalence of Transition Systems

For a basic transition system P, we denote by $\mathcal{R}(P)$ the set of all reduced behaviors generated by P.

Let P_1 and P_2 be two basic transition systems and $\mathcal{O} \subseteq \Pi_1 \cap \Pi_2$ be a set of variables, specified to be the observable variables for both systems. The systems P_1 and P_2 are defined to be *equivalent* (relative to $\mathcal{O}$), denoted by

$$P_1 \ \sim \ P_2,$$

if $\mathcal{R}(P_1) = \mathcal{R}(P_2)$. This definition fulfills our wish to consider programs P_1 and P_2 equivalent: $P_1 \sim P_2$.

It is important to note that the comparison of two programs for being equivalent is not restricted to the comparison of their final values. Thus, the following two programs are not considered equivalent:

$$Q_1 :: \quad [\textbf{out } x\text{: } \textbf{integer where } x = 0; \quad x := 2]$$

$$Q_2 :: \quad [\textbf{out } x\text{: } \textbf{integer where } x = 0; \quad x := 1; \ x := x + 1]_.$$

This is because the reduced behaviors they generate are respectively

$$\sigma_1^r: \quad \langle 0 \rangle \ , \ \langle 2 \rangle \ , \ \langle 2 \rangle \ , \ \dots$$

$$\sigma_2^r: \quad \langle 0 \rangle \ , \ \langle 1 \rangle \ , \ \langle 2 \rangle \ , \ \langle 2 \rangle \ , \ \dots .$$

On the other hand, Q_1 is equivalent (relative to the observable set $\{x\}$) to the program Q_3 given by

$$Q_3 :: \quad [\textbf{out } x\text{: } \textbf{integer where } x = 0; \ [\textbf{local } t\text{: } \textbf{integer}; \ \ t := 1; \ x := t + 1]]_,$$

which also has σ_1^r as its only reduced behavior.

Congruence of Statements

The definition presented earlier is adequate for comparing entire programs, viewing them as transition systems. However, when we consider statements in a text program, we need a more stringent notion of equivalence.

Consider, for example, the two statements

$$T_1 :: \quad [x := 1; \ x := 2]$$

$$T_2 :: \quad [x := 1; \ x := x + 1].$$

If we view them as the bodies of programs they are certainly equivalent. For example, the two programs

$$P_1 :: \quad [\textbf{out } x\text{: } \textbf{integer where } x = 0; \ T_1]$$

$$P_2 :: \quad [\textbf{out } x\text{: } \textbf{integer where } x = 0; \ T_2]$$

are equivalent. This is because both programs have the single reduced behavior

$$\sigma^r: \quad \langle 0 \rangle \ , \ \langle 1 \rangle \ , \ \langle 2 \rangle \ , \ \langle 2 \rangle \ , \ \dots .$$

On the other hand, our expectations about equivalent statements is that they would be completely interchangeable. That means that the behavior of a program containing T_1 will not change when we replace an occurrence of T_1 with T_2. This is not the case with the two preceding statements.

Consider, for example, the two programs

$$Q_1 :: \quad [\textbf{out } x:\ \textbf{integer where } x = 0;\ [T_1 \parallel x := 0]]$$

$$Q_2 :: \quad [\textbf{out } x:\ \textbf{integer where } x = 0;\ [T_2 \parallel x := 0]].$$

Obviously Q_2 can be obtained from Q_1 by replacing T_1 with T_2. But Q_1 and Q_2 are not equivalent. Listing the reduced behaviors of Q_1, we obtain the set

$$\langle 0 \rangle ,\ \langle 1 \rangle ,\ \langle 2 \rangle ,\ \langle 2 \rangle ,\ \cdots$$

$$\langle 0 \rangle ,\ \langle 1 \rangle ,\ \langle 0 \rangle ,\ \langle 2 \rangle ,\ \langle 2 \rangle ,\ \cdots$$

$$\langle 0 \rangle ,\ \langle 1 \rangle ,\ \langle 2 \rangle ,\ \langle 0 \rangle ,\ \langle 0 \rangle ,\ \cdots$$

The different behaviors correspond to the different ways the statement $x := 0$ can be interleaved with the two substatements of T_1.

The set of reduced behaviors of Q_2 is given by

$$\langle 0 \rangle ,\ \langle 1 \rangle ,\ \langle 2 \rangle ,\ \langle 2 \rangle ,\ \cdots$$

$$\langle 0 \rangle ,\ \langle 1 \rangle ,\ \langle 0 \rangle ,\ \langle 1 \rangle ,\ \langle 1 \rangle ,\ \cdots$$

$$\langle 0 \rangle ,\ \langle 1 \rangle ,\ \langle 2 \rangle ,\ \langle 0 \rangle ,\ \langle 0 \rangle ,\ \cdots$$

It follows that the two programs are not equivalent, and therefore we should not consider T_1 and T_2 interchangeable.

Based on the preceding discussions we will now define the following notions.

Let $P[S]$ be a *program context*, which is a program in which *statement variable* S appears as one of the statements. For example,

$$Q[S] :: \quad [\textbf{out } x:\ \textbf{integer where } x = 0;\ [S \parallel x := 0]]$$

is a program context.

Let $P[S_1]$ and $P[S_2]$ be the programs obtained by replacing statement variable S with the concrete statements S_1 and S_2, respectively. For example, programs Q_1 and Q_2 can be interpreted as $Q[T_1]$ and $Q[T_2]$ for the program context $Q[S]$ defined earlier.

Statements S_1 and S_2 are defined to be *congruent*, denoted by

$$S_1 \approx S_2,$$

if $P[S_1] \sim P[S_2]$ for every program context $P[S]$.

Examples

There are several obvious congruences that express some basic properties of the concatenation, selection, and cooperation statements.

- Commutativity

Both the selection and cooperation constructions are commutative. This is expressed by the congruences

$$[S_1 \text{ or } S_2] \approx [S_2 \text{ or } S_1] \qquad [S_1 \| S_2] \approx [S_2 \| S_1].$$

- Associativity

The concatenation, selection, and cooperation constructions are all associative. This is expressed by the congruences

$$[S_1;\ [S_2;\ S_3]] \approx [[S_1;\ S_2];\ S_3] \approx [S_1;\ S_2;\ S_3].$$

$$[S_1 \text{ or } [S_2 \text{ or } S_3]] \approx [[S_1 \text{ or } S_2] \text{ or } S_3] \approx [S_1 \text{ or } S_2 \text{ or } S_3]$$

$$[S_1 \ \| \ [S_2 \| S_3]] \approx [[S_1 \| S_2] \ \| \ S_3] \approx [S_1 \ \| \ S_2 \ \| \ S_3].$$

- Skip

Another interesting congruence is

$$S \approx [S;\ \textbf{skip}],$$

which holds for any statement S.

On the other hand, the statements

$$S_1 :: \quad [\textbf{await } x]$$

$$S_2 :: \quad [\textbf{skip};\ m :\ \textbf{await } x]$$

are not congruent. To see this, consider the program context

$$P[S] :: \quad \begin{bmatrix} \textbf{out } x: \textbf{ boolean where } x = \text{F} \\ \ell_0:\ [S \text{ or } [\textbf{await } \neg x]];\ \ell_1:\ x := \text{T}:\ \widehat{\ell_1} \end{bmatrix}.$$

Program $P[S_1]$ has only one computation (listing the values of π and x):

$$\langle \{\ell_0\},\ \text{F} \rangle,\ \langle \{\ell_1\},\ \text{F} \rangle,\ \langle \{\widehat{\ell_1}\},\ \text{T} \rangle,\ \langle \{\widehat{\ell_1}\},\ \text{T} \rangle,\ \ldots.$$

This is because the statement **await** x cannot be selected while $x = \text{F}$.

On the other hand, program $P[S_2]$ has the following two computations:

$$\langle \{\ell_0\},\ \text{F} \rangle,\ \langle \{\ell_1\},\ \text{F} \rangle,\ \langle \{\widehat{\ell_1}\},\ \text{T} \rangle,\ \langle \{\widehat{\ell_1}\},\ \text{T} \rangle,\ \ldots$$

$$\langle \{\ell_0\},\ \text{F} \rangle,\ \langle \{m\},\ \text{F} \rangle,\ \langle \{m\},\ \text{F} \rangle,\ \ldots.$$

The second computation represents a deadlock situation where the statement [**skip**; m: **await** x] has been selected when $x = \text{F}$.

Taking the reduced behaviors of both programs (relative to the observable variable x), we obtain for $P[S_1]$ the set of reduced behaviors consisting of the single behavior

$$\langle \text{F} \rangle,\ \langle \text{T} \rangle,\ \langle \text{T} \rangle,\ \ldots,$$

while for $P[S_2]$ we obtain the reduced behaviors

$$\langle \text{F} \rangle \, , \, \langle \text{T} \rangle \, , \, \langle \text{T} \rangle \, , \, \cdots$$

$$\langle \text{F} \rangle \, , \, \langle \text{F} \rangle \, , \, \cdots .$$

This shows that S_1 is not congruent to S_2.

- *await-while*

  A less obvious but conceptually important congruence is the following:

  $$\textbf{await } c \;\; \approx \;\; \textbf{while } \neg c \textbf{ do skip}.$$

This points out that one way to implement the **await** statement is by busy-waiting. Thus, while the two programs

$$P_1 :: \quad \big[\textbf{out } x\text{: boolean where } x = \text{F}; \; \ell_0\text{: await } x\big]$$

$$P_2 :: \quad \big[\textbf{out } x\text{: boolean where } x = \text{F}; \; \ell_0\text{: while } (\neg x) \textbf{ do } \ell_1\text{: skip}\big]$$

produce the different computations

$$\sigma_1\text{:}\quad \langle \{\ell_0\}, \text{F} \rangle \, , \, \langle \{\ell_0\}, \text{F} \rangle \, , \, \cdots$$

$$\sigma_2\text{:}\quad \langle \{\ell_0\}, \text{F} \rangle \, , \, \langle \{\ell_1\}, \text{F} \rangle \, , \, \langle \{\ell_0\}, \text{F} \rangle \, , \, \langle \{\ell_1\}, \text{F} \rangle \, , \, \cdots ,$$

their reduced behavior is identical:

$$\sigma_1^r \; = \; \sigma_2^r \; = \; \langle \text{F} \rangle \, , \, \langle \text{F} \rangle \, , \, \cdots .$$

In **Problem 1.3**, the reader will compare several statements and identify pairs of congruent statements among them.

Implementation Versus Emulation

There are two possible relations that hold between two programs P_1 and P_2 and that may allow the replacement of P_1 by P_2. Such a replacement is desirable, for example, in the case that P_1 is expressed in terms of high-level constructs that are not directly available on a considered machine, while P_2 contains only constructs available on that machine. A case in point is the replacement of the statement **await** c by the busy-waiting loop **while** $\neg c$ **do skip**.

The first relation is that of emulation. We say that P_2 *emulates* P_1 if they are equivalent, i.e., if their sets of reduced behaviors are equal. This notion is obviously symmetric and implies that P_1 also emulates P_2. The decision of which program should replace the other depends on the application.

Another relation is that of implementation. We say that P_2 *implements* P_1 if the set of reduced behaviors of P_2 is a subset of the set of reduced behaviors of P_1.

To illustrate this relation, consider the programs

$$P_1 ::
\begin{bmatrix}
\textbf{out } x, y: \textbf{ integer where } x = 0, \; y = 0 \\
\textbf{loop forever do} \\
\quad [x := x + 1 \textbf{ or } y := y + 1]
\end{bmatrix}$$

and

$$P_2 ::
\begin{bmatrix}
\textbf{out } x, y: \textbf{ integer where } x = 0, \; y = 0 \\
\textbf{loop forever do} \\
\quad [x := x + 1; \; y := y + 1]
\end{bmatrix}$$

Clearly, program P_1 allows all computations that continuously increment x or increment y. This means that any behavior that increments either x or y or both infinitely many times is an acceptable computation. On the other hand, the deterministic program P_2 picks a single particular computation of the infinitely many computations allowed by P_1. It picks a computation in which the incrementations of x and y precisely alternate. According to our definition of implementation, which is based on inclusion between the sets of reduced behaviors, program P_2 implements P_1.

These two definitions extend in a straightforward way to similar relations between statements. Let $P[S]$ denote a program context, i.e., a program in which the statement variable S appears as one of the statements.

We say that statement S_2 *emulates* statement S_1 if $P[S_2]$ emulates $P[S_1]$ for every program context $P[S]$. Clearly S_2 emulates S_1 iff S_2 is congruent to S_1. Thus, the statement **while** $\neg c$ **do skip** emulates the statement **await** c.

We say that statement S_2 *implements* statement S_1 if $P[S_2]$ implements $P[S_1]$ for every program context $P[S]$. Thus $x := x + 1$ implements $[[x := x + 1]$ **or** $[y := y + 1]]$.

Note that $S_2 = $ **await** x does not implement $S_1 = [$**await** $x]$ **or** $[$**await** $y]$. To see this, consider the program context $P[S]$ given by:

$$\begin{bmatrix}
\textbf{local } x, y: \textbf{ boolean where } x = \text{F}, \; y = \text{T} \\
\textbf{out } \quad z: \qquad \textbf{integer where } z = 0 \\
\quad S; \qquad z := 1
\end{bmatrix}$$

Program $P[S_1]$ generates the reduced behavior (listing values of z)

$$\langle 0 \rangle, \; \langle 1 \rangle, \; \langle 1 \rangle, \; \dots,$$

while program $P[S_2]$ generates the reduced behavior

$$\langle 0 \rangle, \; \langle 0 \rangle, \; \dots.$$

Therefore, S_2 does not implement S_1. On the other hand **await**$(x \vee y)$ implements S_1.

1.7   Grouped Statements

The definition of the semantics of the text language established a set of transitions associated with each statement. This implies that an atomic step, corresponding to a single transition taken in a computation, consists of the execution of at most one statement of the program. In some cases we want to group together several statements and have the whole group executed to completion in one atomic step.

Consequently, we extend the shared-variables text language by a new type of statement called a grouped statement.

The Grouped Statement

We begin by defining a class of statements, to which we refer as *elementary statements*. These are statements that can be grouped together.

The elementary statements are defined as follows:

- skip, assignment, and await statements are elementary.

- If S, S_1, ..., S_k are elementary statements, then so are

  when c **do** S,   **if** c **then** S_1 **else** S_2, $[S_1$ **or** ... **or** $S_k]$, $[S_1; ...; S_k]$.

Note, in particular, that any statement that contains a cooperation or a while statement is not elementary.

If S is an elementary statement, then

$$\langle S \rangle$$

is a *grouped* statement.

As an example of a grouped statement, consider

$$\langle y := y - 1;\ \textbf{await } y = 0;\ y := 1 \rangle,$$

which is obtained by grouping the (elementary) concatenation statement

$$y := y - 1;\ \textbf{await } y = 0;\ y := 1.$$

Execution of this grouped statement calls for the uninterrupted and successful execution of the three statements participating in the group in succession. Thus, if initially $y = 1$, this grouped statement can be executed, yielding a final value of $y = 1$. If y is different from 1, then the **await** $y = 0$ statement cannot be successfully executed after the decrementation of y. In this case, the grouped statement is considered disabled. It follows that this grouped statement is congruent to the statement

$$\textbf{await } y = 1.$$

This interpretation implies that execution of a grouped statement cannot be started unless its successful termination is guaranteed.

The Transition Associated with a Grouped Statement

With each grouped statement $\ell \colon \langle S \rangle$, where S is an elementary statement, we associate one or more transitions defined by appropriate transition relations.

To study the transitions associated with a grouped statement, we introduce first the notion of the product of two transitions.

Product of Transitions

Let τ_1 and τ_2 be two transitions. We define a new transition, called the *product of* τ_1 *and* τ_2, denoted by $\tau_1 \circ \tau_2$, as

$$s'' \in \tau_1 \circ \tau_2(s) \quad \text{iff} \quad \text{there exists an } s',$$
$$\text{such that } s' \in \tau_1(s) \text{ and } s'' \in \tau_2(s').$$

Thus, the $(\tau_1 \circ \tau_2)$-successors of s can be obtained by the application of τ_1 to s, followed by the application of τ_2 to the resulting states.

Assume that τ_1 and τ_2 are given by the relations

$$\rho_{\tau_1} \colon C_1 \wedge (\bar{y}' = \bar{e}_1) \qquad \text{and} \qquad \rho_{\tau_2} \colon C_2 \wedge (\bar{y}' = \bar{e}_2),$$

where, with no loss of generality, we may assume that ρ_{τ_1} and ρ_{τ_2} have the same list of modifiable variables $\bar{y} = (y_1, \ldots, y_k)$. Then the transition relation for the product $\tau_1 \circ \tau_2$ is given by

$$\rho_{\tau_1 \circ \tau_2} = \rho_{\tau_1} \circ \rho_{\tau_2} \colon \quad C_1 \wedge C_2[\bar{e}_1/\bar{y}] \wedge (\bar{y}' = \bar{e}_2[\bar{e}_1/\bar{y}]).$$

We use the notation $\varphi[\bar{e}_1/\bar{y}]$ to denote the formula φ in which we replace every free occurrence of y_i with e^i, $i = 1, \ldots, k$, where $\bar{e}_1 = (e^1, \ldots, e^k)$.

Consider, for example, the case that the transition relations for τ_1 and τ_2 are given by

$$\rho_{\tau_1} \colon \quad (x > y) \wedge (x' = x - y) \wedge (y' = y)$$
$$\rho_{\tau_2} \colon \quad (x < y) \wedge (x' = x) \wedge (y' = y - x).$$

Then the transition relation for the product is given by

$$\rho_{\tau_1 \circ \tau_2} \colon \quad (x > y) \wedge (x < y)[(x-y)/x] \wedge \left(x' = x[(x-y)/x] \right) \wedge$$
$$\left(y' = (y - x)[(x-y)/x] \right),$$

which is equivalent to

$$(x > y) \land (x - y < y) \land (x' = x - y) \land \big(y' = y - (x - y)\big) \leftrightarrow$$
$$(y < x < 2 \cdot y) \land (x' = x - y) \land (y' = 2 \cdot y - x).$$

This shows that τ_1 and τ_2 can be taken in succession only if $y < x < 2 \cdot y$, and when taken they change x to $x - y$, and change y to $2 \cdot y - x$.

Transitions for $\langle S \rangle$

We present an inductive definition of the transitions associated with the grouped statement $\langle S \rangle$ for each elementary statement S.

- If S is a skip, assignment, or await statement, then $\langle S \rangle$ is associated with a single transition $\tau_{\langle S \rangle}$, such that

$$\tau_{\langle S \rangle} = \tau_S.$$

  This is because these three statements execute in one step in any case, so grouping has no effect on them.

- Let S be the statement

  $$\ell: \textbf{when } c \textbf{ do } \tilde{\ell}: \tilde{S}.$$

  For each transition $\tilde{\tau}$ in $trans(\langle \tilde{S} \rangle)$ with transition relation $\tilde{\rho}$, we include in $trans(\langle S \rangle)$ a transition τ with transition relation

  $$\rho: \quad ([\ell] \in \pi) \land c \land \tilde{\rho}[\pi \dot{-} [\ell] + [\tilde{\ell}]/\pi].$$

  This construction implies that the execution of S in one step requires finding c true and proceeding to execute $\tilde{S}$ in one step.

- Let S be the statement

  $$\ell: \textbf{if } c \textbf{ then } \ell_1: S_1 \textbf{ else } \ell_2: S_2.$$

  For each transition $\hat{\tau}_1 \in trans(\langle S_1 \rangle)$ with transition relation $\hat{\rho}_1$ we include in $trans(\langle S \rangle)$ a transition τ_1 with relation

  $$\rho_1: \quad ([\ell] \in \pi) \land c \land \hat{\rho}_1[\pi \dot{-} [\ell] + [\ell_1]/\pi].$$

  For each transition $\hat{\tau}_2 \in trans(\langle S_2 \rangle)$ with transition relation $\hat{\rho}_2$, we include in $trans(\langle S \rangle)$ a transition τ_2 with relation

  $$\rho_2: \quad ([\ell] \in \pi) \land (\neg c) \land \hat{\rho}_2[\pi \dot{-} [\ell] + [\ell_2]/\pi].$$

  Thus, to execute S in one step, we should either find c true and proceed to execute S_1 in one step, or find c false and proceed to execute S_2 in one step.

- If S is the statement $[S_1 \textbf{ or } \cdots \textbf{ or } S_k]$, then

  $$trans(\langle S \rangle) = trans(\langle S_1 \rangle) \cup \cdots \cup trans(\langle S_k \rangle).$$

  Thus, to execute S in one step, we should be able to execute one of $S_1, \ldots, S_k$ in one step.

- Let S be the statement

  $[S_1; S_2]$.

  For each transition $\tau_1 \in trans(\langle S_1 \rangle)$ with relation ρ_1 and each transition $\tau_2 \in trans(\langle S_2 \rangle)$ with relation ρ_2, we include in $trans(\langle S \rangle)$ a transition τ with relation

  $\rho\colon \rho_1 \circ \rho_2$.

  Thus, to execute S in one step, we should be able to execute S_1 in one step, immediately followed by execution of S_2 in one step.

Consider, for example, the case that $\Pi = \{\pi, x, y\}$. Suppose we wish to compute $\rho_{\langle S \rangle}$, where S is the concatenation statement

$$\ell\colon \begin{bmatrix} \ell_1\colon\ x := x + y \\ \ell_2\colon\ y := x - y \\ \ell_3\colon\ x := x - y \end{bmatrix} :\widehat{\ell}.$$

Let ρ_1, ρ_2, and ρ_3 denote the transition relations for ℓ_1, ℓ_2, and ℓ_3, respectively. For simplicity we will omit the dependence of these relations on π and consider only its dependence on x and y.

We compute successively:

$$
\begin{aligned}
\rho_1 \circ \rho_2 \quad &= \quad [(x' = x + y) \wedge (y' = y)] \circ [(x' = x) \wedge (y' = x - y)] \;\leftrightarrow \\
&\quad \left(x' = x[(x+y)/x]\right) \wedge \left(y' = (x - y)[(x+y)/x]\right) \;\leftrightarrow \\
&\quad (x' = x + y) \wedge \left(y' = ((x+y) - y)\right) \;\leftrightarrow \\
&\quad (x' = x + y) \wedge (y' = x).
\end{aligned}
$$

$$
\begin{aligned}
\rho_1 \circ \rho_2 \circ \rho_3 \;=\; &(\rho_1 \circ \rho_2) \circ \rho_3 \;= \\
&[(x' = x + y) \wedge (y' = x)] \circ [(x' = x - y) \wedge (y' = y)] \;\leftrightarrow \\
&\left(x' = (x - y)[(x+y,x)/(x,y)]\right) \wedge \left(y' = y[(x+y,x)/(x,y)]\right) \;\leftrightarrow \\
&\left(x' = ((x+y) - x)\right) \wedge (y' = x) \;\leftrightarrow \\
&(x' = y) \wedge (y' = x).
\end{aligned}
$$

Thus the full $\rho_{\langle S \rangle}$ is given by

$$\rho_{\langle S \rangle}\colon \quad ([\ell] \in \pi) \wedge (\pi' = \pi \doteq [\ell] + [\widehat{\ell}]) \wedge (x' = y) \wedge (y' = x).$$

1.8   Semaphore Statements

We now consider the *semaphore*, which is a special mechanism for synchronization between parallel statements. We introduce semaphores and the statements associated with them as additional statements in the shared-variables text model. Similar extensions can be made to the diagram model.

The Need for Semaphores

One of the main problems in coordinating parallel processes is the management of access to shared resources. Consider a particular version of program BINOM as represented in Fig. 1.8. In this version, statements ℓ_1 and m_2 of Fig. 1.3, which modify shared variable b, have each been split into two statements. The first statement references b and computes an updated value for it, which is stored in a local variable. The second statement copies the updated value from the local variable to b. This program is representative of a general situation in which a transaction involving a shared resource needs several statements for its completion.

Unfortunately, this version is incorrect, in the sense that not all computations yield as their final result the correct value of $\binom{n}{k}$. To illustrate this, consider a computation for the inputs $n = 3$, $k = 2$. The final result for these inputs should be $b = \binom{3}{2} = \frac{3 \cdot 2}{1 \cdot 2} = 3$. For each state in this computation, we list the values of π, y_1, y_2, b, t_1, t_2. We present only some of the intermediate states in the computation, partitioning it into several segments:

$$(1) \quad \langle \{\ell_0, m_0\}, 3, 1, 1, -, - \rangle \xrightarrow{P_1} \dots \xrightarrow{P_1}$$

$$(2) \quad \langle \{\ell_0, m_0\}, 2, 1, 3, 3, - \rangle \xrightarrow{P_2} \dots \xrightarrow{P_2}$$

$$(3) \quad \langle \{\ell_0, m_3\}, 2, 1, 3, 3, 3 \rangle \xrightarrow{P_1} \dots \xrightarrow{P_1}$$

$$(4) \quad \langle \{\widehat{\ell_0}, m_3\}, 1, 1, 6, 6, 3 \rangle \xrightarrow{P_2}$$

$$(5) \quad \langle \{\widehat{\ell_0}, m_4\}, 1, 1, 3, 6, 3 \rangle \xrightarrow{P_2} \dots \xrightarrow{P_2}$$

$$(6) \quad \langle \{\widehat{\ell_0}, m_2\}, 1, 2, 3, 6, 3 \rangle \xrightarrow{P_2}$$

$$(7) \quad \langle \{\widehat{\ell_0}, m_3\}, 1, 2, 3, 6, 1 \rangle \xrightarrow{P_2} \dots \xrightarrow{P_2}$$

$$(8) \quad \langle \{\widehat{\ell_0}, \widehat{m_0}\}, 1, 3, 1, 6, 1 \rangle \longrightarrow \dots .$$

In segment (1), P_1 acts alone, multiplying b by 3. In segment (2), P_2 is active and computes $(b \textbf{ div } y_2) = (3 \textbf{ div } 1) = 3$ in t_2, which should be eventually assigned to b. However the segment stops short of assigning 3 to b and remains at m_3 with $t_2 = 3$. In segment (3), P_1 continues and completes the necessary

$$
\begin{array}{l}
\textbf{in} \quad k,\ n \ : \textbf{integer where } 0 \le k \le n \\
\textbf{local } y_1,\ y_2 \text{: integer where } y_1 = n,\ y_2 = 1 \\
\textbf{out} \quad b \qquad : \textbf{integer where } b = 1
\end{array}
$$

$$
P_1 ::
\begin{bmatrix}
\textbf{local } t_1 : \textbf{integer} \\
\ell_0: \textbf{while } y_1 > (n-k) \textbf{ do} \\
\qquad \begin{bmatrix}
\ell_1: t_1 := b \cdot y_1 \\
\ell_2: b := t_1 \\
\ell_3: y_1 := y_1 - 1
\end{bmatrix} \\
: \widehat{\ell_0}
\end{bmatrix}
$$

$$\parallel$$

$$
P_2 ::
\begin{bmatrix}
\textbf{local } t_2 : \textbf{integer} \\
m_0: \textbf{while } y_2 \le k \textbf{ do} \\
\qquad \begin{bmatrix}
m_1: \textbf{await } (y_1 + y_2) \le n \\
m_2: t_2 := b \textbf{ div } y_2 \\
m_3: b := t_2 \\
m_4: y_2 := y_2 + 1
\end{bmatrix} \\
: \widehat{m_0}
\end{bmatrix}
$$

Fig. 1.8. Program BINOM — with split statements.

multiplication of b by 2, after which it terminates. At that point P_2 is reactivated and completes the assignment of $t_2 = 3$ to b, as described in the step at segment (4). Clearly, this destructive assignment restores b to an outdated version and completely cancels the effect of the multiplication of b by 2 done by P_1 in segment (3).

From now on, there is no way to salvage the computation. At segment (5), P_2 gets to the point where it divides b by 2. Since b has the wrong value, the division of 3 by 2 at segment (6) does leave a remainder, and its result, which is also the value on termination, is $b = 1$. This, of course, is different from the correct result, which is $\binom{3}{2} = 3$.

The mishap has been caused by unwanted interference by P_1 in the middle of the sequence

$$
t_2 := b \textbf{ div } y_2 \ ; \ b := t_2
$$

of P_2. A similar interference can happen if P_2 interferes in the middle of the sequence

$$t_1 := b \cdot y_1 \ ; \ b := t_1$$

of P_1.

In order to correct such situations, we have to prevent unwanted interference in the middle of critical sequences, such as the computations of new values for b.

One way to prevent such unwanted interferences is already available to us using the grouped statement. It is an easy matter to enclose statements ℓ_1, ℓ_2 and m_2, m_3 within a grouped statement (i.e., $\langle \ell_1; \ell_2 \rangle$ and $\langle m_2; m_3 \rangle$, respectively). This ensures that ℓ_1 and ℓ_2 are always executed consecutively, and so are m_2 and m_3. In fact, this solution brings us back to a correct program that is equivalent to program BINOM of Fig. 1.3.

However, this solution may be considered too crude in the following sense. Enclosing a sequence of statements within a single grouped statement is really a *locking* device. It disallows any action by a parallel process until the process executing the sequence completes. This total locking may be considered too indiscriminating, when the aim is to do as much parallel processing as possible. For example, while executing $\ell_1; \ell_2$, the only parallel statements we want to exclude are m_2 and m_3. We do not object to any of the other parallel statements, such as m_0, m_1, m_4, being interleaved between ℓ_1 and ℓ_2. Unnecessarily severe locking reduces the degree of concurrency possible in the execution. Therefore, we should be interested in more discriminate locking and in protective mechanisms that enable us, for example, to lock out m_2 and m_3 but to allow m_0, m_1 and m_4 while executing the sequence $\ell_1; \ell_2$.

General constructs that achieve such locking and coordination between processes are referred to as *synchronization constructs*. Actually, program BINOM of Fig. 1.3 already contains one synchronization statement, m_1, which causes P_2 to wait until P_1 lowers the value of y_1 to be at most $n - y_2$. For more complicated synchronization between processes, modern concurrent programming languages offer several synchronization constructs.

Semaphore Statements

In this section, we consider one set of such synchronization constructs, the semaphore statements.

There are two *semaphore* statements:

- A *request* statement

    request(r).

- A *release* statement

release(r).

Integer variable r is called a *semaphore variable*. It is required that semaphore variables be modified only by semaphore statements. In particular, a semaphore variable cannot appear on the left-hand side of an assignment.

The traditional notations for the semaphore statements are $P(r)$ for the request and $V(r)$ for the release statements. Some texts use the terminology **wait**(r) and **signal**(r).

The transitions corresponding to the semaphore statements are defined as follows:

- *request*

  With the statement

  ℓ: **request**(r) : $\widehat{\ell}$,

  we associate a transition τ_ℓ, whose transition relation is given by

  $$\rho_\ell: \quad ([\ell] \in \pi) \ \wedge \ (r > 0) \ \wedge \ (\pi' = \pi \div [\ell] + [\widehat{\ell}]) \ \wedge \ (r' = r - 1).$$

- *release*

  With the statement

  ℓ: **release**(r) : $\widehat{\ell}$,

  we associate a transition τ_ℓ, whose transition relation is given by

  $$\rho_\ell: \quad ([\ell] \in \pi) \ \wedge \ (\pi' = \pi \div [\ell] + [\widehat{\ell}]) \ \wedge \ (r' = r + 1).$$

Note that the transition corresponding to the **request**(r) statement is equivalent to the transition corresponding to the grouped statement

$$\langle \textbf{await} \ r > 0; \ r := r - 1 \rangle.$$

Similarly, the transition corresponding to the **release**(r) statement is equivalent to the transition corresponding to

$$r := r + 1.$$

However, as we will see in the next chapter, the semaphore statements differ from the grouped statements shown earlier by having additional requirements concerning the frequency of their activation.

Use of Semaphores for Mutual Exclusion

Assume that semaphore variable r is initialized to 1. This is usually the case in most programs. A process reaching a **request**(r) statement will proceed beyond it only if $r > 0$, and will set r to 0. In case the process attempting to perform a **request**(r) finds $r \le 0$, it waits at that location until r becomes positive. This usually will be caused by another process performing a **release**(r)

statement. Thus, a location containing a **request**(r) statement can be used as a checkpoint, synchronizing the process with other processes containing **request**(r) and **release**(r) statements on the same semaphore variable r.

Consider program MUX-SEM presented in Fig. 1.9, which achieves mutual exclusion by semaphores.

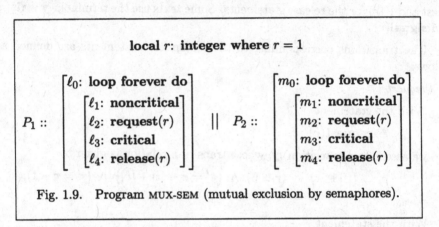

Fig. 1.9.   Program MUX-SEM (mutual exclusion by semaphores).

In this program we use the construct

> **loop forever do** S

to stand for **while** T **do** S. The **loop-forever** form emphasizes that the considered statement is perpetual and is intended to run continuously, never terminating.

The program represents a typical situation in which two processes engage in their activities essentially independently, but need now and then to coordinate their accesses to a shared resource. This shared resource may represent a shared variable or a device, such as a disk or printer, that needs to be accessed exclusively, i.e., protected from interference.

In this program, the independent activity of each process is schematically represented by the single statement **noncritical**. This statement may stand for an arbitrary complex statement that represents all the processing that requires no coordination with the other process. In general, we do not even require the eventual termination of this statement. Nontermination of the noncritical statement corresponds to the situation in which a certain process needs no further accesses to the shared resource, and hence may stay forever in the uncoordinated part.

Statment **critical** (usually referred to as the *critical statement* or *critical section*) represents all the activity that has to be performed in protected mode. For this activity, we require eventual termination. Nontermination of the critical statement corresponds to one process appropriating the shared resource and never releasing it to the other process. This is, in general, an unacceptable behavior.

An important assumption about both statements is that they do not modify any of the variables that are used in the protocol for coordination between the two processes. In the case of program MUX-SEM this means that neither of these statements modifies semaphore variable r.

The *mutual exclusion problem* is to devise a protocol, such as the program represented in Fig. 1.9, that contains the two schematic **noncritical** and **critical** statements as well as some coordination statements. The role of the coordination statements is to guarantee exclusive execution of the critical sections, i.e., while one of the processes is in its critical statement, the other is not. The coordinating statements usually refer to variables that are employed only for coordination purposes. We therefore assume that neither the noncritical nor the critical sections modify these coordination variables.

The program in Fig. 1.9 presents one of the classical solutions to the mutual exclusion problem, where coordination is achieved by semaphores. It is not difficult to see that mutual exclusion of the critical sections is indeed maintained in this program.

Assume, for example, that P_1 arrives first at ℓ_2 when r is 1. It proceeds beyond ℓ_2 while setting r to 0. As long as P_1 is at ℓ_3 or ℓ_4, r remains 0. Consequently, if the other process P_2 attempts to proceed beyond its **request**(r) statement m_2, it will be suspended there since the enabling condition $r > 0$ is false. It must wait for r to turn positive, which can only be caused by P_1 performing **release**(r) at ℓ_4. Similarly, when P_2 is anywhere at m_3 or m_4, r is 0, and P_1 is then barred from entering its critical section.

The solution of the mutual exclusion problem by semaphores easily generalizes to the case of several processes. In Fig. 1.10 we present a program containing k processes, where mutual exclusion is coordinated by semaphore variable r.

An argument similar to the one presented earlier, shows that if any process manages to perform a request statement and enters its critical section, this causes r to become 0, preventing any of the other processes from entering their own critical sections.

In **Problem 1.4**, the reader will examine additional programs proposed as possible solutions to the mutual exclusion problem.

Example (binomial coefficient with protected sections)

We now show how to modify program BINOM of Fig. 1.8 to avoid the unwanted interference and restore the correctness of the program. This illustrates the application of the general solution of the mutual exclusion problem to a concrete program.

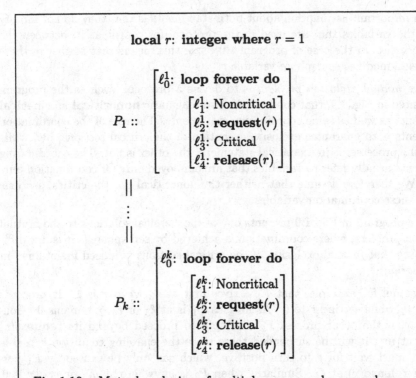

local r: integer where $r = 1$

$$P_1 :: \left[\begin{array}{l} \ell_0^1 \text{: loop forever do} \\ \left[\begin{array}{l} \ell_1^1 \text{: Noncritical} \\ \ell_2^1 \text{: request}(r) \\ \ell_3^1 \text{: Critical} \\ \ell_4^1 \text{: release}(r) \end{array} \right] \end{array} \right]$$

$\parallel$

$\vdots$

$\parallel$

$$P_k :: \left[\begin{array}{l} \ell_0^k \text{: loop forever do} \\ \left[\begin{array}{l} \ell_1^k \text{: Noncritical} \\ \ell_2^k \text{: request}(r) \\ \ell_3^k \text{: Critical} \\ \ell_4^k \text{: release}(r) \end{array} \right] \end{array} \right]$$

Fig. 1.10.   Mutual exclusion of multiple processes by semaphores.

To prevent the unwanted interference, it is necessary to protect each of the sequences $\ell_1; \ell_2$ and $m_2; m_3$ from interference by the other sequence. The protection is done using semaphore variable r. The modified BINOM program is presented in Fig. 1.11.

The protected critical sections are $\ell_{2,3}$ (statements ℓ_2, ℓ_3) and $m_{3,4}$ (statements m_3, m_4), respectively. Their mutual exclusion ensures that each computed value of b is assigned to b without any interference.

Note that we may view release statements ℓ_4 and m_5 as parts of the critical sections preceding them. This is because when P_1, say, is in front of the release statement at ℓ_4, r is still 0, thereby barring P_2 from passing m_2. It follows that the maximal regions, which are guaranteed to be exclusive from one another, are $\ell_{2..4}$ (i.e., ℓ_2, ℓ_3, ℓ_4) and $m_{3..5}$ (i.e., m_3, m_4, m_5).

This BINOM program is again correct, and all its computations yield the final value $b = \binom{n}{k}$.

in k, n : **integer where** $0 \leq k \leq n$
local y_1, y_2, r: **integer where** $y_1 = n$, $y_2 = 1$, $r = 1$
out b : **integer where** $b = 1$

$P_1 ::$

$$\left[\begin{array}{l} \textbf{local } t_1\text{: } \textbf{integer} \\ \ell_0\text{: } \textbf{while } y_1 > (n - k) \textbf{ do} \\ \quad \left[\begin{array}{l} \ell_1\text{: } \textbf{request}(r) \\ \quad \boxed{\begin{array}{l} \ell_2\text{: } t_1 := b \cdot y_1 \\ \ell_3\text{: } b := t_1 \end{array}} \\ \ell_4\text{: } \textbf{release}(r) \\ \ell_5\text{: } y_1 := y_1 - 1 \end{array}\right] \end{array}\right]$$

$\|$

$P_2 ::$

$$\left[\begin{array}{l} \textbf{local } t_2\text{: } \textbf{integer} \\ m_0\text{: } \textbf{while } y_2 \leq k \textbf{ do} \\ \quad \left[\begin{array}{l} m_1\text{: } \textbf{await } (y_1 + y_2) \leq n \\ m_2\text{: } \textbf{request}(r) \\ \quad \boxed{\begin{array}{l} m_3\text{: } t_2 := b \textbf{ div } y_2 \\ m_4\text{: } b := t_2 \end{array}} \\ m_5\text{: } \textbf{release}(r) \\ m_6\text{: } y_2 := y_2 + 1 \end{array}\right] \end{array}\right]$$

Fig. 1.11.   Program BINOM — with protected sections.

Other Uses of Semaphores

When used in order to protect critical sections, the semaphore statements usually appear in request-release pairs within the same process. The protected sections are then defined as the area delimited by the pairs. However, semaphores may be used in a variety of additional ways for signaling and synchronization between processes.

Example (producer-consumer)

Consider program PROD-CONS (Fig. 1.12), which models a producer-consumer

local r, ne, nf: **integer where** $r = 1$, $ne = N$, $nf = 0$
b : **list of integer where** $b = \Lambda$

$Prod ::$
$$
\begin{bmatrix}
\textbf{local } x\text{: integer} \\
\ell_0\text{: } \textbf{loop forever do} \\
\begin{bmatrix}
\ell_1\text{: } \textbf{compute } x \\
\ell_2\text{: } \textbf{request}(ne) \\
\ell_3\text{: } \textbf{request}(r) \\
\boxed{\ell_4\text{: } b := b \bullet x} \\
\ell_5\text{: } \textbf{release}(r) \\
\ell_6\text{: } \textbf{release}(nf)
\end{bmatrix}
\end{bmatrix}
$$

$\|$

$Cons ::$
$$
\begin{bmatrix}
\textbf{local } y\text{: integer} \\
m_0\text{: } \textbf{loop forever do} \\
\begin{bmatrix}
m_1\text{: } \textbf{request}(nf) \\
m_2\text{: } \textbf{request}(r) \\
\boxed{m_3\text{: } (y, b) := \big(hd(b),\ tl(b)\big)} \\
m_4\text{: } \textbf{release}(r) \\
m_5\text{: } \textbf{release}(ne) \\
m_6\text{: } \textbf{use } y
\end{bmatrix}
\end{bmatrix}
$$

Fig. 1.12.   Program PROD-CONS (producer-consumer).

situation. In the second line of the declaration, we omitted the mode of b, implying that it has the same mode **local** as the preceding line.

Producer *Prod* computes a value and stores it in x, using only variables local to the process. The details of the computation are irrelevant, and we use the generic statement "**compute** x" to represent this activity. It then appends x to the end of buffer b at ℓ_4. After successfully appending x to b, it cycles back to compute the next value of x.

Consumer *Cons*, acting in parallel, removes elements from the top of the buffer and deposits them in y. After successfully obtaining such an element from

b, it proceeds to use the value for some internal computations. This activity is generically represented by the statement "**use** y"; it is also constrained to use only variables local to process *Cons*.

The buffer is represented by a list b, whose initial value is the empty list Λ. Adding an element x to the end of b is accomplished by the *append* operation $b \bullet x$. The first element (head) of the buffer b is retrieved by the list function $hd(b)$, and removal of this element from the buffer is accomplished by replacing b with its tail $tl(b)$. It is assumed that the maximal capacity of the buffer is $N > 0$.

In order to ensure correct synchronization between the processes, which also guarantees that the buffer never overflows, we use three semaphore variables:

- Semaphore variable r ensures that access to the buffer is protected and provides mutual exclusion between the statements ℓ_4 and m_3, in which b is accessed and modified. Whenever one of the processes starts accessing and updating b, the other process cannot access b until the previous access is completed.

Note that in the presented program, the entire transaction (access and update) involving buffer b is completed within a single statement in each process. As a result, by definition, this transaction is uninterruptible since it is accomplished by a single transition. Yet, to represent the more general situation, in which it may take several statements to complete the transaction, we provide protection using semaphore r.

- Semaphore variable ne ("number of empties") contains the number of free available slots in the buffer b. It protects b from overflowing. The producer is not allowed to deposit a value in the buffer if $ne = 0$. Before depositing a value in b, process *Prod* decrements ne by 1 (in ℓ_2). Since initially $ne = N$, the producer cannot deposit more than N items that have not been removed by the consumer. The consumer, on the other hand, increments ne by 1 (in m_5) whenever it removes an item and creates a new vacancy.

- Semaphore variable nf ("number of fulls") contains the number of items currently in the buffer. It is initialized to 0, incremented by the producer (in ℓ_6) whenever a new item is deposited, and decremented by the consumer (in m_1) before an item is removed. This ensures that the consumer does not attempt to remove an item from an empty buffer.

Note that while the statements for semaphore r appear in request-release pairs that enclose protected sections, semaphores ne and nf are used differently as unidirectional signaling devices. Thus, we may view nf as a signal generated by the producer's **release**(nf) statement and sensed by the consumer's **request**(nf) statement. Symmetrically, the ne signal is generated by the consumer's **release**(ne) statement and sensed by the producer's **request**(ne) statement. In both cases, a missing signal causes the sensing process to wait at the corresponding synchronization point until the expected signal arrives.

Thus, when buffer b is empty and $ne = N$, the producer can perform at least N **request**(ne) statements before it may get suspended due to lack of cooperation from the consumer. Similarly, when b is full and $nf = N$, the consumer can perform at least N **request**(nf) statements before it may get suspended.

1.9   Region Statements

The semaphore statements discussed in the previous section provide powerful synchronization constructs. However, they have been criticized for being unstructured and for not enforcing a disciplined methodology. A more structured statement, the region statement, achieves similar goals, in particular the protection of critical sections, and provides additional testing capabilities.

This mechanism uses a resource declaration.

- *Resource Declaration*

  Among the declarations, both at the beginning of the program and at the head of blocks, we allow declarations of resources of the form

  $\quad r$: **resource protecting** $(y_1, \ldots, y_n)$.

  This declaration aggregates several variables $y_1, \ldots, y_n$ into a set called a *resource*, which is given the name r. We say that each of the variables $y_1, \ldots, y_n$ belongs to resource r. Each shared variable of the program, i.e., variable that is referenced in more than one process, must belong to precisely one resource.

- *Region Statement*

  The *region statement* has the general form

  $\quad$ **region** r **when** c **do** S.

  In this statement r is a resource name, c is a boolean expression, and S is a statement not containing any cooperation statement or other region statement. We refer to c as the *guard condition* of the region statement and to S as the *body* of the region statement or the *critical section* protected by this statement. The only shared variables that may be referenced within c or S must belong to r.

Let $S_1, \ldots, S_k$ be all the statements appearing as the body of a region statement for resource r, i.e., in the context

$\quad$ **region** r **when** c_i **do** S_i.

To specify the transitions associated with the region statement, we define the auxiliary control predicate

$$free(r): \quad \bigwedge_{i=1}^{k} (\neg in\_S_i).$$

Predicate $free(r)$ characterizes all the states in which no statement S_i that is protected by the resource r is currently executing, i.e., control is not in front of S_i or any of its substatements. We may refer to such a situation by saying that resource r is *free*.

Using this predicate, we specify the transition τ_ℓ associated with the region statement

$$\ell: \textbf{region } r \textbf{ when } c \textbf{ do } \widetilde{\ell} : \widetilde{S}$$

by the transition relation

$$\rho_\ell: \quad ([\ell] \in \pi) \ \wedge \ free(r) \ \wedge \ c \ \wedge \ (\pi' = \pi \doteq [\ell] + [\widetilde{\ell}]).$$

Thus, a successful execution of τ_ℓ requires that condition c be true and that no other statement protected by r is currently executing.

With the addition of the region statement, we add the following rule to the definition of the label equivalence relation $\sim_L$.

• For a region statement $S = \textbf{region } r \textbf{ when } c \textbf{ do } \widetilde{S}$, we have

$$post(S) \ \sim_L \ post(\widetilde{S}).$$

Example (producer-consumer with region statements)

In Fig. 1.13 we present a solution to the producer-consumer problem using region statements. Compare this PROD-CONS program with the one using semaphores in Fig. 1.12. The identification of the critical and noncritical sections is made syntactically clear in the region version.

Process *Prod* consists of a noncritical section, which computes x ("producing"), followed by a critical section, which handles the communication of the produced value to process *Cons*. The critical section may be executed only exclusively (i.e., when resource r protecting buffer b is free), and then only when b is not full. When *Prod* succeeds in executing its critical section, it appends x to the end of b.

Process *Cons* also alternates between a critical and a noncritical section. In the critical section, executed only when resource r is free and the buffer is nonempty, the first element of the buffer is copied into y and removed from the buffer. In the noncritical section, *Cons* uses the value obtained in y for some computations ("consuming").

By the definition of region statements, it is clear that the two processes can never coreside in their respective critical sections. ◢

In **Problem 1.5**, the reader will present an implementation of the region statement in terms of other statements.

$$\boxed{\begin{array}{c}
\textbf{local } b\text{: list of integer where } b = \Lambda \\
r\text{: resource protecting } b \\[1em]
Prod :: \left[\begin{array}{l}
\textbf{local } x\text{: integer} \\
\textbf{loop forever do} \\
\quad \left[\begin{array}{l}
\textbf{compute } x \\
\textbf{region } r \textbf{ when } |b| < N \textbf{ do} \\
\quad b := b \bullet x
\end{array}\right]
\end{array}\right] \\[3em]
\parallel \\[2em]
Cons :: \left[\begin{array}{l}
\textbf{local } y\text{: integer} \\
\textbf{loop forever do} \\
\quad \left[\begin{array}{l}
\textbf{region } r \textbf{ when } |b| > 0 \textbf{ do} \\
\quad (y,\ b) := \big(hd(b),\ tl(b)\big) \\
\textbf{use } y
\end{array}\right]
\end{array}\right]
\end{array}}$$

Fig. 1.13.   Program PROD-CONS — with region statements.

Comparing Semaphores to Region Statements

The region statement is a more structured and powerful construct and leads to cleaner and more readable programs than semaphores. However, its implementation is more expensive than that of the semaphore. A satisfactory implementation of a semaphore has only to keep track of the current value of the semaphore and the identity of the processes suspended (waiting) at a request statement for that semaphore. An implementation of a region statement, on the other hand, has to keep track not only of the current status of the resource (occupied or free) and the identities of the waiting processes, but also of the status (true or false) of their individual guard conditions. A process can execute its protected statement only when both the resource is free and the guard condition currently holds.

Synchronization Within Selection Statements

In all the examples considered up to this point, the synchronization statements, such as the semaphore request statement or the region statement, appear in the context of concatenations, but never as immediate substatements of a selection statement. This means that whenever a process reaches a synchronization statement that is currently disabled, it has no choice but to wait until (if ever) it becomes enabled. This implies that execution of the synchronization statement is essential for the continuation of the computation.

In many situations, a synchronization is desirable at some point but not absolutely essential for the continuation. In other situations, several synchronizations are possible, and we would like to select any one of them that is currently enabled. These situations call for synchronization statements as immediate substatements of a selection statement. We illustrate such a case in the following example.

$$
\begin{array}{l}
\textbf{local } b[1],\ \ldots,\ b[m]\textbf{: list of integer} \\
\qquad\qquad \textbf{where } b[1] = \Lambda,\ \ldots,\ b[m] = \Lambda \\
r[1] \qquad\qquad\quad\textbf{: resource protecting } b[1] \\
\vdots \\
r[m] \qquad\qquad\quad\textbf{: resource protecting } b[m]
\end{array}
$$

$$
\overset{\ell}{\underset{i=1}{\big\Vert}}\ Prod[i] ::
\begin{bmatrix}
\textbf{local } x[i]\textbf{: integer} \\
\textbf{loop forever do} \\
\begin{bmatrix}
\textbf{compute } x[i] \\
\overset{m}{\underset{j=1}{\textbf{OR}}}
\begin{bmatrix}
\textbf{region } r[j] \textbf{ when } |b[j]| < N \textbf{ do} \\
b[j] := b[j] \bullet x[i]
\end{bmatrix}
\end{bmatrix}
\end{bmatrix}
$$

$$\big\Vert$$

$$
\overset{n}{\underset{k=1}{\big\Vert}}\ Cons[k] ::
\begin{bmatrix}
\textbf{local } y[k]\textbf{: integer} \\
\textbf{loop forever do} \\
\begin{bmatrix}
\overset{m}{\underset{j=1}{\textbf{OR}}}
\begin{bmatrix}
\textbf{region } r[j] \textbf{ when } |b[j]| > 0 \textbf{ do} \\
(y[k],\, b[j]) := (hd(b[j]),\ tl(b[j]))
\end{bmatrix} \\
\textbf{use } y[k]
\end{bmatrix}
\end{bmatrix}
$$

Fig. 1.14. Program PROD-CONS — with multiple producers and consumers.

Example (producer-consumer with multiple producers and consumers)

Program PROD-CONS (Fig. 1.14) is a generalization of the producer-consumer PROD-CONS program of Fig. 1.13 to the case that there are ℓ producers and n consumers communicating via m buffers. Figure 1.14 actually contains a *program scheme* that has to be instantiated for each concrete value of ℓ, m, and n. A basic assumption is that of full homogeneity, meaning that all values produced by all the producers are equally valid and useful to all the consumers. Consequently, a producer may choose to deposit its current value in any buffer that has an available slot, and a consumer may choose to read and remove a value from any buffer that contains an unused value.

Following this assumption, each producer $Prod[i]$ has a selection statement that nondeterministically selects an available resource $r[j]$ protecting a nonfull $(|b[j]| < N)$ buffer. Once selected, the producer deposits the computed value $x[i]$ in $b[j]$. Similarly, each consumer $Cons[k]$ has a selection statement that nondeterministically selects an available resource $r[j]$ protecting a nonempty buffer $(|b[j]| > 0)$. It then proceeds to remove the value from buffer $b[j]$ into $y[k]$.

1.10   Model 3: Message-Passing Text

In the two previous models, diagrams and shared-variables text languages, communication between parallel statements was done by shared variables. Some higher-level statements, such as semaphore and region statements, were introduced to provide synchronization, which can be regarded as limited communication.

In the present model, which we obtain by modifying the shared-variables text language, communication between parallel statements is carried out by explicit message passing. Thus, we disallow communication by shared variables and introduce new primitive statements that send and receive messages. Message passing also induces synchronization because a message cannot be received before it has been sent, and a process may choose to wait until a particular message arrives.

In sending and receiving messages, processes do not name their communication partners directly. Instead, the communication statements name a channel. In order to establish communication between two processes, one process must send a message via some channel, and the other process must request an input from the same channel. This naming convention leads to a better encapsulation of processes, since a process only has to know the names of the channels through which it communicates, not the names of all the potential partners that may access each channel. It also allows many-to-many communication through a single channel by having several processes send to and several processes receive from the same channel. In some programming languages, channels are referred to as *ports*.

Two modifications to the shared-variables text language are necessary to obtain a pure message-passing language text. The first modification disallows the use of shared variables for communication between parallel statements and omits the special synchronization statements based on shared variables, i.e., the semaphore and region statements. The second modification introduces new communication statements based on message passing.

Note that the first modification is necessary only in order to get closer to traditional pure message-passing languages, such as CSP, but in principle we can consider programs that allow communication between processes both by shared variables (and their associated synchronization statements) and by message-passing statements.

Communication Statements

Several new constructs are introduced to provide the capability of communication by message passing.

- *Channel Declaration*

  Channels are declared at the head of blocks by a *channel declaration*:

  $$\text{mode } \alpha_1, \alpha_2, \ldots, \alpha_n: \textbf{ channel of } \text{type}.$$

  This declaration identifies $\alpha_1, \ldots, \alpha_n$ as channels through which messages of the specified type can be sent and received.

  If not otherwise specified, the channels are initialized to Λ, the empty sequence (list) of messages.

  Sometimes we may want to preload the channels with a given sequence of messages that will be specified in the declaration, e.g.,

  $$\alpha: \textbf{ channel of integer where } \alpha = [1, 2].$$

  This declaration specifies α as a channel of integers that initially contains 1 as the first message and 2 as the second message.

- *Send Statement*

  The *send* statement has the form

  $$\alpha \Leftarrow e,$$

  where α is a channel name and e is an expression whose value is to be sent via channel α. The type of the channel and of the expression must match.

- *Receive Statement*

  The *receive* statement has the form

  $$\alpha \Rightarrow u,$$

  where α is a channel name and u is a variable. The type of the channel and of the variable must match. Execution of this statement reads and removes the first message (value) currently held in α and stores it in u.

The send and receive statements appear in different syntactic forms in various languages. Some languages present statements

$$\alpha \Leftarrow e \quad \text{and} \quad \alpha \Rightarrow u$$

as

send e **to** α and   **receive** u **from** α.

A prevalent notation, introduced in the language CSP, represents these statements as

$$\alpha!e \quad \text{and} \quad \alpha?u.$$

We refer to the group of statements consisting of the synchronization statements request, release, and region and the communication statements send and receive as *coordination statements*.

Buffering Capability

Channels may be endowed with a buffering capability. This means that they are able to hold some messages that have been sent but not yet requested. Usually, and this is the convention we follow here unless explicitly stated otherwise, the messages are kept in the order sent. In this case, buffering channels may be viewed as queues (or lists) of pending messages and the send and receive statements described as appending and removing elements from a queue.

The declaration of a channel specifies its buffering capacity. Three possible levels of buffering may be considered: unbounded, bounded, and no buffering. The transition relations associated with the send and receive statements depend on the level of buffering and are separately discussed for each case.

Unbounded Buffering

Channels with unbounded buffering capacity are declared by

α: **channel** $[1..]$ **of** type.

For each such declaration, we add to the set of state variables Π a new variable α. The domain of this variable consists of lists of elements of the declared type. Thus, if channel α is declared as

α: **channel** $[1..]$ **of integer**,

the new state variable α ranges over lists of integers.

List α represents the messages that have been written to channel α by some send statements and have not yet been read by a receive statement.

- With the send statement

$$\ell: \ \alpha \Leftarrow e : \widehat{\ell},$$

we associate a transition τ_ℓ, whose transition relation is given by

$$\rho_\ell: \quad ([\ell] \in \pi) \;\wedge\; \left(\pi' = \pi \dot- [\ell] + [\widehat{\ell}]\right) \;\wedge\; (\alpha' = \alpha \bullet e).$$

The data part of the assertion ρ_ℓ describes the new value of α as being obtained by appending the value of e to the end of the old value of α.

- With the receive statement

  $$\ell: \; \alpha \Rightarrow u : \widehat{\ell},$$

  we associate a transition τ_ℓ, whose transition relation is given by

  $$\rho_\ell: \begin{bmatrix} ([\ell] \in \pi) \;\wedge\; (|\alpha| > 0) \\ \wedge \\ \left(\pi' = \pi \dot- [\ell] + [\widehat{\ell}]\right) \;\wedge\; (u' = hd(\alpha)) \;\wedge\; (\alpha' = tl(\alpha)) \end{bmatrix}.$$

  The data part of ρ_ℓ states that transition τ_ℓ is enabled only if channel α is currently nonempty and, when executed, its effect is to deposit the first element (head) of α in u and to remove this element (retaining the tail) from α.

In the case that no initializing **where** clause appears in the channel declaration, we add the clause $(\alpha = \Lambda)$ to the initial condition Θ. If the channel declaration contains an initializing clause of the form

  $$\textbf{where } \alpha \; = \; \text{list-expression},$$

we add, instead, the clause $(\alpha = \text{list-expression})$ to Θ.

These definitions imply that the send statement $\alpha \Leftarrow e$ is always enabled when control is at the statement. In contrast, the receive statement $\alpha \Rightarrow u$ is enabled only when the channel is nonempty.

Variable α, added to the state variables, is similar to control variable π in being an auxiliary variable. This means that it is required for the representation of a message-passing program as a transition system, but it cannot be explicitly referenced as a variable by statements in the program.

Bounded Buffering

A channel with bounded buffering capacity is declared by

  $$\alpha: \textbf{channel } [1..N] \textbf{ of } \text{type},$$

where constant or input variable N specifies the maximal capacity of channel α. This means that the size of α can never exceed N, and a statement that attempts to send an additional element to a full channel will be delayed until the size of the list of pending messages contained in the buffer drops below the maximum. This will happen only when one of the processes reads a message from α.

As is the case with unbounded buffering, we add a variable α to the set of state variables. The domain of α is again that of lists of elements of the declared type. Here, however, it is sufficient to consider lists of length not exceeding N.

The transition associated with a receive statement that refers to α is identical to the one specified for an unbounded channel.

- With the send statement

$$\ell: \ \alpha \Leftarrow e : \widehat{\ell},$$

referring to bounded channel α, we associate a transition τ_ℓ, whose transition relation is given by

$$\rho_\ell: \quad \left[([\ell] \in \pi) \ \wedge \ (|\alpha| < N) \ \wedge \ (\pi' = \pi \doteq [\ell] + [\widehat{\ell}]) \ \wedge \ (\alpha' = \alpha \bullet e) \right].$$

Thus, for bounded channels, the send statement can be performed only if it does not cause the size of α to exceed N.

The additions to the initial condition Θ are defined as in the unbounded case.

Message-passing systems using channels with positive buffering capacity, i.e., unbounded or bounded with a positive N, are called *asynchronously communicating* (AC) systems. The name emphasizes that the send and receive statements require no direct synchronization between the communicating processes. It may require some synchronization between a process and the channel it addresses, such as the execution of a receive statement being delayed until the channel becomes nonempty and the execution of a send statement being delayed until the channel becomes nonfull (in the bounded case).

No Buffering

Channels with no buffering capacity are declared simply by

$$\alpha: \ \textbf{channel of type}.$$

Such a channel cannot hold messages even for a short duration. Therefore, communication along such a channel allows no delay between the sending and receiving of a message. Consequently, send and receive statements can only be performed simultaneously. This implies that any process reaching either a send or a receive statement delays its execution until another process is ready to perform the matching statement. Two parallel statements are considered to be *matching* if they form an $\alpha \Leftarrow e$, $\alpha \Rightarrow u$ pair for some e and u and for the same channel α. When two matching statements are jointly ready to execute, their execution is atomic and simultaneous and the effect is equivalent to the assignment

$$u := e.$$

To express this in the semantic framework we have been using, we associate with each pair of matching send and receive statements

$$\ell_1: \ \alpha \Leftarrow e : \widehat{\ell_1} \qquad \ell_2: \ \alpha \Rightarrow u : \widehat{\ell_2},$$

a corresponding joint transition $\tau_{\langle \ell_1, \ell_2 \rangle}$, whose transition relation is given by

$$\rho_{\langle \ell_1, \ell_2 \rangle}: \quad \left[(\{\ell_1, \ell_2\} \subseteq \pi) \wedge (\pi' = \pi - \{\ell_1, \ell_2\} \cup \{\widehat{\ell}_1, \widehat{\ell}_2\}) \wedge (u' = e) \right].$$

Thus, transition $\tau_{\langle \ell_1, \ell_2 \rangle}$ is enabled only if both at_ℓ_1 and at_ℓ_2 hold simultaneously. This is tested by the inclusion $\{\ell_1, \ell_2\} \subseteq \pi$. When executed, the transition causes joint progress in the two processes containing the communication statements, simultaneously replacing $[\ell_1]$ by $[\widehat{\ell}_1]$, and $[\ell_2]$ by $[\widehat{\ell}_2]$. It also performs the communication itself, assigning to u the value of the expression e.

Note that the transition $\tau_{\langle \ell_1, \ell_2 \rangle}$ is associated with the two statements ℓ_1 and ℓ_2.

Let

$$\ell: \ \alpha \Leftarrow e$$

be a send statement. Denote by $match(\ell)$ the set of statements (represented by their labels) that match statement ℓ. As defined, $match(\ell)$ consists of all the receive statements of the form

$$m: \ \alpha \Rightarrow u$$

for some u and m, such that m is parallel to ℓ.

We define $trans(\ell)$, the set of transitions associated with statement ℓ, to be the set of transitions $\tau_{\langle \ell, m \rangle}$ for all $m \in match(\ell)$, that is,

$$trans(\ell) \ = \ \{ \tau_{\langle \ell, m \rangle} \mid m \in match(\ell) \}.$$

Similar definitions hold for the case that ℓ is a receive statement.

The case of no buffering is not the same as the case of buffering with $N = 0$. Buffering with $N = 0$ does not allow any send statement to be executed, since the buffer is always full to its capacity 0. The case of no buffering, on the other hand, allows a send statement to be executed, provided it is executed simultaneously with a matching receive statement.

Note that state variable α is not needed in π for the case of no buffering.

Example

Consider the program presented in Fig. 1.15.

This program has the following possible computation (listing for each state the values of π, x, y).

$$\langle \{\ell_0, m_0\}, \ \text{T}, \ \text{T} \rangle \ \xrightarrow{\ell_0^{\text{T}}} \ \langle \{\ell_1, m_0\}, \ \text{T}, \ \text{T} \rangle \ \xrightarrow{m_0^{\text{T}}}$$

$$\langle \{\ell_1, m_1\}, \ \text{T}, \ \text{T} \rangle \ \xrightarrow{\langle \ell_1, m_1 \rangle} \ \langle \{\ell_2, m_0\}, \ \text{T}, \ \text{T} \rangle \ \xrightarrow{\ell_4}$$

$$
\boxed{
\begin{array}{c}
\textbf{local } \alpha\text{: } \textbf{channel of boolean} \\[4pt]
P_1 :: \begin{bmatrix}
\textbf{local } x\text{: } \textbf{boolean where } x = \text{T} \\
\ell_0\text{: } \textbf{while } x \textbf{ do} \\
\quad \begin{bmatrix} \ell_1\text{: } \alpha \Leftarrow \text{T} \\ \ell_2\text{: } [\ [\ell_3\text{: } x := \text{T}] \textbf{ or } [\ell_4\text{: } x := \text{F}]\ ] \end{bmatrix} \\
\ell_5\text{: } \alpha \Leftarrow \text{F} \\
:\widehat{\ell_5}
\end{bmatrix} \\[10pt]
\| \\[10pt]
P_2 :: \begin{bmatrix}
\textbf{local } y\text{: } \textbf{boolean where } y = \text{T} \\
m_0\text{: } \textbf{while } y \textbf{ do } [m_1\text{: } \alpha \Rightarrow y] \\
:\widehat{m_0}
\end{bmatrix}
\end{array}
}
$$

Fig. 1.15.   No-buffering channel.

$$
\langle \{\ell_0,\ m_0\},\ \text{F},\ \text{T} \rangle \xrightarrow{m_0^{\text{T}}} \langle \{\ell_0,\ m_1\},\ \text{F},\ \text{T} \rangle \xrightarrow{\ell_0^{\text{F}}}
$$

$$
\langle \{\ell_5,\ m_1\},\ \text{F},\ \text{T} \rangle \xrightarrow{\langle \ell_5, m_1 \rangle} \langle \{\widehat{\ell_5},\ m_0\},\ \text{F},\ \text{F} \rangle \xrightarrow{m_0^{\text{F}}}
$$

$$
\langle \{\widehat{\ell_5},\ \widehat{m_0}\},\ \text{F},\ \text{F} \rangle \longrightarrow \cdots .
$$

Note that the two send statements ℓ_1 and ℓ_5 match the single receive statement m_1. ◢

The unbuffered mode of communication is called *synchronous communication* and has been referred to as *handshaking* or *rendezvous communication*. Systems communicating by this mode of communication are called *synchronously communicating* (SC) systems.

In **Problem 1.6**, the reader will consider augmentation of the state variables by additional control variables that record details about the last communication performed.

Examples

We present three examples that illustrate implementation of the producer-consumer problem in each of the three different message-passing models. Since the producer-consumer problem can be viewed as the construction of a bounded-buffer communication between processes, it is natural to consider the bounded buffering implementation first.

Example (producer-consumer with bounded buffering)

Consider the implementation of the producer-consumer problem using message passing. Obviously, the producer-consumer problem is a paradigm for bounded-buffer communication between processes. Therefore, it is not surprising that when bounded-buffer communication is available as a primitive statement, the resulting program becomes trivial.

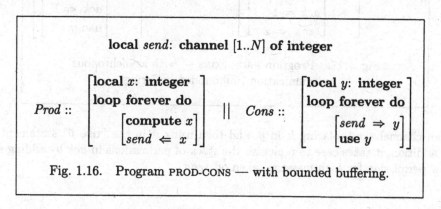

Fig. 1.16.   Program PROD-CONS — with bounded buffering.

In Fig. 1.16 we present the PROD-CONS program using bounded-buffering channels.

Example (producer-consumer with unbounded buffering)

A more interesting situation is the implementation of the producer-consumer problem using unbounded-buffering channels or channels with bounded buffering in which the actual bound on the buffering capacity is greater than the bound N specified in the problem. The requirement is that the channel should never hold more than N pending messages irrespective of the actual buffering capacity of the channel. This is accomplished in program PROD-CONS of Fig. 1.17 by establishing an acknowledgment channel ack leading from the consumer to the producer.

The producer process in this program behaves very much as before, except that it removes one message from channel ack before sending x through channel $send$. We may view the messages in channel ack as permission to send one message through $send$. Their particular value is of no importance and we use the value 1. Hence, the role of the receive statement $ack \Rightarrow t$ is to remove one "permission" from ack. The actual value placed into t is immaterial.

The initial value of channel ack is a sequence of N messages with value 1, implying N "permissions." The cycle of the consumer consists of reading a value

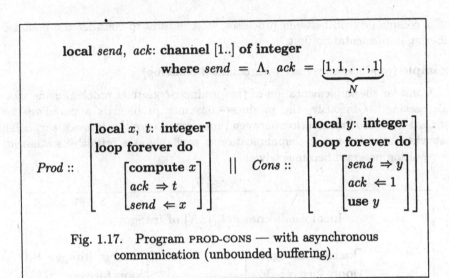

$$\text{local } send,\ ack\text{: channel } [1..] \text{ of integer}$$
$$\text{where } send = \Lambda,\ ack = \underbrace{[1,1,\ldots,1]}_{N}$$

$$Prod ::
\begin{bmatrix}
\text{local } x,\ t\text{: integer} \\
\text{loop forever do} \\
\quad \begin{bmatrix}
\text{compute } x \\
ack \Rightarrow t \\
send \Leftarrow x
\end{bmatrix}
\end{bmatrix}
\quad \| \quad Cons ::
\begin{bmatrix}
\text{local } y\text{: integer} \\
\text{loop forever do} \\
\quad \begin{bmatrix}
send \Rightarrow y \\
ack \Leftarrow 1 \\
\text{use } y
\end{bmatrix}
\end{bmatrix}$$

Fig. 1.17.   Program PROD-CONS — with asynchronous
communication (unbounded buffering).

from channel *send*, placing it in y, and then using it in the "**use** y" statement. In addition, it takes care to replenish the stock of permissions in *ack* by adding a new permission for each message taken off *send*.

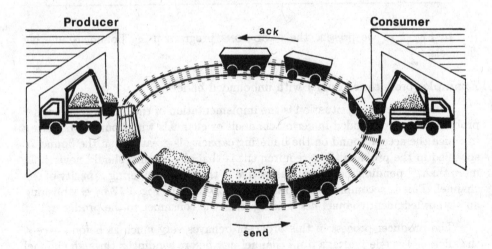

Fig. 1.18.   Pictorial representation of program PROD-CONS
with unbounded buffering.

A pictorial representation of the relation between channels *send* and *ack* is drawn in Fig. 1.18. Messages carrying values of x are drawn as loaded cars traveling on the *send* track from the producer to the consumer. The *ack* messages are drawn as empty cars traveling in the opposite direction. Drawing the channels *send* and *ack* as two sides of a single loop is justified by the fact that the producer needs an empty car, obtained from channel *ack*, before it can send a loaded car along channel *send*. Similarly, as soon as the consumer receives a loaded car from channel *send*, it sends an empty one along channel *ack*.

The correctness of the program is indeed based on the tight reciprocal relation between the two channels expressed by the invariant

$$|ack| + |send| \leq N.$$

This invariant ensures that $|send| \leq N$, as required.

Note the similarity between this solution and the one using semaphores (Fig. 1.12). Channel *ack* plays an identical role to that of semaphore variable *ne*, counting empty slots. ◢

In the third example, an implementation of the producer-consumer problem with synchronous communication, we use an extended version of the communication statements, called *conditional communication* statements.

We therefore pause to introduce these additional statements.

Conditional Communication Statements

In many cases, the readiness of a process to participate in a communication also depends on some internal condition. In these cases, we want to combine the send and receive statements with a test of a boolean expression. This leads to the introduction of two conditional communication statements.

The *conditional send* statement has the form

$$\alpha \Leftarrow e \textbf{ provided } c,$$

where α is a (declared) channel, e is an expression whose type is compatible with the type of α, and c is a boolean expression. The intended meaning of the conditional send statement is that it can perform the implied communication only if c evaluates to T. If c is true, then this statement behaves as the unconditional send statement.

The *conditional receive* statement has the form

$$\alpha \Rightarrow u \textbf{ provided } c,$$

with a similar interpretation.

The conditional send and receive statements can also be explained in terms of appropriate grouped statements, given by

$$\langle \textbf{when } c \textbf{ do } \alpha \Leftarrow e \rangle \qquad \text{and} \qquad \langle \textbf{when } c \textbf{ do } \alpha \Rightarrow u \rangle.$$

This shows that we consider these statements atomic and allow their execution only on states in which both c is true and the associated communication is possible.

From now on, we will view the unconditional communication statements as special cases of the corresponding conditional statements where $c = \mathrm{T}$.

We will present the transitions corresponding to the conditional communication statements, distinguishing again between the asynchronous and synchronous cases.

Asynchronous Communication

For the case of asynchronous channels (positive buffering capability), we define the transitions as follows:

- With the conditional send statement

  $$\ell:\ \alpha \Leftarrow e \textbf{ provided } c : \widehat{\ell},$$

we associate the transition τ_ℓ, whose transition relation is given by

$$\rho_\ell: \quad \begin{bmatrix} ([\ell] \in \pi) \ \wedge\ (|\alpha| < N_\alpha) \ \wedge\ c \\ \wedge \\ (\pi' = \pi \doteq [\ell] + [\widehat{\ell}]) \ \wedge\ (\alpha' = \alpha \bullet e) \end{bmatrix}.$$

Note that it differs from the transition relation for the unconditional case by having c as an additional clause. Parameter N_α denotes the upper limit declared for α in the bounded case. In the unbounded case, the clause $|\alpha| < N_\alpha$ is omitted.

- With a conditional receive statement

  $$\ell:\ \alpha \Rightarrow u \textbf{ provided } c : \widehat{\ell},$$

we associate the transition τ_ℓ, whose transition relation is given by

$$\rho_\ell: \quad \begin{bmatrix} ([\ell] \in \pi) \ \wedge\ (|\alpha| > 0) \ \wedge\ c \\ \wedge \\ (\pi' = \pi \doteq [\ell] + [\widehat{\ell}]) \ \wedge\ (u' = hd(\alpha)) \ \wedge\ (\alpha' = tl(\alpha)) \end{bmatrix}.$$

The additions to the state variables Π and to the initial condition Θ are identical to those of the unconditional case of asynchronous channels.

Synchronous Communication

For the case of synchronous channels (no buffering capability), we consider two matching communication statements

$$\ell_1:\ \alpha \Leftarrow e \textbf{ provided } c_1 : \widehat{\ell}_1 \qquad \text{and} \qquad \ell_2:\ \alpha \Rightarrow u \textbf{ provided } c_2 : \widehat{\ell}_2,$$

and define the joint transition $\tau_{\langle \ell_1, \ell_2 \rangle}$ associated with them by:

$$\rho_{\langle \ell_1, \ell_2 \rangle}: \begin{bmatrix} (\{\ell_1, \ell_2\} \subseteq \pi) \ \wedge \ c_1 \ \wedge \ c_2 \\ \wedge \ (\pi' = \pi - \{\ell_1, \ell_2\} \cup \{\widehat{\ell_1}, \widehat{\ell_2}\}) \ \wedge \ (u' = e) \end{bmatrix}.$$

Note that the case that one of the communication statements is unconditional is also covered by taking c_1 or c_2 to be T.

We illustrate the usefulness of the conditional communication statements with a program that implements the producer-consumer problem by synchronous communication.

Example (producer-consumer without buffering)

Since synchronous channels do not have built-in buffers, we implement the buffer as a third process. In program PROD-CONS presented in Fig. 1.19, the process *Buff* mediates between the sending needs of *Prod* and the receiving needs of *Cons*.

---

local pb, bc: **channel of integer**

$Prod ::$
$$\begin{bmatrix} \text{local } x: \textbf{integer} \\ \textbf{loop forever do} \\ \quad [\text{compute } x; \ pb \Leftarrow x] \end{bmatrix}$$

$\|$

$Buff ::$
$$\begin{bmatrix} \text{local } y: \textbf{integer} \\ \quad\quad b: \textbf{list of integer where } b = \Lambda \\ \textbf{loop forever do} \\ \quad \begin{bmatrix} pb \Rightarrow y \textbf{ provided } |b| < N; \ b := b \bullet y \\ \textbf{or} \\ bc \Leftarrow hd(b) \textbf{ provided } |b| > 0; \ b := tl(b) \end{bmatrix} \end{bmatrix}$$

$\|$

$Cons ::$
$$\begin{bmatrix} \text{local } z: \textbf{integer} \\ \textbf{loop forever do} \\ \quad [bc \Rightarrow z; \ \text{use } z] \end{bmatrix}$$

Fig. 1.19.   Program PROD-CONS — with synchronous communication.

There are two communication channels in this program. Channel *pb* connects *Prod* to *Buff* and channel *bc* connects *Buff* to *Cons*.

$$\boxed{Prod} \xrightarrow{\ \ pb\ \ } \boxed{Buff} \xrightarrow{\ \ bc\ \ } \boxed{Cons}$$

Process *Buff* has an internal buffer b in which it stores the values received from *Prod* and not yet sent to *Cons*. The communication pattern of *Prod* and *Cons* is simple. They regularly alternate between computation and communication.

The body of process *Buff* is an endlessly repeated selection statement, which offers two communication alternatives to the environment. Both are conditional on two factors. The first factor is a local condition on variable b, represented by the boolean expressions $|b| < N$ and $|b| > 0$. The second factor, which is always present in synchronous communication, is the availability of a matching communication partner.

It is vital in this example to test both factors simultaneously. Communicating first and testing the local condition later may lead to transmitting the head of an empty list. Testing the local condition first and committing to a particular communication based on this test may lead to waiting for a sluggish partner while the other, more agile, partner is waiting for us.

Consequently, we use conditional communication statements in *Buff*. The implications of the conditional communication statements appearing as two alternatives of the selection statement are the following:

(a) The communication will be performed only if both conditions are simultaneously satisfied, i.e., the boolean condition holds and a matching communication partner is available.

(b) As long as no communication is performed, no commitment has been made, and both alternatives are left open until one of them becomes enabled. ⏌

In **Problem 1.7**, the reader will critically examine the representation of asynchronous communication by allocating a single buffer variable to each asynchronous channel.

Comparison of the Synchronous and Asynchronous Models

The implementation of bounded buffering in terms of synchronous communication identifies a general transformation from an arbitrary program, using asynchronous communication with buffering, into a program using synchronous communication. The transformation entails defining, for each channel α, a new process P_α, to which we may refer as the *server* for α, which carries out the tasks of the asynchronous channel α in the original program. Process P_α has an internal buffer b_α and is ready to communicate with all the readers and writers of the channel α in the original program.

This transformation shows that, as far as communication capabilities are considered, synchronous communication is a more primitive concept than asynchronous communication. It has to explicitly define constructs such as the internal buffer and a server process in order to provide the same functionality that is already built into the asynchronous communication regime. Indeed, the seminal paper introducing synchronous communication via the language CSP motivates the choice of this mode of communication (the unbuffered one) as being the most basic and primitive one conceivable, and one on which higher-level modes of communication, such as buffered communication, can be implemented.

Moreover, as it later emerges, when we consider the synchronization capabilities of the different models, synchronous communication offers some advantages over the asynchronous versions. This is because the execution of a synchronous communication immediately provides the sender with an acknowledgment that the communication has taken place. In the asynchronous case, such an acknowledgment has to be explicitly programmed. We can observe this fact by comparing the simpler synchronous program of Fig. 1.19 with the more complex asynchronous program of Fig. 1.17. The latter includes explicit code for managing the acknowledgment using channel *ack*.

A Fair Server

A typical problem in concurrent programming is that of a fair server. The problem can be stated by describing a single process, called the *server* S, that is expected to provide services to N customer processes, called $P[1], \ldots, P[N]$, respectively. The server can serve only one customer at a time.

For simplicity and conciseness, we describe the services provided by the server as computing a function $f(x)$, for a nonzero argument x submitted by one of the customer processes. Clearly, this can represent the general situation of a server computing a response to a request made by a customer process.

It is required that the server eventually respond to any request made by one of the customer processes. A program that satisfies this requirement is called a *fair server*, as it is eventually fair to all customers.

Fair Server Using Shared Variables

In Fig. 1.20 we present program FAIR-SERVER, which implements a fair server using shared variables. This program uses the array $X[1..N]$ for input of arguments to the server and the array $Y[1..N]$ for output from the server to the customers. Array X is initially 0, that is, $X[1] = \cdots = X[N] = 0$.

The customer processes are represented by $P[j]$, $j = 1, \ldots, N$. These processes alternate between doing other activity and requiring the services of S. When a process $P[j]$ needs the services of S, it places an argument in $X[j]$. By assumption, arguments are always different from zero. After $P[j]$ places an argument in $X[j]$, it waits for $X[j]$ to become zero again. When it does, $P[j]$ assumes that the expected result is available in $Y[j]$ and proceeds to use it.

---

local X: **array** $[1..N]$ **of integer where** $X = 0$
            Y: **array** $[1..N]$ **of integer**

$$S :: \begin{bmatrix} \text{local } i\text{: integer where } i = 1 \\ \ell_0\text{: loop forever do} \\ \quad \begin{bmatrix} \ell_1\text{: if } X[i] \neq 0 \text{ then} \\ \quad \begin{bmatrix} \ell_2\text{: } Y[i] := f(X[i]) \\ \ell_3\text{: } X[i] := 0 \end{bmatrix} \\ \ell_4\text{: } i := i \oplus_N 1 \end{bmatrix} \end{bmatrix}$$

$\parallel$

$$\mathop{\parallel}\limits_{j=1}^{N} P[j] :: \begin{bmatrix} \text{local } u,\ v\text{: integer} \\ m_0\text{: loop forever do} \\ \quad \begin{bmatrix} m_1\text{: Other Activity} \\ m_2\text{: compute } u \\ m_3\text{: } X[j] := u \\ m_4\text{: await } X[j] = 0 \\ m_5\text{: } v := Y[j] \\ m_6\text{: use } v \end{bmatrix} \end{bmatrix}$$

Fig. 1.20.   Program FAIR-SERVER — a fair server
using shared variables.

Process S repeatedly scans array X, searching for nonzero elements. When it finds such an element in $X[i]$, it applies f to it and places the result in $Y[i]$. Subsequently, it sets $X[i]$ to zero, signaling that the result is ready. At the end of the loop body S advances to the next position. The expression $i \oplus_N 1$ denotes the next value of i in cyclic order over the range $1..N$; it is equal to $(i \bmod N) + 1$.

Fair Server Using Message Passing

In Fig. 1.21 we present a message-passing version of a solution for the fair-server problem. It is valid for both synchronous and asynchronous channels. The customer processes communicate with the server by two arrays of channels $\alpha[1..N]$ and $\beta[1..N]$. Arguments are sent to the server through the α channels and the results are retrieved through the β channels.

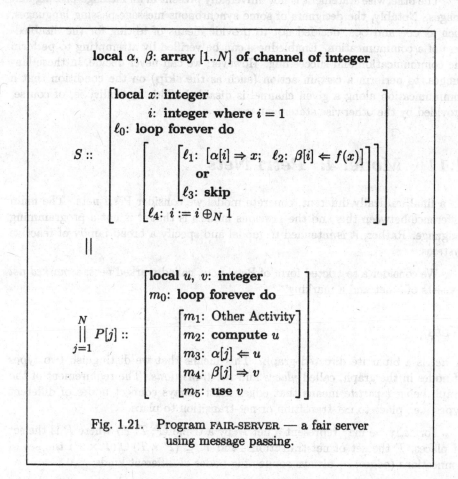

Fig. 1.21. Program FAIR-SERVER — a fair server
using message passing.

The selection statement in the body of the loop ℓ_0 presents a nondeterministic choice between serving process $P[i]$ and skipping to the next process. Clearly, $P[i]$ will not be served unless it has requested service that can be sensed by the receive statement ℓ_1 being enabled.

Differently from the case of the shared-variables program (Fig. 1.21), though, it is possible that $P[i]$ has requested service but the server may choose to ignore this request on this round. This can happen if server S chooses to execute ℓ_3 even though ℓ_1 is enabled.

In **Problem 1.8**, the reader will rectify this situation by using the otherwise statement, introduced in Problem 1.3, to construct a program in which the server cannot ignore a requesting $P[i]$.

The otherwise statement is not universally present in all message-passing languages. Notably, the designers of some synchronous message-passing languages, such as CSP and CCS, decided not to provide means of testing for the disabledness of a communication. Enabledness can be verified by attempting to perform the communication and succeeding. However, we can never decide, in these languages, to perform a certain action (such as the **skip**) on the condition that a communication along a given channel is disabled. This capability is, of course, provided by the otherwise statement.

1.11   Model 4:   Petri Nets

As a final, radically different, concrete model we consider Petri nets. The main difference between this and the previous models is that it is not a programming language. Rather, it is intended to model and specify a broad family of reactive systems.

We consider a restricted form of Petri nets, called marked nets; a *marked net* consists of a net and a marking.

Nets

A *net* is a bipartite directed graph. This means that we distinguish two types of nodes in the graph, called *places* and *net-transitions*. The requirement of the graph being *bipartite* means that edges must always connect nodes of different types, i.e., place to net-transition or net-transition to place.

Formally we may represent a net N by a triple $\langle P, T, F \rangle$ where P is the set of places, T the set of net-transitions, and $F \subseteq (P \times T) \cup (T \times P)$ the set of connections (edges) — always connecting nodes of different kinds.

For a net-transition $t \in T$ we define the *pre-set* of t, denoted by $^\bullet t$, as the set of places connected to t:

$$^\bullet t \;=\; \big\{ p \in P \mid (p,t) \in F \big\}.$$

The *post-set* of t, denoted by $t^\bullet$, is the set of places to which t is connected:

$$t^\bullet \;=\; \big\{ p \in P \mid (t,p) \in F \big\}.$$

Similarly, we define for a place $p \in P$,

$$^\bullet p \; = \; \{t \in T \mid (t,p) \in F\}$$

and

$$p^\bullet \; = \; \{t \in T \mid (p,t) \in F\}.$$

Marking

Let N be a net with places $P = \{p_1, \ldots, p_m\}$. A *marking* over N is a vector $\bar{y} = y[1], \ldots, y[m]$ of natural numbers, having a component $y[i]$ corresponding to each place p_i, $i = 1, \ldots, m$. Markings can be added and subtracted according to the usual rules of vector addition and subtraction.

Markings can also be compared

$$\bar{y} \geq \bar{y}' \quad \text{iff} \quad y[i] \geq y'[i] \text{ for every } i = 1, \ldots, m.$$

For a set of places $A \subseteq P$, C_A denotes the characteristic marking of A:

$$C_A[i] \; = \; \text{if } p_i \in A \text{ then } 1 \text{ else } 0.$$

Graphical Representation

Graphically we represent nets as directed graphs with nodes of two types. Places are drawn as circles, net-transitions as squares. Edges, representing the connections F, are drawn connecting places to net-transitions and net-transitions to places. A marking $\bar{y}$ over a net is represented by drawing tokens within places. For each place p_i in P we draw $y[i]$ tokens inside the circle representing p_i.

Example (a marked net)

Fig. 1.22 gives an example of a marked net.

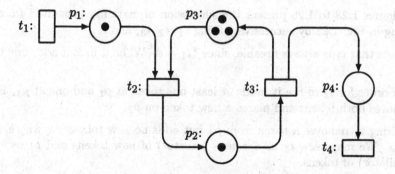

Fig. 1.22. A marked net.

In this net:

$$P = \{p_1, p_2, p_3, p_4\},$$
$$T = \{t_1, t_2, t_3, t_4\},$$
$$F = \{(t_1, p_1), (p_1, t_2), (p_3, t_2), (t_2, p_2), (p_2, t_3), (t_3, p_3), (t_3, p_4), (p_4, t_4)\}.$$

The pre-sets and post-sets of the transitions are given by

$$\begin{aligned}
{}^\bullet t_1 &= \phi, & t_1^\bullet &= \{p_1\}, \\
{}^\bullet t_2 &= \{p_1, p_3\}, & t_2^\bullet &= \{p_2\}, \\
{}^\bullet t_3 &= \{p_2\}, & t_3^\bullet &= \{p_3, p_4\}, \\
{}^\bullet t_4 &= \{p_4\}, & t_4^\bullet &= \phi.
\end{aligned}$$

The marking $\bar{y}$ shown in the diagram is:

$$y[1] = 1, \qquad y[2] = 1, \qquad y[3] = 3, \qquad y[4] = 0.$$

Firing

The basic operation on marked nets is the firing of a net-transition t in T. A net-transition t is defined to be *fireable* under the marking $\bar{y}$ if $\bar{y} \geq C_{\bullet t}$, that is, if $y[i] \geq 1$ for each $p_i \in {}^\bullet t$.

The *firing* of a transition t transforms the marking $\bar{y}$ into the marking $\bar{y}'$ defined by

$$\bar{y}' = \bar{y} - C_{\bullet t} + C_{t \bullet}.$$

It can be described as the removal of a token from each $p \in {}^\bullet t$ and the addition of a token to each $p \in t^\bullet$. The condition of fireability ensures that the removal process can be completed.

Example (marking after firing)

Figures 1.23 to 1.26 present the succession of markings generated from the marking in Fig. 1.22 by successively firing t_1, t_2, t_3, and t_4.

Note that t_1 is always fireable, since ${}^\bullet t_1 = \phi$. When it fires it adds one token to p_1.

In order for t_2 to fire it needs at least one token at p_1 and one at p_3. Firing t_2 removes both tokens and places a new token on p_2.

Firing t_4 removes a token from p_4 but adds no new tokens anywhere, since $t_4^\bullet = \phi$. We may view t_1 as a *source* (creator) of new tokens and t_4 as a *sink* (annihilator) of tokens.

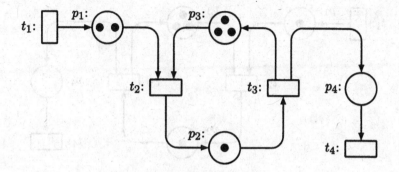

Fig. 1.23. Marking after firing t_1.

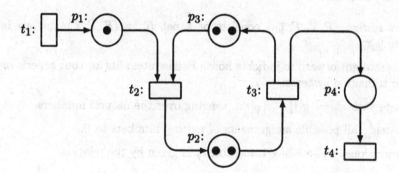

Fig. 1.24. Marking after firing t_1, t_2.

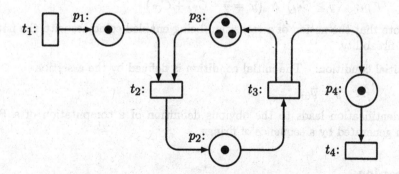

Fig. 1.25. Marking after firing t_1, t_2, t_3.

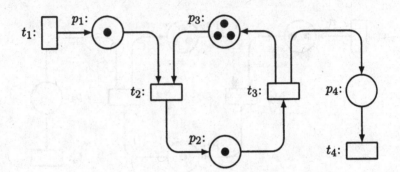

Fig. 1.26.   Marking after firing t_1, t_2, t_3, t_4.

Petri Systems

A *Petri system* $\langle P, T, F, \overline{y}_0 \rangle$ consists of a net $N = \langle P, T, F \rangle$ and an *initial marking* $\overline{y}_0$.

It is straightforward to indicate how a Petri system fits into our generic model of basic transition systems:

- State variables: $y[1], \ldots, y[m]$, ranging over the natural numbers.

- States: all possible assignments of natural numbers to $\overline{y}$.

- Transitions: The idling transition τ_I is given by the relation

    ρ_I: T.

Each net-transition t in T is taken to be a diligent transition of the transition system. The transition relation for a net-transition t in T is naturally defined by:

$$\rho_t: \quad (\overline{y} \geq C_{\bullet t}) \ \wedge \ (\overline{y}' = \overline{y} - C_{\bullet t} + C_{t \bullet}).$$

Note that the notion of a transition being enabled coincides with the notion of fireability.

- Initial condition: The initial condition is defined by the assertion

    Θ: $\overline{y} = \overline{y}_0$.

This identification leads to the obvious definition of a computation of a Petri system generated by a sequence of firings.

Examples

Let us consider the application of Petri systems for the modeling of reactive systems.

Example (producer-consumer)

The Petri system of Fig. 1.27 provides a model for the producer-consumer system. Among the solutions we have already provided for this problem, this solution is closest to the solution of the PROD-CONS program of Fig. 1.17.

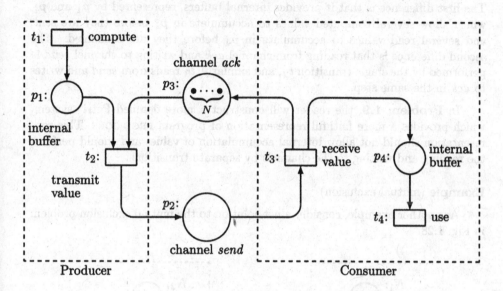

Fig. 1.27.   Producer-consumer Petri system.

We can identify the producer as the subnet consisting of t_1, p_1, and t_2 and the consumer as the subnet consisting of t_3, p_4, and t_4.

Transition t_1 represents the **compute** statement, generating a value that is represented as a new token placed into p_1. Place p_1 represents an unbounded internal buffer in which values are stored until they are transmitted to the consumer. Transition t_2 represents the combined process of reading an element from channel *ack* and transmitting an element taken from p_1 to channel *send*. Place p_2 represents the *send* channel containing elements that have been transmitted by the producer and not yet collected by the consumer. Transition t_3 represents the combined action of reading a value from channel *send*, which is then stored in the unbounded internal buffer p_4 and transmitting an acknowledging token to channel *ack*. Place p_3 represents channel *ack* counting the number of empty slots in channel *send*. Transition t_4 represents the *use* statement, consuming one element from buffer p_4.

The initial marking of this system consists of N tokens at p_3. This corresponds to the initial loading of channel *ack* with N messages, representing permissions.

This model differs from the PROD-CONS program of Fig. 1.17 in two aspects. The first difference is that it provides internal buffers, represented by p_1 and p_4, which allow several computed values to accumulate in p_1 before they are sent, and several read values to accumulate in p_4 before they are consumed. The second difference is that reading from channel *ack* and writing to channel *send* is performed by the single transition t_2, and similarly, t_3 reads from *send* and writes to *ack* in the same step.

In **Problem 1.9**, the reader will construct a more detailed Petri system, which provides a more faithful representation of program PROD-CONS. This representation should not allow internal accumulation of values and should perform the reading and writing to the channels by separate transitions.

Example (mutual exclusion)

As another example, consider a net solution to the mutual exclusion problem in Fig. 1.28.

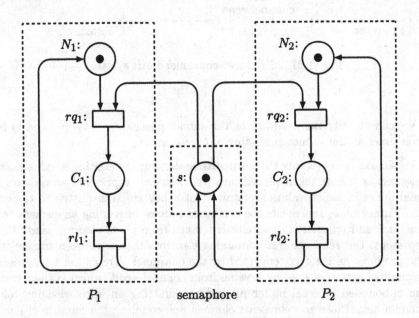

Fig. 1.28. Mutual exclusion Petri system.

In this diagram, process P_1 alternates between a noncritical section represented by N_1 and a critical section represented by C_1. Similarly, P_2 alternates between the noncritical N_2 and the critical C_2. Place s represents a semaphore variable; it contains a token iff the semaphore variable equals 1. Initially, process P_1 is at N_1, process P_2 is at N_2, and $s = 1$, represented by having tokens at N_1, N_2, and s. At that point two transitions are enabled, namely, rq_1 and rq_2, representing **request** statements. When one of them is performed, the appropriate process moves to its C location while s becomes 0. Exit from the critical section is associated with one of the rl_1 and rl_2 transitions, representing **release** statements. It causes the appropriate process to revert to its noncritical section and s to increase to 1.

The initial marking of this system consists of one token each at N_1 and N_2, representing the initial location of the two processes as noncritical, and one token at s, representing an initial value of 1 for the semaphore variable.

This example can be used to illustrate one of the powerful proof techniques associated with nets.

Consider the set of places and transitions

$$C = \{s, \ rq_1, \ C_1, \ rl_1, \ rq_2, \ C_2, \ rl_2\}.$$

This set satisfies the following two requirements:

(a) For each transition t in C, $|{}^{\bullet}t \cap C| = |t^{\bullet} \cap C|$. That is, for each transition in C the number of its successor places in C equals the number of its predecessor places in C.

(b) For each place p in C, $({}^{\bullet}p \cup p^{\bullet}) \subseteq C$. That is, all the transitions placing tokens and removing tokens from p are in C.

A subnet satisfying these requirements has the property that the number of tokens in C remains invariant. This is because, by (b), no transition outside C can deposit tokens in C or remove tokens from C and, by (a), every transition in C removes and places exactly the same number of tokens in C.

Since the subnet C specified earlier satisfies the two requirements, the number of tokens in C at any stage of a computation equals the number of tokens in C at the initial marking, namely, 1. This shows that mutual exclusion is guaranteed, because a violation of mutual exclusion implies tokens at both C_1 and C_2, i.e., 2 tokens in C.

Problems

Problem 1.1 (an irreproducible while statement)   page 39

Consider program SB of Fig. 1.29.

out x: integer where $x = 0$

$$\ell_0: \begin{bmatrix} [\ell_1: \textbf{while } x \geq 0 \textbf{ do } [\ell_2: x := x + 1 : \widehat{\ell_2}]] \\ \textbf{or} \\ [\ell_3: \textbf{await } x > 0] \end{bmatrix} : \widehat{\ell_0}$$

Fig. 1.29. Program SB (strangely behaving).

(a) Show that this program has a terminating computation.

This terminating computation may appear to be counterintuitive. We can trace the problem to the label equivalence $\widehat{\ell_2} \sim_L \ell_1$. One way out of this difficulty is to disallow while statements as children of selection statements.

Another solution is to consider a different version of a while statement

$$\ell_1: [\text{WHILE } c \text{ DO } [\ell_2: S: \widehat{\ell_2}]]: \widehat{\ell_1},$$

for which $\widehat{\ell_2} \not\sim_L \ell_1$.

(b) Define transitions and transition relations for the WHILE statement presented earlier. Show that the version of program SB in which the while statement has been replaced by a WHILE statement has no terminating computation.

Problem 1.2 (translation of text to diagram)   page 39

(a) Show that a sequential text program, i.e., a program without cooperation statements, can be translated to an equivalent diagram program.

(b) Show that a text program of the form

$$[\text{declaration}; [S_1 \| \ldots \| S_m]],$$

where each S_i is a sequential statement, can be translated to an equivalent diagram program.

*(c) Show that a text program that does not contain the variable size constructs $\overset{n}{\underset{i=1}{\textbf{OR}}}[S_i]$ or $\overset{n}{\underset{i=1}{\|}} S_i$ can be translated to an equivalent diagram program. In this translation you may have to add some auxiliary variables and instructions that establish additional communication between the processes. A statement such as $S_1; [S_2 \| S_3]; S_4$ may require several diagram processes for its execution. These processes may signal one another to announce the initiation and termination of the statement $S_2 \| S_3$.

(d) Translate the schematic text program

$$[S_1; \ [S_2\|S_3]; \ S_4; \ [S_5\|S_6\|S_7]; \ S_8]$$

to a diagram program. Assume that each S_i, $i = 1, \ldots, 8$, is a sequential statement which has already been translated into a diagram D_i with a single entry location ℓ_i and a single exit location m_i.

Problem 1.3 (otherwise statement)   page 50

Define a new statement, called the otherwise statement. If S_1 and S_2 are statements, then

$$S_1 \ \textbf{otherwise} \ S_2$$

is an *otherwise* statement. We refer to S_1 and S_2 as the *children* of the otherwise statement.

The intended meaning of this statement is:

■   If S_1 is currently enabled, S_2 is ignored, and the first step in the execution of S_1 is performed. Subsequent steps continue to execute the rest of S_1 if more than one step is necessary.

■   If S_1 is currently disabled, S_1 is ignored. Subsequent steps are committed to the execution of S_2.

Thus, we give priority to S_1 over S_2, provided execution of S_1 can commence immediately. Note that when deciding to ignore S_1, it is not checked whether S_2 is enabled.

Let S be the statement

$$\ell: \ [[\ell_1 : S_1] \ \textbf{otherwise} \ [\ell_2 : S_2]]$$

The label equivalences related to this statement are

$$\ell \sim_L \ell_1$$

and

$$post(S_1) \sim_L post(S_2) \sim_L post(S).$$

The transitions associated with S are given by

$$trans(S) \ = \ trans(S_1) \cup \{\tau_\ell\}.$$

These transitions consist of all the transitions associated with S_1 plus the unique transition τ_ℓ attributed to S, whose transition relation is given by

$$\rho_\ell \ = \ ([\ell] \in \pi) \ \wedge \ (\neg enabled(S_1)) \ \wedge \ (\pi' = \pi \,\dot-\, [\ell] + [\ell_2]).$$

Thus, the single transition τ_ℓ, attributed to S itself, is allowed to ignore S_1 and commit to the execution of S_2, only from a state in which no transition of $trans(S_1)$ is enabled. Note that τ_ℓ does not start the execution of S_2, but only decides to discard S_1.

Consequently, if control is at S it may proceed to execute a transition of S_1 or take τ_ℓ if no transition of S_1 is enabled.

Using these definitions, indicate which of the following statements are congruent. Whenever you claim that two statements are not congruent, justify it by describing an environment that causes the two to behave differently:

(a) [when c_1 do S_1] or [when c_2 do S_2]

(b) [when c_1 do S_1] otherwise [when c_2 do S_2]

(c) if c_1 then S_1 else [when c_2 do S_2]

(d) [[when c_1 do S_1] otherwise [when c_2 do S_2]] or [when c_2 do S_2]

(e) [[when c_1 do S_1] otherwise [when c_2 do S_2]] otherwise [when c_2 do S_2].

Problem 1.4 (mutual exclusion)   page 61

Program TRY-MUX of Fig. 1.30 is suggested as a solution to the mutual exclusion problem.

(a) Is it an acceptable solution? Justify your answer.

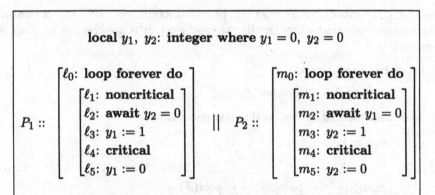

Fig. 1.30.   Program TRY-MUX (proposed solution to mutual exclusion).

(b) The same question for a program in which statements ℓ_2 and ℓ_3 are interchanged and so are statements m_2 and m_3.

(c) The same question for program TURN of Fig. 1.31.

Problem 1.5 (implementation of region statement)   page 67

Show how to implement region statements by other statements (including semaphores) of the shared-variables language. Introduce an integer variable r

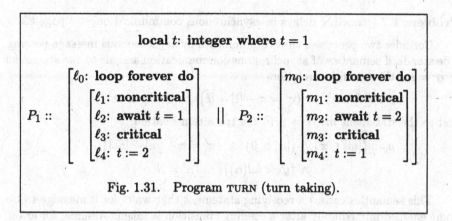

local t: integer where $t = 1$

$$P_1 :: \begin{bmatrix} \ell_0: \textbf{loop forever do} \\ \begin{bmatrix} \ell_1: \textbf{noncritical} \\ \ell_2: \textbf{await } t = 1 \\ \ell_3: \textbf{critical} \\ \ell_4: t := 2 \end{bmatrix} \end{bmatrix} \quad \| \quad P_2 :: \begin{bmatrix} m_0: \textbf{loop forever do} \\ \begin{bmatrix} m_1: \textbf{noncritical} \\ m_2: \textbf{await } t = 2 \\ m_3: \textbf{critical} \\ m_4: t := 1 \end{bmatrix} \end{bmatrix}$$

Fig. 1.31. Program TURN (turn taking).

for each resource, whose value is 0 whenever a statement protected by a region statement is executing, and 1 otherwise.

Show how to transform the statement

region r **when** c **do** S

to a statement that uses either semaphores or grouped statements but no region statement. The transformed program should preserve the intended meaning of the region statement, i.e.,

(1) no two statements protected by the same resource may execute at the same time;

(2) when the program commits to S, c must be true.

Problem 1.6 (variables recording last communication)   page 76

For message-passing programs, there are advantages in having state variables that identify whether the last transition taken was a communication transition, and if so identify the channel and the value communicated. Assume that we add the following state variables:

- *ind* — ranging over *send*, *receive*, or *none*.
  This variable identifies whether the last transition taken was a send transition, a receive transition, or any other transition.

- *chan* — records the name of the channel on which the last communication took place.

- *val* — records the last value communicated.

Explain the extensions needed to the definitions of the initial condition Θ and the transition relations. Note that the transition relations associated with noncommunicating statements should also be modified.

Problem 1.7 (modeling delays in asynchronous communication)   page 82

Consider two processes that communicate by asynchronous message passing. The standard semantics of asynchronous communication assigns to the statement $\ell\colon \alpha \Leftarrow e\colon \widehat{\ell}$ the transition relation

$$\rho_\ell\colon\ ([\ell] \in \pi)\ \wedge\ (\pi' = \pi \div [\ell] + [\widehat{\ell}])\ \wedge\ (\alpha' = \alpha \bullet e)$$

and to the statement $m\colon \alpha \Rightarrow y\colon \widehat{m}$ the transition relation

$$\rho_m\colon\ ([m] \in \pi) \wedge (|\alpha| > 0) \wedge (\pi' = \pi \div [m] + [\widehat{m}])$$
$$\wedge\ (y' = hd(\alpha))\ \wedge\ (\alpha' = tl(\alpha)).$$

This semantics causes a receiving statement that waits for a message to become enabled immediately after a sending transition is taken. Assume, for example, that one process contains the program segment

$$\cdots\ \alpha \Leftarrow 1;\ \beta \Leftarrow 2\ \cdots$$

and a parallel process contains the statement

$$\cdots\ m\colon\ [[m_1\colon\ \alpha \Rightarrow x]\ \textbf{or}\ [m_2\colon\ \beta \Rightarrow y]]\ \cdots,$$

where these are the only statements addressing α or β. Then, transition m_1 always becomes enabled before m_2.

In real systems there may be different delays associated with channels α and β. As a result, even though the message on α is sent before the message on β, the β-message may arrive earlier than the α-message.

A more realistic modeling of delayed transmission is obtained by breaking the single buffer α, used in the standard semantics, into two buffers: α_S and α_R. The transitions associated with statements $\ell\colon \alpha \Leftarrow e\colon \widehat{\ell}$ and $m\colon \alpha \Rightarrow y\colon \widehat{m}$ are

$$\rho_\ell^d\colon\ ([\ell] \in \pi)\ \wedge\ (\pi' = \pi \div [\ell] + [\widehat{\ell}])\ \wedge\ (\alpha_S' = \alpha_S \bullet e)$$
$$\rho_m^d\colon\ ([m] \in \pi) \wedge (|\alpha_R| > 0) \wedge (\pi' = \pi \div [m] + [\widehat{m}])$$
$$\wedge\ (y' = hd(\alpha_R))\ \wedge\ (\alpha_R' = tl(\alpha_R)).$$

In addition, we have a spontaneous transition (i.e., not associated with any statement) defined by

$$\rho_\alpha^d\colon\ (|\alpha_S| > 0)\ \wedge\ (\alpha_R' = \alpha_R \bullet hd(\alpha_S))\ \wedge\ (\alpha_S' = tl(\alpha_S)).$$

This transition removes the first element of α_S and appends it to the end of α_R.

We refer to this version of the transitions as the *delayed* version and to computations using these transitions as a *delayed computations*.

(a) Consider program OBS-ORD in Fig. 1.32, which uses the otherwise statement introduced in Problem 1.3. Show that this program has a delayed computation that leads to a final state that cannot be obtained by any standard computation.

$$
\begin{array}{l}
\textbf{out} \quad z \quad : \textbf{integer where } z = 0 \\
\textbf{local } \alpha,\ \beta \colon \textbf{channel } [1..] \textbf{ of integer}
\end{array}
$$

$$
P :: \begin{bmatrix} \ell_0 \colon \alpha \Leftarrow 1 \\ \ell_1 \colon \beta \Leftarrow 2 \end{bmatrix} \quad \| \quad Q :: \begin{bmatrix} m_0 \colon \beta \Rightarrow z \\ m_1 \colon \begin{bmatrix} m_2 \colon \alpha \Rightarrow z \\ \textbf{otherwise} \\ m_3 \colon \textbf{skip} \end{bmatrix} \end{bmatrix}
$$

Fig. 1.32. Program OBS-ORD (observing order of arrival).

This shows that delayed computations model behaviors that cannot be captured by the standard semantics.

*(b) Consider a program P containing no otherwise statements. Assume that the auxiliary variables α, α_R, and α_S are not observable. Show that the set of reduced standard computations equals the set of reduced delayed computations.

This shows that, without otherwise statements, a program cannot distinguish between standard and delayed semantics.

Problem 1.8 (a really fair server)   page 86

The program presented in Fig. 1.21 is suggested as the message-passing analog of program FAIR-SERVER of Fig. 1.20, which uses shared variables. However, as explained in the text, the two programs are not fully similar. In particular, the shared-variables program guarantees that once process $P[j]$ requests a service it will be served on the next time that $i = j$, i.e., the next time that S examines the status of $P[j]$. This is not true of the program in Fig. 1.21. Server S may decide to ignore a requesting $P[j]$ an unbounded number of times by choosing to perform ℓ_3 rather than ℓ_1.

Using the otherwise statement, construct a message-passing program that, similar to the shared-variables program, can guarantee that each requesting process will be served the very next time it is examined by S. Explain why this is the case for the program you construct.

Problem 1.9 (program PROD-CONS using Petri nets)   page 92

The net presented in Fig. 1.27 differs from program PROD-CONS of Fig. 1.17 on two major points. The first is that it allows accumulation of internal values in the buffers, represented by the places p_1 and p_4, before they are shipped out or consumed, respectively. The second difference is that each of the transitions t_2 and t_3 reads and writes on the channels in a single action. Construct a more detailed net that represents more closely the PROD-CONS program of Fig. 1.17. It should allow at most one value that is computed and not yet sent, and at most one value that is read and not yet consumed. It should also perform the reading and writing on the two channels by separate transitions. Give an interpretation to the places appearing in your net, where some places may be interpreted as buffers holding values, while others may be interpreted as locations in the program, and a token being there construed as control reaching those locations.

Bibliographic Notes

Transition systems as a generic model for concurrent programs were introduced by Keller [1976]. Representation of concurrent programs by *transition diagrams* is advocated by Lamport [1983d]. The basic notion of modeling concurrency by *interleaving* was first used by Dijkstra [1965]. The term "interleaving" was coined by Dijkstra [1971]. These references and Dijkstra [1968a] have laid the foundations for the model used throughout this book, emphasizing the interplay between concurrency and *nondeterminism*.

Of the various mechanisms for communication between processes considered here, *shared variables* is the mechanism used by Dijkstra [1965] for formulating the mutual exclusion problem. Several variants of *message passing*, including both bounded and unbounded buffering, are considered by Dijkstra [1968a], who also introduced in the same paper synchronization by *semaphores*. *Asynchronous message passing* has been used by Kahn [1974] as the basis for his data-flow model of parallelism.

Synchronous message passing in the style used here, where sender and receiver are distinguished, was introduced first by Hoare [1978]. In this paper, which introduces the language CSP, Hoare justifies the choice of this communication mechanism by identifying it as a more primitive mechanism than that of buffered message passing and as the closest to the hardware level. This mechanism is the one used in the programming language OCCAM. The same mechanism in a more abstract setting, which concentrates on the synchronization induced by synchronous message passing, was adopted in the language CCS by Milner [1980]. These ideas are further developed and refined by Milner [1989].

When focusing on synchronous message passing as a (handshaking) synchronization mechanism, one may drop the distinction between sender and receiver and require all processes (generalizing to more than 2) that refer to a given channel to synchronize on an abstract action referring to this channel. This is the communication mode adopted by Hoare [1984], where the emphasis is on specification and description of concurrent systems rather than on programming. Actually, the notion of several concurrent processes synchronizing on joint actions reaches back to the work of Campbell and Habermann [1974] and additional developments by Lauer, Shields and Best [1979].

We can trace the origins of some of the other statements in our programming language. As mentioned above, *semaphores* were first introduced by Dijkstra [1968a], where they were used for solving the mutual exclusion and other synchronization problems. The paper also shows how to simulate a general integer semaphore by a binary one. Dijkstra [1971] considers a parallel semaphore.

The *region* and *await* statements were introduced by Lamport [1976]. The *cooperation* statement, allowing a sequential process to spawn several parallel ones in mid-execution, is modeled after the *parbegin* statement of Dijkstra [1968a]. The notion of *guarded command*, which is the basis for our diagram language and an inspiration for the *when* statement, was first introduced by Dijkstra [1975] and further elaborated by Dijkstra [1976].

An important element of the guarded command language of Dijkstra [1976] (see also Gries [1981]) is the nondeterministic choice *if* statement which, in our language, is represented as a *selection* statement with *when* statements as children. In the shared-variables model, this construct is convenient but not absolutely necessary. It can always be programmed by a *while* statement that checks the guards one at a time and executes the statement associated with the first guard found to be true. The situation is different in the message-passing model, where the construct of waiting for an incoming input on one of several channels cannot be programmed without guarded selection. This was first pointed out by Hoare [1978] and is now recognized as one of the most important elements of message-passing languages.

Petri nets, first introduced by Petri [1962], is an extensively studied formalism for the description and analysis of concurrent systems. A modern introduction to net theory is given by Reisig [1985]. Another introduction is by Peterson [1981].

Our approach to the *semantics* of concurrent programs by which a program is uniquely identified by the set of its *reduced behaviors* is one of the simplest approaches possible. The decision to identify two computations that differ only by *stuttering* follows Lamport [1983d]. The notion of statement congruence induced by program equivalence is inspired by Hennessy and Milner [1985] and by the general algebraic approach to program semantics promoted by Milner [1980].

There are many additional mechanisms for communication and synchronization which have been proposed in the literature and will not be considered here. In principle, all of them can be represented in the transition systems model. Two surveys of synchronization mechanisms and comparison of their expressive power are Andrews and Schneider [1983] and Ben-Ari [1990].

Some of these mechanisms are *secretaries* proposed by Dijkstra [1971], *monitors* introduced by Hoare [1974], *remote calls* implemented in ADA, *concurrent logic programming* developed by Shapiro [1989], *broadcast* communication employed in I/O automata proposed by Lynch and Tuttle [1987], and also used in

Statecharts by Harel [1987].

It is interesting to compare the approach to the representation of concurrent programs proposed in this book to the *Unity* approach taken by Chandy and Misra [1988]. While we adopt *transition systems* as a generic model but prefer to use a higher level structured programming language for presenting programs, the *Unity* language can be described as programming directly at the transition system level. In that it is closer to our diagram language which has only one type of executable statement: a guarded assignment.

Considering the main examples presented in this chapter, the *mutual exclusion* problem was first formulated by Dijkstra [1965], together with a proposed solution which is proven to be *safe* (i.e., mutual exclusion maintained) and deadlock free. As observed by Knuth [1966], this solution is not free of *individual starvation*. Knuth [1966] provided solutions that are free of individual starvation but allow one process to overtake its competitor an unbounded number of times. An improved solution was presented by de Bruijn [1967].

The first correct solution for two processes which overcomes all these problems is described by Dijkstra [1968a] and attributed to Dekker. The first fully correct solution for n processes, called the *bakery algorithm*, was presented by Lamport [1974]. It is safe, deadlock free, and starvation free with bounded overtaking, but is not finite state as it uses unbounded counters. An improved version was presented by Lamport [1976], where the question of *atomicity* of statements is examined more carefully. It is shown there that for $n = 2$ the algorithm can be made finite state.

The first finite state solution for n processes, which ensures all the other requirements, was given by Peterson [1983b].

The *producer-consumer* problem was formulated by Dijkstra [1968a], and solved using semaphores.

Chapter 2
Modeling Real Concurrency

An essential element of the generic model used in this book is that concurrency is represented by *interleaving*. This means that, according to the formal model, two parallel processes never execute their statements at precisely the same instant, but take turns in executing atomic transitions. Formally, when one of them executes an atomic transition, the other is inactive. This model of computation is very convenient for the formalization, analysis, and manipulation of concurrent programs.

However, actual concurrent systems are usually composed of several independent processors, each of them executing a program of its own (a *process* in our terminology). In such systems, the execution of statements in different processors usually overlaps rather than interleaves. We refer to this behavior as *overlapped execution*.

A crucial question is how to reconcile the formal notion of interleaved computations, defined in our models, and the notion of overlapped executions, as realized on actual systems.

Two problems have to be resolved to achieve this reconciliation. The first problem is that of interference, and the second is independent progress.

• *Interference*

Interleaved execution provides a higher degree of protection from interference than is available in overlapped execution. This is because interleaved execution requires that when a transition is taken, all other transitions are inactive, so no interference during a transition is possible.

Consider, for example, the following statement:

when $y = y$ **do** S.

In interleaved computations, the condition $y = y$ is tested in one atomic step, so it always yields the value T. In comparison, overlapped execution (under naive implementation, with no optimization) of this statement will reference y twice.

If, precisely between these two references, an overlapped statement performed by a concurrent processor changes y, the testing processor may find the condition to be false.

There are two possible solutions to the interference problem: we can either admit more interference in the interleaved computations or require more protection in the overlapped executions. These solutions will be discussed in the following sections.

• *Independent Progress*

The problem of *independent progress* is that, in an overlapped execution, the computation of each process keeps advancing, since each processor is independently responsible for its own progress. In an interleaved computation, the only requirement is that enabled transitions be continuously chosen and executed. There is nothing to disallow a computation in which only transitions from one process are ever chosen. Such a computation ensures progress of the preferred process, but keeps all other processes stagnant.

The solution of this problem is to impose more restrictions on the basic model, guaranteeing progress for all processes in the interleaved computations. Such restrictions will be presented in the sections on fairness.

2.1 Interleaving and Concurrency

In this section, we will compare the behavior of programs under overlapped execution with their interleaved computations.

Overlapped Execution

Consider the simple program $A1$ in Fig. 2.1. The overlapped execution of this program on a system consisting of two independent processors sharing a common memory yields $\{0, 1, 2\}$ as the set of possible outcomes for y.

---

out y: integer where $y = 1$

$$P_1 :: \quad [\ell_0: y := y + 1 : \widehat{\ell_0}] \quad || \quad P_2 :: \quad [m_0: y := y - 1 : \widehat{m_0}]$$

Fig. 2.1.   Program $A1$.

To see this, realize that execution of an assignment statement, such as $y :=y + 1$, usually consists of three distinct steps:

- *Fetch step*: The value in the shared-memory location corresponding to y is fetched and stored in a local register.

- *Compute step*: The register is incremented, with the resulting value possibly being deposited in another local register.

- *Store step*: The value in the result register is stored in the shared-memory location corresponding to y.

The partition of execution of an assignment into these three steps is common to many other statements. More complicated assignments may have several fetch steps, depending on the number of variables appearing in their right-hand sides.

When we consider program $A1$, there are such steps in the execution of assignments by both processes P_1 and P_2. We identify four of these steps as *critical events*, in the sense that the relative ordering between them determines the final outcome of the execution. They are the events of fetching and storing values from and to the shared-memory location corresponding to y. We describe the critical events of this program as:

P_1 reads value m from y, denoted by $r_1(m)$

P_1 writes value m to y, denoted by $w_1(m)$

P_2 reads value m from y, denoted by $r_2(m)$

P_2 writes value m to y, denoted by $w_2(m)$.

Furthermore, we assume that these critical events are *atomic*, in the sense that they cannot overlap. For simple data types, this is usually guaranteed by the underlying hardware: while one process is accessing a memory location, no other process may access the same location.

In an overlapped execution of program $A1$, these events can occur in several orders, some of which are listed here:

E_1: $r_1(1)$, $w_1(2)$, $r_2(2)$, $w_2(1)$, yielding $y = 1$

E_2: $r_1(1)$, $r_2(1)$, $w_1(2)$, $w_2(0)$, yielding $y = 0$

E_3: $r_1(1)$, $r_2(1)$, $w_2(0)$, $w_1(2)$, yielding $y = 2$.

This shows how an overlapped execution of this program can yield the three possible results 0, 1, and 2, depending on the relative ordering of the critical events of the execution. Note that we do not consider the calculation step critical, since it operates only on internal registers that are not accessible to the other process.

The situation illustrated here is general. In any concurrent program it is always possible to identify some events in the execution of the program as *critical events*, such that their relative ordering in time uniquely determines the final result of the execution as well as its observable behavior, i.e., the sequence of values assumed by the observed variables. For programs that communicate by shared variables, these events are the reading and writing to the shared variables.

It is important to note that the set of behaviors described here is not unique to the particular implementation considered, i.e., two independent processors sharing a common memory. Precisely the same set of behaviors is exhibited in a uniprocessor environment where concurrency is implemented by multiprogramming. In such systems, a single processor simulates concurrency by alternating execution of parallel tasks that correspond to the parallel processes in our programs. The decision to switch from one task to another may be based on interrupts by a timer or external events. Consider, for example, the sequence of critical events called E_3. It is easy to envision a scenario in which the processor is executing the $r_1(1)$ event for process P_1, and just then being interrupted by a timer and switching to the task corresponding to P_2, where it proceeds to perform $r_2(1)$ followed by $w_2(0)$. It may then return to P_1 to complete the pending $w_1(2)$ operation.

Interleaved Computation

Consider now the possible results of computations of program $A1$ (Fig. 2.1), as defined in our model of basic transition system. The computational model assigns to program $A1$ two transitions ℓ_0 and m_0 (shorthand notation for τ_{ℓ_0} and τ_{m_0}) corresponding to the assignment statements in P_1 and P_2. Thus, the only possible computations of program $A1$ in our interleaved model are the following:

$$\langle \{\ell_0, m_0\}, 1 \rangle \xrightarrow{\ell_0} \langle \{\widehat{\ell}_0, m_0\}, 2 \rangle \xrightarrow{m_0} \langle \{\widehat{\ell}_0, \widehat{m}_0\}, 1 \rangle \cdots$$

$$\langle \{\ell_0, m_0\}, 1 \rangle \xrightarrow{m_0} \langle \{\ell_0, \widehat{m}_0\}, 0 \rangle \xrightarrow{\ell_0} \langle \{\widehat{\ell}_0, \widehat{m}_0\}, 1 \rangle \cdots .$$

In the interleaved model only one final result is possible: $y = 1$.

This seems to indicate that interleaved computation fails to capture the full range of behaviors exhibited by overlapped execution.

However, the problem is not in the interleaving model per se, but in the assignment of atomic transitions to statements in the program. According to the rules we gave for our programming language, each assignment statement is represented as a single atomic transition. This representation leads to the undesirable effect that a transition such as ℓ_0 (corresponding to $y := y + 1$) forces the two critical events r_1 and w_1 to happen in one step, thereby precluding the possibility of any of the critical events r_2, w_2 occurring after r_1 but before w_1. Indeed it is these possibilities that led to the outcomes 0 and 2, which the interleaved computation failed to produce.

One possible solution to this difficulty is that an assignment such as $y := y+1$ in program $A1$ should be associated with two atomic transitions, say τ'_{ℓ_0} and τ''_{ℓ_0}.

The first transition τ'_{ℓ_0} should perform the fetch substep, while τ''_{ℓ_0} should perform the store substep. The calculation substep can be absorbed into either τ'_{ℓ_0} or τ''_{ℓ_0}.

Finer Granularity

There is another solution to the problem of discrepancy between interleaved computation and overlapped execution. This solution, which is the one we follow, is to modify program $A1$ in such a way that any atomic transition generated according to the rules as originally given, i.e., one transition per assignment statement, contains at most one critical event. Such a modification is presented by program $A2$ of Fig. 2.2.

$$
\boxed{
\begin{array}{c}
\textbf{out } y\text{: integer where } y = 1 \\[2mm]
P_1 :: \begin{bmatrix} \textbf{local } t_1\text{: integer} \\ \ell_0\text{: } t_1 := y \\ \ell_1\text{: } y := t_1 + 1 : \widehat{\ell_1} \end{bmatrix}
\quad \| \quad
P_2 :: \begin{bmatrix} \textbf{local } t_2\text{: integer} \\ m_0\text{: } t_2 := y - 1 \\ m_1\text{: } y := t_2 : \widehat{m_1} \end{bmatrix}
\end{array}
}
$$

Fig. 2.2.   Program $A2$ (finer version of program $A1$).

Each of the assignments of program $A1$ has been broken into two successive assignments in $A2$. The first assignment in each sequence performs the fetch substep, while the second assignment performs the store substep. To emphasize that the exact timing of the calculation substep is immaterial (as long as it comes after fetching and before storing), we have included it in the storing assignment in P_1 and in the fetching assignment in P_2. Note that local variables t_1 and t_2 represent the internal registers of the two independent processors.

The interleaved computations of $A2$ re-create all the overlapped executions of $A2$, which in turn are identical to the overlapped executions of program $A1$. To see this, we will illustrate three computations of $A2$ leading to the final results 1, 0, and 2. We represent the states occurring in these computations by listing the values assumed by the variables π, y, t_1, and t_2.

σ_1: $\langle \{\ell_0, m_0\},\ 1,\ -,\ - \rangle \xrightarrow{\ell_0} \langle \{\ell_1, m_0\},\ 1,\ 1,\ - \rangle \xrightarrow{\ell_1}$

$\quad\quad \langle \{\widehat{\ell_1}, m_0\},\ 2,\ 1,\ - \rangle \xrightarrow{m_0} \langle \{\widehat{\ell_1}, m_1\},\ 2,\ 1,\ 1 \rangle \xrightarrow{m_1} \langle \{\widehat{\ell_1}, \widehat{m_1}\},\ 1,\ 1,\ 1 \rangle \cdots$,

$\quad\quad\quad\quad\quad\quad\quad\quad\quad\quad\quad\quad\quad\quad\quad\quad\quad\quad\quad\quad\quad\quad\quad\quad$ yielding $y = 1$.

σ_2: $\langle \{\ell_0, m_0\},\ 1,\ -,\ - \rangle \xrightarrow{\ell_0} \langle \{\ell_1, m_0\},\ 1,\ 1,\ - \rangle \xrightarrow{m_0}$

$$\langle \{\ell_1, m_1\}, \ 1, \ 1, \ 0 \rangle \xrightarrow{\ell_1} \langle \{\widehat{\ell_1}, m_1\}, \ 2, \ 1, \ 0 \rangle \xrightarrow{m_1} \langle \{\widehat{\ell_1}, \widehat{m_1}\}, \ 0, \ 1, \ 0 \rangle \cdots ,$$

yielding $y = 0$.

$\sigma_3:$ $\langle \{\ell_0, m_0\}, \ 1, \ -, \ - \rangle \xrightarrow{\ell_0} \langle \{\ell_1, m_0\}, \ 1, \ 1, \ - \rangle \xrightarrow{m_0}$

$$\langle \{\ell_1, m_1\}, \ 1, \ 1, \ 0 \rangle \xrightarrow{m_1} \langle \{\ell_1, \widehat{m_1}\}, \ 0, \ 1, \ 0 \rangle \xrightarrow{\ell_1} \langle \{\widehat{\ell_1}, \widehat{m_1}\}, \ 2, \ 1, \ 0 \rangle \cdots ,$$

yielding $y = 2$.

We summarize this discussion by observing that, while for program $A1$, over-lapped executions and interleaved computations differ, they coincide for program $A2$. The difference between the two programs is that in program $A2$ each assignment contains at most one reference to a shared variable and hence can cause at most one critical event.

The number of critical events contained in a single atomic transition determines the *granularity* of the transition. The fewer critical events in a transition, the finer the granularity. Under our convention of associating one atomic transition with each assignment, we may describe program $A2$ as a *refinement* of program $A1$, and describe it as a program of a *finer* grain of atomicity (finer granularity) than that of $A1$.

2.2 Limiting the Critical References

In the previous discussion, we loosely identified the critical events in an execution as the reading or writing of shared variables. Here we would like to give a more precise definition of the events in the program that should be considered critical. We first consider shared-variable programs with no semaphore or region statements.

We define reading and writing references as follows:

- Statement **skip** is defined to have no writing references and no reading references.

- The assignment statement

$$(u_1, \ldots, u_k) := (e_1, \ldots, e_k)$$

is defined to have a writing reference to each variable $u_1, \ldots, u_k$ and reading references to all the variables appearing in $e_1, \ldots, e_k$.

- The statements

$$\textbf{await } c, \quad \textbf{when } c \textbf{ do } S, \quad \textbf{if } c \textbf{ then } S_1 \textbf{ else } S_2, \quad \textbf{while } c \textbf{ do } S$$

are defined to have reading references to all the variables appearing in c.

This definition captures the reading and writing references that are attributed to the statement itself, as distinct from references that can be attributed to one of its proper substatements. For example, we attribute to the statement **when** c **do** S only the reading references performed in the evaluation of c. Any reference appearing within S will be attributed to the smallest statement in which it appears.

If we consider an extended language that allows subscripted expressions, we should also add the following:

- The subscripted reference

$$u[e]$$

is defined to have a reading reference to all the variables appearing in e, independent of the context in which the subscripted reference appears. Thus, the assignment

$$u[v + 1] := w[x]$$

contains a writing reference to u and reading references to v, w, and x.

Consider program $A3$ of Fig. 2.3. It contains several reading and writing references to variables y_1 and y_2. However, we claim that only the reference to y_1 should be considered critical. To justify this claim, observe that y_2 is not referenced by P_1, so it is not actually a "shared" variable. It follows that the references of P_2 to y_2 are not critical because their precise timing, relative to the actions of P_1, cannot influence the behavior of the program.

$$\textbf{out } y_1, y_2 \textbf{: integer where } y_1 = 1$$

$$P_1 :: \begin{bmatrix} \ell_0: y_1 := 2 \\ \ell_1: y_1 := y_1 + 1 \end{bmatrix} \quad || \quad P_2 :: \begin{bmatrix} m_0: y_2 := y_1 + 1 \\ m_1: y_2 := y_1 + y_2 \end{bmatrix}$$

Fig. 2.3. Program $A3$.

A more subtle argument shows that the reading reference to y_1 by P_1 in ℓ_1 need not be considered critical. P_1 is the only process that writes on y_1 in this program. Consequently, the value read from y_1 by P_1 is always the value that P_1 has last written on it, regardless of how many actions of P_2 intervene between these two events.

Critical References

Based on the preceding discussion we present the following definitions:

A reference to a variable occurring in a statement S is *critical* if:

■   It is a writing reference to a variable that has reading or writing references in a statement parallel to S or

■   It is a reading reference to a variable that has writing references in a statement parallel to S.

An alternative but equivalent definition of critical references may be based on the following.

For a statement S, define a variable to be:

●   *private* to S if no statement parallel to S references it.

●   *public* in S if both S and some statement parallel to S reference it.

●   *local* to S if S is a block statement and the variable is declared as **local** at its head.

●   *owned* by S if the only references to the variable in statements parallel to S are reading references.

Obviously, a variable that is private to S is owned by S, and a variable that is local to S is private to S.

For example, in program A3 (Fig. 2.3), variable y_2 is private to statements m_0 and m_1 and process P_2. Variable y_1 is public for all statements in the program, but is owned by P_1 and its substatements, because they are the only statements that can modify it.

Using this terminology, we present an alternative but equivalent definition of critical references.

A reference to a variable occurring in a statement S is *critical* if:

■   It is a writing reference to a variable that is not private to S or

■   It is a reading reference to a variable that is not owned by S.

The LCR Restriction for Statements

We say that a statement S satisfies the *limited-critical-reference* restriction (LCR restriction, for short) if each of the transitions associated with S performs at most one critical reference.

It is important to realize that the restriction applies to the number of critical references that are attributed to each transition associated with S, and not to the total number of critical references contained in S. For example, assuming that x and y are public variables, the statement

$$\ell_0: \textbf{when } x > 0 \textbf{ do } \ell_1: y := 1$$

satisfies the LCR restriction, even though it contains two critical references. The reason is that the reference to x is attributed to the transition τ_{ℓ_0}, while the reference to y is attributed to the transition τ_{ℓ_1}. In terms of transitions, two transitions are involved in the complete execution of ℓ_0: τ_{ℓ_0} and τ_{ℓ_1}. Each of these transitions performs one critical reference.

The preceding definition is expressed as a restriction on the transitions associated with a statement. Instead, it can be formulated as a syntactic restriction on the statements themselves.

- Statement **skip** always satisfies the LCR restriction.

- For an assignment $\bar{u} := \bar{e}$, the restriction is that, together, $\bar{u}$ and $\bar{e}$ contain at most one critical reference.

- For the statements

  $$\textbf{await } c, \quad \textbf{when } c \textbf{ do } \widetilde{S}, \quad \textbf{if } c \textbf{ then } S_1 \textbf{ else } S_2, \quad \textbf{while } c \textbf{ do } \widetilde{S}$$

  the restriction is that c contains at most one critical reference.

- The

  concatenation, selection, cooperation, and block

  statements, which have no unique transitions of their own, are always taken as satisfying the LCR restriction.

- By definition, any grouped statement $\langle S \rangle$ satisfies the LCR restriction. This is because, even if S contains more than one critical reference, the execution of $\langle S \rangle$ (including overlapped execution) must be atomic and allows no occurrence of other critical events until it is completed.

- No explicit restriction is specified for the synchronization statements: *request*, *release*, and *region*. Each is considered to have a single critical reference, since their built-in protection mechanism prevents interference.

- The situation is particularly simple in the case of message-passing programs. In such programs, any two parallel processes that refer to the same variable can have only reading references to that variable, which may therefore be considered *owned* by both of them. This is, for example, the situation with an input variable, which may be read by all processes in the program. The only resources that can be critically referenced in such programs are the channels.

  Consequently, for message-passing programs, all the basic statements are considered to have zero critical references attributed to them, except for the communication statements send and receive, which have a single critical reference, even in their conditional form.

We refer to a statement S such that all substatements of S satisfy the LCR restriction as an LCR *statement*.

LCR Programs

A program is defined to be an LCR *program* if all its statements satisfy the LCR restriction.

The preceding discussion suggests the following:

Claim

If P is an LCR program, then interleaving computations and overlapped executions of P yield the same set of behaviors.

Example (binomial coefficient)

Consider program BINOM of Fig. 2.4 (see also Fig. 1.3).

$$
\begin{aligned}
&\textbf{in}\quad\; k,\, n\; : \textbf{integer where } 0 \le k \le n\\
&\textbf{local } y_1,\, y_2 : \textbf{integer where } y_1 = n,\, y_2 = 1\\
&\textbf{out}\quad b\quad\; : \textbf{integer where } b = 1
\end{aligned}
$$

$$
P_1 :: \begin{bmatrix} \ell_0: \textbf{while } y_1 > (n-k) \textbf{ do}\\ \begin{bmatrix} \ell_1: b := b \cdot y_1\\ \ell_2: y_1 := y_1 - 1 \end{bmatrix} \end{bmatrix}
$$

$$
\|
$$

$$
P_2 :: \begin{bmatrix} m_0: \textbf{while } y_2 \le k \textbf{ do}\\ \begin{bmatrix} m_1: \textbf{await } (y_1 + y_2) \le n\\ m_2: b := b \textbf{ div } y_2\\ m_3: y_2 := y_2 + 1 \end{bmatrix} \end{bmatrix}
$$

Fig. 2.4.   Program BINOM (binomial coefficient).

Variables k and n are input variables. They are not written by any process, and hence are owned by both P_1 and P_2. Variable y_2 is private to P_2. Variable

y_1 is public but owned by P_1, as P_1 is the only process writing to it. Variable b is public and not owned by any process, since it is modified by both processes.

The following statements have no critical references directly attributed to them:

ℓ_0: **while** $y_1 > (n - k)$ **do** $\ldots$

m_0: **while** $y_2 \leq k$ **do** $\ldots$

m_3: $y_2 := y_2 + 1$.

This is because y_1 is owned by P_1, so reading references to y_1 by P_1 are noncritical, k and n are owned by both P_1 and P_2, and y_2 is private to P_2.

The following statements each have a single critical reference (the critical references are boxed):

ℓ_2: $\boxed{y_1} := y_1 - 1$

m_1: **await** $\left(\boxed{y_1} + y_2 \right) \leq n$.

This is because the reading references to y_1 in ℓ_2 and to y_2 in m_1 are noncritical.

The following statements each have two critical references, the references to b:

ℓ_1: $\boxed{b} := \boxed{b} \cdot y_1$

m_2: $\boxed{b} := \boxed{b}$ **div** y_2.

Since these statements violate the LCR requirement, BINOM in this form is not an LCR program.

We can transform a non-LCR program into an LCR program by refining each of the offending statements into a sequence of smaller LCR statements, introducing additional local variables if necessary. Applying this transformation to program BINOM of Fig. 2.4 yields program BINOM of Fig. 2.5. The critical references in the program are boxed.

To obtain this version of BINOM, we refined

$b := b \cdot y_1$

in Fig. 2.4 into the sequence

$t_1 := b \cdot y_1; \; b := t_1,$

and the statement

$b := b$ **div** y_2

into the sequence

$t_2 := b$ **div** $y_2; \; b := t_2$.

$$\begin{aligned}
&\textbf{in} \quad\ k, \ n \ : \textbf{integer where } 0 \le k \le n\\
&\textbf{local } y_1, \ y_2\textbf{: integer where } y_1 = n, \ y_2 = 1\\
&\textbf{out} \quad\ b \quad\ : \textbf{integer where } b = 1
\end{aligned}$$

$$P_1 :: \begin{bmatrix} \textbf{local } t_1\textbf{: integer}\\ \ell_0\textbf{: while } y_1 > (n-k) \textbf{ do}\\[4pt] \begin{bmatrix} \ell_1\text{: } t_1 := \boxed{b} \cdot y_1\\[4pt] \ell_2\text{: } \boxed{b} := t_1\\[4pt] \ell_3\text{: } \boxed{y_1} := y_1 - 1 \end{bmatrix} \end{bmatrix}$$

$\|$

$$P_2 :: \begin{bmatrix} \textbf{local } t_2\textbf{: integer}\\ m_0\textbf{: while } y_2 \le k \textbf{ do}\\[4pt] \begin{bmatrix} m_1\text{: } \textbf{await} \left(\boxed{y_1} + y_2 \right) \le n\\[4pt] m_2\text{: } t_2 := \boxed{b} \textbf{ div } y_2\\[4pt] m_3\text{: } \boxed{b} := t_2\\[4pt] m_4\text{: } y_2 := y_2 + 1 \end{bmatrix} \end{bmatrix}$$

Fig. 2.5.   Program BINOM — LCR version.

The program presented in Fig. 2.5 is now an LCR program.

Extra Protection is Needed

While the version of program BINOM in Fig. 2.5 is satisfactory in the sense of being an LCR program, it is unfortunately incorrect. It is no longer guaranteed to compute $\binom{n}{k}$ in all of its possible computations. We refer the reader to Section 1.8, where a computation of this program producing a wrong result, for the inputs $n = 3$, $k = 2$, is demonstrated.

The solution to this problem, as given in that section, was to introduce additional protection that prevents interference by a parallel process between the statements ℓ_1 and ℓ_2, and between m_2 and m_3. The protection was provided by viewing $\{\ell_1, \ell_2\}$ and $\{m_2, m_3\}$ as critical sections and enclosing them within a

$$
\begin{array}{ll}
\textbf{in} \quad k,\, n & : \textbf{integer where } 0 \le k \le n \\
\textbf{local } y_1,\, y_2,\, r\colon & \textbf{integer where } y_1 = n,\ y_2 = 1,\ r = 1 \\
\textbf{out} \quad b & : \textbf{integer where } b = 1
\end{array}
$$

$P_1 ::$
$$
\begin{bmatrix}
\textbf{local } t_1\colon \textbf{integer} \\
\ell_0\colon \textbf{while } y_1 > (n-k) \textbf{ do} \\[4pt]
\quad
\begin{bmatrix}
\ell_1\colon \textbf{request}(r) \\[3pt]
\quad
\begin{bmatrix}
\ell_2\colon t_1 := b \cdot y_1 \\
\ell_3\colon b := t_1
\end{bmatrix} \\[3pt]
\ell_4\colon \textbf{release}(r) \\
\ell_5\colon y_1 := y_1 - 1
\end{bmatrix}
\end{bmatrix}
$$

$\parallel$

$P_2 ::$
$$
\begin{bmatrix}
\textbf{local } t_2\colon \textbf{integer} \\
m_0\colon \textbf{while } y_2 \le k \textbf{ do} \\[4pt]
\quad
\begin{bmatrix}
m_1\colon \textbf{await } (y_1 + y_2) \le n \\
m_2\colon \textbf{request}(r) \\[3pt]
\quad
\begin{bmatrix}
m_3\colon t_2 := b \textbf{ div } y_2 \\
m_4\colon b := t_2
\end{bmatrix} \\[3pt]
m_5\colon \textbf{release}(r) \\
m_6\colon y_2 := y_2 + 1
\end{bmatrix}
\end{bmatrix}
$$

Fig. 2.6.   Program BINOM — with semaphores.

request-release pair of semaphore statements. The resulting program (Fig. 2.6) is a correct LCR program and properly computes $\binom{n}{k}$.

Every Program Has an LCR Refinement

The transformation carried out on the program of Fig. 2.4 to obtain its refined version, presented in Fig. 2.5, can be generalized to show that any program has an LCR refinement. We will sketch the major steps in such a transformation. For simplicity, we consider only programs with no grouped statements.

Restricting Critical References to Assignments

The first major step in the transformation removes multiple critical references from all statements, except for assignments. We perform the following transformations on all statements that contain a non-LCR condition, i.e., a condition c that contains more than one critical reference. Variable t is a new local boolean variable appearing in these transformations. The replacing statement repeatedly evaluates the condition c and stores its boolean value in t, until $t = $ T is detected. Then the while statement terminates and S is executed. The same transformation also applies to statement **await** c, by taking S to be **skip**.

- Replace each statement of the form

     if c **then** S_1 **else** S_2

  where c is non-LCR, by

     $[t := c;\ \ \textbf{if}\ t\ \textbf{then}\ S_1\ \textbf{else}\ S_2]$.

- Replace each statement of the form

     while c **do** S

  where c is non-LCR, by

     $[t := c;\ \ \textbf{while}\ t\ \textbf{do}\ [S;\ t := c]]$.

- Replace each statement of the form

     when c **do** S,

  that is not a child of a selection statement, and where c is non-LCR, by

     $[t := \text{F};\ \textbf{while}\ \neg t\ \textbf{do}\ [t := c]\ ;\ S]$.

We cannot use this transformation for the case that the when statement is a child of a selection statement. This is because the first statement of the translation, $t := $ F, is always enabled, and it may cause us to select an alternative whose condition is never true.

Consequently, we have to consider separately the case of a selection statement whose children are when statements.

- Replace each statement of the form

$$
\begin{bmatrix}
\textbf{when}\ c_1\ \textbf{do}\ S_1 \\
\textbf{or} \\
\vdots \\
\textbf{or} \\
\textbf{when}\ c_k\ \textbf{do}\ S_k
\end{bmatrix}
$$

  where, together, $c_1, \ldots, c_k$ contain more than one critical reference, by

$$\left[\begin{array}{l} t_1 := \text{F}; \ \ldots; \ t_k := \text{F} \\ \textbf{while } \neg(t_1 \vee \cdots \vee t_k) \textbf{ do} \\ \quad (t_1, \ldots, t_k) := (c_1, \ldots, c_k) \\ \left[\begin{array}{l} \textbf{when } t_1 \textbf{ do } S_1 \\ \quad \textbf{or} \\ \quad \vdots \\ \quad \textbf{or} \\ \textbf{when } t_k \textbf{ do } S_k \end{array}\right] \end{array}\right]$$

The variables $t_1, \ldots, t_k$ are new local boolean variables.

The case of a *mixed selection statement*, where some of the children are when (or await) statements and others are not, is dealt by uniformly representing all the latter statements as fictitious when statements. Thus, we deal with a selection of the form

$$[\textbf{when } c \textbf{ do } S] \textbf{ or } [y := e],$$

as though it has the form

$$[\textbf{when } c \textbf{ do } S] \textbf{ or } [\textbf{when } \text{T} \textbf{ do } y := e].$$

Refining Assignments

Let

$$(u_1, \ldots, u_k) := (e_1, \ldots, e_k)$$

be a multiple assignment statement (possibly $k = 1$) that contains more than one critical reference. Let $\bar{v} = v_1, \ldots, v_m$ be the list of variables to which the assignment has critical reading references.

We replace this assignment with the statement

$$\left[\begin{array}{l} t_1 := v_1; \ \ldots; \ t_m := v_m \\ u_1 := e_1[\bar{t}/\bar{v}]; \ \ldots; \ u_k := e_k[\bar{t}/\bar{v}] \end{array}\right].$$

The expression $e[\bar{t}/\bar{v}]$ is obtained from e by replacing each occurrence of v_i by t_i, $i = 1, \ldots, m$. Here, each t_i is a new local variable of the type of v_i.

In case some u_i is a subscripted variable of the form $u[e]$, the list $v_1, \ldots, v_m$ should also contain all the variables to which e has critical references, and e must be replaced by $e[\bar{v}/\bar{t}]$. Consider, for example, the statement

$$u[i+1] := x + y + 2,$$

where the references to i, x, and y are critical. The transformation described here replaces this statement with

$$\begin{bmatrix} t_1 := i; \ t_2 := x; \ t_2 := y \\ u[t_1 + 1] := t_2 + t_3 + 2 \end{bmatrix}.$$

The result of applying the two described transformations is summarized by the following claim:

Claim

For every program P, there exists an LCR refinement $\widetilde{P}$ such that the interleaved execution of $\widetilde{P}$ and the overlapped executions of both P and $\widetilde{P}$ yield the same set of behaviors.

Every Program Has an LCR Equivalent

Unfortunately, as was the case for program BINOM, if the original program P is not an LCR program then the refinement $\widetilde{P}$ is not equivalent to P. While all the replacements carried out in the first group of transformations are based on valid congruences, the refinement of an assignment may lead to a noncongruent statement.

To remedy the situation, we introduce semaphore statements protecting each refinement of an assignment.

We replace each statement

$$\begin{bmatrix} t_1 := v_1; \ \ldots; \ t_m := v_m \\ u_1 := e_1[\bar{t}/\bar{v}]; \ \ldots; \ u_k := e_k[\bar{t}/\bar{v}] \end{bmatrix}$$

obtained from a refinement of the assignment

$$(u_1, \ldots, u_k) := (e_1, \ldots, e_k)$$

with the statement

$$\begin{bmatrix} \textbf{request}(r) \\ \quad t_1 := v_1; \ \ldots; \ t_m := v_m \\ \quad u_1 := e_1[\bar{t}/\bar{v}]; \ \ldots; \ u_k := e_k[\bar{t}/\bar{v}] \\ \textbf{release}(r) \end{bmatrix}$$

This transformation uses a common semaphore variable r to protect all refinements of assignment statements. It is initialized to 1 at the program's head. The semaphore statements that refer to r ensure that the complete sequence is executed with no interference from other statements that may refer to the variables critically referenced in the original assignment.

The effect of this last transformation can be summarized by the following claim:

Claim

For every program P, there exists an LCR program $\widehat{P}$ that is equivalent to P.

The program obtained by these transformations is not the most efficient one. Usually it contains much more severe protection from interference than is actually necessary. In **Problem 2.1**, the reader will define a transformation that eliminates some unnecessary protection and applies to programs that contain grouped statements.

Example (producer-consumer with two lists)

In Fig. 2.7 we present a program in which a producer process communicates with a consumer process using two shared lists. The producer chooses nondeterministically between the lists b_1 and b_2. The produced value x is appended to the selected list. Shared variables s_1 and s_2 record the current lengths of b_1 and b_2. The producer can select a list b_i, $i = 1, 2$, only if its length s_i is currently lower than the bound N_i. On appending x to b_i, variable s_i is incremented by 1.

Symmetrically, the consumer selects a list b_i with nonzero length, i.e., $s_i > 0$, removes the first element of the selected list and places it in y, decrements s_i, and finally uses the value y.

Fig. 2.8 is the LCR translation of this program. The figure contains only the translation of the producer, but that of the consumer is straightforward. ⬛

Semantically Critical References

The protection provided by the semaphores in program BINOM in Fig. 2.6 ensures that P_2 cannot access b while P_1 performs the sequence of statements

$$\ell_2\colon\ t_1 := b \cdot y_1$$

$$\ell_3\colon\ b := t_1.$$

This is because all the accesses of P_2 to b are contained in the critical section $m_{3,4}$, which cannot coexecute together with $\ell_{2,3}$. Consequently, the two references to b in the statements at ℓ_2 and ℓ_3 should not be considered 'critical,' because no reference to b by a parallel statement can be interleaved between them.

Let us reconsider the definition of critical references. It defines a reference to a variable y in a statement S to be critical if there are references of a particular type to y in a statement S' that is parallel to S. The notion of parallelism considered there was *syntactic*, i.e., S and S' were substatements of two distinct children of a cooperation statement.

Since the notion of critical reference is determined by the possibility of interference, we should consider a reference within a statement S as critical only if

$$\text{local } b_1, \ b_2 \text{: list of integer where } b_1 = b_2 = \Lambda$$
$$s_1, \ s_2 \text{: integer where } s_1 = s_2 = 0$$

$$Prod :: \left[\begin{array}{l} \text{local } x \text{: integer} \\ \text{loop forever do} \\ \left[\begin{array}{l} \ell_0 \text{: compute } x \\ \ell_1 \text{:} \left[\begin{array}{l} \ell_2 \text{: when } s_1 < N_1 \text{ do } [b_1 := b_1 \bullet x; \ s_1 := s_1 + 1] \\ \text{or} \\ \ell_3 \text{: when } s_2 < N_2 \text{ do } [b_2 := b_2 \bullet x; \ s_2 := s_2 + 1] \end{array} \right] \end{array} \right] \end{array} \right]$$

$$\|$$

$$Cons :: \left[\begin{array}{l} \text{local } y \text{: integer} \\ \text{loop forever do} \\ \left[\begin{array}{l} m_0 \text{:} \left[\begin{array}{l} m_1 \text{: when } s_1 > 0 \text{ do } (y, \ b_1) := \big(hd(b_1), \ tl(b_1)\big) \\ \qquad s_1 := s_1 - 1 \\ \text{or} \\ m_2 \text{: when } s_2 > 0 \text{ do } (y, \ b_2) := \big(hd(b_2), \ tl(b_2)\big) \\ \qquad s_2 := s_2 - 1 \end{array} \right] \\ m_3 \text{: use } y \end{array} \right] \end{array} \right]$$

Fig. 2.7. Program PROD-CONS — producer-consumer with two lists.

the parallel statement S' containing other references to the same variable can be executed at the same time as S. This suggests that we can relax the definition (calling fewer references critical) by interpreting the parallel relation semantically.

Let $\ell: S$ and $\ell': S'$ be two (syntactically) parallel statements in a program P. S and S' are called *semantically parallel* if there exists a reachable state s of P such that both $[\ell]$ and $[\ell']$ are contained in $s[\pi]$.

For example, the statements ℓ_1 and m_3 in the program of Fig. 2.9 are semantically parallel, while the statements ℓ_2 and m_3 are not.

We define a reference to a variable in a statement S to be *semantically critical* if it is:

• a reading reference to a variable that has a writing reference in a semantically parallel statement S', or

local b_1, b_2: **list of integer where** $b_1 = b_2 = \Lambda$
s_1, s_2: **integer where** $s_1 = s_2 = 0$
r : **integer where** $r = 1$

Prod ::

$$\begin{bmatrix} \textbf{local } x \quad : \textbf{integer} \\ \textbf{local } t_1,\ t_2: \textbf{boolean} \\ \quad t_3,\ t_4: \textbf{integer} \\ \quad t_5,\ t_6: \textbf{list of integer} \\ \textbf{loop forever do} \\ \begin{bmatrix} \ell_0: \textbf{compute } x \\ t_1 := \text{F} \ ;\ t_2 := \text{F} \\ \textbf{while } \neg(t_1 \vee t_2) \textbf{ do} \\ \quad [t_1 := (s_1 < N_1);\ t_2 := (s_2 < N_2)] \\ \begin{bmatrix} \begin{bmatrix} \textbf{when } t_1 \textbf{ do} \\ \begin{bmatrix} \textbf{request}(r);\ t_5 := b_1 \bullet x;\ b_1 := t_5;\ \textbf{release}(r) \\ \textbf{request}(r);\ t_3 := s_1 + 1;\ s_1 := t_3;\ \textbf{release}(r) \end{bmatrix} \\ \textbf{or} \\ \begin{bmatrix} \textbf{when } t_2 \textbf{ do} \\ \begin{bmatrix} \textbf{request}(r);\ t_6 := b_2 \bullet x;\ b_2 := t_6;\ \textbf{release}(r) \\ \textbf{request}(r);\ t_4 := s_2 + 1;\ s_2 := t_4;\ \textbf{release}(r) \end{bmatrix} \end{bmatrix} \end{bmatrix} \end{bmatrix} \end{bmatrix}$$

$\|$

Cons :: ...

Fig. 2.8. Program PROD-CONS — LCR version.

- a writing reference to a variable that has a reading or writing reference in a semantically parallel statement S'.

We say that a statement S (similarly a program P) satisfies the limited semantically critical reference restriction if each substatement of S has at most one semantically critical reference attributed to it.

Consequently, we modify our definition of LCR statements (LCR programs) to refer to semantic rather than syntactic critical references as follows:

From now on, the notions of critical reference and LCR statement (LCR program) are to be interpreted as semantic critical reference and semantic LCR statement (LCR program), respectively.

Semantically restricted LCR programs enjoy the same advantages as syntactically restricted LCR programs. Their overlapped and interleaved executions coincide.

Example

With the more liberal definition of LCR programs, we can rewrite program BINOM of Fig. 2.6, reuniting the sequence of assignments to b, in each process, into a single assignment. This is allowed since, due to mutual exclusion, the statements $\{\ell_2, \ell_3\}$ of P_1 are not semantically parallel to the statements $\{m_3, m_4\}$ of P_2, even though they are syntactically parallel to them. The resulting BINOM program is presented in Fig. 2.9.

$$
\begin{aligned}
&\textbf{in} \quad k, n \quad : \textbf{integer where } 0 \le k \le n\\
&\textbf{local } y_1, y_2, r: \textbf{integer where } y_1 = n,\ y_2 = 1,\ r = 1\\
&\textbf{out} \quad b \qquad : \textbf{integer where } b = 1
\end{aligned}
$$

$$
P_1 :: \begin{bmatrix} \ell_0: \textbf{while } y_1 > (n-k) \textbf{ do} \\ \begin{bmatrix} \ell_1: \textbf{request}(r) \\ \ell_2: b := b \cdot y_1 \\ \ell_3: \textbf{release}(r) \\ \ell_4: y_1 := y_1 - 1 \end{bmatrix} \end{bmatrix}
$$

$$\|$$

$$
P_2 :: \begin{bmatrix} m_0: \textbf{while } y_2 \le k \textbf{ do} \\ \begin{bmatrix} m_1: \textbf{await } (y_1 + y_2) \le n \\ m_2: \textbf{request}(r) \\ m_3: b := b \textbf{ div } y_2 \\ m_4: \textbf{release}(r) \\ m_5: y_2 := y_2 + 1 \end{bmatrix} \end{bmatrix}
$$

Fig. 2.9. Program BINOM — with reunited assignments.

We point out that the question of whether a given set of locations is simultaneously reachable in a program P is generally undecidable. This implies that, while checking whether a program satisfies the syntactic LCR restriction is easy, the question of whether it satisfies the semantic restriction is undecidable. Consequently, we will be able to use the more liberal definition only in some cases.

Merging Statements

So far, we have used the LCR requirement as a criterion for deciding whether statements presented as atomic should be refined into smaller statements. However, it can also serve as justification for merging smaller statements into larger ones, either using the grouped statement or performing a transformation inverse to refinement.

In fact, we can describe the passage from the program in Fig. 2.6 to the program in Fig. 2.9 as a merging transformation. In this transformation we merged statements ℓ_2 and ℓ_3 in Fig. 2.6 into the single statement ℓ_2 in Fig. 2.9, and merged m_3 and m_4 in Fig. 2.6 into the single m_3 in Fig. 2.9.

The motivation for striving toward coarser granularity is that it simplifies the analysis of the behavior of programs. Clearly, merging smaller statements together leads to a program with a smaller number of transitions and control locations. As we will see later, the complexity of analyzing a program depends on the number of transitions and control locations associated with the transitions. Consequently, any reduction in the number of transitions simplifies the analysis.

By the claims presented earlier, if S is an elementary statement having at most one critical reference, then we can replace S by the grouped statement $\langle S \rangle$ to obtain an equivalent program. The implication of the grouping is that the whole statement must be executed uninterrupted in one step of the computation.

Example (binomial coefficient)

As an additional example of the grouping transformation, we present program BINOM in Fig. 2.10, which can be obtained by grouping some of the statements in the program in Fig. 2.9.

The grouping we have performed consists of the following:

- the release statement of P_1 has been grouped with the assignment. This is allowed since the multiplication does not contain any (semantically) critical references.

- the request statement of P_2 has been grouped with the division statement, which does not contain any (semantically) critical references.

- the release statement of P_2 has been grouped with the incrementation of y_2, which is a variable local to P_2.

$$\textbf{in} \quad k, n \quad : \textbf{integer where } 0 \leq k \leq n$$

$$\textbf{local } y_1, y_2, r: \textbf{integer where } y_1 = n, y_2 = 1, r = 1$$

$$\textbf{out} \quad b \quad : \textbf{integer where } b = 1$$

$$
P_1 :: \begin{bmatrix}
\ell_0: \textbf{ while } y_1 > (n - k) \textbf{ do} \\[2mm]
\begin{bmatrix}
\ell_1: \textbf{ request } \left(\boxed{r} \right) \\[2mm]
\ell_2: \left\langle \begin{matrix} b := b \cdot y_1 \\ \textbf{release } \left(\boxed{r} \right) \end{matrix} \right\rangle \\[2mm]
\ell_3: \boxed{y_1} := y_1 - 1
\end{bmatrix}
\end{bmatrix}
$$

$$\|$$

$$
P_2 :: \begin{bmatrix}
m_0: \textbf{ while } y_2 \leq k \textbf{ do} \\[2mm]
\begin{bmatrix}
m_1: \textbf{ await } \boxed{y_1} + y_2 \leq n \\[2mm]
m_2: \left\langle \begin{matrix} \textbf{request}\left(\boxed{r} \right) \\ b := b \textbf{ div } y_2 \end{matrix} \right\rangle \\[2mm]
m_3: \left\langle \begin{matrix} \textbf{release}\left(\boxed{r} \right) \\ y_2 := y_2 + 1 \end{matrix} \right\rangle
\end{bmatrix}
\end{bmatrix}
$$

Fig. 2.10.   Program BINOM — with coarser granularity.

Obviously, the program in Fig. 2.10 has fewer transitions and control locations than the program in Fig. 2.9 and yet is equivalent to it.

With Statement

A statement that may facilitate the construction of LCR programs is the with statement. Its form is:

$$\textbf{with } x \textbf{ do } S,$$

where x is a variable and S is a statement whose only references to x are reading references. This statement can be viewed as an abbreviation for the following block statement:

$$[\textbf{local } t; \ t := x; \ S[t/x]]$$

This statement includes a definition of a new local variable t, a single assignment of x to t, and a copy of S in which all the references to x have been replaced by references to t.

The effect of the with statement is to reduce all the critical reading references to x in S to a single one.

Thus, if x is a public variable and y is private, the statement

$$y := \boxed{x} \cdot 2; \ y := y + \boxed{x}$$

has two critical references, and therefore cannot be merged by grouping. On the other hand, the statement

$$\textbf{with } \boxed{x} \ \textbf{do } [y := x \cdot 2; \ y := y + x]$$

contains only a single critical reference, so it can be grouped to obtain an equivalent statement.

In **Problem 2.2**, the reader will show that refinement of a non- LCR program P may yield a program that is not equivalent to P, but refinement of LCR programs is an equivalence transformation.

2.3 Justice (Weak Fairness)

In the rest of this chapter, we complete our computational model by introducing various notions of *fairness*. All these notions impose additional restrictions on the computations allowed by the computational model. Their main purpose is to exclude computations that do not correspond to actual executions of real concurrent systems.

In the following sections we introduce several types of fairness requirements. Following the detailed description and analysis of each type, we formulate the notion of a *fair transition system*, which incorporates a set of fairness requirements into the model of a basic transition system. We adopt the notion of a fair transition system as the complete computational model in subsequent chapters.

The Need for Fairness

In the previous sections, we compared interleaving computations of a program with its behavior under overlapped executions. Our main concern has been to show that interleaving computations do not miss any behaviors manifested by concurrent executions of the programs we study. We argued that if the limited-critical-reference (LCR) restriction is satisfied, then all overlapped behaviors are represented by the interleaving model.

In the following sections we are concerned with the dual question: Are there, perhaps, behaviors that correspond to interleaving computations but could never be manifested by concurrent executions?

It is not difficult to come up with an example of a computation that can never arise in an actual concurrent execution.

Unfair Computations

Consider program $A4$ presented in Fig. 2.11.

$$
\begin{array}{c}
\textbf{local } x\text{: } \textbf{boolean where } x = \text{T} \\
y\text{: } \textbf{integer where } y = 0 \\
\\
P_1 :: \left[\begin{array}{l} \ell_0\text{: } \textbf{while } x \textbf{ do} \\ \quad \ell_1\text{: } y := y + 1 \\ : \widehat{\ell_0} \end{array} \right] \quad \| \quad P_2 :: \left[m_0\text{: } x := \text{F} : \widehat{m}_0 \right]
\end{array}
$$

Fig. 2.11.   Program $A4$.

This program has four diligent transitions, to which we refer by the labels of the statements associated with them.

ℓ_0^{T}:   finding $x = \text{T}$ and moving from ℓ_0 to ℓ_1.

ℓ_0^{F}:   finding $x = \text{F}$ and moving from ℓ_0 to $\widehat{\ell}_0$.

ℓ_1:   moving from ℓ_1 to ℓ_0 and incrementing y by 1.

m_0:   moving from m_0 to $\widehat{m}_0$ and setting x to F .

A state in a computation of this program can be represented by listing the values assumed by the variables π, x, and y.

The interleaving model admits the following divergent (nonterminating) computation of this program, obtained by executing only statements of P_1 and ignoring P_2 completely:

$$
\langle \{\ell_0, m_0\}, \text{ T, } 0 \rangle \xrightarrow{\ell_0^{\text{T}}} \langle \{\ell_1, m_0\}, \text{ T, } 0 \rangle \xrightarrow{\ell_1}
$$

$$
\langle \{\ell_0, m_0\}, \text{ T, } 1 \rangle \xrightarrow{\ell_0^{\text{T}}} \langle \{\ell_1, m_0\}, \text{ T, } 1 \rangle \xrightarrow{\ell_1}
$$

$$\langle\{\ell_0, m_0\},\ T,\ 2\rangle \xrightarrow{\ell_0^T} \langle\{\ell_1, m_0\},\ T,\ 2\rangle \xrightarrow{\ell_1} \cdots .$$

On the other hand, if this program were actually to be run on two parallel processors, then the processor running P_2 would eventually perform the transition m_0 and terminate, causing the other processor to also terminate within two additional steps. Consequently, a concurrent execution could never give rise to a computation such as the preceding one, which suggests modifying the interleaving model to exclude this computation.

Clearly, the element missing from the interleaving model is a formalization of the fact that each independent processor in a real concurrent system keeps performing its statements, unhindered by execution of other processors. Thus, the basic model of interleaved computations has to be restricted to ensure that no single process is consistently neglected, as was the case with P_2 in the preceding computation. We refer to this additional restriction as *justice*, describing the preceding computation as unjust to P_2, never giving it a chance to perform its next statement. In the literature, the notion of justice is also referred to as *weak fairness*.

Justice

The major role of justice is to ensure that, in the interleaved representation, processes progress independently, as they do in the overlapped execution of multiprocessor systems. Assume that some process P_i depends on a single transition τ for its progress, and consider a computation in which τ is continually enabled (from a certain point on). In a multiprocessor system this transition will eventually be executed and, if we wish to capture this behavior in the interleaved representation, we must require that a transition that is continually enabled is eventually taken.

Consider, on the other hand, program $A4'$ in Fig. 2.12.

$$\begin{array}{c} \textbf{local } x: \textbf{boolean where } x = T \\ y: \textbf{integer where } y = 0 \end{array}$$

$$P_1 :: \begin{bmatrix} \ell_0: \textbf{while } x \textbf{ do} \\ \quad \ell_1: y := y + 1 \end{bmatrix} \quad \Big\| \quad P_2 :: \begin{bmatrix} m_0: \textbf{await } even(y) \\ m_1: x := F \end{bmatrix}$$

Fig. 2.12.   Program $A4'$.

Here, progress (and termination) of P_2 depends on the successful activation of await statement m_0. However, unlike the previous case, the transition (associated with) m_0 is no longer continually enabled in a computation that consistently executes transitions from P_1. It is disabled on all states in which y is odd. How would an overlapped execution of such a program behave?

We should realize that the await statement is usually not a primitive instruction available on a machine. Instead, it is usually implemented by a small loop that repeatedly tests for the expected condition. Thus, the actual program that will be run will resemble the program presented in Fig. 2.13.

$$\text{local } x: \textbf{boolean where } x = \text{T}$$
$$y: \textbf{integer where } y = 0$$

$$P_1 :: \begin{bmatrix} \ell_0\text{: } \textbf{while } x \textbf{ do} \\ \quad \ell_1\text{: } y := y + 1 \end{bmatrix} \parallel P_2 :: \begin{bmatrix} m_0\text{: } \textbf{while } \neg \ even(y) \textbf{ do skip} \\ m_1\text{: } x := \text{F} \end{bmatrix}$$

Fig. 2.13.   Program $A4''$.

Now, the infinitely many states in which statement m_0 in program $A4'$ is disabled correspond to infinitely many states in which the termination condition of loop m_0 in program $A4''$ is false. While many overlapped executions of program $A4''$ terminate, there are also many executions in which each sampling of the condition $even(y)$ by loop m_0 happens to fall in a state at which y is odd. Such executions will not terminate.

These considerations suggest that if a transition such as m_0 in program $A4'$ is not continuously enabled, then justice does not require eventual activation of that transition, nor the progress of the process containing it.

We can view justice as defining the minimal level of attention to be paid to processes in the program. It tells the scheduler that builds up a computation that it cannot forever ignore a transition that is continually enabled beyond some point. As we will see later, there are higher levels of attention that can be paid to processes to ensure overall progress of the program. These more attentive modes of fairness will be discussed in the following sections.

Justice Requirements

Consider an infinite sequence of states σ: $s_0, s_1, \ldots, s_k, \ldots$.

- For a transition τ in $\mathcal{T}$, we say that τ is *enabled* at position k if τ is enabled on s_k.

- For a transition τ in $\mathcal{T}$, we say that τ is *taken* at position k if

$$s_{k+1} \in \tau(s_k).$$

Thus, τ is taken at position k if s_{k+1} can be obtained by applying τ to s_k. Note that we do not claim that τ is the transition actually taken at this point in σ, but only that it is a transition that can explain the transformation from s_k to s_{k+1}. In fact, sometimes several transitions τ can be considered as taken at the same position k.

We say that a computation σ is *just with respect to a transition* τ if

> it is not the case that τ is continually enabled beyond some position $k \geq 0$ without being taken beyond k.

We observe that this definition is equivalent to the following:

> It is not the case that τ is continually enabled beyond some position, but is taken only a finite number of times.

In general, for a given transition system P, we specify a set of transitions $\mathcal{J} \subseteq \mathcal{T}$, and require that computations be just with respect to each $\tau \in \mathcal{J}$. We refer to $\mathcal{J}$ as the *justice set* of P.

We say that a computation is *just* with respect to $\mathcal{J}$ if it is just with respect to each transition τ in $\mathcal{J}$.

In most cases we take $\mathcal{J} = \mathcal{T}_D$, i.e., we require that computations be just with respect to all diligent transitions of the program. Therefore, whenever we do not mention the set $\mathcal{J}$ explicitly, it is implied that $\mathcal{J} = \mathcal{T}_D$, and a computation is called *just* if it is just with respect to $\mathcal{T}$. There are few exceptions to this rule, which we will discuss later, and in these cases we mention $\mathcal{J}$ explicitly.

In the literature, one often finds several variations for the formulation of the justice requirement. We will list some of these variations. They are all logically equivalent to our formulation.

- Either τ is disabled infinitely many times or it is taken infinitely many times.

- If τ is continually enabled from a certain position on, then it is taken infinitely many times.

In the literature, justice is sometimes referred to as *weak fairness*.

Justice Distinguishes Concurrency from Nondeterminism

Consider the simple program presented in Fig. 2.14.

We claim that the following computation of this program (listing values of π, x, and y) is just:

$$\langle \ell_0, 0, 0 \rangle \xrightarrow{\tau_1} \langle \ell_1, 1, 0 \rangle \xrightarrow{\tau_1'} \langle \ell_0, 1, 0 \rangle \xrightarrow{\tau_1}$$

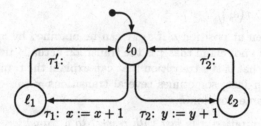

out x, y: **integer where** $x = y = 0$

Fig. 2.14. Competing transitions.

$$\langle \ell_1, 2, 0 \rangle \xrightarrow{\tau_1'} \langle \ell_0, 2, 0 \rangle \longrightarrow \cdots.$$

Even though this computation consistently takes only the τ_1 and τ_1' transitions, it is also just with respect to τ_2. This is because τ_2 is not continually enabled beyond any point.

It is interesting to note that this program is not equivalent to the program in Fig. 2.15, in which τ_1 and τ_2 now belong to parallel processes. For the program in Fig. 2.15, the following sequence, which again takes only τ_1 and τ_1', is not just:

$$\langle \ell_0, m_0, 0, 0 \rangle \xrightarrow{\tau_1} \langle \ell_1, m_0, 1, 0 \rangle \xrightarrow{\tau_1'} \langle \ell_0, m_0, 1, 0 \rangle \xrightarrow{\tau_1} \cdots.$$

This sequence is not just towards τ_2, because τ_2 is continually enabled from the start, and yet it is never taken.

out x, y: **integer where** $x = y = 0$

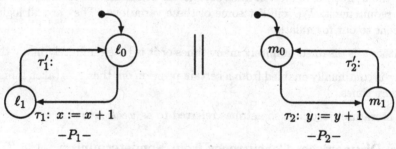

Fig. 2.15. Parallel transitions.

These two examples illustrate that once justice is introduced into the model, concurrency is no longer fully equivalent to nondeterminism. Justice certainly distinguishes between the case that τ_1 and τ_2 belong to the same process (as in Fig. 2.14), and the case that τ_1 and τ_2 are parallel (as in Fig. 2.15).

In **Problem 2.3**, the reader will consider a simpler form of a justice requirement for transitions obeying some restrictions and which can be described as *non-self-looping* transitions.

2.4 Implications of the Justice Requirements

Some implications of the justice requirement are not immediately apparent. We discuss several of them.

Fairness in Selection is Not Guaranteed

Consider program $A5$ of Fig. 2.16. As usual, we ask the question, do all computations of this program terminate?

$$
\textbf{local } x: \textbf{ boolean where } x = \text{F}
$$

$$
P_1 :: \quad [\ell_0: \textbf{ await } x] \quad || \quad P_2 :: \quad
\begin{bmatrix}
m_0: \textbf{ while } (\neg x) \textbf{ do} \\
m_1: \begin{bmatrix} m_2: \textbf{ skip} \\ \textbf{or} \\ m_3: x := \text{T} \end{bmatrix}
\end{bmatrix}
$$

Fig. 2.16. Program $A5$ — no fairness in selection.

The crucial question is whether the periodic computation

$$
\langle \{\ell_0, m_0\}, \text{ F} \rangle \xrightarrow{m_0^{\text{T}}} \langle \{\ell_0, m_1\}, \text{ F} \rangle \xrightarrow{m_2} \langle \{\ell_0, m_0\}, \text{ F} \rangle \xrightarrow{m_0^{\text{T}}} \cdots
$$

is acceptable. In particular, is it just to all transitions? Transition ℓ_0 has no grounds for complaint, since it is never enabled. Similarly, m_0^{F} is always disabled. Transitions m_0^{T} and m_2 certainly cannot complain, since they are repeatedly taken.

The question is, are we just to m_3? According to the definition we are, since m_3, while being enabled infinitely often, is not continually enabled beyond any point. Thus, the preceding behavior is acceptable as a computation, and this means that the program of Fig. 2.16 has a divergent (nonterminating) computation.

We may summarize this observation by saying that justice does not guarantee fairness in selection between competing transitions. It allows a process, such as P_2, to consistently prefer m_2 to m_3.

Transition Versus Process Justice

The justice requirements, as stated earlier, guarantee the eventual progress of a process only if some particular transition in the process is continually enabled. On the other hand, it allows computations in which, at any state, some transition of the process is enabled, yet no transition of the process is ever activated. Thus, the continual enabledness of a process does not guarantee its eventual progress.

Example

Consider program $A6$ of Fig. 2.17. It consists of a process P_1 that tries, in the statement ℓ_0, to select between two alternative statements ℓ_1 and ℓ_2, based on whether it succeeds in detecting x or $(\neg x)$ as true. In parallel, P_2 keeps alternating the truth value of x.

$$
\boxed{
\begin{array}{l}
\textbf{local } x,\ y\colon \textbf{ boolean where } x = \text{F},\ y = \text{T} \\[2ex]
P_1 :: \quad \left[\ell_0\colon \begin{bmatrix} \ell_1\colon \textbf{ when } x \textbf{ do } y := \text{F} \\ \textbf{or} \\ \ell_2\colon \textbf{ when } (\neg x) \textbf{ do } y := \text{F} \end{bmatrix} \right] \\[4ex]
\quad || \\[2ex]
P_2 :: \quad \begin{bmatrix} m_0\colon \textbf{ while } y \textbf{ do} \\ \quad [m_1\colon x := \neg x] \end{bmatrix}
\end{array}
}
$$

Fig. 2.17. Program $A6$ — detained program.

Consider the following computation σ (listing the values of π, x, and y) in which no transition of P_1 is ever taken and statements m_0^T and m_1 are repeatedly executed in a periodic order, i.e.,

$$
\langle \{\ell_0, m_0\},\ \text{F},\ \text{T} \rangle \xrightarrow{m_0^T} \langle \{\ell_0, m_1\},\ \text{F},\ \text{T} \rangle \xrightarrow{m_1}
$$

$$\langle \{\ell_0, m_0\},\ \text{T},\ \text{T}\rangle \ \xrightarrow{m_0^{\text{T}}} \ \langle \{\ell_0, m_1\},\ \text{T},\ \text{T}\rangle \ \xrightarrow{m_1}$$

$$\langle \{\ell_0, m_0\},\ \text{F},\ \text{T}\rangle \ \xrightarrow{m_0^{\text{T}}} \ \langle \{\ell_0, m_1\},\ \text{F},\ \text{T}\rangle \ \cdots .$$

Obviously, at any state of σ either ℓ_1 or ℓ_2 is enabled, which means that some transition of P_1 is always enabled.

However, since m_1 alternately changes x to T and F, there are infinitely many states at which ℓ_1 is disabled and infinitely many states at which ℓ_2 is disabled. It follows that while some transition of P_1 is always enabled, neither ℓ_1 nor ℓ_2 is continually enabled.

Consequently, the infinite computation given here is just according to our definition and hence is acceptable. ◢

Some researchers have proposed a different notion of justice, which may be called *process justice*.

Let P be a process in a (diagram or text) program. We say that P is *enabled* at position $j \geq 0$ if some transition of P is enabled at this position. Consequently, P is continually enabled beyond position k if for every $j \geq k$, there exists a transition of P enabled at j. Different transitions of P may be enabled at different j-positions. The process P is considered to be *taken* (or *activated*) at position j if some transition of P is taken at j.

Process justice requires for each process P that

> it is not the case that the process P is continually enabled beyond some position $k \geq 0$, while no transition of the process is taken beyond k.

According to this definition, computation σ of program $A6$ in Fig. 2.17 is not process just, since at any state of this computation either ℓ_1 or ℓ_2 is enabled, and therefore the process P_1 is continually enabled. Yet, no transition of P_1 is taken. It follows that, according to this definition, program $A6$ has no infinite computations and always terminates.

Process justice is a stronger notion (more restrictive) than the notion of justice we proposed earlier to which, for comparison sake, we refer as *transition justice*. It is certainly a viable assumption that may be adopted in certain contexts.

In this book, we prefer to assume only transition justice, and we offer the following reasons for this preference.

We should realize that the when statement is usually not a primitive instruction available on most machines. This is certainly the case with a selection of several when statements. A typical implementation of statement ℓ_0 of process P_1

in Fig. 2.17 is given by the statement

$$
\tilde{\ell}_0: \begin{bmatrix} \textbf{local } done: \textbf{ boolean where } done = \text{F} \\ \textbf{while } (\neg \ done) \textbf{ do} \\ \quad \begin{bmatrix} \ell_1: \textbf{if } x \textbf{ then } [y := \text{F}; \ done := \text{T}] \\ \textbf{else} \\ \ell_2: \textbf{if } (\neg x) \textbf{ then } [y := \text{F}; \ done := \text{T}] \end{bmatrix} \end{bmatrix}
$$

This implementation alternately samples x and $\neg x$ and proceeds to perform the body of ℓ_1 or ℓ_2 on finding a true value. It is not difficult to see that if we substitute this statement for the statement ℓ_0 in program $A6$, the resulting program will have divergent computations according to any version of justice requirements.

Since we would like to consider $\tilde{\ell}_0$ an acceptable implementation for statement ℓ_0, we must allow the original program $A6$ to have divergent computations as well. This is supported by our notion of transition justice but not by process justice.

We may summarize this discussion by saying that, according to transition justice (the justice assumption adopted in this book), the fact that a process is continually enabled, from a certain point on, does not guarantee its eventual activation. It is only when a particular transition of this process is continually enabled that justice guarantees eventual activation of the process.

Scheduling for Justice

Consider an imaginary scheduler whose role is to decide at each step which transition among all those that are currently enabled should be taken next. In multiprogramming systems, such a task is usually performed by a component of the operating system, which is called the *scheduler*.

Assume that the objective of the scheduler is to construct a just computation. What policy can it use to guarantee this objective? It seems reasonable that if the scheduler observes that some transition, such as τ_2 in the computation of the program in Fig. 2.15, has been continually enabled for the last several steps but not taken, then eventually τ_2 must be scheduled. This is because if such a situation is ignored forever, then an unjust computation such as the one shown earlier is generated.

Consequently, any effective policy that tries to ensure justice cannot wait forever to verify that indeed a transition τ is continually enabled for all positions up to infinity. Having to act, based on observing only a finite prefix of the computation, any such policy must activate a transition if it has remained continually enabled for a sufficiently long period. Actual policies may differ in their interpretations of what "sufficiently long" means.

To provide a concrete example, consider algorithm J-SCHED presented in Fig. 2.18. In order to perform the scheduling task, we have enriched the programming language with a new data type **transition** and the operations $enabled(\tau)$ and $take(\tau)$ that, respectively, test whether transition τ is enabled, and cause the activation of τ.

---

local q: **list of transition where** $q = (\tau_I, \tau_1, \ldots, \tau_k)$
τ: **transition**

loop forever do

$$\left[\begin{array}{l} (\tau,\ q) := \big(hd(q),\ tl(q)\big) \\ \textbf{if } enabled(\tau) \textbf{ then } take(\tau) \\ q := q \bullet \tau \end{array}\right]$$

Fig. 2.18.   Algorithm J-SCHED — a scheduler for justice.

Assume that the justice set of the considered program is $\mathcal{J} = \{\tau_1, \ldots, \tau_k\}$. This abstract algorithm uses a variable τ to hold individual transitions and a list q for holding a queue of transitions waiting their turn. Initially, q is loaded with all the just transitions of the considered program, together with τ_I. On each round, the scheduler places the transition at the head of the queue into variable τ and removes it from the queue. It then examines this transition for being enabled and activates it if it is enabled. In any case the transition is returned to the end of the queue.

This scheduling algorithm is not guaranteed to generate all possible just computations of a given program, but it generates only just computations.

Justice Cannot Be Measured

Consider the program in Fig. 2.19.

This program has the following computation (listing the values of variables π, y, and z):

$$\langle \{\ell_0, m_0\}, 0, 0 \rangle \xrightarrow{\ell_0, \ell_1} \langle \{\ell_0, m_0\}, 1, 0 \rangle \xrightarrow{\ell_0, \ell_1} \langle \{\ell_0, m_0\}, 2, 0 \rangle \xrightarrow{\ell_0, \ell_1}$$
$$\langle \{\ell_0, m_0\}, 3, 0 \rangle \xrightarrow{m_0, m_1}$$

$$\textbf{out } y, \; z\textbf{: integer where } y = 0, \; z = 0$$

$$P_1 :: \begin{bmatrix} \ell_0\text{: \textbf{loop forever do}} \\ \ell_1\text{: } y := y + 1 \end{bmatrix} \; \| \; P_2 :: \begin{bmatrix} m_0\text{: \textbf{loop forever do}} \\ m_1\text{: } z := z + 1 \end{bmatrix}$$

Fig. 2.19.   Two counters.

$$\langle \{\ell_0, m_0\}, \; 3, \; 1 \rangle \xrightarrow{\ell_0, \ell_1} \langle \{\ell_0, m_0\}, \; 4, \; 1 \rangle \xrightarrow{\ell_0, \ell_1} \langle \{\ell_0, m_0\}, \; 5, \; 1 \rangle \xrightarrow{\ell_0, \ell_1}$$

$$\langle \{\ell_0, m_0\}, \; 6, \; 1 \rangle \xrightarrow{m_0, m_1}$$

$$\langle \{\ell_0, m_0\}, \; 6, \; 2 \rangle \longrightarrow \cdots .$$

This computation is just, even though P_2 is consistently discriminated against, being allowed only one transition for each three of P_1.

Note that when referring to the transitions associated with a **loop forever** statement, such as ℓ_0, we write ℓ_0 instead of ℓ_0^T. This is because the other transition, ℓ_0^F, is always disabled.

Thus, justice is not associated with any quantitative measure of even-handedness. We could easily conceive of a scheduling that would discriminate even more against P_2, such as:

1 step of P_1 followed by 1 step of P_2, then
10 steps of P_1 followed by 1 step of P_2, then
100 steps of P_1 followed by 1 step of P_2, $\cdots$.

Even this schedule yields a just computation according to our definition.

This indicates that justice is a very weak requirement that makes no assumption about the ratio of speeds of the different processors. Thus, the schedule presented earlier corresponds to a processor P_1 that gets progressively faster than its partner as the computation proceeds.

Making the assumption of justice as weak as we did is advantageous from the point of view of verification. This is because a program that has been proven correct over this more general model would certainly behave correctly in a more realistic implementation. Thus, weaker restrictions and more generality in the model lead to increased robustness of the verification results.

One may wonder whether a concept as weak as justice can ever be implemented in its full generality. Indeed, it can be demonstrated that any actual implementation of a fair construct has stronger fairness properties than the weak definition we adopt here. For example, each implementation of a fair choice between two alternatives usually has a bound on how long the first alternative can be chosen before the implementation switches to the other choice.

However, justice and the other fairness requirements discussed later are suggested as a useful abstraction that generalizes many actual implementations, rather than a goal to be implemented in its full generality and full weakness. An analogous situation is the concept of real numbers, which also can never be implemented in full generality by a finite program but are considered very useful abstractions for reasoning about programs.

Unjust Transitions

As we have already mentioned, normally we require that all diligent transitions be just, i.e., $\mathcal{J} = \mathcal{T}_D$. Here we would like to present one exception, a transition for which justice is intentionally not required.

Consider program MUX-SEM for ensuring mutual exclusion by semaphores, presented in Fig. 2.20 (see also Fig. 1.9).

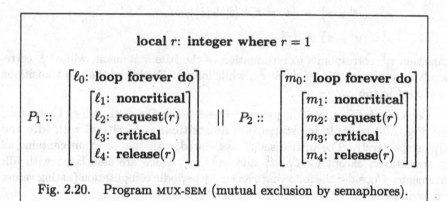

Fig. 2.20.   Program MUX-SEM (mutual exclusion by semaphores).

This program contains the two schematic statements **noncritical** and **critical**. As explained in Chpater 1, these statements stand for arbitrary sections of code that can be described as the noncritical and critical sections, respectively. These sections may contain additional activities whose internal details are irrelevant for the coordination problem of mutual exclusion. When introduced in Chapter 1, these statements were not associated with transitions. The assignment of transition semantics to statements **critical** and **noncritical** is based on the three following assumptions about the behavior of the critical and noncritical sections represented by these statements:

- Execution within the sections does not modify the values of the synchronization variables of the exclusion protocol, e.g., variable r in Fig. 2.20.

- The critical section always terminates.

- The noncritical section need not terminate.

The last assumption represents the possibility that from a certain point on, a process has no further need for accessing the critical section.

In principle, we could consider statements **critical** and **noncritical** as two new statements with which we associate transitions. Instead, we choose to equate them to other statements.

Statement **critical** is taken as another name for **skip**. It satisfies the requirements of not tampering with the protocol variables and termination.

Statement **noncritical** is taken as another name for a new statement **idle**, not to be confused with the idling transition τ_I. With the statement

$$\ell: \textbf{idle} : \widehat{\ell},$$

we associate two transitions, τ_ℓ^T and τ_ℓ^F. Their transition relations ρ_ℓ^T and ρ_ℓ^F, respectively, are given by

$$\rho_\ell^T: \ ([\ell] \in \pi) \ \wedge \ (\pi' = \pi \div [\ell] + [\widehat{\ell}])$$

$$\rho_\ell^F: \ ([\ell] \in \pi) \ \wedge \ (\pi' = \pi).$$

Transition τ_ℓ^T corresponds to termination of the **idle** statement, while τ_ℓ^F corresponds to a decision to remain at ℓ a while longer. Neither of the two transitions is included in the justice set $\mathcal{J}$.

Consider, for example, the program presented in Fig. 2.21, which is obtained from Fig. 2.20 by replacing statements **noncritical** and **critical** with **idle** and **skip**, respectively. The justice set $\mathcal{J}$ associated with this program contains all the transitions, except for ℓ_1^T, ℓ_1^F and m_1^T, m_1^F which are associated with idle statements. Consider the following eventually periodic computation (listing values of π and r)

$$\cdots \ \langle \{\ell_1, m_1\}, 1 \rangle \ \xrightarrow{m_1, m_2, \ell_1^T} \ \langle \{\ell_2, m_3\}, 0 \rangle \ \longrightarrow \ \cdots$$

$$\langle \{\ell_2, m_1\}, 1 \rangle \ \longrightarrow \ \cdots \ \langle \{\ell_3, m_1\}, 0 \rangle \ \longrightarrow \ \cdots \ \langle \{\ell_2, m_1\}, 1 \rangle \ \longrightarrow \ \cdots .$$

This computation is just (with respect to $\mathcal{J}$), even though from a certain point on, m_1^T is continually enabled and never taken. This is because $m_1^T \notin \mathcal{J}$. This computation represents the situation that from a certain point on, P_2 loses interest in entering the critical section.

We point out that the introduction of the idle statement is not absolutely necessary in order to model this phenomenon. Instead we can use the following statement

$$\boxed{\begin{array}{c}
\textbf{local } r\textbf{: integer where } r = 1 \\[4pt]
P_1 :: \begin{bmatrix} \ell_0\text{: } \textbf{loop forever do} \\ \quad \begin{bmatrix} \ell_1\text{: } \textbf{idle} \\ \ell_2\text{: } \textbf{request}(r) \\ \ell_3\text{: } \textbf{skip} \\ \ell_4\text{: } \textbf{release}(r) \end{bmatrix} \end{bmatrix} \quad \Big\| \quad P_2 :: \begin{bmatrix} m_0\text{: } \textbf{loop forever do} \\ \quad \begin{bmatrix} m_1\text{: } \textbf{idle} \\ m_2\text{: } \textbf{request}(r) \\ m_3\text{: } \textbf{skip} \\ m_4\text{: } \textbf{release}(r) \end{bmatrix} \end{bmatrix}
\end{array}}$$

Fig. 2.21. Representing sections by **idle** and **skip**.

$$\begin{bmatrix} \textbf{local } t\textbf{: boolean where } t = \text{T} \\[4pt] \textbf{while } t \textbf{ do} \quad \begin{bmatrix} t := \text{F} \\ \textbf{or} \\ \textbf{skip} \end{bmatrix} \end{bmatrix}$$

This statement represents a loop that can nondeterministically choose to stay in place or terminate. Indeed, this statement is congruent to the idle statement, provided the context does not place them at the front of a selection statement. There are, however, obvious advantages to the idle statement, which represents the same behavior using only two transitions.

It is interesting to note that another possible modeling of the idling behavior is provided by the statement

$$\textbf{skip or } [\textbf{skip; await } \text{F}].$$

This statement makes a nondeterministic choice between termination and remaining stuck forever in a hopeless waiting situation.

In **Problem 2.4**, the reader will, among other things, justify these claims.

2.5   *Compassion (Strong Fairness)*

While justice requirements are adequate to ensure the progress of processes that do not contain synchronization or communication statements, they are not sufficient to characterize the expected behavior of synchronization and communication statements that require tight coordination with other processes. In the following, we will consider a stronger notion of fairness, which will be associated with the coordination statements of the language. We will use the standard example of mutual exclusion in order to compare the expressive power of the different coordination statements under the associated fairness requirement.

Justice is Not Enough

We illustrate the inadequacy of justice by the standard solution to the mutual exclusion problem, using semaphores. Consider program MUX-SEM in Fig. 2.20, which represents this solution.

This program has the following periodic computation, where each state lists the values of variables π and r:

$$\sigma: \quad \langle\{\ell_0, m_0\}, 1\rangle \longrightarrow \cdots \longrightarrow \langle\{\ell_2, m_2\}, 1\rangle \overset{\ell_2}{\longrightarrow}$$

$$\langle\{\ell_3, m_2\}, 0\rangle \overset{\ell_3}{\longrightarrow} \langle\{\ell_4, m_2\}, 0\rangle \overset{\ell_4}{\longrightarrow} \langle\{\ell_0, m_2\}, 1\rangle \overset{\ell_0}{\longrightarrow}$$

$$\langle\{\ell_1, m_2\}, 1\rangle \overset{\ell_1}{\longrightarrow} \langle\{\ell_2, m_2\}, 1\rangle \overset{\ell_2}{\longrightarrow} \langle\{\ell_3, m_2\}, 0\rangle \longrightarrow \cdots.$$

This computation represents a situation in which, even though process P_2 is continually waiting at m_2, requesting admission to its critical section, it is never admitted. Nevertheless computation σ is just, i.e, satisfies all the justice requirements. In particular it is just with respect to m_2, even though this transition is never taken. This is because m_2 is disabled infinitely many times, for instance, on all occurrences of the state $\langle\{\ell_3, m_2\}, 0\rangle$.

On the other hand, a satisfactory solution to the mutual exclusion problem should ensure that both P_1 and P_2 are eventually admitted to their critical sections. A computation such as σ should not be acceptable. Indeed, a reasonable implementation of semaphores will guarantee fairness in responding to request statements. This type of fairness is not adequately captured by the notion of justice, and a stronger type of fairness is needed.

The conclusion is that for some transitions τ, in particular, transitions corresponding to synchronization constructs such as semaphore statements, activation is required not only if τ is continually enabled beyond some point, but also if τ is enabled infinitely many times, as are the request statements in program MUX-SEM.

Compassion Requirement

The precise concept we would like to capture is: a process detained at a synchronization statement that is enabled infinitely many times will eventually progress.

We say that a computation $\sigma: s_0, s_1, \ldots$ is *compassionate with respect to a transition* τ if

> it is not the case that τ is enabled infinitely many times but not taken beyond some position $k \geq 0$.

We observe that this definition is equivalent to the following:

> It is not the case that τ is enabled infinitely many times but is taken only finitely many times.

Note that the main difference between a justice requirement and a compassion requirement is that the phrase "continually enabled beyond some position" has been replaced with "enabled infinitely many times."

In general, for a given transition system P, we specify a set of transitions $C \subseteq T$ and require that computations be compassionate with respect to each $\tau \in C$. We refer to C as the *compassion set* of P.

We say that a computation of P is *compassionate* if it is compassionate with respect to each transition in C, the compassion set of P.

Alternative but equivalent formulations of the compassion requirement for τ that are encountered in the literature are:

- Either τ is enabled only finitely many times or it is taken infinitely many times.

- If τ is enabled infinitely many times, then it is taken infinitely many times.

In the literature, compassion is sometimes referred to as *strong fairness*.

In the following, we will identify the compassion requirements that are associated with the different types of coordination statements that appear in the various concrete models.

Justification of Names

We may owe the readers some explanation for the terms justice and compassion given to the two types of fairness. We may view scheduling a transition as a reward for being frequently enabled. On the other hand, being disabled can be viewed as a transgression, for which some of the requirements may punish the transition by not scheduling it.

Clearly, justice commits to scheduling a transition only if beyond a certain point it has stopped transgressing and is continually enabled.

Compassion, on the other hand, completely ignores states of disabledness. It commits to schedule a transition whenever the transition is infinitely often enabled.

Scheduling for Compassion

It is interesting to compare the requirements of a scheduler for compassion with those of a scheduler for justice. As we have seen in the previous section, to ensure just scheduling it is enough to ensure that each just transition is considered now

local q : list of transitions where $q = (\tau_I, \tau_1, \ldots, \tau_k)$
τ : transition
i : integer
done: boolean

loop forever do

$$
\left[
\begin{array}{l}
i := 1;\ done := \text{F} \\
\textbf{while } \neg done \textbf{ do} \\
\quad \left[
\begin{array}{l}
\textbf{if } enabled\,(q[i]) \textbf{ then} \\
\quad \left[
\begin{array}{l}
\tau := q[i] \\
take(\tau) \\
q := q - \{\tau\} \\
q := q \bullet \tau \\
done := \text{T}
\end{array}
\right] \\
i := i + 1
\end{array}
\right]
\end{array}
\right]
$$

Fig. 2.22.   Algorithm C-SCHED — a scheduler for compassion.

and then. If the transition happens to be disabled precisely when it is considered, it is just too bad but no special effort is necessary to avoid such situations.

This approach is unacceptable for scheduling a compassionate transition. It may lead to a situation in which a compassionate transition τ is enabled infinitely many times yet is never taken because it happened to be disabled each time its turn came up. Thus, to ensure compassionate scheduling, it is necessary to pay more attention to the enabledness status of transitions.

Assume that the compassion set of a program is $\mathcal{C} = \{\tau_1, \ldots, \tau_k\}$. The abstract algorithm C-SCHED presented in Fig. 2.22 is proposed as a concrete example of a scheduler for compassion. For simplicity we assume that the justice set is empty.

At each round, the scheduler begins scanning the queue of pending transitions from the top, looking for the enabled transition that is closest to the head of the queue. Since τ_I is always in the queue, one such transition will be found. Once found, the transition is activated, removed from the queue, and placed at its end. This reintroduces the transition into the queue with the lowest possible priority.

It is not difficult to see that, similar to the justice scheduler, this algorithm does not generate all compassionate computations, but each computation it generates is compassionate. This is because each time a transition τ is enabled but not taken, it gets closer to the head of the queue. If it is enabled infinitely many times it must be taken repeatedly.

In **Problem 2.5**, the reader will construct an algorithm that generates sequences that are diligent, just, and compassionate, i.e., computations.

2.6 Synchronization Statements

The first concrete model we consider is that of shared-variables text programs. In this model we classify the following as synchronization statements:

$$\text{request,} \qquad \text{release,} \qquad \text{region.}$$

A transition associated with a synchronization statement is called a *synchronization transition*.

For a shared-variables text program P, the compassion set C is the set of all synchronization transitions in P.

For example, the compassion set for program MUX-SEM in Fig. 2.20 is $\{\ell_2, \ell_4, m_2, m_4\}$. Compassion for this program excludes the offending computation σ in which the synchronization transition m_2 is never activated. This computation is excluded because m_2 is enabled infinitely many times but never taken.

Mutual Exclusion with Semaphores

We show that when compassion is observed, the program in Fig. 2.20 provides a straightforward and satisfactory solution to the mutual-exclusion problem. Compassion is sufficient to guarantee individual accessibility to each of the processes. That is, each process P_i, $i = 1, 2$, interested in entering its critical section, is guaranteed to eventually succeed.

To see this, assume that process P_1 waits at ℓ_2 to gain entry to critical section ℓ_3. The **request**(r) statement at ℓ_2 is enabled whenever $r > 0$.

- If beyond a certain point, r is continually positive, then P_1 must progress to ℓ_3 by the requirement of justice with respect to ℓ_2.

- Otherwise, if r is not continually positive beyond some point, r must be zero sometimes. This is possible only when the other process performs its **request**(r) statement at m_2. But then, P_2 must eventually perform the **release**(r) statement at m_4 (due to the assumption that critical sections always terminate). Each execution of the **release**(r) causes r to become positive again. It follows that, in this case, r is positive infinitely many times. By compassion with respect to ℓ_2, it follows that P_1 must eventually progress and execute ℓ_3.

Mutual Exclusion by Region Statements

The solution of Fig. 2.23 to the mutual-exclusion problem, using region statements, is similar to the semaphore solution. It uses only part of the power of these statements, as we can tell by observing that no when part is included. The argument that compassion with respect to the region statements guarantees individual accessibility is identical to the one presented for the semaphore case.

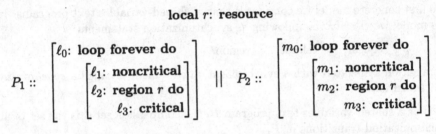

Fig. 2.23.   Mutual exclusion by region statements.

2.7   Communication Statements

The message-passing models use the communication statements send and receive instead of synchronization statements. Consequently, to attain expressive power equivalent to that of the shared-variables model, we associate compassion requirements with the communication statements.

Let S be a communication statement, i.e., a statement of the general form

$$\alpha \Leftarrow e \ \textbf{provided} \ c \qquad \text{or} \qquad \alpha \Rightarrow u \ \textbf{provided} \ c.$$

Let τ in $trans(S)$ be one of the transitions associated with statement S; for the synchronous case there may be more than one transition associated with S, depending on the number of matching communication statements parallel to S. We refer to τ as a *communication transition*.

For a message-passing text program P, the compassion set $\mathcal{C}$ is the set of all communication transitions in P.

Let us study the implications of the compassion requirement for synchronously communicating systems.

Example

Program $A7$ in Fig. 2.24 consists of two processes. Process P_1 has a loop containing a nondeterministic choice between statements ℓ_2 and ℓ_3. If it chooses ℓ_2, P_1 sends F over synchronous channel α and sets x to F. If it chooses ℓ_3, no communication takes place and x retains its initial value T. Process P_2 also has a loop in which it tries to read a value from α into y. Clearly, if P_1 ever chooses ℓ_2 then both x and y get the value F and the program terminates. The question we wish to explore is whether the program always terminates.

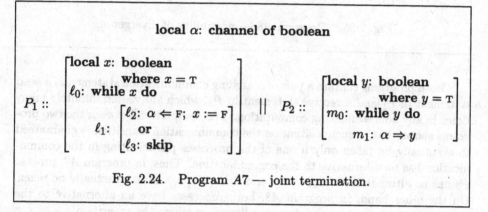

Fig. 2.24. Program $A7$ — joint termination.

It is not difficult to see that the only nonterminating computation this program may have is the periodic computation

$$\cdots \ \langle\{\ell_1, m_1\},\ \text{T},\ \text{T}\rangle \xrightarrow{\ell_3} \langle\{\ell_0, m_1\},\ \text{T},\ \text{T}\rangle \xrightarrow{\ell_0} \langle\{\ell_1, m_1\},\ \text{T},\ \text{T}\rangle \longrightarrow \cdots.$$

This computation is not compassionate with respect to the communication transition $\tau_{\langle \ell_2, m_1 \rangle}$, which is infinitely often enabled but never taken. Consequently, all admissible computations terminate.

For comparison, consider program $A8$ presented in Fig. 2.25. In program $A7$ process P_2 cannot progress beyond m_1 unless a communication takes place, while in program $A8$, P_2 has an alternative to the communication, represented by the skip statement m_3.

Program $A8$ has the following nonterminating computation:

$$\sigma: \ \langle\{\ell_0, m_0\},\ \text{T},\ \text{T}\rangle \xrightarrow{\ell_0} \langle\{\ell_1, m_0\},\ \text{T},\ \text{T}\rangle \xrightarrow{\ell_3} \langle\{\ell_0, m_0\},\ \text{T},\ \text{T}\rangle$$
$$\xrightarrow{m_0} \langle\{\ell_0, m_1\},\ \text{T},\ \text{T}\rangle \xrightarrow{m_3} \langle\{\ell_0, m_0\},\ \text{T},\ \text{T}\rangle \longrightarrow \cdots.$$

This computation is both just and compassionate. Compassion follows from the fact that the only communication transition, $\tau_{\langle \ell_2, m_2 \rangle}$, is never enabled on σ.

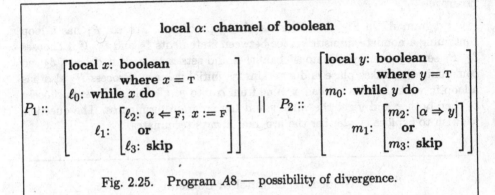

Fig. 2.25.   Program $A8$ — possibility of divergence.

Both programs contain a pair of matching communication statements, a send statement in P_1 and a receive statement in P_2, which are visited infinitely many times in any nonterminating computation. The comparison between the two programs shows that in such a situation the communication transition is guaranteed to eventually be taken only if one of the processes participating in the communication has no alternative to the communication. Thus, in program $A7$, process P_2 has no alternative to m_1, so the transition $\tau_{\langle \ell_2, m_2 \rangle}$ must eventually be taken. On the other hand, in program $A8$, both processes have an alternative to the communication, so computations are allowed in which the transition $\tau_{\langle \ell_2, m_2 \rangle}$ is never taken.

In **Problem 2.6**, the reader will consider an alternative set of   fairness requirements to which we refer as *set-fairness*.

Mutual Exclusion by Synchronous Communication

To demonstrate that the compassion requirements associated with the synchronous communication model endow it with a power similar to that of the fair shared-variables model, we present in Fig. 2.26 a solution to the mutual exclusion problem using synchronous communication.

In this program, as in most solutions based on message passing, it is necessary to introduce a special process A, whose role is to arbitrate between processes P_1 and P_2. Processes P_1 and P_2 talk directly only with the arbiter process A, using channels α_1 and α_2, respectively. A message T communicated via α_i from P_i to A signals that P_i requests and is granted permission to enter the critical section. A message F communicated via channel α_i signals a release of that permission by process P_i. Note that since synchronous communication is performed simultaneously at the sending and receiving ends, each message carries with it immediate acknowledgment.

$$
\textbf{local } \alpha_1, \alpha_2\textbf{: channel of boolean}
$$

$$
P_1 ::
\begin{bmatrix}
\ell_0\text{: } \textbf{loop forever do} \\
\quad
\begin{bmatrix}
\ell_1\text{: noncritical} \\
\ell_2\text{: } \alpha_1 \Leftarrow \text{T} \\
\ell_3\text{: critical} \\
\ell_4\text{: } \alpha_1 \Leftarrow \text{F}
\end{bmatrix}
\end{bmatrix}
$$

$\parallel$

$$
A ::
\begin{bmatrix}
\textbf{local } y\textbf{: boolean} \\
k_0\text{: } \textbf{loop forever do} \\
\quad k_1\text{: }
\begin{bmatrix}
[k_2\text{: } \alpha_1 \Rightarrow y;\ k_3\text{: } \alpha_1 \Rightarrow y] \\
\textbf{or} \\
[k_4\text{: } \alpha_2 \Rightarrow y;\ k_5\text{: } \alpha_2 \Rightarrow y]
\end{bmatrix}
\end{bmatrix}
$$

$\parallel$

$$
P_2 ::
\begin{bmatrix}
m_0\text{: } \textbf{loop forever do} \\
\quad
\begin{bmatrix}
m_1\text{: noncritical} \\
m_2\text{: } \alpha_2 \Leftarrow \text{T} \\
m_3\text{: critical} \\
m_4\text{: } \alpha_2 \Leftarrow \text{F}
\end{bmatrix}
\end{bmatrix}
$$

Fig. 2.26. Program MUX-SYNCH (mutual exclusion
by synchronous communication).

Each of the competing processes P_i, $i = 1, 2$ attempts to send T via channel
α_i. If it succeeds, it enters the critical section. On termination of the critical
section, P_i sends F via α_i. A cycle in an execution of arbiter A begins by a
selection between receiving from channel α_1 and channel α_2. On selecting channel
α_i, the arbiter permits P_i to enter its critical section. Arbiter A then waits for a
release signal from P_i, which is another message, F, transmitted via α_i.

The actual value of the messages transmitted in this protocol is irrelevant.
What is significant is that the communication has taken place, implying a synchronization between the participating processes. Our choice of transmitting T
for obtaining permission and F for its release is arbitrary.

To show that the solution ensures accessibility to each of the processes, we observe that due to compassion with respect to $\tau_{\langle \ell_2, k_2 \rangle}$, it is impossible for P_1 to be waiting forever at ℓ_2 while A visits k_1 (hence k_2) infinitely many times. A similar argument ensures accessibility for P_2.

Mutual Exclusion by Asynchronous Communication

Next, we consider the case of communication by asynchronous message passing. By our general definition, we require compassion for each transition associated with an asynchronous communication statement of the general form

$$\alpha \Leftarrow e \textbf{ provided } c \qquad \text{or} \qquad \alpha \Rightarrow u \textbf{ provided } c.$$

A solution to the mutual exclusion problem, using asynchronous communication, is presented by program MUX-ASYNCH in Fig. 2.27.

This program resembles program MUX-SYNCH in Fig. 2.26 for mutual exclusion by synchronous communication. The main difference is due to the fact that unlike the synchronous case, an asynchronous message does not carry its own acknowledgment, so it has to be programmed explicitly. Indeed, the single send statement at ℓ_2 in Fig. 2.26 is split in Fig. 2.27 into a send at ℓ_2 followed by a receive at ℓ_3, which reads the acknowledgment $\beta_1 \Leftarrow \text{T}$ sent by A. A similar replacement has been done for the statement of m_2.

In **Problem 2.7**, the reader will examine the implications of the notion of set-fairness defined in Problem 2.6 for the behavior of asynchronously communicating programs.

2.8   Summary: Fair Transition Systems

Having considered the two types of fairness requirements that seem useful and desirable on the one hand and implementable on the other, we now present a general definition that summarizes these two cases.

As we recall from the previous chapter, a basic transition system $\langle \Pi, \Sigma, \mathcal{T}, \Theta \rangle$ consists of the following components:

- Π — a finite set of state variables
- Σ — a set of states
- $\mathcal{T}$ — a finite set of transitions
- Θ — an initial condition.

We augment the formalism of basic transition systems by adding the following two components:

local α_1, α_2, β_1, β_2: **channel** [1..] **of boolean**

$$P_1 ::\quad \begin{bmatrix} \text{local } x_1\text{: boolean} \\ \ell_0\text{: loop forever do} \\ \begin{bmatrix} \ell_1\text{: noncritical} \\ \ell_2\text{: } \alpha_1 \Leftarrow \text{T} \\ \ell_3\text{: } \beta_1 \Rightarrow x_1 \\ \ell_4\text{: critical} \\ \ell_5\text{: } \alpha_1 \Leftarrow \text{F} \end{bmatrix} \end{bmatrix}$$

$\|$

$$A ::\quad \begin{bmatrix} \text{local } y\text{: boolean} \\ k_0\text{: loop forever do} \\ k_1\text{:} \quad \begin{bmatrix} [k_2\text{: } \alpha_1 \Rightarrow y;\ k_3\text{: } \beta_1 \Leftarrow \text{T};\ k_4\text{: } \alpha_1 \Rightarrow y] \\ \textbf{or} \\ [k_5\text{: } \alpha_2 \Rightarrow y;\ k_6\text{: } \beta_2 \Leftarrow \text{T};\ k_7\text{: } \alpha_2 \Rightarrow y] \end{bmatrix} \end{bmatrix}$$

$\|$

$$P_2 ::\quad \begin{bmatrix} \text{local } x_2\text{: boolean} \\ m_0\text{: loop forever do} \\ \begin{bmatrix} m_1\text{: noncritical} \\ m_2\text{: } \alpha_2 \Leftarrow \text{T} \\ m_3\text{: } \beta_2 \Rightarrow x_2 \\ m_4\text{: critical} \\ m_5\text{: } \alpha_2 \Leftarrow \text{F} \end{bmatrix} \end{bmatrix}$$

Fig. 2.27. Program MUX-ASYNCH (mutual exclusion
by asynchronous communication).

- $\mathcal{J} \subseteq \mathcal{T}$ — a justice set of transitions.

- $\mathcal{C} \subseteq \mathcal{T}$ — a compassion set of transitions.

We refer to the basic system augmented with these two components as a *fair transition system*.

Computations

Given a fair transition system $P = \langle \Pi, \Sigma, \mathcal{T}, \Theta, \mathcal{J}, \mathcal{C} \rangle$, we define a *computation* of P to be an infinite sequence of states

$$\sigma: \; s_0, \; s_1, \; s_2, \; \ldots$$

satisfying the following requirements:

- *Initiation*: $s_0 \models \Theta$, that is, the first state s_0 is *initial*.

- *Consecution*: For each pair of consecutive states s_i, s_{i+1} in σ, there exists a transition τ in $\mathcal{T}$, such that $s_{i+1} \in \tau(s_i)$. That is, s_{i+1} is a τ-successor of s_i.

- *Diligence*: The sequence contains either infinitely many diligent steps (i.e., τ-steps for $\tau \neq \tau_I$) or a terminal state s, i.e., $\tau(s) = \phi$ for all $\tau \neq \tau_I$.

- *Justice*: For each τ in $\mathcal{J}$ it is not the case that τ is continually enabled beyond some position in σ but taken only finitely many times.

- *Compassion*: For each τ in $\mathcal{C}$ it is not the case that τ is enabled infinitely many times in σ but taken only finitely many times.

From now on, we refer to sequences that satisfy these five conditions above as *computations* of P, to sequences that satisfy the first two conditions as *runs* of P, and to runs that also satisfy the requirement of diligence as *diligent runs*.

We refer to the requirements of initiation and consecution as the *finitary* requirements, because they only constrain the finite prefixes of a computation. We refer to the requirements of diligence, justice, and compassion as the *infinitary* or *fairness* requirements. These requirements constrain the entire infinite computation. The difference between the two can be explained as follows.

If an infinite sequence of states violates one of the finitary requirements, there is always a finite prefix of the sequence in which this violation can be detected. A violation of the initiation requirement can already be detected at s_0. A violation of the consecution requirement is always detectable as a pair of states s_i, s_{i+1} such that s_{i+1} is not a τ-successor of s_i for any $\tau \in \mathcal{T}$. Thus, the finite prefix $s_0, \ldots, s_i, s_{i+1}$ is already faulty and no extension of it can be a computation.

Violation of the infinitary (fairness) requirements, on the other hand, can never be detected in a finite prefix. Every finite sequence that satisfies the finitary requirements can be extended into an infinite sequence that satisfies all five requirements and is, therefore, a computation.

In **Problems 2.8** to **2.12**, the reader will compare various notions of fairness and study their effect on the validity of certain transformations.

2.9 Fairness in Petri Nets

Even though in some aspects, such as richness of data structures, the Petri net model is much simpler than the other models, it contains a much richer range of synchronization possibilities. Consequently, we proceed gradually from simpler to more complicated cases, while introducing the different notions of fairness that can be associated with nets.

Justice

For each transition t in the net we require justice with respect to t. This requirement excludes computations in which t is continually enabled beyond some position in the computation but not taken beyond that position.

Compassion for Nonunary Net-Transitions

In the previous models, the most complicated case we encountered was a communication transition belonging to two disjoint processes. In Petri nets, we can construct transitions that feed from n different places, and therefore represent n-way synchronization.

We classify net-transitions according to the number of places from which they feed. We call a net-transition t *unary* if it feeds from a single place, i.e., $|^\bullet t| = 1$. Otherwise, we call it nonunary. We interpret nonunary net-transitions as representing coordination between parallel components in the net. Consequently, we associate compassion requirements with all the nonunary net-transitions as follows.

For each nonunary net-transition t, we require compassion with respect to t. This requirement excludes computations in which t is enabled infinitely many times but is fired only finitely many times.

In **Problem 2.13**, the reader will consider the alternative notion of set-fairness for nonunary net-transitions.

Mutual Exclusion

In Fig. 2.28 we present the Petri net solution to the mutual exclusion problem. Here, the competing processes are represented by the subnets P_1 and P_2, the critical sections by the subnets C_1 and C_2, and the noncritical sections by the subnets N_1 and N_2.

The solution represents the possibility that either of the competing processes may choose to remain in its noncritical section from a certain point on. This

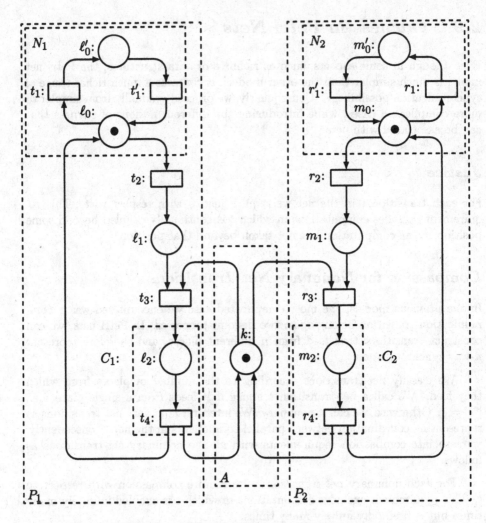

Fig. 2.28.   Mutual exclusion by Petri systems.

possibility is modeled by the transitions t_1, t'_1, r_1, and r'_1, which represent internal processing in the noncritical sections.

Node k serves as a semaphore, communicating either with P_1 via t_3 or with P_2 via r_3. We show that the assumptions of justice for all transitions and compassion for nonunary transitions ensure a fair solution, i.e., each of the processes that is interested in entering its critical section eventually does so. Consider a case in which P_1 is waiting at ℓ_1, i.e., y_{ℓ_1}, the state variable describing the marking at place ℓ_1, equals 1. If $y_k = 1$ continually, transition t_3 is continually enabled and by justice must eventually be activated. Another case in which P_1 is held up at

ℓ_1 and fails to arrive at ℓ_2 is when k repeatedly interacts with P_2, consistently ignoring t_3. However, such a computation enables t_3 infinitely many times while never taking it. It therefore violates the compassion requirement with respect to binary transition t_3 and is disallowed. Consequently, any admissible computation must eventually activate t_3, which causes P_1 to proceed to ℓ_3.

2.10   *Semantic Considerations of Fairness*

Fairness Prevents Finite Distinguishability

The main approach followed in the book for defining the semantics of a program P is to interpret P as a transition system and consider its computations. As pointed out in Section 1.6, this semantic is too discerning and distinguishes between programs we would prefer to consider equivalent. Consequently, we proposed in that section a more abstract semantic consisting of $\mathcal{R}(P)$, the set of reduced behaviors generated by the program (transition system) P. By definition, $\mathcal{R}(P)$ is a set of infinite sequences.

In the classical treatment of semantics of programs, there is a certain reluctance of dealing with sets of infinite objects. Instead, it is strongly advocated to represent such objects by the (possibly infinite) set of their finite approximations. This recommendation leads to semantic domains that are (possibly infinite) sets of finite (finitely representable) objects.

Consequently, if two programs have different semantics, i.e., are inequivalent, they must differ by a finite object that belongs to the semantics of one of them but not to the other. We refer to this property as *finite distinguishability*. Instead, all the reasonable semantics proposed for sequential programs have this property.

In the case of infinite sequences, the naturally suggested notion of finite approximation is that of a finite prefix. For an infinite sequence σ: $s_0, s_1, \ldots$, we call the finite sequence $\widehat{\sigma}$: $s_0, \ldots, s_k$ a *prefix* of σ, and denote $\widehat{\sigma} \prec \sigma$.

For a program P, $\mathcal{F}(P)$ denotes the set of all prefixes of the sequences in $\mathcal{R}(P)$, i.e., the set of prefixes of reduced behaviors of P. We refer to $\mathcal{R}(P)$ and $\mathcal{F}(P)$ as the *infinitary* and *finitary semantics* of P, respectively.

Consider, for example, program $B1$ of Fig. 2.29. The set of reduced behaviors (assuming y to be the only observable variable) for this program (i.e., its infinitary semantics $\mathcal{R}(B1)$) consists of sequences of the form

$$\sigma_n: \quad \langle 0 \rangle, \; \langle 1 \rangle, \; \ldots, \; \langle n \rangle, \; \langle n \rangle, \; \langle n \rangle, \; \ldots$$

for each $n \geq 0$. The reduced behavior σ_n corresponds to a computation in which P_2 sets x to F and P_1 finds it to be false precisely when $y = n$.

$$
\boxed{
\begin{array}{c}
\textbf{out}\quad y\text{: integer where } y = 0 \\
\textbf{local } x\text{: boolean where } x = \text{T} \\[1em]
P_1 :: \begin{bmatrix} \textbf{while } x \textbf{ do} \\ \quad y := y + 1 \end{bmatrix} \;\|\; P_2 :: \begin{bmatrix} x := \text{F} \end{bmatrix}
\end{array}
}
$$

Fig. 2.29.   Program $B1$ — always terminating.

Taking prefixes of these sequences, we obtain for the finitary semantics $\mathcal{F}(B1)$ a set of finite sequences

$$
\widehat{\sigma}_{k,\ell}: \quad \langle 0 \rangle, \; \langle 1 \rangle, \; \ldots, \; \underbrace{\langle k \rangle, \; \langle k \rangle, \; \ldots, \; \langle k \rangle}_{\ell}
$$

and for each $k \geq 0$ and $\ell \geq 1$.

$$
\boxed{
\begin{array}{c}
\textbf{out}\quad y\text{: integer where } y = 0 \\
\textbf{local } x\text{: boolean where } x = \text{T} \\[1em]
P_1 :: \begin{bmatrix} \textbf{while } x \textbf{ do} \\ \quad y := y + 1 \end{bmatrix} \;\|\; P_2 :: \begin{bmatrix} x := \text{F} \\ \textbf{or} \\ \textbf{skip} \end{bmatrix}
\end{array}
}
$$

Fig. 2.30.   Program $B2$ — sometimes terminating.

Next, let us consider program $B2$ of Fig. 2.30. Program $B2$ differs from $B1$ in that process P_2 of $B2$ has a nondeterministic choice between setting x to F or terminating without modifying x. Consequently, while all computations of $B1$ terminate, $B2$ has some nonterminating computations.

Constructing the infinitary semantics $\mathcal{R}(B2)$, we observe that in addition to the sequences σ_n, for each $n \geq 0$, $\mathcal{R}(B2)$ also contains the sequence

$$
\sigma_\omega: \quad \langle 0 \rangle, \; \langle 1 \rangle, \; \ldots, \; \langle n \rangle, \; \langle n + 1 \rangle, \; \ldots
$$

in which x assumes as values all the natural numbers. This reduced behavior corresponds to the nonterminating computations. It follows that $\mathcal{R}(B1) \subset \mathcal{R}(B2)$, which implies that programs $B1$ and $B2$ are not equivalent.

On the other hand, computing the finitary semantics $\mathcal{F}(B2)$, we observe that

$\mathcal{F}(B2) = \mathcal{F}(B1)$. This is because σ_ω can only contribute to $\mathcal{F}(B2)$ prefixes of the form $\widehat{\sigma}_{k,1}$: $\langle 0 \rangle, \langle 1 \rangle, \ldots, \langle k-1 \rangle, \langle k \rangle$, which are also prefixes of σ_k.

Thus, the semantics of fair transition system do not enjoy the finite distinguishability property. Programs $B1$ and $B2$ are not equivalent and can be distinguished by their infinitary semantics, i.e., σ_ω is a reduced behavior of $B2$ but not of $B1$. Nevertheless, these two programs cannot be distinguished by their finitary semantics, as $\mathcal{F}(B1) = \mathcal{F}(B2)$.

We can easily identify fairness as the element responsible for this phenomenon.

A transition system is called *finitely branching* if its set of transitions is finite and, for each state s and transition τ, the successor set $\tau(s)$ is finite. Obviously, all the transition systems we have so far considered are finitely branching.

The following claim establishes fairness as guilty of the loss of finite distinguishability.

Claim

Let P_1 and P_2 be two finitely branching transition systems whose justice and compassion sets are empty, i.e., $\mathcal{J} = \mathcal{C} = \emptyset$. Then

$$\mathcal{R}(P_1) = \mathcal{R}(P_2) \quad \text{iff} \quad \mathcal{F}(P_1) = \mathcal{F}(P_2).$$

The claim states that (finitely branching) transition systems with no fairness requirements have the finite distinguishability property.

Fairness and Random Choice

As observed in the preceding discussion, finite distinguishability is ensured, provided the following two conditions are satisfied:

- There are no fairness requirements.

- The models are finite branching.

It is no coincidence that these two conditions appear together. As we will show in the following discussion, the phenomena of fairness and infinitely branching transitions are closely related.

Let us first introduce a simple infinitely branching transition. Consider the choice statement

$$\ell: \ \mathbf{choose}(z) : \widehat{\ell},$$

where z is a variable that has been declared an integer. The intended meaning of this statement is that it assigns a random positive integer value to the variable z.

No assumptions are made about the probabilistic distribution of the values assigned to z. This is a purely nondeterministic statement.

The transition relation ρ_ℓ associated with this statement is given by

$$\rho_\ell: \quad ([\ell] \in \pi) \;\wedge\; (\pi' = \pi \doteq [\ell] + [\hat\ell]) \;\wedge\; (z' > 0).$$

Note that the formula expressing ρ_ℓ is more general than the standard form of transition relations we have considered so far. In the standard form, primed variables appear only as arguments for an equality statement, e.g., $z' = e$. The preceding formula contains the conjunct $z' > 0$, which allows z in the next state to assume an arbitrary positive integer value.

We now show that extending the programming language with random choice, or alternately introducing justice leads to the same expressive power.

Emulating Random Assignment by Justice

Consider program $B3$ presented in Fig. 2.31.

$$
\begin{array}{c}
\textbf{out}\quad z: \textbf{integer where } z = 0 \\
\textbf{local } x: \textbf{boolean where } x = \text{T} \\
y: \textbf{integer where } y = 1
\end{array}
$$

$$
P_1 :: \left[
\begin{array}{l}
\left[\begin{array}{l}
\textbf{while } x \textbf{ do} \\
\quad\quad y := y + 1
\end{array}\right] \\
z := y
\end{array}\right]
\quad \Big|\Big| \quad
P_2 :: \ [x := \text{F}]
$$

Fig. 2.31.   Program $B3$ — emulating random choice.

It is not difficult to see that the set of reduced behaviors of this program (listing the values of z) consists of the sequences

$$\langle 0 \rangle, \ \langle n \rangle, \ \langle n \rangle, \ \dots$$

for each $n > 0$. This is precisely the set of reduced behaviors for the program

$$
B_3' :: \left[
\begin{array}{l}
\textbf{out } z: \textbf{integer where } z = 0 \\
\textbf{choose}(z)
\end{array}\right].
$$

This shows that program $B3$ emulates program $B3'$, whose body consists of the random choice **choose**(z), in its full generality, i.e., program $B3$ is equivalent to $B3'$.

Emulating Justice by Random Choice

It is outside the scope of this book to present a full proof that shows how to emulate an arbitrary program under the assumption of justice, using random assignment. Instead, we will show how to emulate the single example of program $B4$ of Fig. 2.32. Program $B5$ of Fig. 2.33 proposes an emulation of program $B4$.

$$
\textbf{out}\quad y: \textbf{integer where } y = 0 \\
\textbf{local } x: \textbf{boolean where } x = \text{T}
$$

$$
P_1 :: \begin{bmatrix} \textbf{while } x \textbf{ do} \\ \quad y := y + 1 \end{bmatrix} \quad \| \quad P_2 :: \; [x := \text{F}]
$$

Fig. 2.32. Program $B4$.

$$
\textbf{out}\quad y: \textbf{integer where } y = 0 \\
\textbf{local } u: \textbf{integer}
$$

$$
P_1 : \begin{bmatrix} \textbf{choose}(u) \\ \textbf{while } u > 1 \textbf{ do} \\ \begin{bmatrix} y := y + 1 \\ u := u - 1 \end{bmatrix} \end{bmatrix}
$$

Fig. 2.33. Program $B5$ — emulating program $B4$.

It is not difficult to see that both programs $B4$ and $B5$ generate a set of reduced behaviors consisting of the sequences

$$
\langle 0 \rangle, \; \langle 1 \rangle, \; \ldots, \; \langle n - 1 \rangle, \; \langle n \rangle, \; \langle n \rangle, \; \langle n \rangle, \ldots
$$

for every $n \geq 0$. Consequently, they are equivalent.

In the literature one often sees sweeping statements claiming that fairness cannot be implemented. What is actually meant is that fairness cannot be implemented in its full generality, i.e., cannot be emulated. That is, we can never construct a program P_2 that, with no fairness assumptions at all, can generate all the computations that P_1 can generate.

This indeed is the case, as long as we consider only finitely branching programs. We have already claimed that in order to emulate justice or any other type of fairness we need an infinitely branching program, such as allowing random assignments.

A Complete Scheduler for Justice

To illustrate our claim that with the availability of random choice fairness can be fully emulated, we present in Fig. 2.34 a complete scheduler for justice. Unlike the scheduler for justice, algorithm J-SCHED, presented in Fig. 2.18 which only claimed that each generated sequence is just, the scheduler of Fig. 2.34, algorithm FJ-SCHED, is also claimed to be *complete*, that is, every just sequence can be generated by algorithm FJ-SCHED.

---

local pr : **array** $[1..k]$ **of integer**
$\quad\quad$ z, i: **integer**

for $i := 1$ **to** k **do**
$\quad$ $[\textbf{choose}(z);\ pr[i] := z]$

loop forever do

$$\begin{bmatrix} \textbf{let } i \textbf{ be such that} \\ \quad pr[i] = min\{pr[1], \ldots, pr[k]\} \\ \textbf{if } enabled(\tau_i) \textbf{ then } take(\tau_i) \\ \textbf{choose}(z) \\ pr[i] := pr[i] + z \end{bmatrix}$$

Fig. 2.34.   Algorithm FJ-SCHED — complete scheduler for justice.

To simplify the presentation, we assume that $C = \emptyset$ and that $\mathcal{J} = \mathcal{T} = \{\tau_1, \ldots, \tau_k\}$.

The algorithm uses an array $pr[1..k]$ to hold priorities for the various transitions, where a lower number denotes a higher priority. The algorithm starts by assigning random priorities to all the transitions.

The main cycle of the algorithm chooses i such that $pr[i]$ is minimal. If there are several such, one of them is chosen nondeterministically. If τ_i is enabled it is taken. Then the priority of τ_i is incremented (priority lowered) by a random $z > 0$.

It is not difficult to see that each sequence generated by this algorithm is just. Let us indicate the arguments for completeness.

Let σ: $s_0, s_1, \ldots$ be a just sequence. Based on σ, we can construct a justification sequence

$$J: \quad \tau_1^0, \ \tau_2^0, \ \ldots, \ \tau_{m_0}^0, \ \tau_1^1, \ \ldots, \ \tau_{m_1}^1, \ \ldots,$$

where

$\tau_1^0, \ldots, \tau_{m_0-1}^0$ are all the transitions disabled on s_0,

$\tau_{m_0}^0$ is the transition leading from s_0 to s_1,

$\tau_1^1, \ldots, \tau_{m_1-1}^1$ are the transitions disabled on s_1,

$\tau_{m_1}^1$ is the transition leading from s_1 to s_2,

$\ldots$.

Let $i \in \{1, \ldots, k\}$. Since σ is just, τ_i must appear infinitely many times in J. Let $j_1, j_2, \ldots$ be the sequence of positions at which τ_i appears in J. It is possible to arrange the random choices taken in computing values to $pr[i]$ so that $pr[i]$ will be successively assigned the values $j_1, j_2, \ldots$.

It is obvious that if this is the case then algorithm FJ-SCHED will examine transitions precisely according to their appearance in J and will generate the sequence σ.

In **Problem 2.14**, the reader will construct a complete scheduler that ensures diligence, justice, and compassion.

Problems

Problem 2.1 (efficient LCR transformation)   page 119

The transformation presented in Section 2.2, transforming an arbitrary program to an equivalent LCR program, uses a single semaphore variable r to protect all sequences of assignments obtained by decomposing non-LCR assignments. This introduces in some cases unnecessary protection. For example, the transformed program may contain in parallel processes the following two segments

   request(r); $t_1 := x$; $u := t_1$;   **release**(r)

   request(r); $t_2 := y$; $w := t_2$;   **release**(r).

The common semaphore r guarantees that these two segments are never executed at the same time. The purpose of this protection is to prevent interference between the two segments. However, since the sets of variables referenced by the two segments are disjoint, the segments do not interfere with one another even without the protection, which is unnecessary in this case. The cost of unnecessary protection is that the execution of one of the segments may be delayed because the other segment is executing.

Define a more refined transformation that avoids such unnecessary locking and delays. In defining the transformation, consider programs that contain grouped statements. The resulting program should not contain any grouped statements, but may use semaphores.

*Problem 2.2 (robustness under refinement of statements)   page 125

Let P_1 be a program containing the statement

$\ell: z := x + y.$

Let P_2 be a program obtained from P_1 by replacing statement ℓ by the concatenation

$\widetilde{\ell}: [t := x; \ z := t + y],$

where t is a new variable, not present in P_1. In comparing P_1 to P_2, assume that t is unobservable.

(a) Show that if P_1 is an LCR program, then P_2 is equivalent to P_1.

(b) Give an example of a non-LCR program P_1 such that P_2 is not equivalent to P_1. Show a reduced behavior of one of the programs that cannot be generated by the other.

Consider a similar situation of programs P_3 and P_4. Program P_3 contains the statement

$\ell: \textbf{if } x \vee y \textbf{ then } S_1 \textbf{ else } S_2,$

and program P_4 replaces ℓ with the statement

$\widetilde{\ell}: \textbf{if } x \textbf{ then } S_1 \textbf{ else } (\textbf{if } y \textbf{ then } S_1 \textbf{ else } S_2).$

(c) Are P_3 and P_4 equivalent when P_3 is an LCR program? Are they equivalent when P_3 may be a non-LCR program? If you claim equivalence prove it. If you claim inequivalence, show an example.

Problem 2.3 (justice for non-self-looping transitions)   page 131

A transition τ is called non-self-looping if τ is disabled on any state resulting from taking τ, i.e., if $s' \in \tau(s)$ then τ is disabled on s'.

(a) Show that a diligent run σ of a program P is just with respect to a non-self-looping transition τ iff τ is disabled on infinitely many states of σ.

(b) Self-looping transitions naturally appear in diagram programs and Petri nets. For example, transition τ_0 in the diagram at the top of the next page is self-looping.

Show that, for a self-looping transition τ, the requirement of justice is not the same as requiring that τ is disabled infinitely many times. This can be shown by displaying a computation that satisfies one of the requirements but not the other.

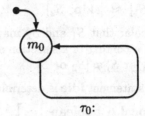

τ_0:

Problem 2.4 (different variants of conditional, while, and idle)   page 139

In this problem we introduce different variants of the conditional, while, and idle statements and compare them with the standard versions.

(a) Consider the statement

$$\ell: \text{IF } c \text{ THEN } \ell_1: S_1 \text{ ELSE } \ell_2: S_2.$$

This statement is associated with a single (just) transition τ_ℓ, whose transition relation ρ_ℓ is given by

$$\rho_\ell: \ ([\ell] \in \pi) \ \wedge \ \Big[(c \wedge \pi' = \pi \doteq [\ell] + [\ell_1]) \ \vee \ (\neg c \wedge \pi' = \pi \doteq [\ell] + [\ell_2])\Big].$$

Show that, in general, an IF-THEN-ELSE statement is not congruent to the standard **if-then-else** statement. That is, display a program context $P[S]$ and a statement IF c THEN S_1 ELSE S_2 such that

$$P[\text{IF } c \text{ THEN } S_1 \text{ ELSE } S_2] \not\sim P[\text{if } c \text{ then } S_1 \text{ else } S_2].$$

(b) Consider the statement

$$\ell: \big[\text{WHILE } c \text{ DO } [\widetilde{\ell}: \widetilde{S}]\big]: \widehat{\ell}.$$

This statement is associated with a single (just) transition τ_ℓ, whose transition relation ρ_ℓ is given by

$$\rho_\ell: \ ([\ell] \in \pi) \ \wedge \ \Big[(c \wedge \pi' = \pi \doteq [\ell] + [\widetilde{\ell}]) \ \vee \ (\neg c \wedge \pi' = \pi \doteq [\ell] + [\widehat{\ell}])\Big].$$

Show that, in general, a WHILE statement is not congruent to the standard **while** statement.

(c) Consider the statement

$$\ell: \text{IDLE}: \widehat{\ell}.$$

This statement is associated with a single just transition τ_ℓ, whose transition relation ρ_ℓ is given by

$$\rho_\ell: \ ([\ell] \in \pi) \ \wedge \ \Big[(\pi' = \pi \doteq [\ell] + [\widehat{\ell}]) \ \vee \ (\pi' = \pi)\Big].$$

Show that statement IDLE is congruent to **idle**.

(d) Two statements S_1 and S_2 are called *deterministically congruent* if

·

$$[\textbf{skip};\ S_1]\ \approx\ [\textbf{skip};\ S_2].$$

Note, in particular that S_1 and S_2 may be deterministically congruent but their embedding in a context of a selection statement may lead to noncongruent statements, i.e., $[S_1 \textbf{ or } S] \not\approx [S_2 \textbf{ or } S]$.

Show that the statement **idle** is deterministically congruent to the statement

$$\left[\begin{array}{c} \textbf{local } t\text{: boolean} \\ t := \text{T} \\ \textbf{while } t \textbf{ do } [\textbf{skip or } t := \text{F}] \end{array}\right]$$

and to the statement

$$\textbf{skip or } [\textbf{skip};\ \textbf{await } \text{F}],$$

but not to the statement

$$\textbf{skip or await } \text{F}.$$

(e) To which of the three statements in (d) is **idle** congruent (rather than deterministically congruent)? Justify your answer.

Problem 2.5 (scheduling for justice and compassion)   page 143

Algorithm J-SCHED (Fig. 2.18) guaranteed generation of just sequences while algorithm C-SCHED (Fig. 2.22) guaranteed compassionate sequences. However, each of these algorithms completely ignored the other fairness requirement. Propose an algorithm that generates sequences that are diligent, just, and compassionate. Assume that the set of transitions T is partitioned into three disjoint subsets $\mathcal{J}$, $\mathcal{C}$, and $\mathcal{R}$, where $\mathcal{R}$ denotes the set of transitions that are neither just nor compassionate. You may assume that the idling transition τ_I belongs to $\mathcal{R}$.

Problem 2.6 (set-fairness)   page 146

A different approach to fairness is based on the notion of set-fairness. A *set-fairness requirement* consists of a pair (E, T), where E and T are sets of transitions, $E \subseteq T \subseteq \mathcal{T}$. A computation is defined to be *just* with respect to (E, T) if

it is not the case that E is continually enabled beyond some position, while T is taken only finitely many times.

Recall that E is enabled at position $k \geq 0$ if some transition $\tau \in E$ is enabled at k, and T is taken at k if some transition $\tau \in T$ is taken at k.

A computation is defined to be *compassionate* with respect to requirement (E, T) if

it is not the case that E is enabled infinitely many times, while T is taken only finitely many times.

Note that a fairness requirement of either type of the form $(\{\tau\}, \{\tau\})$ is equivalent to the standard requirement of justice or compassion for transition τ.

A set-fair transition system $P^S = \langle \Pi, \Sigma, \mathcal{T}, \Theta, \mathcal{J}^S, \mathcal{C}^S \rangle$ contains, in addition to Π, Σ, $\mathcal{T}$, and Θ, the components $\mathcal{J}^S$ and $\mathcal{C}^S$, each of which is a set of set-fairness requirements. A sequence σ is defined to be a computation of P^S if, in addition to the usual requirements of initiation, consecution, and diligence, it is just with respect to each $(E, T) \in \mathcal{J}^S$, and compassionate with respect to each $(E, T) \in \mathcal{C}^S$.

A given text program is associated with set-fairness requirements as follows:

- For each transition τ associated with a skip, assignment, await, or cooperation statement, we include the (set-) justice requirement

  $(\{\tau\}, \{\tau\})$.

  Thus, for these transitions, the set-fairness requirements coincide with the standard fairness requirements.

- For each statement $\ell\!:\! S$ where S is a conditional or while statement, we include the justice requirement

  $(\{\ell^T, \ell^F\}, \{\ell^T, \ell^F\})$.

- For each synchronization or communication statement S, i.e., a request, release, region, send, or receive statement, we include the compassion requirement

  $\left(trans(S), \ trans\big(Comp(S)\big) \right)$,

  where $trans(S)$ is the set of transitions associated with S (a single transition for all but synchronous communication statements), and $trans\big(Comp(S)\big)$ are the transitions associated with statements competing with S.

Consider, for example, program MUX-SYNCH of Fig. 2.26. Transition $\tau_{\langle \ell_2, k_2 \rangle}$ participates in the following compassion requirements

$$\left(\{\tau_{\langle \ell_2, k_2 \rangle}, \ \tau_{\langle \ell_2, k_3 \rangle}\}, \ \{\tau_{\langle \ell_2, k_2 \rangle}, \ \tau_{\langle \ell_2, k_3 \rangle}\} \right)$$

$$\left(\{\tau_{\langle \ell_2, k_2 \rangle}, \ \tau_{\langle \ell_4, k_2 \rangle}\}, \ \{\tau_{\langle \ell_2, k_2 \rangle}, \ \tau_{\langle \ell_4, k_2 \rangle}, \ \tau_{\langle m_2, k_4 \rangle}, \ \tau_{\langle m_4, k_4 \rangle}\} \right)$$

$$\left(\{\tau_{\langle m_2, k_4 \rangle}, \ \tau_{\langle m_4, k_4 \rangle}\}, \ \{\tau_{\langle m_2, k_4 \rangle}, \ \tau_{\langle m_4, k_4 \rangle}, \ \tau_{\langle \ell_2, k_2 \rangle}, \ \tau_{\langle \ell_4, k_2 \rangle}\} \right)$$

obtained by considering statements ℓ_2, k_2, and k_4, respectively.

(a) Consider program $B3$ presented in Fig. 2.35.

  (1) Show that under the standard fairness requirements, this program has a nonterminating computation.

  (2) Show that assuming set-fairness all computations of the program terminate.

local x, y: **boolean** where $x = $ F, $y = $ T

ℓ_0: [**if** x **then** ℓ_1: $y := $ F **else** ℓ_2: $y := $ F] : ℓ_3

||

m_0: [**while** y **do** m_1: $x := \neg x$] : m_2

Fig. 2.35.   Program $B3$ — undecided conditional.

(b) Consider program $A8$ presented in Fig. 2.25.

   (1) Show that under standard fairness this program always terminates.

   (2) Show that under set-fairness the program also terminates.

(c) Consider the program presented in Fig. 2.36.

local α: **channel of boolean**

$P_1 ::$
$\begin{bmatrix} \text{local } x\text{: boolean} \\ \qquad \text{where } x = \text{T} \\ \ell\text{: while } x \text{ do} \\ \qquad \begin{bmatrix} \ell_2\text{: } \alpha \Leftarrow \text{F}; \ x := \text{F} \\ \ell_1\text{:} \quad \textbf{or} \\ \ell_3\text{: } \alpha \Leftarrow \text{T} \end{bmatrix} \end{bmatrix}$
$\quad || \quad$
$P_2 ::$
$\begin{bmatrix} \text{local } y\text{: boolean} \\ \qquad \text{where } y = \text{T} \\ m_0\text{: while } y \text{ do} \\ \qquad m_1\text{: } \alpha \Rightarrow y \end{bmatrix}$

Fig. 2.36.   Fair communication.

   (1) Show that under standard fairness this program terminates.

   (2) Show that under set-fairness this program has a nonterminating compu-
       tation.

Problem 2.7 (impact of set-fairness on fairness in selection)   page 148

   Consider program MUX-ASYNCH in Fig. 2.27.

(a) Show that under standard fairness this program ensures accessibility for both
processes. That is, P_1 cannot remain stuck forever at ℓ_3 and P_2 cannot remain
stuck forever at m_3.

$$\text{local } \alpha, \ \beta\text{: channel of integer}$$

$$
S ::
\begin{bmatrix}
\textbf{local } x\text{: } integer \\
\ell_0\text{: } \textbf{loop forever do} \\
\quad
\begin{bmatrix}
\ell_1\text{: } \textbf{compute}(x) \\
\ell_2\text{: } \alpha \Leftarrow x
\end{bmatrix}
\end{bmatrix}
$$

$$\|$$

$$
B_\beta ::
\begin{bmatrix}
\textbf{local } b\text{: list of integer where } b = \Lambda \\
\quad\quad y\text{: } \textbf{integer} \\
m_0\text{: } \textbf{loop forever do} \\
m_1\text{: }
\begin{bmatrix}
m_2\text{: } \alpha \Rightarrow y; \ m_3\text{: } b := b \bullet y \\
\textbf{or} \\
m_4\text{: } \beta \Leftarrow hd(b) \ \textbf{provided } |b| > 0; \ m_5\text{: } b := tl(b)
\end{bmatrix}
\end{bmatrix}
$$

$$\|$$

$$
R ::
\begin{bmatrix}
\textbf{local } z\text{: integer} \\
k_0\text{: } \textbf{loop forever do} \\
k_1\text{: }
\begin{bmatrix}
k_2\text{: } \beta \Rightarrow z; \ k_3\text{: } \textbf{use}(z) \\
\textbf{or} \\
k_4\text{: } \textbf{skip}
\end{bmatrix}
\end{bmatrix}
$$

Fig. 2.37. Program SYNCH-BUF (implementation of a buffer by synchronous communication).

(b) Show that under set-fairness accessibility to both processes is not guaranteed.

This demonstrates that standard fairness associates a certain degree of fairness in selection with communication statements, which is not the case with set-fairness. In the case of program MUX-ASYNCH, this is a disadvantage of set-fairness.

Problem 2.8 (services to intermittent receiver)   page 150

Consider program SYNCH-BUF of Fig. 2.37. This program consists of a sender process S that keeps generating messages, a receiver process R that nondeterministically chooses between reading a message and skipping, and a buffer process B_β.

(a) Show that this program has a computation in which no messages are transmitted on channel β.

(b) Consider program IMP-BUF given by

local α, β, γ: **channel of integer**

$$S \parallel B_\gamma \parallel Serv \parallel R$$

where S and R are the same as in Fig. 2.37, B_γ is process B_β in which references to channel β are replaced by references to γ, and process $Serv$ is given by

$$Serv :: \begin{bmatrix} \textbf{local } t\textbf{: integer} \\ n_0\text{: } \textbf{loop forever do} \\ \quad [n_1\text{: } \gamma \Rightarrow t;\ n_2\text{: } \beta \Leftarrow t] \end{bmatrix}.$$

Show that all computations of program IMP-BUF transmit in finitely many messages on channel β. We may claim the combination $B_\gamma \parallel Serv$ to be a better buffer, since it ensures that all messages sent by S are eventually received by R.

**Problem 2.9 (robustness under spacing transformation)   page 150

(a) Restricting attention to programs with no synchronous communication statements, show the congruence

$$S \approx [S;\ \textbf{skip}],$$

for every statement S.

(b) The combination of synchronous communication and standard fairness destroys this property. Consider program CONTIG presented in Fig. 2.38.

(1) Show that under standard fairness this program always terminates.

(2) Consider program NCONTIG obtained from CONTIG by replacing statement ℓ_1: $\alpha \Leftarrow \tau$, by the statement ℓ_1: $[\alpha \Leftarrow \tau; \textbf{skip}]$. Show that program NCONTIG has a nonterminating computation.

(3) Show that under set-fairness both CONTIG and NCONTIG have nonterminating computations.

(c) More generally, show that under set-fairness, statements S and $[S; \textbf{skip}]$ are congruent even for programs that contain synchronous communication.

Problem 2.10 (generalized fairness)   page 150

A uniform approach to a variety of fairness requirements is provided by the notion of generalized fairness. Assume a first-order language $\mathcal{L}$ that includes the two predicates $enabled(\tau)$ and $taken(\tau)$ for each $\tau \in \mathcal{T}$. We refer to formulas of $\mathcal{L}$ as *local formulas*. Given a local formula φ, it is obvious how to evaluate the boolean value of φ at a position of a computation σ. In particular, $enabled(\tau)$ is true at position i if τ is enabled there, and $taken(\tau)$ is true at i if τ is taken there.

$$
\begin{array}{c}
\textbf{local } x,\ y,\ z\textbf{: boolean where } x = \text{T},\ y = \text{T} \\
\alpha,\ \beta \quad \textbf{: channel of boolean}
\end{array}
$$

$$
P_1 :: \left[
\begin{array}{l}
\ell_0\text{: \textbf{while } } x \textbf{ do} \\
\quad \left[
\begin{array}{l}
\ell_1\text{: } \alpha \Leftarrow \text{T};\ \ell_2\text{: } \left[
\begin{array}{l}
\ell_3\text{: } \beta \Rightarrow x;\ \ell_4\text{: } \alpha \Leftarrow \text{F} \\
\textbf{or} \\
\ell_5\text{: \textbf{skip}}
\end{array}
\right]
\end{array}
\right] \\
\text{: } \ell_6
\end{array}
\right]
$$

$$\|$$

$$
P_2 :: \left[
\begin{array}{l}
m_0\text{: \textbf{while } } y \textbf{ do} \\
\quad \left[
\begin{array}{l}
m_1\text{: } \alpha \Rightarrow y;\ m_2\text{: } \left[
\begin{array}{l}
m_3\text{: } \beta \Leftarrow \text{F};\ m_4\text{: } \alpha \Rightarrow y \\
\textbf{or} \\
m_5\text{: \textbf{skip}}
\end{array}
\right]
\end{array}
\right] \\
\text{: } m_6
\end{array}
\right]
$$

Fig. 2.38.   Program CONTIG (contiguous communications).

A *generalized fairness requirement* is a pair (φ, ψ) of two local formulas φ and ψ.

A sequence of states σ: $s_0, s_1, \ldots$ is said to *satisfy* the generalized fairness requirement (φ, ψ) if

> it is not the case that σ contains infinitely many φ-positions, but only finitely many ψ-positions.

An equivalent formulation of this requirement is the following:

> Either σ contains only finitely many φ-positions
> or it contains infinitely many ψ-positions.

Note that the trivial fairness requirements (φ, T) and (F, ψ), for arbitrary φ and ψ, are satisfied by every sequence of states.

To ensure that the generalized fairness requirements do not lead to a system with an empty set of computations, we impose certain restrictions on the fairness requirements. Let P be a basic transition system. A generalized fairness requirement (φ, ψ) is defined to be *feasible* for P if, for every computation prefix of P

$$s_0, \ldots, s_k$$

such that φ holds at position k, there exists a transition τ and a state $s_{k+1} \in \tau(s_k)$, such that ψ holds at position k of the computation prefix

$$s_0, \ldots, s_k, s_{k+1}.$$

This definition ensures that from any P-accessible φ-state, it is possible within one computation step to obtain a ψ-state. By a repeated application of this extension, we can show that there always exists a computation that satisfies the feasible fairness requirement (φ, ψ).

(a) Let $(\varphi_1, \psi_1), \ldots, (\varphi_m, \psi_m)$ be a finite set of generalized fairness requirements feasible for P, and let $s_0, \ldots, s_k$ be a computation segment of program P. Show that the segment $s_0, \ldots, s_k$ can be extended to a run of P that satisfies all these general fairness requirements.

All the fairness requirements we have considered can be represented as generalized fairness requirements. Consider, for example, the justice requirement for a non-self-looping transition τ. The requirement is that τ must be disabled on infinitely many positions. This requirement can be formulated as the generalized fairness requirement

$$\big(\text{T},\ \neg enabled(\tau)\big).$$

(b) Formulate diligence as a generalized fairness requirement. Show it to be feasible.

(c) Formulate the justice requirement with respect to (a possibly self-looping) transition τ as a generalized fairness requirement. Show it to be feasible.

(d) Formulate the compassion requirement with respect to τ as a generalized fairness requirement. Show it to be feasible.

**Problem 2.11 (justice alone does not improve termination)   page 150

Let P be a program whose processes communicate by synchronous message passing but share no common variables. Assume that P has no otherwise statements. Recall that a diligent run of P is a state sequence that satisfies the requirements of initiation, consecution, and diligence, but not necessarily the requirements of justice and compassion. A just run of P is a diligent run that satisfies the requirement of justice.

Show that all diligent runs of P terminate iff all just runs of P terminate.

This result can be interpreted as stating that without the requirement of compassion justice does not improve the termination properties of synchronously communicating programs.

Problem 2.12 (fair selection)   page 150

In some cases it is useful to have a selection statement that chooses fairly between its enabled children.

A *fair-selection* statement S has the form

$$S :: \quad [S_1 \textbf{ fair-or } S_2 \textbf{ fair-or } \cdots \textbf{ fair-or } S_k],$$

for some $k \geq 2$. It is syntactically required that S have no competing statements in the program to which it belongs.

A fair-selection statement behaves identically to a selection statement as far as transitions and structural relations (such as the predicate at_S) are concerned. It differs from the selection statement in being associated with a particular set of fairness requirements, to which we refer as *selection fairness*.

For a transition τ that is associated with a statement S, i.e., $\tau \in trans(S)$, we say that τ is *syntactically enabled* at a state s if at_S holds at s.

A selection fairness requirement for a transition τ demands that

it is not the case that

- τ is syntactically enabled infinitely many times;

- beyond a certain point, τ is enabled at all positions at which it is syntactically enabled;

- τ is taken only finitely many times.

We can view selection fairness as relativized justice, where continual enabledness of τ is replaced by enabledness of τ on all states at which τ is syntactically enabled.

For each fair-selection statement

$$S :: \quad [S_1 \textbf{ fair-or } \cdots \textbf{ fair-or } S_k],$$

and each transition τ in $trans(S_i)$, $i = 1, \ldots, k$, we require selection fairness with respect to τ.

This requirement excludes computations in which S_i (equivalently S) is visited infinitely many times and from a certain point on τ is enabled on each of these visits, but τ is taken only finitely many times.

(a) Consider the programs in Figs. 2.39 and 2.40. Show that all computations of the program in Fig. 2.39 terminate, but there are nonterminating computations of the program in Fig. 2.40.

(b) We saw in Problem 2.7 that when replacing standard fairness with set-fairness, program MUX-ASYNCH in Fig. 2.27 cannot guarantee accessibility to both processes.

Consider a modified version of this program, obtained by replacing statement k_1 with

$$k_1: \quad \begin{bmatrix} k_2: & [\alpha_1 \Rightarrow y; & \beta_1 \Leftarrow \text{T}; & \alpha_1 \Rightarrow y] \\ & \textbf{fair-or} & & \\ k_3: & [\alpha_2 \Rightarrow y; & \beta_2 \Leftarrow \text{T}; & \alpha_2 \Rightarrow y] \end{bmatrix}$$

local x: **boolean where** $x = \text{T}$

ℓ_0: **while** x **do** ℓ_1: $\begin{bmatrix} \ell_2\text{: \textbf{skip}} \\ \textbf{fair-or} \\ \ell_3\text{: } x := \text{F} \end{bmatrix}$

Fig. 2.39. Fair selection (terminating program).

local x, y: **boolean where** $x = \text{T}, \ y = \text{T}$

ℓ_0: **while** x **do** ℓ_1: $\begin{bmatrix} \ell_2\text{: } y := \neg y \\ \textbf{fair-or} \\ \ell_3\text{: \textbf{when} } y \textbf{ do } x := \text{F} \end{bmatrix}$

Fig. 2.40. Fair selection (nonterminating program).

Show that under set-fairness together with selection fairness, the modified program guarantees accessibility to both processes.

(c) Formulate fair selection as a generalized fairness requirement. Show that it is feasible.

(d) Construct a program, using the random choice statement **choose**(z), that emulates the program

$$\begin{bmatrix} \textbf{out } x, y\text{: \textbf{integer where} } x = 0, \ y = 0 \\ \textbf{loop forever do} \begin{bmatrix} x := x + 1 \\ \textbf{fair-or} \\ y := y + 1 \end{bmatrix} \end{bmatrix}.$$

Problem 2.13 (set-fairness for Petri nets)   page 151

Problem 2.9 showed that set-fairness is robust with respect to the transformation replacing a statement S by $[S; \textbf{skip}]$. This means that if program P' is obtained from P by such a replacement then under set-fairness, P is equivalent to P'. As shown in that problem, the same is not true under standard fairness.

When considering Petri nets, the relevant transformation is place refinement, depicted in Fig. 2.41.

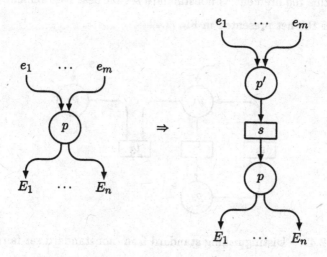

Fig. 2.41   Place Refinement.

We define set-fairness requirements for Petri nets.

- For each net-transition t, we include the justice requirement

$$(\{t\}, \{t\}).$$

Thus, the set-justice requirements coincide with the standard justice requirements.

- Let t be a net-transition that feeds from places $p_1, \ldots, p_n$, $n > 0$, i.e., $p_1, \ldots, p_n$ are all the places p such that $t \in p^\bullet$. For each subset $P \subseteq \{p_1, \ldots, p_n\}$ of size $n - 1$, we include the compassion requirement

$$\left(\{t\}, \bigcup_{p \in P} p^\bullet\right).$$

Thus, if t is enabled infinitely many times it is required that transitions feeding from places in P are taken infinitely many times.

For example, for t that feeds from p_1 and p_2, we include the compassion requirements

$$(\{t\}, p_1^\bullet) \qquad \text{and} \qquad (\{t\}, p_2^\bullet).$$

(a) An alternative and simpler compassion requirement for a net-transition t feeding from places $p_1, \ldots, p_n$ is

$$\left(\{t\}, \bigcup_{i=1}^{n} p_i^\bullet \right).$$

We refer to this requirement as nonstandard set-fairness requirement.

Consider the net presented in Fig. 2.42.

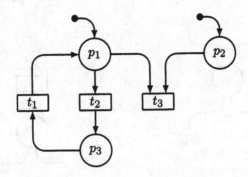

Fig. 2.42. Distinguishing standard from nonstandard set-fairness

(1) Show that under set-fairness all computations of this net terminate.

(2) Show that under nonstandard set-fairness this net has a nonterminating computation.

(b) Consider nets N and N' presented in Figs. 2.43 and 2.44, respectively. Clearly N' is obtained from N by applying place refinements to p_2 and p_3.

(1) Show that under standard fairness all computations of N fire t_3, while N' has computations that never fire t_3.

(2) Show that under set-fairness both N and N' have computations that never fire t_3.

(c) Let N be a net, some of whose places are identified as observable. Let N' be a net obtained from N by refining some of the nonobservable places. Show that under set-fairness the set of reduced behaviors of N' is equal to that of N. This shows that set-fairness is robust with respect to place refinement.

Problem 2.14 (complete scheduler for fairness)   page 159

Algorithm FJ-SCHED of Fig. 2.34 presents a complete scheduler for justice, using random choice. Construct an algorithm, using random choice, that is a complete scheduler for computations. That is, any sequence generated by the algorithm is diligent, just, and compassionate (soundness), and any diligent, just, and compassionate sequence can be generated by the algorithm (completeness).

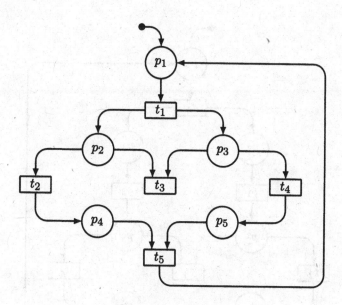

Fig. 2.43.   Net N.

Give arguments in support of the claim that your algorithm is both sound and complete.

Bibliographic Notes

This chapter deals with two central topics: the *atomicity* of statements and their possible *interference*, and the various notions of *fairness*.

The necessity of atomicity in statements that refer to shared variables was first observed by Dijkstra [1965]. Lamport [1976] discusses the reader-writers problem introduced by Courtois, Heymans and Parnas [1971] (solved there using semaphores). The solution given by Lamport [1976] uses the *region* and *await* constructs, and then provides implementations of these constructs using queues and atomic actions on shared memory in a *distributed* system. Similar to the *bakery* algorithm, these implementations potentially lead to an infinite number of states, even though the original problem is finite state. The queuing ideas can be traced to Knuth [1966].

Our analysis of interleaved computations, leading to the LCR restriction, is based on the identification of the mechanism by which statements in the shared-variables model interfere with one another. The problem of interference has been studied in the literature, mainly with the goal of identifying cases where state-

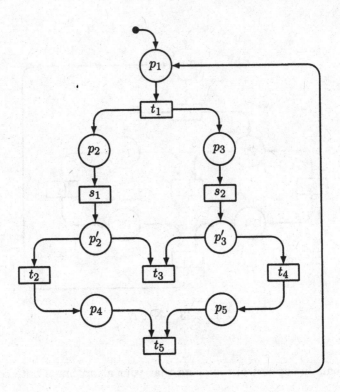

Fig. 2.44.   Net N'.

ments do not interfere at all with one another. Sufficient syntactic condition
for noninterference were given by Bernstein [1966]. Semantic rules that extend
the syntactic ones were presented by Best and Lengauer [1989]. Syntactic rules
that ensure noninterference were given by Reynolds [1978, 1989]. Proof-theoretic
notions of noninterference were described by Owicki and Gries [1976a].

The simplest notion of fairness, to which we refer as *justice*, is an inevitable
logical conclusion of the two premises underlying the interleaving model which
were postulated by Dijkstra:

- Nothing may be assumed about the relative speeds of the N computers; we
  may not even assume their speed to be constant in time (Dijkstra [1965]).

- "We now request that a process, once initiated, will — sooner or later — get
  the opportunity to complete its actions" (Dijkstra [1968a]).

One of the first researchers to realize that fairness, which is essential to the abstract representation of concurrency, complicates the mathematical semantics of
programs and necessitates working with monotonic operators rather than with
continuous ones, as advocated by Scott's thesis, was Park [1980]. He studied

fairness in the context of data-flow languages, focusing on the *fair-merge* process as the main implementer of fairness. In his work he also pointed out the connection of fairness with *maximal fixpoints*, while the sequential program theory works mainly with *minimal fixpoints*. Related investigations are reported in Park [1981a, 1983]. The connection of fairness to fixpoints is further elaborated by Stomp, de Roever and Gerth [1989].

In the context of shared-variables programs (and more general transition systems), Lehmann, Pnueli and Stavi [1981] propose three levels of fairness, two of which are justice and compassion (compassion is called there *fairness*). Best [1984] extends these notions to an infinite hierarchy.

The connection between fairness and unbounded nondeterminism has been identified by Apt and Olderog [1983], who propose a transformation from a fair program to a program that does not assume fairness but contains a nondeterministic choice of a natural number, similar to our **choose**(x) statement. A more general transformation from fair concurrency to unbounded nondeterminism was given by Harel [1986]. A general investigation of unbounded nondeterminism is reported by Apt and Plotkin [1986].

Fairness in general transition systems was considered by Queille and Sifakis [1983]. Fairness in CCS was considered by Costa and Stirling [1984] and extended to an asynchronous variant of CCS by Darondeau [1985]. Fairness in Petri nets was first studied by Best [1984] and further analyzed by Kwiatkowska [1989]. Several fairness notions in an automata framework were examined by Priese, Rehrmann and Willecke-Klemme [1987], and Vardi [1985].

A comprehensive survey of the diverse notions of fairness that have been proposed was presented by Francez [1986]. The paper by Apt, Francez and Katz [1988] examines the effectiveness and utility of adopting various notions of fairness. It has been instrumental in our final decision about the fairness notions adopted in the definition of a fair transition system.

The use of fairness for representing qualitative aspects of probabilistic systems was studied in Pnueli [1983], Pnueli and Zuck [1986b], and Vardi [1985].

It is interesting to compare the notion of fairness adopted in *Unity* (Chandy and Misra [1988]) with the requirement of justice. By definition, *Unity* assignments are always enabled. In that case the requirement of justice can be simplified to the requirement that each assignment is executed infinitely many times. This indeed is the standard fairness notion required by *Unity*.

Part II

Specifications

Chapter 3

Temporal Logic

In the preceding chapters, we introduced the concept of a fair transition system as a model for reactive systems. Following the general definition, we presented several concrete languages for concurrent systems and showed how they can all be cast in the general framework of transition systems.

In the introduction, we claimed that the appropriate semantics for reactive systems must be *behavioral*, i.e., it must talk about the ongoing behavior of the system. Consistent with this observation, we take the semantics of a reactive system to be its behavior, as represented by the set of computations.

In this chapter, we introduce the language of temporal logic as a tool for the specification of reactive systems. By *specification* we mean the description of the desired behavior or operation of the system, while avoiding references to the method or details of its implementation.

Viewing a program as a generator of a set of computations, we expect that a specification of a program should provide an alternative characterization, hopefully more descriptive and less operational, of the set of computations generated by the program.

The language of temporal logic defines predicates over infinite sequences of states. For brevity we refer to sequences of states simply as *sequences*. Thus, each formula of temporal logic is (in general) satisfied by some sequences and falsified by some other sequences. Interpreted over a computation, such a formula expresses a property of the computation.

For example, consider a program P implementing mutual exclusion between processes P_1 and P_2. The following are examples of properties of computations of P that can be expressed in temporal logic:

p_0: For all states of the computation, it is never the case that P_1 and P_2 occupy their critical sections at the same state.

p_1: If a computation σ contains a state at position $j \geq 0$ in which P_1 is waiting to enter the critical section, then σ also contains a state at a position $k \geq j$ in which P_1 is inside the critical section. That is, whenever P_1 wishes to enter its critical section, it will eventually do so.

p_2: The same requirement as p_1 but for process P_2.

These properties are true of some sequences and false of others.

If a property p is true of all computations generated by a program P, then we call p a *valid property* of P. Thus if p_0, p_1, and p_2 are valid properties of a program P, then P should be considered an acceptable solution to the mutual-exclusion problem. This suggests that the set of properties p_0, p_1, and p_2 can be viewed as a *specification* of the mutual-exclusion problem.

Since our language has the conjunction operator $\wedge$, we can always combine a list of properties, such as p_0, p_1, and p_2, into a single property given by $p_0 \wedge p_1 \wedge p_2$. Clearly, a sequence satisfies the conjunction iff it satisfies each of the properties separately.

We may view a property (equivalently, a set of properties) as a specification for a program. It specifies any program all of whose computations satisfy (or have) the property. This shows that a specification rarely specifies a unique program. The relation of implementation (or satisfaction) holding between a program and its specification can be viewed as an inclusion relation. Let $Sat(p)$ be the set of all sequences that satisfy property p and $\mathcal{C}(P)$ the set of all sequences that are computations of P. Then, we say that P *implements the specification* p, or P *satisfies* p, if the set of computations of P is contained in the set of sequences satisfying p, i.e., $\mathcal{C}(P) \subseteq Sat(p)$.

This approach, in which a specification is given by a list of properties, enjoys the important advantage of incrementality. By this we mean that if, after developing a specification, we suddenly realize that the specification is incomplete, we can always rectify the situation by adding one or more missing properties as additional conjuncts in an incremental fashion.

3.1 State Formulas

The language of temporal logic is built from a state language, used to construct state formulas, and a set of logical and temporal operators. By applying the logical and temporal operators to the state formulas, we construct general temporal formulas.

A state formula can be evaluated at a certain position $j \geq 0$ in a sequence, and it expresses properties of the state s_j occurring at this position. The state language that we introduce here is adequate for reasoning about the concrete programming languages that we consider. Other languages, admitting additional constructs, may require some extensions of the state language.

State Language

The state language is an extension of the underlying language that was introduced in Section 1.1 and used there for the definition of the syntax of programming languages and for the expression of transition relations.

The Vocabulary

The vocabulary $\mathcal{V}$ of the state language consists of a countable set of typed variables. Some of these variables, called *data variables*, range over data domains provided in the programming language, such as booleans, integers, lists, and sets. Other variables, called *control variables*, assume as values locations in programs. The type of each variable indicates the domain over which the variable ranges. We usually refer to boolean variables as *propositions*.

As mentioned in Section 1.1, the variables are partitioned into rigid and flexible variables. A *rigid variable* must have the same value in all states of a computation, while a *flexible variable* may assume different values in different states of the computation. All variables that are taken as state variables of transition systems are flexible. Rigid data variables are mainly used for specification purposes, i.e., they do not appear in the program itself and are used to relate values at different states in the sequence. For example, in order to state that the value of flexible variable y in state s' is greater by one than its value in state s, where both s and s' appear in the same sequence, we may use the rigid variable u and state that if $y = u$ in s then $y = u + 1$ in s'.

Other Symbols

In addition to the variables of vocabulary $\mathcal{V}$, we also have constants, functions, and predicates. We agree to view constants as 0-ary functions.

The constants, functions, and predicates are concrete individual elements, concrete functions, and concrete predicates over their respective domains.

For example, we have constants F, T, over the booleans; $0, 1, 2, \ldots$ over the integers; Λ (the empty list) over lists; and ϕ (the empty set) over sets. We have the function symbols $\vee$, $\wedge$ over the booleans; $+$, $-$ over the integers; $\bullet$ (adding an element to the front of a list), $*$ (appending two lists), hd (taking the head of a nonempty list), tl (taking the tail of a nonempty list) over lists; and $\cup$, $\cap$ over sets. We also have the predicate symbols $>$, $<$ over integers; $null$ (testing the list for emptiness) over lists; and $\subseteq$, $\in$ over sets.

The symbol for equality, $=$, is used for comparing two elements of the same type.

In the following, let $V \subseteq \mathcal{V}$ be a subset of the vocabulary. Using the variables in V and the constants, functions, and predicates over the corresponding domains, we can construct expressions and formulas over V.

Expressions over V

Expressions are constructed as follows:

- Every variable $x \in V$ is an expression over V.

- If $e_1, \ldots, e_m$ are expressions over V and f is a function of arity m ($m \geq 0$), then $f(e_1, \ldots, e_m)$ is an expression over V. In particular (when $m = 0$), every constant is an expression.

Thus, $x + 3y$, $hd(u) \bullet tl(v)$, and $A \cup B$ are examples of expressions.

Atomic Formulas over V

- Every proposition $x \in V$, i.e., a variable x of type boolean, is an atomic formula over V.

- If P is a predicate of arity m ($m > 0$), and $e_1, \ldots, e_m$ are expressions over V of types compatible with the arguments of P, then $P(e_1, \ldots, e_m)$ is an atomic formula over V. In particular, for e_1, e_2, expressions of the same type over V, $e_1 = e_2$ is an atomic formula over V.

Thus, $x > y + 1$, $null(u)$, and $x \in A \cup B$ are examples of atomic formulas.

Boolean Formulas over V

We define the set of *boolean formulas* over V as follows:

- Every atomic formula over V is a boolean formula.

- If p and q are boolean formulas over V, then so are the constructs

$$\neg p \qquad p \vee q \qquad p \wedge q \qquad p \rightarrow q \qquad p \leftrightarrow q,$$

formed by the boolean connectives: $\neg$ (negation), $\vee$ (disjunction), $\wedge$ (conjunction), $\rightarrow$ (implication), and $\leftrightarrow$ (equivalence).

Thus, $\neg(x > y) \wedge null(v)$ is an example of a boolean formula.

State Formulas (Assertions) over V

- Every boolean formula over V is a state formula over V.

- If p is a state formula over V, then so are the constructs

$$\exists u\colon p \qquad \forall u\colon p$$

using the variable $u \in V$ and the quantifiers: $\exists$ (existential) and $\forall$ (universal).

- If p and q are state formulas over V, then so are:

$$\neg p \qquad p \vee q \qquad p \wedge q \qquad p \rightarrow q \qquad p \leftrightarrow q.$$

State formulas without quantification and whose only variables are boolean (propositions) are called *propositional state formulas*. For example, $\forall x \forall y \colon (x > y + 1) \rightarrow \exists v \colon null(v)$ is a state formula, while $(p \leftrightarrow q) \rightarrow r$ is a propositional state formula.

An occurrence of a variable u is called *free* if it does not fall in the scope of a quantification over u. A variable u is called *free* in a formula p if all its occurrences in p are free.

Semantics of State Formulas

Next we consider the semantics of the different constructs, showing how to evaluate them over states.

Models over V

We define a *state s over V* to be an interpretation that assigns to each variable $u \in V$ a value from the appropriate domain, denoted by

$$s[u].$$

A *model σ over V* is an infinite sequence of the form

$$\sigma \colon s_0, \; s_1, \; s_2, \; \ldots ,$$

where each s_i is a state over V.

A model must always satisfy the requirement of *rigidity*, which states that if u is a rigid variable and s_i, s_j are two states in the same sequence, then $s_i[u] = s_j[u]$.

Evaluating Expressions

Let s be a state over V, and e an expression over V. We inductively define the value of e at s, denoted by $s[e]$.

- The value of a (possibly boolean) variable $x \in V$ is $s[x]$.

- For the expression $f(e_1, \ldots, e_m)$, we define

$$s[f(e_1, \; \ldots, \; e_m)] \; = \; f(s[e_1], \; \ldots, \; s[e_m]).$$

That is, function f is applied to the values of $e_1, \ldots, e_m$ at s.

Evaluating Boolean Formulas

The value of a boolean formula φ over a state s, denoted by $s[\varphi]$, is defined as follows:

- For the atomic formula $P(e_1, \ldots, e_m)$, we define

$$s[P(e_1, \ldots, e_m)] = P(s[e_1], \ldots, s[e_m]).$$

- For boolean formulas constructed by boolean connectives, we define

$$
\begin{aligned}
s[\neg p] &= \neg s[p] \\
s[p \vee q] &= s[p] \vee s[q] \\
s[p \wedge q] &= s[p] \wedge s[q] \\
s[p \rightarrow q] &= s[p] \rightarrow s[q] \\
s[p \leftrightarrow q] &= s[p] \leftrightarrow s[q].
\end{aligned}
$$

Consider, for example, a state s over $V = \{x, y, z\}$ given by

$$s = \langle x{:}\,0,\ y{:}\,1,\ z{:}\,2 \rangle.$$

The previous definitions yield that the value of the boolean formula

$$(x + z = 2 \cdot y) \rightarrow (y > z)$$

is

$$
\begin{aligned}
s\big[(x + z = 2 \cdot y) &\rightarrow (y > z)\big] \\
&= \big(s[x] + s[z] = 2 \cdot s[y]\big) \rightarrow \big(s[y] > s[z]\big) \\
&= \big((0 + 2 = 2 \cdot 1) \rightarrow (1 > 2)\big) = (\textsc{t} \rightarrow \textsc{f}) \\
&= \textsc{f}.
\end{aligned}
$$

Evaluating State Formulas

Let s, s' be two states over V and $x \in V$ a variable. We say that s' is an *x-variant* of s if

$$s'[y] = s[y] \qquad \text{for every } y \in V{-}\{x\}.$$

That is, s' and s may disagree on at most the interpretation given to variable x.

Given a state s and a state formula p, both over V, we define the notion of *p holding* at s

$$s \Vvdash p,$$

by cases on the form of state formula p:

- For a boolean formula,

$$s \Vvdash p \quad \text{iff} \quad s[p] = \textsc{t}.$$

- For quantification over a variable u, we have:

  - $s \Vvdash \exists u{:}\,p$ iff $s' \Vvdash p$ for some s' over V that is a u-variant of s.

  - $s \Vvdash \forall u{:}\,p$ iff $s' \Vvdash p$ for all s' over V that are u-variants of s.

- For the boolean connectives applied to state formulas, we have:

  ■ $s \Vdash \neg p$ iff $s \nVdash p$.

  That is, $\neg p$ holds at state s iff p does not.

  ■ $s \Vdash p \vee q$ iff $s \Vdash p$ or $s \Vdash q$.

  That is, $p \vee q$ holds at s iff either p or q does.

  Since the other boolean operators, $\wedge$, $\rightarrow$, $\leftrightarrow$, can be expressed in terms of disjunction ($\vee$) and negation ($\neg$), the corresponding definitions can be deduced from the previous two.

If $s \Vdash p$, we say that s satisfies p and we refer to s as a *p-state*. If s satisfies p, we define $s[p] = \mathrm{T}$, otherwise, $s[p] = \mathrm{F}$.

For example, consider a state s over vocabulary $V = \{x, y\}$ whose interpretation is given by

$$\langle x{:}\,0, \ y{:}\,1 \rangle.$$

It is easy to see that s satisfies the state formula $(x = 0) \vee (y = 0)$, but does not satisfy the formula $(x = 0) \wedge (y = 0)$. On the other hand, it satisfies the formula $\exists y\colon \big[(x = 0) \wedge (y = 0)\big]$, because the state $s'\colon \langle x{:}\,0, \ y{:}\,0 \rangle$, which is a y-variant of s, does satisfy $(x = 0) \wedge (y = 0)$.

For a state formula p, we say that p is *state-satisfiable* if there exists a state s such that $s \Vdash p$. We say that p is *state-valid* if for all states s, $s \Vdash p$. It is sufficient to consider in these definitions only states over a vocabulary V that contains only the variables appearing in p. For example, let x be an integer variable. Then the formula $0 < x < 2$ is state-satisfiable, since there exists a state, namely, $s\colon \langle x{:}\,1 \rangle$, such that $s \Vdash 0 < x < 2$. On the other hand, the formula $\neg(0 < x < 1)$ is state-valid since $0 < x < 1$ is false at all states.

The two state formulas p and q are *state-equivalent* if, for every state s, $s \Vdash p$ iff $s \Vdash q$. This is the same as stating that the formula $p \leftrightarrow q$ is state-valid. Thus, under the assumption that x is an integer variable, the formula $0 < x < 2$ is state-equivalent to the formula $x = 1$.

The notions of state-satisfiability, state validity, and state-equivalence can be relativized to a more restricted set of states. Let C be a set of sequences. We say that a state s is *C-accessible* if there exists a sequence $\sigma \in C$, $\sigma = s_0, s_1, \ldots, s_j, \ldots$ and a position $j \geq 0$, such that $s = s_j$, i.e., s appears at position j in σ. Consequently, for state formulas p and q, we say that

- p is *C-state-satisfiable* if $s \Vdash p$ for some C-accessible state s.

- p is *C-state-valid* if $s \Vdash p$ for all C-accessible states s.

- p and q are *C-state-equivalent* if for every C-accessible state s, $s \Vdash p$ iff $s \Vdash q$.

3.2   Temporal Formulas: Future Operators

A temporal formula is constructed from state formulas to which we apply temporal operators, boolean connectives, and quantification. The temporal operators are partitioned into two groups: the future and past operators. We first consider the future operators.

For each of the operators and subformulas allowed in a temporal formula, we present a definition of its interpretation in a given model. This definition is based on the notion of a formula p holding at a position j, $j \geq 0$, in a sequence σ, denoted by

$$(\sigma, j) \models p.$$

Note the use of $\models$ for holding over sequences and the use of $\Vdash$ for holding over states.

State Formulas

For a state formula p,

$$(\sigma, j) \models p \quad \text{iff} \quad s_j \Vdash p,$$

where σ: s_0, s_1, ..., s_j, ...

For example, in the following table we represent a sequence over the vocabulary $V = \{x, y\}$ by listing on separate lines: the position $j = 0, 1, \ldots$, the interpretation of x by s_j, the interpretation of y by s_j, and the evaluation of the state formula $x = y$ over s_j.

j	0	1	2	3	$\cdots$
x	1	2	3	4	$\cdots$
y	5	4	3	2	$\cdots$
$x = y$	F	F	T	F	$\cdots$

It follows that $x = y$ holds at position 2 of this sequence, i.e., $(\sigma, 2) \models (x = y)$, but does not hold at any other position.

Boolean Operators

- For a negation $\neg p$, we define

$$(\sigma, j) \models \neg p \quad \text{iff} \quad (\sigma, j) \not\models p.$$

Thus, $\neg p$ holds at position j iff p does not.

- For a disjunction $p \vee q$, we define

$$(\sigma, j) \models p \vee q \quad \text{iff} \quad (\sigma, j) \models p \text{ or } (\sigma, j) \models q.$$

Thus, $p \lor q$ holds at position j iff either p or q does.

For illustration, we display the evaluation of some boolean combinations of formulas.

j	0	1	2	3	$\cdots$
x	1	2	3	4	$\cdots$
y	5	4	3	2	$\cdots$
$x = y$	F	F	T	F	$\cdots$
$\neg(x = y)$	T	T	F	T	$\cdots$
$x < y$	T	T	F	F	$\cdots$
$\neg(x = y) \lor x < y$	T	T	F	T	$\cdots$

It is clear how to extend these definitions to the other boolean operators, $\land$, $\rightarrow$, and $\leftrightarrow$, using their definition in terms of $\lor$ and $\neg$.

The *Next* Operator $\bigcirc$

If p is a temporal formula, then so is $\bigcirc p$, read as *next p*. Its semantics is defined by

$$(\sigma, j) \vDash \bigcirc p \quad \text{iff} \quad (\sigma, j+1) \vDash p.$$

Thus, $\bigcirc p$ holds at position j iff p holds at the next position $j + 1$.

The following table illustrates the evaluation of the formula $(x = 0) \land \bigcirc(x = 1)$, which holds for all positions j such that $x = 0$ at j and $x = 1$ at $j + 1$. We assume the examined sequence to be periodic.

j	0	1	2	3	4	5	6	$\cdots$
x	0	0	1	1	0	0	1	$\cdots$
$x = 0$	T	T	F	F	T	T	F	$\cdots$
$x = 1$	F	F	T	T	F	F	T	$\cdots$
$\bigcirc(x = 1)$	F	T	T	F	F	T	T	$\cdots$
$(x = 0) \land \bigcirc(x = 1)$	F	T	F	F	F	T	F	$\cdots$

The *Henceforth* Operator $\square$

If p is a temporal formula, then so is $\square p$, read *henceforth p* or *always p*. Its semantics is defined by

$$(\sigma, j) \vDash \square p \quad \text{iff} \quad (\sigma, k) \vDash p \text{ for all } k \geq j.$$

Thus, $\square p$ holds at position j iff p holds at position j and all following positions — "from now on."

We illustrate the evaluation of the formula $\square\,(x > 3)$.

j	0	1	2	3	4	5	6	$\cdots$
x	1	3	2	4	3	5	4	$\cdots$
$x > 3$	F	F	F	T	F	T	T	$\cdots$
$\square\,(x > 3)$	F	F	F	F	F	T	T	$\cdots$

It is interesting to note that the set of positions satisfying $\square\, p$ in a sequence is *upwards closed*. That is, if $\square\, p$ holds at j, then it also holds at any $k \geq j$.

The *Eventually* Operator $\Diamond$

If p is a temporal formula, then so is $\Diamond\, p$, read as *eventually p*. Its semantics is defined by

$$(\sigma, j) \models \Diamond\, p \quad \text{iff} \quad (\sigma, k) \models p \text{ for some } k \geq j.$$

Thus, $\Diamond\, p$ holds at position j iff p holds at some position $k \geq j$.

We illustrate the evaluation of the formula $\Diamond\,(x = 4)$.

j	0	1	2	3	4	5	$\cdots$
x	1	2	3	4	5	6	$\cdots$
$x = 4$	F	F	F	T	F	F	$\cdots$
$\Diamond\,(x = 4)$	T	T	T	T	F	F	$\cdots$

The eventually operator is dual to the henceforth operator. This means that $\Diamond\, p$ holds at a position j iff $\square\,\neg p$ does not hold there.

The set of positions at which $\Diamond\, p$ holds in a sequence is *downwards closed*. That is, if $\Diamond\, p$ holds at position j, then it also holds at any k, $0 \leq k \leq j$.

The *Until* Operator $\mathcal{U}$

The formula $\Diamond\, q$ predicts the eventual occurrence of q and the formula $\square\, p$ states that p will hold continuously from now on. The *until* formula $p\,\mathcal{U}\, q$ (read *p until q*) combines these statements by predicting the eventual occurrence of q and stating that p holds continuously at least until the (first) occurrence of q.

Formally, we define

$$(\sigma, j) \models p\,\mathcal{U}\, q \quad \text{iff} \quad \begin{array}{l} \text{there exists a } k \geq j, \text{ such that } (\sigma, k) \models q, \\ \text{and for every } i,\ j \leq i < k,\ (\sigma, i) \models p. \end{array}$$

The following table illustrates the evaluation of the formula $(3 \le x \le 5)\,\mathcal{U}\,(x = 6)$.

j	0	1	2	3	4	5	6	$\cdots$
x	1	2	3	4	5	6	7	$\cdots$
$3 \le x \le 5$	F	F	T	T	T	F	F	$\cdots$
$x = 6$	F	F	F	F	F	T	F	$\cdots$
$(3 \le x \le 5)\,\mathcal{U}\,(x = 6)$	F	F	T	T	T	T	F	$\cdots$

Note that if position j satisfies formula q, it also satisfies $p\,\mathcal{U}\,q$ for any p (even F). With $k = j$ in the definition, the requirement that p holds at all positions i, such that $j \le i < k = j$, is fulfilled vacuously.

Note also that if $p\,\mathcal{U}\,q$ holds at position j, then $\Diamond q$ also holds there.

The *Unless* (*Waiting-for*) Operator $\mathcal{W}$

The until formula $p\,\mathcal{U}\,q$ guarantees that q will eventually occur. In some cases we need a weaker property, which states that p holds continuously either until the next occurrence of q or throughout the sequence.

This is expressed by the formula $p\,\mathcal{W}\,q$, read p *unless* q (also p *waiting for* q). Using the previously defined operators, its formal definition is given by

$$(\sigma, j) \vDash p\,\mathcal{W}\,q \qquad \text{iff} \qquad (\sigma, j) \vDash p\,\mathcal{U}\,q \text{ or } (\sigma, j) \vDash \Box\, p.$$

We illustrate the evaluation of the formula $\big[(3 \le x \le 5) \vee (x \ge 8)\big]\,\mathcal{W}\,(x = 6)$.

j	0	1	2	3	4	5	6	7	8	$\cdots$
x	1	2	3	4	5	6	7	8	9	$\cdots$
$(3 \le x \le 5) \vee (x \ge 8)$	F	F	T	T	T	F	F	T	T	$\cdots$
$x = 6$	F	F	F	F	F	T	F	F	F	$\cdots$
$\big[(3 \le x \le 5) \vee (x \ge 8)\big]\,\mathcal{W}\,(x = 6)$	F	F	T	T	T	T	F	T	T	$\cdots$

Note that in the interval $2, \dots, 5$ the validity of the unless formula is due to the fact that $x = 6$ eventually occurs at position 5. On the other hand, on the infinite interval $7, 8, \dots$, the unless formula holds because $x \ge 8$ holds at all positions in this interval, even though $x = 6$ never occurs again.

Quantification

Let $\sigma: s_0, s_1, \dots$, and $\sigma': s_0', s_1', \dots$ be two models over V, and $x \in V$ be a variable. We say that σ' is an *x-variant* of σ if for each $j \ge 0$, s_j' is an x-variant of s_j, i.e., differs from s_j by at most the interpretation given to x.

- For an existentially quantified formula, we define

$$(\sigma, j) \models \exists u\colon p \quad \text{iff} \quad (\sigma', j) \models p \text{ for some } \sigma', \text{ a } u\text{-variant of } \sigma.$$

- For a universally quantified formula, we define

$$(\sigma, j) \models \forall u\colon p \quad \text{iff} \quad (\sigma', j) \models p \text{ for every } \sigma', \text{ a } u\text{-variant of } \sigma.$$

For illustration, we display the evaluation of the existentially quantified formula $\exists y\colon \Box(y = x^2)$ over a model $\sigma\colon s_0, s_1, \ldots$, using the y-variant $\sigma'\colon s_0', s_1', \ldots$

j	0	1	2	3	$\cdots$
$s_j[x]$	1	2	3	4	$\cdots$
$s_j[y]$	2	3	4	5	$\cdots$
$s_j'[x]$	1	2	3	4	$\cdots$
$s_j'[y]$	1	4	9	16	$\cdots$
$s_j'[y = x^2]$	T	T	T	T	$\cdots$
$s_j'[\Box(y = x^2)]$	T	T	T	T	$\cdots$
$s_j[\exists y\colon \Box(y = x^2)]$	T	T	T	T	$\cdots$

The preceding definitions apply to quantification over both rigid and flexible variables. However, if u is a rigid variable, any u-variant of σ must assign to u the same value in all states.

Consider, for example, the following model, where x and y are flexible and u is rigid.

$$\sigma\colon \quad \langle x\colon 1, y\colon 2, u\colon 0\rangle, \ \langle x\colon 2, y\colon 3, u\colon 0\rangle, \ \langle x\colon 3, y\colon 4, u\colon 0\rangle, \ \ldots$$

As we have seen, the formula $\exists y\colon \Box(y = x^2)$ holds at position 0 of σ. This is because in the y-variant

$$\sigma'\colon \quad \langle x\colon 1, y\colon 1, u\colon 0\rangle, \ \langle x\colon 2, y\colon 4, u\colon 0\rangle, \ \langle x\colon 3, y\colon 9, u\colon 0\rangle, \ \ldots$$

of σ, $\Box(y = x^2)$ holds at position 0. However, there exists no u-variant of σ such that u is assigned a uniform value throughout the sequence and still $\Box(u = x^2)$ holds at position 0. Consequently, $(\sigma, 0) \models \exists y\colon \Box(y = x^2)$ holds but $(\sigma, 0) \models \exists u\colon \Box(u = x^2)$ does not.

Satisfaction

If $(\sigma, j) \models p$, we say that the model σ *satisfies* p *at position* j and refer to j as a *p-position*.

If formula p holds at position 0 of a model σ, i.e., $(\sigma, 0) \models p$, we write $\sigma \models p$ and say that the model σ *satisfies* the formula p.

Simple Examples

Following are several frequently used formulas and their verbal interpretations. The verbal interpretation characterizes the models σ such that $\sigma \vDash \varphi$ for the considered formula φ, i.e., that φ holds at position 0 of σ. We assume that the subformulas p and q appearing below are state formulas.

- $p \rightarrow \Diamond q$

  This formula states that if the model σ satisfies p it also satisfies $\Diamond q$. A model σ satisfies p if p is true in s_0. It satisfies $\Diamond q$, if for some position $j \geq 0$, q holds at s_j. Consequently, this formula expresses the following property of the model σ:

    if initially p then eventually q.

- $\Box (p \rightarrow \Diamond q)$

  The previous formula stated the property: "if p holds at position j then q holds at some position not smaller than j" for $j = 0$. Adding the henceforth operator in front of the previous formula states that this property holds for all positions $j \geq 0$. Consequently, this formula expresses the following property of σ:

    every p-position coincides with or is followed by a q-position.

- $\Box \Diamond q$

  This formula can be obtained from the previous formula by omitting the p condition (i.e., taking $p = \text{T}$). We therefore obtain a property that states that every position in the sequence coincides with or is followed by a later position satisfying q. Consequently, the formula states that

    the sequence σ contains infinitely many q-positions.

- $\Diamond \Box q$

  Reading the formula from left to right, we obtain the following: there exists a position $j \geq 0$ that satisfies $\Box q$, i.e., there exists a position such that q holds at all later positions. This property can be described as the following property of σ:

    eventually permanently q,

  or equivalently:

    the sequence σ contains only finitely many $\neg q$-positions.

- $(\neg q) \, \mathcal{W} \, p$

  The formula states that either $\neg q$ holds forever or that it holds until an occurrence of p. This means:

    the first q-position must coincide with or be preceded by a p-position.

Note that the implied precedence is not strict, i.e., the first occurrence of q may be simultaneous with an occurrence of p. To express strict precedence we may use the formula:

$$(\neg q) \; \mathcal{W} \; (p \wedge \neg q).$$

- $\Box(p \to \bigcirc p)$

The formula states that the subformula $p \to \bigcirc p$ holds at all positions. The subformula holds at position i either if p is false there or if p is true both at i and at $i+1$. Consequently, this formula expresses the following property:

the successor of every p-state is another p-state.

- $\Box(p \to \Box p)$

The formula states that if p holds at position i, then it also holds at every position $j \geq i$. Therefore, it expresses the following property:

once p, always p.

- $\Box \, \exists u \colon ((x = u) \wedge \bigcirc(x = u + 1))$

The formula refers to a rigid variable u and a flexible variable x. It states that at every position j, there exists a value of u such that, at position j, x equals u and, at the next position $j+1$, x equals $u+1$. It follows that $s_{j+1}[x] = s_j[x] + 1$. This is a way to specify a sequence in which

x increases by 1 from each state to the next.

In **Problem 3.1**, the reader will write some formulas that demonstrate the expressive power of flexible quantification.

3.3   Temporal Formulas: Past Operators

The past temporal operators include a symmetric counterpart to each of the future operators. While a future formula describes a property holding at a suffix of the model, lying to the right of the current position, a past formula describes a property of a prefix of the model, lying to the left of the current position. That is, a future formula at position j describes a property of positions $j, j+1, \ldots$, while a past formula at j describes a property of positions $j, j-1, \ldots, 0$.

The *Previous* Operator $\ominus$

If p is a temporal formula, then so is $\ominus p$, read *previously* p. Its semantics is defined by

$$(\sigma, j) \vDash \ominus p \qquad \text{iff} \qquad (j > 0) \text{ and } (\sigma, j - 1) \vDash p.$$

Thus, $\ominus p$ holds at position j iff j is not the first position in the sequence σ and p holds at position $j - 1$. In particular, $\ominus p$ is false at position 0.

The following table illustrates the evaluation of the formula $x = 1 \wedge \ominus (x = 0)$, which holds at all positions in which x has just *risen*, i.e., positions j such that $x = 1$ at j and $x = 0$ at $j - 1$. For comparison, we also display the evaluation of the formula $x = 0 \wedge \bigcirc (x = 1)$, which detects the same phenomenon of x changing from 0 to 1. Note that the formula using the $\bigcirc$ operator detects the rising of x one position earlier, when x is still 0.

j	0	1	2	3	4	5	6	$\cdots$
x	1	1	0	0	1	1	0	$\cdots$
$(x = 1) \wedge \ominus (x = 0)$	F	F	F	F	T	F	F	$\cdots$
$(x = 0) \wedge \bigcirc (x = 1)$	F	F	F	T	F	F	F	$\cdots$

The *Has-always-been* Operator $\boxminus$

If p is a temporal formula, then so is $\boxminus p$, read *has always been p* (or *always in the past p*). Its semantics is defined by

$$(\sigma, j) \models \boxminus p \quad \text{iff} \quad (\sigma, k) \models p \text{ for all } k, 0 \le k \le j.$$

Thus, $\boxminus p$ holds at position j iff p holds at position j and all preceding positions.

We illustrate the evaluation of the formula $\boxminus (x \le 3)$.

j	0	1	2	3	4	5	$\cdots$
x	1	2	3	4	5	6	$\cdots$
$\boxminus (x \le 3)$	T	T	T	F	F	F	$\cdots$

The set of positions satisfying $\boxminus p$ in a sequence is downwards closed. That is, if $\boxminus p$ holds at position j, then it also holds at any k, $0 \le k \le j$.

The *Once* Operator $\diamondminus$

If p is a temporal formula, then so is $\diamondminus p$, called *once p*. Its semantics is defined by

$$(\sigma, j) \models \diamondminus p \quad \text{iff} \quad (\sigma, k) \models p \text{ for some } k, 0 \le k \le j.$$

Thus, $\diamondminus p$ holds at position j iff p holds at position j or some preceding position.

We illustrate the evaluation of the formula $\diamondminus (x = 4)$.

j	0	1	2	3	4	5	$\cdots$
x	1	2	3	4	5	6	$\cdots$
$\diamondminus (x = 4)$	F	F	F	T	T	T	$\cdots$

The once operator is dual to the has-always-been operator. This means that $\diamondsuit p$ holds at a position j iff $\boxminus \neg p$ does not hold there.

The set of positions at which $\diamondsuit p$ holds in a sequence is upwards closed. That is, if $\diamondsuit p$ holds at a position j, then it also holds at any $k \geq j$.

The *Since* Operator S

The *since* formula $p \, S \, q$ (read p *since* q) states that q has happened in the past and p has held continuously from the position following the (last) occurrence of q to the present.

Formally, we define

$$(\sigma, j) \models p \, S \, q \quad \text{iff} \quad \text{there exists a } k, \, 0 \leq k \leq j, \text{ such that } (\sigma, k) \models q,$$
$$\text{and for every } i, \, k < i \leq j, \, (\sigma, i) \models p.$$

We illustrate the evaluation of the formula $(x \leq 6) \, S \, (x = 3)$.

j	0	1	2	3	4	5	6	$\cdots$
x	1	2	3	4	5	6	7	$\cdots$
$x \leq 6$	T	T	T	T	T	T	F	$\cdots$
$x = 3$	F	F	T	F	F	F	F	$\cdots$
$(x \leq 6) \, S \, (x = 3)$	F	F	T	T	T	T	F	$\cdots$

Note that if position j satisfies the formula q, it also satisfies $p \, S \, q$ for an arbitrary p. This is because we can take $k = j$, which makes the range of positions $i, \, k < i \leq j$, which should satisfy p, empty.

Note also that any position that satisfies $p \, S \, q$ also satisfies $\diamondsuit q$.

The *Back-to* Operator B

In the same way that the unless operator $\mathcal{W}$ provides a weaker version of the until operator $\mathcal{U}$, the *back-to* operator B provides a weaker version of the since operator. The formula $p \, B \, q$ (read p *back to* q) states that p holds continuously at all positions preceding (and including) the present, either to the last occurrence of q or to position 0.

Formally, we define

$$(\sigma, j) \models p \, B \, q \quad \text{iff} \quad (\sigma, j) \models p \, S \, q \text{ or } (\sigma, j) \models \boxminus p.$$

This definition ensures that either p holds continuously at all positions $i, \, 0 \leq i \leq j$, or there exists a position $k, \, 0 \leq k \leq j$, such that $(\sigma, k) \models q$ and $(\sigma, i) \models p$ for all positions $i, \, k < i \leq j$.

We illustrate the evaluation of the formula $(x \neq 4) \, \mathcal{B} \, (x = 6)$.

j	0	1	2	3	4	5	6	7	8	$\cdots$
x	1	2	3	4	5	6	7	8	9	$\cdots$
$x \neq 4$	T	T	T	F	T	T	T	T	T	$\cdots$
$x = 6$	F	F	F	F	F	T	F	F	F	$\cdots$
$(x \neq 4) \, \mathcal{B} \, (x = 6)$	T	T	T	F	F	T	T	T	T	$\cdots$

Note that at position 8, for example, $(x \neq 4) \, \mathcal{B} \, (x = 6)$ holds because $x = 6$ at position 5 and, between positions 6 and 8, x is continuously unequal to 4. On the other hand, $(x \neq 4) \, \mathcal{B} \, (x = 6)$ holds at position 2 because x has been unequal to 4 since the beginning of the computation.

Simple Examples

- $\Box (q \rightarrow \diamondsuit p)$

  The formula states that for each position j, if q holds at j, there must be an earlier position $k \leq j$ satisfying p. That is,

  > every q-position coincides with or is preceded by a p-position.

- $\neg \ominus \text{T}$

  The formula states that there is no previous position that satisfies T. Since all positions that are in the model satisfy T, this is equivalent to the following:

  > there is no previous position.

  Note that this formula always holds at the initial position of every model, and nowhere else. We refer to this formula as *first*.

- $\Box \diamondsuit \textit{first}$

  This formula states that every position coincides with or is preceded by a position satisfying $\textit{first} = \neg \ominus \text{T}$, or equivalently:

  > all positions coincide with or are preceded by the initial position.

  This formula holds at all positions of every model.

Satisfiability and Validity

We extend the definition of satisfaction to the case of a temporal formula p that may contain past operators.

For a formula p and a model σ, we write

$$\sigma \models p \quad \text{if} \quad (\sigma, 0) \models p$$

and say that the model σ *satisfies* the formula p.

The following definitions are introduced:

- A formula p is called *satisfiable* if $\sigma \models p$ for some model σ.

- A formula p is called *valid* if $\sigma \models p$ for all models σ.

These definitions can be relativized to a particular set of models C, such as the set of models corresponding to computations of a particular program. In that case:

- A formula p is called *C-satisfiable* if $\sigma \models p$ for some $\sigma \in C$.

- A formula p is called *C-valid* if $\sigma \models p$ for all $\sigma \in C$.

Note that if formula p has a free variable u, we have the following:

- p is satisfiable iff $\exists u : p$ is satisfiable.

- p is valid iff $\forall u : p$ is valid.

In particular, the second fact is used to specify valid properties of programs without explicitly quantifying over the free variables.

Equivalence, Congruence, and Entailment

Two formulas p and q are *equivalent*, denoted by

$$p \sim q,$$

if $p \leftrightarrow q$ is a valid formula. This means that p and q have the same truth value in the first position of every model.

Two formulas p and q are *congruent*, denoted by

$$p \approx q,$$

if $\Box (p \leftrightarrow q)$ is a valid formula. This means that p and q have the same truth value in all positions of every model.

For example,

$$\text{T} \sim \neg \ominus \text{T},$$

since both are true in the first position of every model. Clearly

$$\text{T} \not\approx \neg \ominus \text{T}$$

since T holds at all positions of every model, while $\neg \ominus \text{T}$ holds only in the first position. An example of a congruence is

$$\Box p \approx \neg \Diamond (\neg p).$$

We introduce the abbreviations

$$p \Rightarrow q \quad \text{for} \quad \Box(p \rightarrow q)$$
$$p \Leftrightarrow q \quad \text{for} \quad \Box(p \leftrightarrow q).$$

The formula $p \Rightarrow q$ holds over σ if $p \rightarrow q$ holds at all positions of σ. Note, in comparison, that the formula $p \rightarrow q$ states only that p implies q at the first position of σ. Thus, $p \Rightarrow q$ is a stronger type of implication, known in modal logic as *entailment*.

The formula $p \Leftrightarrow q$ holds over σ if $p \leftrightarrow q$ holds at all positions of σ. Clearly $p \Leftrightarrow q$ is valid iff $p \approx q$.

A helpful intuition is provided by viewing entailment and congruence as relations between sets of positions. For a given formula p and a model σ, we define $Sat_\sigma(p)$ to be the set of positions $j \geq 0$ such that $(\sigma, j) \vDash p$. That is,

$$Sat_\sigma(p) = \{j \mid (\sigma, j) \vDash p\}.$$

Then it is not difficult to see that

- σ satisfies $p \Rightarrow q$ iff $Sat_\sigma(p) \subseteq Sat_\sigma(q)$.

- σ satisfies $p \Leftrightarrow q$ iff $Sat_\sigma(p) = Sat_\sigma(q)$.

Substitutivity

Both equivalence and congruence imply certain notions of *substitutivity*, i.e., the ability to substitute equals for equals in a formula and obtain a formula with identical meaning. However, some restrictions on the formula into which we substitute must be imposed.

Let $\varphi(u)$ be a formula with some occurrences of the sentence symbol u. The following substitutivity properties hold:

Claim (state substitutivity)

For a state formula $\varphi(u)$ and two formulas p and q,

$$\text{if} \quad p \sim q \quad \text{then} \quad \varphi(p) \sim \varphi(q),$$

where $\varphi(p)$ and $\varphi(q)$ denote the formulas obtained by replacing all occurrences of u by p and q, respectively.

For example, since

$$\text{T} \sim \neg \ominus \text{T},$$

we may conclude that

$$(r \wedge \text{T}) \sim (r \wedge \neg \ominus \text{T}),$$

by considering $\varphi(u) = (r \wedge u)$.

Note that the requirement that $\varphi(u)$ is a state formula is essential, as is illustrated by the counterexample obtained by taking $\varphi(u)$: $\square\, u$,

$$\square\, \text{T} \;\not\approx\; \square(\neg \ominus \text{T}).$$

The two sides are not equivalent since $\square\, \text{T}$ is valid, while $\square(\neg \ominus \text{T})$ is false in any model.

Claim (temporal substitutivity)

For an (unrestricted) temporal formula $\varphi(u)$,

$$\text{if } p \approx q \text{ then } \varphi(p) \approx \varphi(q).$$

For example, since

$$\square\, p \;\approx\; \neg \Diamond \neg p,$$

we may conclude that

$$q\,\mathcal{U}\,(\square\, p) \;\approx\; q\,\mathcal{U}\,(\neg \Diamond \neg p)$$

by considering $\varphi(u) = (q\,\mathcal{U}\,u)$.

Past and Future Formulas

As we defined, a *state formula* is a formula without any temporal operators. We also define the following:

A formula that contains no future operators is called a *past formula*.

A formula that contains no past operators is called a *future formula*.

Thus,

$$p \;\rightarrow\; \diamondsuit\, q$$

is a past formula, while

$$\square(p \rightarrow \Diamond q)$$

is a future formula. Note that state formulas are both future and past formulas.

The Weak Version of *Previous*

The until ($\mathcal{U}$) and since ($\mathcal{S}$) operators each have a weaker version given by the unless ($\mathcal{W}$) and back-to ($\mathcal{B}$) operators, respectively. In a similar way, it is possible to define a weak version of the previous operator, $\ominus$, denoted by $\widetilde{\ominus}$. This weak version can be defined as the operator dual to the strong version, as follows:

$$\text{weak previous: } \widetilde{\ominus}p \;=\; \neg \ominus \neg p.$$

It is straightforward to provide a direct semantic definition, which tells us at what positions in a sequence a formula involving the weak operator holds.

$$(\sigma, j) \vDash \widetilde{\ominus} p \quad \text{iff} \quad \text{either } j = 0 \text{ or } (j > 0 \text{ and } (\sigma, j - 1) \vDash p).$$

Thus the difference between the strong and weak versions is merely that, for any model and any formula p, $\widetilde{\ominus} p$ is always true at the first position, while $\ominus p$ is always false at that position. At all other positions, $\ominus p$ holds iff $\widetilde{\ominus} p$ does.

The weak version of the previous operator provides an alternative definition for the special predicate *first*, which characterizes the first position in a model. We can define

$$\textit{first} \; = \; \widetilde{\ominus} \text{F}.$$

We refer to the operators $\bigcirc$, $\ominus$, and $\widetilde{\ominus}$ as the *immediate* operators. The other temporal operators are called *nonimmediate*.

A Basic Set of Operators

While we have given an independent semantic definition to each of the temporal operators, they are not completely independent. This means that some of them can be expressed by a formula that uses the other operators. Consequently, it is possible to single out a subset of the operators, refer to them as basic, and show how the remaining operators can be expressed in terms of the basic ones. The advantage of this separation is that when we want to establish that a certain property is satisfied by all the operators, it is sufficient to show that it is satisfied by the basic operators and all of their boolean combinations.

A good set of basic operators for the propositional fragment is

$$\neg, \quad \vee, \quad \bigcirc, \quad \mathcal{W}, \quad \widetilde{\ominus}, \quad \mathcal{B}.$$

It is clear how to express the other boolean operators using only $\neg$ and $\vee$.

The following congruences show how the remaining temporal operators can be expressed using the basic ones.

$$\square p \;\approx\; p\,\mathcal{W}\,\text{F} \qquad\qquad \boxminus p \;\approx\; p\,\mathcal{B}\,\text{F}$$

$$\lozenge p \;\approx\; \neg\,\square\,\neg p \qquad\qquad \diamondminus p \;\approx\; \neg\,\boxminus\,\neg p$$

$$p\,\mathcal{U}\,q \;\approx\; (p\,\mathcal{W}\,q) \wedge \lozenge q \qquad\qquad p\,\mathcal{S}\,q \;\approx\; (p\,\mathcal{B}\,q) \wedge \diamondminus q$$

$$\ominus p \;\approx\; \neg\,\widetilde{\ominus}\,\neg p.$$

The Strict Version of the Operators

All our definitions of the meaning of the nonimmediate temporal operators referred to positions k and i, lying to the right or left of the reference position j, using weak inequalities, such as $j \leq k$ or $i \leq j$. This implies that these definitions consider the present to be a part of both the future and the past. We refer to these types of definitions as *reflexive*.

In comparison, it is possible to define a *strict* (nonreflexive) version of all the nonimmediate temporal operators, in which the present is neither a part of the future nor of the past. For each nonimmediate operator, we denote its strict version by placing the symbol $\wedge$ over the operator, e.g., $\widehat{\Box}$.

One way of defining the strict version of these operators is to repeat the semantic definition while replacing each weak inequality of the form $j \leq k, j \leq i$, $k \leq j$, and $i \leq j$, by its strict version $j < k, j < i, k < j$, and $i < j$, respectively.

We take another route, which defines the strict operators by combining the reflexive operator with an appropriate immediate operator, shifting the reference position one position to the left or right. Consequently we define

$$\widehat{\Box}p \ = \bigcirc \Box p \qquad\qquad \widehat{\boxminus}p = \ominus \boxminus p$$

$$\widehat{\Diamond}p \ = \bigcirc \Diamond p \qquad\qquad \widehat{\diamondsuit}p = \ominus \diamondsuit p$$

$$p\,\widehat{\mathcal{U}}\,q \ = \bigcirc(p\,\mathcal{U}\,q) \qquad\qquad p\,\widehat{\mathcal{S}}\,q = \ominus(p\,\mathcal{S}\,q)$$

$$p\,\widehat{\mathcal{W}}\,q = \bigcirc(p\,\mathcal{W}\,q) \qquad\qquad p\,\widehat{\mathcal{B}}\,q = \ominus(p\,\mathcal{B}\,q).$$

By using $\ominus$ in the definition of $\widehat{\diamondsuit}$ and $\widehat{\mathcal{S}}$, and $\ominus$ in the definition of $\widehat{\boxminus}$ and $\widehat{\mathcal{B}}$, we ensure that the strict past operators satisfy duality relations similar to those holding among the reflexive past operators.

These definitions show how to define the strict version of the nonimmediate operators in terms of their reflexive version. It is also possible to go in the other direction and express the reflexive version of these operators in terms of their strict version. This is shown by the following congruences:

$$\Box p \ \approx \ p \wedge \widehat{\Box}p \qquad\qquad \boxminus p \ \approx \ p \wedge \widehat{\boxminus}p$$

$$\Diamond p \ \approx \ p \vee \widehat{\Diamond}p \qquad\qquad \diamondsuit p \ \approx \ p \vee \widehat{\diamondsuit}p$$

$$p\,\mathcal{U}\,q \ \approx \ q \vee [p \wedge (p\,\widehat{\mathcal{U}}\,q)] \qquad\qquad p\,\mathcal{S}\,q \ \approx \ q \vee [p \wedge (p\,\widehat{\mathcal{S}}\,q)]$$

$$p\,\mathcal{W}\,q \ \approx \ q \vee [p \wedge (p\,\widehat{\mathcal{W}}\,q)] \qquad\qquad p\,\mathcal{B}\,q \ \approx \ q \vee [p \wedge (p\,\widehat{\mathcal{B}}\,q)].$$

In fact, one of the interesting observations about the strict operators is that the pair of operators $(\widehat{\mathcal{U}}, \widehat{\mathcal{S}})$ constitutes a minimal set of basic operators for the temporal language we consider here. This is established by the following chain of congruences, showing how the rest of the strict operators, as well as the immediate ones, can be defined in terms of those two.

$$\widehat{\Diamond}p \ \approx \ \mathrm{T}\,\widehat{\mathcal{U}}\,p \qquad\qquad \widehat{\diamondsuit}p \ \approx \ \mathrm{T}\,\widehat{\mathcal{S}}\,p$$

$$\widehat{\Box}p \ \approx \ \neg\widehat{\Diamond}\neg p \qquad\qquad \widehat{\boxminus}p \ \approx \ \neg\widehat{\diamondsuit}\neg p$$

$$p \widehat{W} q \approx \Box p \lor (p \widehat{U} q) \qquad p \widehat{B} q \approx \boxminus p \lor (p \widehat{S} q)$$
$$\bigcirc p \approx \text{F} \widehat{U} p \qquad\qquad \ominus p \approx \text{F} \widehat{S} p.$$

Consider, for example, the justification for the congruence $\bigcirc p \approx \text{F} \widehat{U} p$. By the semantic definition, $(\sigma, j) \models \text{F} \widehat{U} p$ iff there exists some $k > j$ such that $(\sigma, k) \models p$ and for all i, $j < i < k$, $(\sigma, i) \models \text{F}$. Since no position in σ can satisfy F, this requirement is equivalent to $k = j + 1$, which claims that $(\sigma, j + 1) \models p$, i.e., $(\sigma, j) \models \bigcirc p$.

In **Problem 3.2**, we present a long list of formulas and the reader will identify the valid formulas among them.

In **Problem 3.3**, the reader will consider some additional temporal operators and explore the relations between these operators and the standard ones.

In **Problem 3.4**, the reader will consider the effect of duplicating states on the validity of formulas.

3.4 Basic Properties of the Temporal Operators

In the application of temporal logic to the specification of program properties, and later to the verification of these properties over concrete programs, we need the ability to perform transformations and carry out inferences involving temporal formulas. Such transformations may replace one formula with an equivalent one with a simpler form or deduce one formula from another that implies it.

Some basic properties and relations that the temporal operators satisfy and some basic inference rules are helpful in carrying out such inferences and equivalence transformations. In this section, we will present a list of some useful properties and rules. All the listed properties are to be interpreted as *validities*, i.e., formulas that hold over all models. Clearly, stating a validity $p \Leftrightarrow q$ is the same as claiming the congruence $p \approx q$.

Schemes and Their Validity

When stating properties of the operators by claiming certain formulas to be valid, we rarely use fully interpreted formulas. More often we use formula schemes containing one or more sentence symbols.

For example, claiming the duality of the operators $\Box$ and $\Diamond$, we may write the formula scheme

FS: $\quad \neg \Box p \Leftrightarrow \Diamond \neg p$

and claim it to be valid. This formula scheme uses the sentence symbol p and stands for the infinitely many formulas that can be obtained from the scheme by replacing p by an arbitrary temporal formula. To formulas obtained by such replacements, we refer as *instantiations* of the scheme FS.

Claiming the scheme FS to be valid amounts to the claim that all instantiations of the scheme are valid formulas.

In some cases we may explicitly restrict the type of instantiations that may be applied to a given sentence symbol. For example, the scheme

$$p \leftrightarrow \Box\, p$$

is valid only for the cases that p stands for a rigid state formula, i.e., a formula in which all variables and propositions are rigid. This means that the sentence symbol p can only be instantiated by rigid state formulas.

To simplify the presentation we will refer to formula schemes simply as formulas.

Some formula schemes use parameterized sentence symbols of the form $p(u_1, \ldots, u_k)$ to stand for an arbitrary formula that has free occurrences (i.e., unbounded by quantification) of the variables $u_1, \ldots, u_k$. We refer to such schemes as *parameterized schemes* while schemes all of whose sentence symbols are not parameterized are called *simple schemes*.

Monotonicity

Let $\varphi(u)$ be a formula scheme with one or more occurrences of the sentence symbol u.

We define an occurrence of u to be *positive* (*of positive polarity*) in φ if it does not occur in a subformula of the form $p \leftrightarrow q$ and it is embedded in an even (explicit or implicit) number of negations. Note that an occurrence of u in p in the context $p \rightarrow q$ counts as an (implicit) negation, because $p \rightarrow q$ is equivalent to $(\neg p) \vee q$. Similarly, an occurrence of u in φ is defined to be *negative* (*of negative polarity*) if it does not occur in a subformula of the form $p \leftrightarrow q$ and it is embedded in an odd number of negations.

The problem with an equivalence $p \leftrightarrow q$ is that it actually represents a disjunction $(p \wedge q) \vee (\neg p \wedge \neg q)$ in which p appears once positively and once negatively. Thus, every occurrence of u in $p \leftrightarrow q$ is both positive and negative. In order to apply any of the rules given here to a formula containing equivalences, it is therefore necessary to expand any $p \leftrightarrow q$ subformula into $(p \wedge q) \vee (\neg p \wedge \neg q)$.

Note that for every unary temporal operator $\mathcal{A}$, p occurs positively in $\mathcal{A}p$; and for every binary temporal operator $\mathcal{R}$, p and q occur positively in $p\,\mathcal{R}\,q$.

There are two general monotonicity properties for the case that all occurrences of u in $\varphi(u)$ have *uniform polarity*, i.e., are all positive or all negative.

Positive Occurrences

In the case of positive occurrences, we have the following property:

Claim (positive polarity)

If all occurrences of u in $\varphi(u)$ are positive, then

$$(p \Rightarrow q) \rightarrow (\varphi(p) \Rightarrow \varphi(q))$$

is valid.

As before $\varphi(p)$ and $\varphi(q)$ denote the result of substituting p and q, respectively, for all the occurrences of u in $\varphi(u)$.

This property states that in any computation, if every p-position is also a q-position, then every position satisfying $\varphi(p)$ also satisfies $\varphi(q)$.

This general property states, in particular, that all the unary temporal operators are monotonic. This is shown by considering special cases of the formula $\varphi(u)$, leading to the validities

$$(p \Rightarrow q) \rightarrow (\Diamond p \Rightarrow \Diamond q) \qquad \text{(taking } \varphi(u) = \Diamond u\text{)}$$

$$(p \Rightarrow q) \rightarrow (\boxminus p \Rightarrow \boxminus q) \qquad \text{(taking } \varphi(u) = \boxminus u\text{)}.$$

Monotonicity of the binary operators follows from a stronger version of the claim. Let $\varphi(u_1, u_2)$ be a formula with two sentence symbols u_1 and u_2.

If all occurrences of u_1 and u_2 in $\varphi(u_1, u_2)$ are positive, then

$$[(p_1 \Rightarrow q_1) \land (p_2 \Rightarrow q_2)] \rightarrow (\varphi(p_1, p_2) \Rightarrow \varphi(q_1, q_2))$$

is valid.

From this general formula we can derive the validity

$$[(p_1 \Rightarrow q_1) \land (p_2 \Rightarrow q_2)] \rightarrow (p_1 \,\mathcal{U}\, p_2 \Rightarrow q_1 \,\mathcal{U}\, q_2).$$

Monotonicity for all the other binary operators is similarly implied.

To increase our understanding of the property of monotonicity, we recall the interpretation of the entailment $p \Rightarrow q$ over a model σ as the inclusion of the set of positions satisfying p in the set of positions satisfying q, that is, $Sat_\sigma(p) \subseteq Sat_\sigma(q)$.

With this interpretation, the property of monotonicity claims that if u is positive in $\varphi(u)$ then

$$Sat_\sigma(p) \subseteq Sat_\sigma(q) \qquad \text{implies} \qquad Sat_\sigma(\varphi(p)) \subseteq Sat_\sigma(\varphi(q)).$$

That is, by increasing the set of positions at which p holds, we can only increase the set of positions at which $\varphi(p)$ holds.

The situation is similar for the binary operators. Consider, for example, the formula $p \,\mathcal{U}\, r$ and a position j in σ. Assume that $p \Rightarrow q$, and therefore q holds at least at all positions at which p holds, and perhaps at some more. Then clearly, if $p\,\mathcal{U}\,r$ holds at j then so does $q\,\mathcal{U}\,r$. It follows that

$$Sat_\sigma(p\,\mathcal{U}\,r) \subseteq Sat_\sigma(q\,\mathcal{U}\,r).$$

Negative Occurrences

In the case of negative occurrences, we have the following symmetric property.

    Claim (negative polarity)

    If all occurrences of u in $\varphi(u)$ are negative, then

$$(p \Rightarrow q) \;\to\; (\varphi(q) \Rightarrow \varphi(p))$$

    is valid.

For example, we may use this general property to conclude the validity

$$(p \Rightarrow q) \;\to\; (\neg \Diamond q \Rightarrow \neg \Diamond p).$$

We have a similar claim for the formula $\varphi(u_1, u_2)$.

Substitutivity

For completeness, we also list substitutivity as a property, restricted to the computations for which $p \Leftrightarrow q$.

    Claim (substitution)

    For an arbitrary formula $\varphi(u)$,

$$(p \Leftrightarrow q) \;\to\; (\varphi(p) \Leftrightarrow \varphi(q))$$

    is valid.

This property states that on any computation such that the set of p-positions coincides with the set of q-positions, a position satisfies $\varphi(p)$ iff it satisfies $\varphi(q)$. We have a similar claim for the formula $\varphi(u_1, u_2)$.

    We may use this property to derive the validity

$$(\neg \Box p)\,\mathcal{U}\,(\Diamond \neg q) \;\Leftrightarrow\; (\Diamond \neg p)\,\mathcal{U}\,(\neg \boxminus q)$$

based on the validities

$$\neg \Box p \Leftrightarrow \Diamond \neg p \quad \text{and} \quad \Diamond \neg q \Leftrightarrow \neg \boxminus q.$$

Reflexivity

We list again the relations that hold between the reflexive versions of the non-immediate operators and their strict versions. Here, however, we list them as validities.

Future Operators

For the future operators we have

FR1. $\Box p \Leftrightarrow (p \wedge \widehat{\Box} p)$

FR2. $\Diamond p \Leftrightarrow (p \vee \widehat{\Diamond} p)$

FR3. $p\,\mathcal{U}\,q \Leftrightarrow (q \vee [p \wedge p\,\widehat{\mathcal{U}}\,q])$

FR4. $p\,\mathcal{W}\,q \Leftrightarrow (q \vee [p \wedge p\,\widehat{\mathcal{W}}\,q])$.

Past Operators

For the past operators we have

PR1. $\boxminus p \Leftrightarrow (p \wedge \widehat{\boxminus} p)$

PR2. $\diamondminus p \Leftrightarrow (p \vee \widehat{\diamondminus} p)$

PR3. $p\,\mathcal{S}\,q \Leftrightarrow (q \vee [p \wedge p\,\widehat{\mathcal{S}}\,q])$

PR4. $p\,\mathcal{B}\,q \Leftrightarrow (q \vee [p \wedge p\,\widehat{\mathcal{B}}\,q])$.

Entailments

The previous valid formulas are formulated as equivalences; they imply some entailments that are often used.

For the future operators we have

FR5. $\Box p \Rightarrow p$ $\qquad p\,\mathcal{U}\,q \Rightarrow (p \vee q)$ $\qquad p\,\mathcal{W}\,q \Rightarrow (p \vee q)$

FR6. $p \Rightarrow \Diamond p$ $\qquad q \Rightarrow p\,\mathcal{U}\,q$ $\qquad q \Rightarrow p\,\mathcal{W}\,q$.

For the past operators we have

PR5. $\boxminus p \Rightarrow p$ $\qquad p\,\mathcal{S}\,q \Rightarrow (p \vee q)$ $\qquad p\,\mathcal{B}\,q \Rightarrow (p \vee q)$

PR6. $p \Rightarrow \diamondminus p$ $\qquad q \Rightarrow p\,\mathcal{S}\,q$ $\qquad q \Rightarrow p\,\mathcal{B}\,q$.

Strictness

The previous set of properties showed how to express the reflexive operators in terms of the strict ones. It is also possible to represent the strict operators in terms of the reflexive ones, using the next and previous operators.

These relations are given by

FS1. $\widehat{\Box} p \Leftrightarrow \bigcirc \Box p$ $\qquad\qquad$ PS1. $\widehat{\boxminus} p \Leftrightarrow \ominus \boxminus p$

FS2. $\widehat{\Diamond} p \Leftrightarrow \bigcirc \Diamond p$ $\qquad\qquad$ PS2. $\widehat{\diamondminus} p \Leftrightarrow \ominus \diamondminus p$

FS3. $p\,\widehat{\mathcal{U}}\,q \Leftrightarrow \bigcirc(p\,\mathcal{U}\,q)$ $\qquad\qquad$ PS3. $p\,\widehat{\mathcal{S}}\,q \Leftrightarrow \ominus(p\,\mathcal{S}\,q)$

FS4. $p \widehat{W} q \Leftrightarrow \bigcirc (p W q)$ PS4. $p \widehat{B} q \Leftrightarrow \widetilde{\ominus} (p B q)$.

Expansion

Combining the reflexivity formulas FR1–FR4 and the strictness formulas FS1–FS4, respectively, we obtain the following expansion formulas:

FE1. $\Box p \Leftrightarrow (p \wedge \bigcirc \Box p)$

FE2. $\Diamond p \Leftrightarrow (p \vee \bigcirc \Diamond p)$

FE3. $p \mathcal{U} q \Leftrightarrow (q \vee [p \wedge \bigcirc (p \mathcal{U} q)])$

FE4. $p W q \Leftrightarrow (q \vee [p \wedge \bigcirc (p W q)])$.

Similar properties hold for the past operators.

Duality

Each of the operators has a dual. Usually the dual of a strong operator is related to its weak version.

For the future operators we have

FU1. $\neg \Box p \Leftrightarrow \Diamond \neg p$ $\neg \Diamond p \Leftrightarrow \Box \neg p$

FU2. $\neg (p \mathcal{U} q) \Leftrightarrow (\neg q) W (\neg p \wedge \neg q)$ $\neg (p W q) \Leftrightarrow (\neg q) \mathcal{U} (\neg p \wedge \neg q)$

FU3. $\neg \bigcirc p \Leftrightarrow \bigcirc \neg p$.

Properties FU1 and FU2 are stated for the reflexive version of the operator. Corresponding properties hold for the strict version. Property FU3 states that the next operator $\bigcirc$ is self-dual.

Similar properties, PU1 and PU2, hold for the past operators. The two previous operators are dual to one another

PU3. $\neg \ominus p \Leftrightarrow \widetilde{\ominus} \neg p$ $\neg \widetilde{\ominus} p \Leftrightarrow \ominus \neg p$.

Weak and Strong Operators

In addition to the duality relations holding between the weak and strong operators, it is often the case that a strong operator can be expressed as a conjunction of the weak operator and some additional requirement. Similarly, the weak operator can often be expressed as a disjunction of the strong operator and another alternative. These relations are

FWS1. $p \mathcal{U} q \Leftrightarrow (p W q \wedge \Diamond q)$ $p W q \Leftrightarrow (p \mathcal{U} q \vee \Box p)$.

For the past operators we have

PWS1. $p\mathcal{S}q \Leftrightarrow (p\mathcal{B}q \wedge \diamondsuit q)$ $p\mathcal{B}q \Leftrightarrow (p\mathcal{S}q \vee \boxminus p)$

PWS2. $\ominus p \Leftrightarrow (\widetilde{\ominus}p \wedge \ominus \text{T})$ $\widetilde{\ominus}p \Leftrightarrow (\ominus p \vee \widetilde{\ominus}\text{F}).$

Property PWS2 uses $\ominus \text{T}$ to characterize positions that are not first in the sequence and uses $\widetilde{\ominus}\text{F} = \textit{first}$ to characterize the first position in the computation.

Several important entailments can be derived from these equivalences. One kind of entailment states that the strong version always entails the weaker version. For example,

$$p\mathcal{U}q \Rightarrow p\mathcal{W}q \qquad \ominus p \Rightarrow \widetilde{\ominus}p.$$

Idempotence

Some of the operators are such that applying them twice yields the same result as a single application. We refer to these operators as *idempotent*. Following are the idempotence properties of the future operators

FI1. $\square\square p \Leftrightarrow \square p$

FI2. $\diamondsuit\diamondsuit p \Leftrightarrow \diamondsuit p$

FI3. $p\mathcal{U}(p\mathcal{U}q) \Leftrightarrow p\mathcal{U}q$ $p\mathcal{W}(p\mathcal{W}q) \Leftrightarrow p\mathcal{W}q$

FI4. $(p\mathcal{U}q)\mathcal{U}q \Leftrightarrow p\mathcal{U}q$ $(p\mathcal{W}q)\mathcal{W}q \Leftrightarrow p\mathcal{W}q.$

The strict operators are not idempotent. Each application adds an additional next operator.

The reflexive past operators satisfy idempotence properties similar to those of the future operators.

Absorption

One of the questions that is extensively studied within modal logic is the number of distinct unary modalities. That is, we consider a long string of unary operators applied to a proposition, $O_1 O_2 \ldots O_k p$, where each O_i is either $\square$ or $\diamondsuit$, and ask how many pairwise nonequivalent combinations like this exist.

By idempotence it is sufficient to consider only alternating strings such that no two adjacent operators are the same. This is because, due to idempotence, in any context,

$$O_1 \cdots \square\square \cdots O_k p \Leftrightarrow O_1 \cdots \square \cdots O_k p,$$

and similarly for an occurrence of $\diamondsuit\diamondsuit$.

The following properties show that any string of alternating $\square$, $\diamondsuit$ operators reduces to a string of length two, retaining the two originally rightmost operators.

FA1. $\Diamond \Box \Diamond p \Leftrightarrow \Box \Diamond p$

FA2. $\Box \Diamond \Box p \Leftrightarrow \Diamond \Box p.$

Using idempotence and these rules, any nonempty string of such operators can be reduced to one of the following four modalities:

$$\Box p \qquad \Diamond p \qquad \Box \Diamond p \qquad \text{or} \qquad \Diamond \Box p.$$

The binary operators have some interesting absorption properties of their own:

FA3. $p \, W \, (p \, \mathcal{U} \, q) \Leftrightarrow p \, W \, q \qquad (p \, \mathcal{U} \, q) \, W \, q \Leftrightarrow p \, \mathcal{U} \, q$

FA4. $p \, \mathcal{U} \, (p \, W \, q) \Leftrightarrow p \, W \, q \qquad (p \, W \, q) \, \mathcal{U} \, q \Leftrightarrow p \, \mathcal{U} \, q.$

Similar properties hold for the past operators.

Commutation Properties of Next and Previous

The next operator commutes over all the nonpast operators, i.e., the future and boolean operators. To establish this, it suffices to state commutation with the basic nonpast operators $\neg$, $\lor$, (trivially) $\bigcirc$, and W. This is stated by the following validities:

CN1. $\bigcirc(\neg p) \Leftrightarrow \neg \bigcirc p$

CN2. $\bigcirc(p \lor q) \Leftrightarrow \bigcirc p \lor \bigcirc q$

CN3. $\bigcirc(p \, W \, q) \Leftrightarrow (\bigcirc p) \, W \, (\bigcirc q).$

Similar commutation relations obviously hold with all the other future operators.

This uniform commutativity property of the next operator can be presented in a more comprehensive manner, as follows. Let $\varphi_{\mathrm{NP}}(p_1, \ldots, p_m)$ be a "no past" formula (scheme) that contains no past operators, such that $p_1, \ldots, p_m$ are all the occurrences of atomic formulas and sentence symbols within φ_{NP}. Then we have the validity

$$\bigcirc \varphi_{\mathrm{NP}}(p_1, \ldots, p_m) \Leftrightarrow \varphi_{\mathrm{NP}}(\bigcirc p_1, \ldots, \bigcirc p_m),$$

where $\varphi_{\mathrm{NP}}(\bigcirc p_1, \ldots, \bigcirc p_m)$ is obtained from φ_{NP} by replacing each occurrence p_i with $\bigcirc p_i$.

Commutation of the Previous Operators

Similar commutation relations hold for the previous operators $\ominus$ and $\widetilde{\ominus}$. However, the situation is complicated by the fact that there are two previous operators that are dual.

The commutation relations with the basic past operators are given by

CP1. $\ominus(\neg p) \Leftrightarrow \neg \widetilde{\ominus} p \qquad\qquad\qquad \widetilde{\ominus}(\neg p) \Leftrightarrow \neg \ominus p$

CP2. $\ominus (p \vee q) \Leftrightarrow \ominus p \vee \ominus q$ $\quad$ $\widetilde{\ominus}(p \vee q) \Leftrightarrow \widetilde{\ominus} p \vee \widetilde{\ominus} q$

CP3. $\ominus (p \mathcal{B} q) \Leftrightarrow (\ominus p) \mathcal{B} (\ominus q)$ $\quad$ $\widetilde{\ominus}(p \mathcal{B} q) \Leftrightarrow (\widetilde{\ominus}p) \mathcal{B} (\widetilde{\ominus}q)$.

Note that according to CP1, when a previous operator commutes with a negation it changes to the dual operator, i.e., $\ominus$ to $\widetilde{\ominus}$ and $\widetilde{\ominus}$ to $\ominus$. Observe that the two previous operators do not commute with one another, that is, $\ominus \widetilde{\ominus} p$ is not congruent to $\widetilde{\ominus} \ominus p$. For example, $\ominus \widetilde{\ominus} p$ is always false at the first position of a model, while $\widetilde{\ominus} \ominus p$ is always true at that position.

Consequently, the comprehensive commutation statement for the previous operators is more modest than the corresponding statement for the next operator.

Let $\varphi_{\mathrm{NF}}(p_1, \ldots, p_m; q_1, \ldots, q_n)$ be a "no future" formula that contains no operators other than $\neg, \vee$, and $\mathcal{B}$. Let $p_1, \ldots, p_m$ be all the positive occurrences of atomic formulas or sentence symbols, i.e., occurrences under an even number of negations. Let $q_1, \ldots, q_n$ be all the negative occurrences, i.e., occurrences under an odd number of negations. Then we claim the following commutation relations

$$\ominus \varphi_{\mathrm{NF}}(p_1, \ldots, p_m; q_1, \ldots, q_n) \Leftrightarrow \varphi_{\mathrm{NF}}(\ominus p_1, \ldots, \ominus p_m; \widetilde{\ominus} q_1, \ldots, \widetilde{\ominus} q_n)$$

$$\widetilde{\ominus} \varphi_{\mathrm{NF}}(p_1, \ldots, p_m; q_1, \ldots, q_n) \Leftrightarrow \varphi_{\mathrm{NF}}(\widetilde{\ominus} p_1, \ldots, \widetilde{\ominus} p_m; \ominus q_1, \ldots, \ominus q_n).$$

We may realize that the problems with the commutation relations among the various immediate operators are always connected with the first position of the sequence. If we move away from the first position, many additional equivalences hold. This can be expressed by the following validities:

NF1. $(\neg \textit{first}) \Rightarrow (\ominus p \leftrightarrow \widetilde{\ominus} p)$

NF2. $(\neg \textit{first}) \Rightarrow (\bigcirc \ominus p \leftrightarrow \ominus \bigcirc p)$.

Property NF1 states, for example, that on all nonfirst positions the strong and weak previous operators are equivalent.

Note that each of the preceding schemes represents a family of valid instantiations. Thus, taking φ_{NP} to be $p \to q$, we obtain

$$\bigcirc (p \to q) \Leftrightarrow (\bigcirc p \to \bigcirc q),$$

which can be instantiated to

$$\bigcirc (\exists x: (x > y) \to \Diamond (y < z)) \Leftrightarrow (\bigcirc \exists x: (x > y) \to \bigcirc \Diamond (y < z))$$

by instantiating p to $\exists x: (x > y)$ and q to $\Diamond (y < z)$.

To see that $\bigcirc$ does not commute with either $\square$ or $\Diamond$, consider the sequence

$$\sigma: \langle x: 0 \rangle, \langle x: 1 \rangle, \ldots.$$

It can be checked that σ satisfies (at position 0) $\square \bigcirc (x = 1)$ and $\bigcirc \Diamond (x = 0)$ but does not satisfy $\bigcirc \square (x = 1)$ or $\Diamond \bigcirc (x = 0)$.

Universal and Existential Operators

Next, we consider the distribution properties of the nonimmediate operators, i.e., excluding the next/previous operators. Some of these operators have a universal character while others have an existential character.

The unary operators

$$\square \qquad \text{and} \qquad \boxminus$$

are universal. The unary operators

$$\diamondsuit \qquad \text{and} \qquad \diamondsuit\hspace{-0.5em}\text{-}$$

are existential. All the binary operators have a split character. They are universal in their first argument and existential in their second argument.

The character of the operator determines how it distributes over disjunction, conjunction, existential quantification, and universal quantification. The universal operators distribute over conjunction and universal quantification. The existential operators distribute over disjunction and existential quantification.

This is expressed by the following properties, stated for the future operators.

FD1. $\square(p \wedge q) \Leftrightarrow (\square p) \wedge (\square q)$ $\square(\forall u\!:p) \Leftrightarrow \forall u\!:\square p$

FD2. $\diamondsuit(p \vee q) \Leftrightarrow (\diamondsuit p) \vee (\diamondsuit q)$ $\diamondsuit(\exists u\!:p) \Leftrightarrow \exists u\!:\diamondsuit p$

FD3. $p\,\mathcal{U}\,(q \vee r) \Leftrightarrow (p\,\mathcal{U}\,q) \vee (p\,\mathcal{U}\,r)$ $p\,\mathcal{U}\,(\exists u\!:q) \Leftrightarrow \exists u\!:(p\,\mathcal{U}\,q)$
       assuming u is not free in p

FD4. $(p \wedge q)\,\mathcal{U}\,r \Leftrightarrow (p\,\mathcal{U}\,r) \wedge (q\,\mathcal{U}\,r)$ $(\forall u\!:p)\,\mathcal{U}\,q \Leftrightarrow \forall u\!:(p\,\mathcal{U}\,q)$
       assuming u is not free in q

FD5. $p\,\mathcal{W}\,(q \vee r) \Leftrightarrow (p\,\mathcal{W}\,q) \vee (p\,\mathcal{W}\,r)$ $p\,\mathcal{W}\,(\exists u\!:q) \Leftrightarrow \exists u\!:(p\,\mathcal{W}\,q)$
       assuming u is not free in p

FD6. $(p \wedge q)\,\mathcal{W}\,r \Leftrightarrow (p\,\mathcal{W}\,r) \wedge (q\,\mathcal{W}\,r)$ $(\forall u\!:p)\,\mathcal{W}\,q \Leftrightarrow \forall u\!:(p\,\mathcal{W}\,q)$
       assuming u is not free in q.

Example

To illustrate that existential operators do not distribute over universal quantification, that is,

$$\diamondsuit(\forall u\!:p) \not\approx \forall u\!:\diamondsuit p,$$

consider the two formulas $\diamondsuit(\forall u\!:p)$ and $\forall u\!:\diamondsuit p$ in the case that $p\!:x \neq u$ and where variable u is rigid.

Consider the model

$$\sigma: \quad \langle x\!:0,\ u\!:2 \rangle,\ \langle x\!:1,\ u\!:2 \rangle,\ \ldots$$

It is easy to show that $\sigma \models \forall u\!: \Diamond(x \neq u)$. To see this, we have to show that all u-variants of σ, i.e., models of the form

$$\sigma_a'\!: \quad \langle x\!:0,\ u\!:a\rangle,\ \langle x\!:1,\ u\!:a\rangle,\ \ldots$$

for every possible value of a, satisfy $\Diamond(x \neq u)$. We consider two cases:

- $a = 0$, then $(\sigma_a', 1) \models (x \neq u)$ as $x = 1$, $u = 0$ at position 1 of σ_a'.

- $a \neq 0$, then $(\sigma_a', 0) \models (x \neq u)$ as $x = 0$, $u = a \neq 0$ at position 0 of σ_a'.

On the other hand, the state formula $\forall u\!: (x \neq u)$ is false on any position, since we can always take $u = x$ at that position. It follows that $\sigma \not\models \Diamond \forall u\!: (x \neq u)$, which shows that the two formulas are not equivalent. ◢

Properties analogous to FD1–FD6 hold for both the strict and past versions of the operators.

In view of the distribution properties of the next and previous operators, these operators have both a universal and an existential character. Their distribution over disjunction and conjunction have been stated in CN2, CN3, CP2, and CP3. The following properties state that they also distribute over quantification:

FD7. $\bigcirc(\exists u\!:p) \Leftrightarrow \exists u\!: \bigcirc p$ $\ominus \exists u\!:p \Leftrightarrow \exists u\!: \ominus p$

FD8. $\bigcirc(\forall u\!:p) \Leftrightarrow \forall u\!: \bigcirc p$ $\ominus \forall u\!:p \Leftrightarrow \forall u\!: \ominus p$.

Similar properties hold for $\widetilde{\ominus}$.

More complicated modalities can also be assigned a restricted universal or existential character. In particular, the combination $\square \Diamond$ has a restricted existential character, while $\Diamond \square$ has a restricted universal character. The restriction is that these modalities distribute over finite disjunctions and conjunctions, but not over existential or universal quantifications.

FD9. $\square \Diamond (p \vee q) \Leftrightarrow \square \Diamond p \vee \square \Diamond q$

FD10. $\Diamond \square (p \wedge q) \Leftrightarrow \Diamond \square p \wedge \Diamond \square q$.

Referring to the *Next* and *Previous* Values of Variables

Consider the model

$$\sigma\!: \quad \langle x\!:0\rangle,\ \langle x\!:1\rangle,\ \ldots,$$

in which x ranges over all the natural numbers. We may wish to express the property, true of this model, which states that for every $i = 0, 1, \ldots$, the value assumed by x at s_{i+1} is greater by one than the value assumed by x at s_i.

This property can be expressed by the formula

$$\square \exists u\!: ((x = u) \wedge \bigcirc(x = u + 1)),$$

which uses quantification over rigid variable u. The formula states that for every position i, there exists a value for u such that $x = u$ at i and $x = u + 1$ at $i + 1$. Since u is rigid, it retains its value from i to $i + 1$, and therefore the formula expresses the required property.

The need to compare expressions in consecutive states arises quite frequently. We therefore extend our syntax to allow reference to the *next value* of a variable x, written x^+.

The needed extension to the definition of the semantics is straightforward. We can no longer talk about the value of expression e at a state, but rather, we must define the value of an expression e at a position i in a model σ, denoted by $val(\sigma, i, e)$.

This can be defined inductively by the following:

- For a variable x,

$$val(\sigma,\ i,\ x)\ =\ s_i[x].$$

- For the next value of a variable,

$$val(\sigma,\ i,\ x^+)\ =\ s_{i+1}[x].$$

That is, the value of x^+ at position i is the value of x at position $i + 1$.

- For a function application,

$$val\big(\sigma,\ i,\ f(e_1,\ \ldots,\ e_m)\big)\ =\ f\big(val(\sigma,\ i,\ e_1),\ \ldots,\ val(\sigma,\ i,\ e_m)\big).$$

For example, the property described earlier, by which x increases by 1 from each state to its successor, can be expressed using the extended syntax by the formula

$$\Box(x^+ = x + 1).$$

We can extend the next-value notation to apply to expressions. The value of e^+ at position j is obtained by evaluating e at position $j + 1$. If e has the form $f(x_1, \ldots, x_n)$, then e^+ is an abbreviation for $f(x_1^+, \ldots, x_n^+)$.

In a completely symmetric way, we can define the *previous value* of a variable x, denoted by x^-. A small problem arises when we attempt to evaluate x^- at the first position of a computation. By convention we agree that in this case x is not evaluated at position $0 - 1 = -1$, which is not a legal position, but at position 0. It follows that, for the first position in a model, $x^- = x$ always holds. The relevant clause in the semantic definition is

- $val(\sigma,\ i,\ x^-)\ =\ s_j[x]$ where $j = \max(i - 1,\ 0)$.

We may use a reference to the previous value in order to rewrite the requirement just considered as

$$\widehat{\Box}(x = x^- + 1).$$

This formula states that at any position that is not the first in the computation, the current value of x is greater by one than the previous value of x.

For expressions e of the form $f(x_1, \ldots, x_m)$ we may write e^- as an abbreviation for $f(x_1^-, \ldots, x_n^-)$. Clearly, the value of e^- at position j is obtained by evaluating e at position 0 if $j = 0$, or evaluating e at position $j - 1$ otherwise.

The notations x^+ and x^- are interchangeable in the sense that one can be expressed by the other. Let $\varphi(x, y)$ be a state formula, having x and y as the only free variables. Then, expressing next values by previous values is based on the congruence

$$\varphi(x, y^+) \iff \bigcirc \varphi(x^-, y).$$

To express previous values by next values, we may use the congruence

$$\varphi(x^-, y) \iff \left(\mathit{first} \wedge \varphi(x, y)\right) \vee \ominus \varphi(x, y^+).$$

The next and previous values of a rigid variable u always equal its current value. This is expressed by the invariants

$$\Box(u = u^+) \qquad \text{and} \qquad \Box(u = u^-).$$

From now on, we will consider (superscript) $+$ and $-$ as temporal operators, where $+$ is considered a future operator and $-$ a past operator. Thus, a past formula should not contain $+$ and a future formula should not contain $-$. An expression that does not contain occurrences of x^+ and x^- is called a *state-expression*. In a state formula, all expressions should be state expressions.

For the case that x is a boolean variable, x^+ and x^- are taken as atomic formulas that are congruent to the formulas $\bigcirc x$ and $(\mathit{first} \wedge x) \vee \ominus x$, respectively.

Semantic Justification

All the properties that have been considered in this section are claimed to be valid. One way of justifying these claims can be based on semantic arguments. Using the definitions of the semantics of the temporal operators, we can interpret each formula as making a claim about propositions holding at certain positions in a mode. We then use normal mathematical arguments to show that the claim is true for every model.

Let us illustrate this technique by justifying the validity of property FU2, claiming the validity of

$$\neg(p \mathcal{U} q) \iff (\neg q) \, \mathcal{W} \, (\neg p \wedge \neg q).$$

This formula claims that, for each position j, φ_1: $\neg(p \mathcal{U} q)$ holds at j iff φ_2: $(\neg q) \, \mathcal{W} \, (\neg p \wedge \neg q)$ holds there.

Following the basic definition, we recall that $p \mathcal{U} q$ holds at j iff there exists a $k \geq j$ such that q holds at k and for every i, $j \leq i < k$, p holds at i. Negating this definition, φ_1: $\neg(p\,\mathcal{U}\,q)$ holds at j iff either q does not hold at any $k \geq j$ or, if k is the smallest index not smaller than j at which q holds, there exists an i, $j \leq i < k$ at which p is false. The latter case can be described by saying that p is false at $i \geq j$ and q is false at positions $j, j+1, \ldots, i$; that is $(\neg q)\,\mathcal{U}\,(\neg p \wedge \neg q)$ holds at j. It follows that $\neg(p\,\mathcal{U}\,q)$ holds at j iff either $\Box\,\neg q$ or $(\neg q)\,\mathcal{U}\,(\neg p \wedge \neg q)$ holds at j iff $(\neg q)\,\mathcal{W}\,(\neg p \wedge \neg q)$ holds at j.

In the next section, we will consider another approach to establishing the validity of a temporal formula.

In **Problem 3.5**, the reader will consider temporal predicates defined as fixpoints of temporal equations.

In **Problem 3.6**, the reader will write several formulas describing certain properties of sequences.

In **Problem 3.7**, the reader will explore normal forms of formulas that do not contain *next* or *previous* operators.

3.5   A Proof System

In the previous section we presented a considerable list of valid temporal formulas. These formulas describe general properties of the temporal operators and identify certain relationships holding among these operators. Note that these formulas are actually *formula schemes*. This means that they may contain sentence symbols, such as p, q, r, $\ldots$, which stand for arbitrary temporal formulas. Thus, when claiming that the formula

$$\Diamond p \Leftrightarrow p \vee \bigcirc \Diamond p$$

is valid, we actually claim that the infinitely many formulas that can be obtained from this scheme, replacing p with arbitrary temporal formulas, are all valid. For example, if we replace the sentence symbol p with the formula $\Diamond q$, we obtain the valid formula

$$\Diamond(\Diamond q) \Leftrightarrow (\Diamond q) \vee \bigcirc \Diamond(\Diamond q).$$

Note the succinct way in which a single valid scheme represents infinitely many valid formulas. We will continue to refer to formulas containing sentence symbols as *formulas*.

Obviously, it is impossible to list all the valid temporal formulas, even if we restrict ourselves to those that arise in actual applications and employ the succinct notation of schemes. Instead, we resort to one of the standard approaches to the presentation of a logical theory, i.e., the effective identification of the valid statements over a particular logic. The approach we adopt is that of a deductive system.

Deductive Systems

A *deductive system* consists of the following elements:

- a set of *axioms*. This is a set of valid formulas that are taken as basic properties of the operators in the language. An example of an axiom is the formula

$$\Box p \Leftrightarrow p \wedge \bigcirc \Box p.$$

- a set of *rules*. Rules provide patterns by which new valid formulas can be derived from other formulas whose validity has been previously established.

A rule has the general form

$$\frac{p_1, \ \ldots, \ p_k}{q},$$

or equivalently,

$$p_1, \ \ldots, \ p_k \ \vdash \ q.$$

A rule consists of a list of formulas $p_1, \ldots, p_k$, called *premises*, and a formula q, called the *conclusion* of the rule. Such a rule states that if we have already established the validity of $p_1, \ldots, p_k$, then we may infer the validity of q.

An example of a rule is the frequently used rule *modus ponens*

$$p, \ p \rightarrow q \ \vdash \ q,$$

which infers the validity of q from the validity of p and $p \rightarrow q$.

Assume that we are given a deductive system H consisting of axiom schemes and rules. We explain how to construct a derivation, called a *proof*, that establishes the validity of a formula, using the axioms and rules.

An important element in the construction of proofs from axioms and rules is the notion of instantiation. Let ψ be a formula (scheme) and $p_1, \ldots, p_r$ some of the sentence symbols appearing in ψ. A *replacement* for $p_1, \ldots, p_r$, which we present as

$$\alpha: \ [p_1 \leftarrow \varphi_1, \ldots, p_r \leftarrow \varphi_r],$$

specifies for each p_i, $i = 1, \ldots, r$, a replacing formula φ_i. We denote by $\psi[\alpha]$ the formula obtained from ψ by replacing all occurrences of $p_1, \ldots, p_r$ with $\varphi_1, \ldots, \varphi_r$, respectively. We refer to $\psi[\alpha]$ as an *instantiation* of ψ.

For example, the formula $\Box \diamondsuit q \vee \diamondsuit \neg \diamondsuit q$ is an instantiation of the formula $\Box p \vee \diamondsuit \neg p$, using the replacement $[p \leftarrow \diamondsuit q]$.

A proof in H is a sequence of lines with each line containing a (possibly temporal) formula p. Such a line states the (proven) validity of p. In presentations of proofs, we usually add to each line a short *justification*, which explains the basis for including this line in the proof. Each line in a proof must be supported by an axiom or application of a rule.

- Using an axiom — Let ψ be an axiom of H and α be a replacement. Then the line $\psi[\alpha]$ can be introduced at any stage of the proof. As justification we identify the axiom scheme ψ that has been used and the instantiation α, when it is not obvious.

- Application of a rule — Let

$$\frac{p_1, \ \dots, \ p_k}{q}$$

be a rule of H and α be a replacement. Assume that the instantiated premises $p_1[\alpha], \dots, p_k[\alpha]$ already appear in previous lines of the proof. Then we may introduce the instantiated conclusion $q[\alpha]$ as the next line in the proof. The justification for this introduction may identify the applied rule, the replacement used α, and the previous lines of the proof that contain the instantiated premises.

Given a proof consisting of the lines $\varphi_1, \dots, \varphi_n$, we say that this is a *proof of* φ_n, the last formula of the proof. We say that φ_n is a *theorem* of the logic. From now on we may use φ_n, or an instantiated version of it, in subsequent proofs as though it were an axiom. The appropriate justification should refer to the name of the theorem and the replacement used for the instantiation.

Example

We illustrate the notion of a deductive system and a proof in this system. Consider the system H_1, defined as follows.

The axioms of H_1 are given by

AX1. $(p \wedge q) \rightarrow p$

AX2. $(p \wedge q) \rightarrow q$.

The only rule of H_1 is $\wedge$-INT:

$$\frac{r \rightarrow s, \qquad r \rightarrow t}{r \rightarrow (s \wedge t)}$$

We wish to present a proof of the scheme $(p \wedge q) \rightarrow (q \wedge p)$. The proof and its justification follow.

1. $(p \wedge q) \rightarrow q$ AX2

2. $(p \wedge q) \rightarrow p$ AX1

3. $(p \wedge q) \rightarrow (q \wedge p)$ $\wedge$-INT $[r \leftarrow p \wedge q, \ s \leftarrow q, \ t \leftarrow p]$ $1, 2$.

Denoting the premises of rule $\wedge$-INT by φ_1 and φ_2 and its conclusion by ψ, it is clear that $\varphi_1[\alpha]$, $\varphi_2[\alpha]$, and $\psi[\alpha]$, where α is the replacement $[r \leftarrow p \wedge q,$

$s \leftarrow q,\ t \leftarrow p]$, are identical to lines 1–3 of the proof, respectively. ⌐

In proofs of program properties we will attempt to be as informal as possible. Therefore, we will only introduce rules that are essential for carrying out the major steps of the proofs. The rules we present are adequate for proving the temporal part of the properties we establish, but we will dwell very little on the formalism by which validity of state formulas is established.

3.6 Axioms for a Proof System

We start our presentation of a proof system for temporal logic with the axioms.

To obtain a system with a small number of operators, we adopt as basic the four temporal operators

$$\bigcirc \qquad \mathcal{W} \qquad \widetilde{\ominus} \qquad \mathcal{B}$$

and consider other operators as derived, where their definitions in terms of the basic ones are

$$\square p = p\mathcal{W}\textsc{f} \qquad\qquad \boxminus p = p\mathcal{B}\textsc{f}$$
$$\diamondsuit p = \neg\,\square\,\neg p \qquad\qquad \diamondsuit p = \neg\,\boxminus\,\neg p$$
$$p\mathcal{U}q = p\mathcal{W}q \wedge \diamondsuit q \qquad\qquad p\mathcal{S}q = p\mathcal{B}q \wedge \diamondsuit q$$
$$\ominus p = \neg\,\widetilde{\ominus}\,\neg p.$$

The Future Axioms

Following are eight axioms dealing with the future operators.

FX0. $\square p \rightarrow p$

FX1. $\bigcirc\neg p \Leftrightarrow \neg\bigcirc p$

FX2. $\bigcirc(p \rightarrow q) \Leftrightarrow (\bigcirc p \rightarrow \bigcirc q)$

FX3. $\square(p \rightarrow q) \Rightarrow (\square p \rightarrow \square q)$

FX4. $\square p \rightarrow \square\bigcirc p$

FX5. $(p \Rightarrow \bigcirc p) \rightarrow (p \Rightarrow \square p)$

FX6. $p\mathcal{W}q \Leftrightarrow \big[q \vee (p \wedge \bigcirc(p\mathcal{W}q))\big]$

FX7. $\square p \Rightarrow p\mathcal{W}q.$

Axiom FX0 states that if p holds at all positions of a model, then in particular it holds at the first position.

Axiom FX1 states that the next operator $\bigcirc$ is self-dual.

Axiom FX2 states that $\bigcirc$ distributes over an implication. It claims that $p \to q$ holds in the next position iff $\bigcirc p \to \bigcirc q$ holds in the current position.

Axiom FX3 states that distributing $\square$ over an implication may only weaken it. It claims that if $p \to q$ holds at all positions following position i, and p holds at all these subsequent positions, then so does q.

Axiom FX4 claims that if p holds at all positions, then $\bigcirc p$ also holds at all positions.

Axiom FX5 can be viewed as a particular form of an induction axiom. Let us consider first a weaker formula that can be derived from FX5:

$$(p \Rightarrow \bigcirc p) \to (p \to \square p).$$

This implication can be rewritten as

$$[(p \Rightarrow \bigcirc p) \wedge p] \to \square p.$$

In this form it can be interpreted as stating that if, whenever p holds at some position, it also holds at the next position, and p is known to hold at the first position, then p holds at all positions.

In its full form, axiom FX5 states that if, whenever p holds at some position, it also holds at the next position, then whenever p holds at position j, it holds also at all following positions $i \geq j$.

Axiom FX6 is one of a family of future expansion formulas that express the truth-value of a future operator at position j as a function of the value of (some of) its arguments at position j, and the value of the same operator at position $j + 1$. For the case of the unless operator $\mathcal{W}$, the expansion formula states that $p \mathcal{W} q$ holds at position j iff either q holds at j, or p holds at j and $p \mathcal{W} q$ holds at $j + 1$. The expansion formulas for the other future operators (listed as properties FE1–FE4 in Section 3.4) are

$$\square p \Leftrightarrow (p \wedge \bigcirc \square p) \qquad \text{for} \quad \square$$
$$\diamondsuit p \Leftrightarrow (p \vee \bigcirc \diamondsuit p) \qquad \text{for} \quad \diamondsuit$$
$$p \mathcal{U} q \Leftrightarrow (q \vee [p \wedge \bigcirc (p \mathcal{U} q)]) \quad \text{for} \quad \mathcal{U}.$$

These formulas can be proven as theorems of the deductive system.

Axiom FX7 identifies $\square p$, that is, all positions $i \geq j$ satisfying p, as one of the ways to satisfy $p \mathcal{W} q$ at j. This is a property that differentiates $\mathcal{W}$ from $\mathcal{U}$.

The Past Axioms

Almost symmetric to the future axioms, we have a corresponding list of past axioms.

PX1. $\ominus p \Rightarrow \widetilde{\ominus} p$

PX2. $\widetilde{\ominus}(p \rightarrow q) \Leftrightarrow (\widetilde{\ominus} p \rightarrow \widetilde{\ominus} q)$

PX3. $\boxminus (p \rightarrow q) \Rightarrow (\boxminus p \rightarrow \boxminus q)$

PX4. $\Box p \rightarrow \Box \widetilde{\ominus} p$

PX5. $(p \Rightarrow \widetilde{\ominus} p) \rightarrow (p \Rightarrow \boxminus p)$

PX6. $p \mathcal{B} q \Leftrightarrow (q \vee [p \wedge \widetilde{\ominus}(p \mathcal{B} q)])$

PX7. $\widetilde{\ominus} \text{F}.$

Note that we do not take the formula $\boxminus p \rightarrow p$, which is the past counterpart of FX0 as an axiom. This is because it can be proven as a theorem of the system.

Axiom PX1 claims that at any position j that $\ominus p$ holds, which ensures that $j > 0$ and p holds at $j - 1$, $\widetilde{\ominus} p$ also holds. It identifies $\widetilde{\ominus}$ as the weaker version of $\ominus$.

Axiom PX2 claims that if $p \rightarrow q$ holds at the position immediately preceding position j (i.e., $j - 1$ if nonnegative), and p also holds there, then so does q.

Axiom PX3 claims that if $p \rightarrow q$ holds at all positions preceding position j, and p holds at all of these positions, then so does q.

Axiom PX4 claims that if p holds at all positions, then $\widetilde{\ominus} p$ also holds at all positions.

Axiom PX5 is a descending induction axiom. It states that if, whenever p holds at some position it also holds at the previous position, then whenever p holds at position j, it holds also at all preceding positions $i \leq j$.

Axiom PX6 is a past expansion formula. A general past expansion formula expresses the value of an operator at position j as a function of the values of its arguments at position j and the value of the operator itself at position $j - 1$, if it exists. For the back-to operator $\mathcal{B}$, the expansion formula states that $p \mathcal{B} q$ holds at position j iff either q holds at j, or p holds at j and $p \mathcal{B} q$ holds at $j - 1$ (if it exists). The expansion formulas for the other past operators are

$$\boxminus p \Leftrightarrow (p \wedge \widetilde{\ominus} \boxminus p) \qquad \text{for } \boxminus$$
$$\diamondsuit p \Leftrightarrow (p \vee \ominus \diamondsuit p) \qquad \text{for } \diamondsuit$$
$$p \mathcal{S} q \Leftrightarrow (q \vee [p \wedge \ominus(p \mathcal{S} q)]) \quad \text{for } \mathcal{S}.$$

These formulas are provable as theorems of the system.

Axiom PX7 is the only one that does not resemble a corresponding future axiom. It states that the first position of every sequence satisfies $\widetilde{\ominus}$F. In general, $(\sigma, j) \vDash \widetilde{\ominus} p$ iff $[(j = 0) \vee (\sigma, j-1) \vDash p]$. Since no position can satisfy F, it follows that $(\sigma, j) \vDash \widetilde{\ominus} \text{F}$ iff $j = 0$. Since temporal validity is always evaluated at the first position, $j = 0$, of every model, $\widetilde{\ominus} \text{F}$ is a valid statement.

The past formula that is the symmetric counterpart of FX7, i.e.,

$$\boxminus p \Rightarrow p \mathcal{B} q,$$

can be proven as a theorem, strongly relying on the axiom PX7.

The Mixed Axioms

The axioms we have considered so far consist of either future formulas (FX0–FX7) or their past counterparts (PX1–PX7), which retain in some cases the operator $\square$.

Two additional axioms intentionally mix future with past.

FX8. $p \Rightarrow \bigcirc \ominus p.$

This axiom states that if p holds at position j, then going forwards one step to position $j + 1$ and then backwards one step, ends up in a position (obviously j again) that also satisfies p. A stronger version of this formula, $p \Leftrightarrow \bigcirc \ominus p$, is actually valid. This can be proven as a theorem of the system.

PX8. $p \Rightarrow \widetilde{\ominus} \bigcirc p.$

This axiom is the past counterpart of FX8. It states that going backwards (if possible) and then forwards from a p-position, ends up again in a p-position.

The State-Tautology Axiom

There are many advantages to a separation of the process of establishing validity of state formulas from that of temporal formulas. For that reason we give no deductive system for the underlying state language. The interested reader may refer to numerous texts on the predicate calculus, including those that take a computational approach and discuss automated procedures for establishing state validity.

The link between state validity and temporal validity that our deductive system provides consists of a single axiom, called the *tautology* axiom, and an interface rule, called the *generalization* rule (which will be presented in a later section).

Let p be a state formula. We remind the reader of the notation $\Vdash p$ claiming the state validity of p, i.e., that p holds on every state, and of the notation $\vDash q$, claiming (for a temporal formula q) that q holds at the first state of every model (sequence of states).

We introduce into our deductive system the following axiom:

Axiom TAU (tautology)

For a state-valid formula p,

$$\models p$$

This axiom allows us to introduce at any step of a proof the line

$\models p$,

for an arbitrary state-valid formula p. By definition, p must be a state formula. The justification for this introduction is the name of axiom TAU.

Some knowledgeable readers may protest at this point that the introduction of axiom TAU immediately makes our deductive system *nonrecursive*. This means that we can no longer examine a proof and effectively check that every step in it is fully justified. In particular, it is impossible to check algorithmically that a formula p, claimed to be state-valid by a proof line $\models p$, is indeed valid.

In all our applications of axiom TAU, the formulas p will be either a propositional tautology whose validity can be effectively checked, or a first-order formula whose validity is self-evident.

A theoretically more satisfying approach might have been to adopt a particular deductive system H_s for proving state validity and then restrict axiom TAU to only those state formulas whose validity can be proven in H_s. However, this requires committing ourselves to the system H_s as the only way that state validity can be established, contrary to our wish for a complete separation between state and temporal reasoning.

3.7 Basic Inference Rules

Next, we introduce a set of basic inference rules as part of the deductive system for temporal logic.

We start with the generalization rule, which enables us to transform state validities into temporal validities.

Generalization and Specialization

Being able to introduce state-valid formulas into our proof, using axiom TAU, we proceed to show how they can be transformed into temporally valid formulas.

This is done by the *generalization* rule GEN.

Rule GEN (generalization)

For a state formula p,

$$\frac{\Vdash\ p}{\vDash\ \Box\, p}$$

This rule is obviously sound for the case that p is a fully interpreted state formula, i.e., contains no sentence symbols. By the premise $\Vdash p$, formula p holds at every possible state. Clearly, p holds at all the states of any particular model $\sigma\colon s_0, s_1, \ldots$, so $\Box\, p$ holds at the first state of σ.

However, the rule is also sound for the case that p is a simple formula scheme that contains sentence symbols. Assume, for example, that p contains the sentence symbol q, e.g., $p\colon q \vee \neg q$. The state validity of the scheme formula p implies that all the state instantiations, i.e., replacing q with state formulas, yield valid formulas. The temporal validity of the conclusion claims that all temporal instantiations, i.e., replacing q with a temporal formula inside $\Box\, p$, yield temporally valid formulas.

Thus, the generalization considered involves not only claiming $\Box\, p$, which means that p holds over all the positions of a model σ. It also extends the range of allowed replacements for the sentence symbols of p, from state formulas to temporal formulas.

Let us illustrate the application of axiom TAU and rule GEN to the proof of the entailment

$$(p \wedge q)\ \Rightarrow\ (q \wedge p).$$

The proof is given by

1. $\Vdash\ (p \wedge q)\ \rightarrow\ (q \wedge p)$ TAU

2. $\Box\,[(p \wedge q)\ \rightarrow\ (q \wedge p)]$ GEN 1

3. $(p \wedge q)\ \Rightarrow\ (q \wedge p)$ Definition of $\Rightarrow$

We may now apply to line 3 the replacement $[p \leftarrow \Box\, r,\ q \leftarrow \Diamond\, t]$ to obtain the valid entailment

$$(\Box\, r\ \wedge\ \Diamond\, t)\ \Rightarrow\ (\Diamond\, t\ \wedge\ \Box\, r).$$

Note that to be compatible with the notation of axiom TAU, we should have presented all the other proof lines, claiming temporal validity, in the form $\vDash p$. However, since most of the lines in a proof claim temporal validity, and only very few claim state validity, we adopt the convention of omitting the symbol for temporal validity, and explicitly write only the symbol for state validity. Consequently each line in our proofs will be either a formula p, with the intended meaning $\models p$, or a state validity claim $\Vdash p$.

The relation between the state validity $\Vdash p$ and the temporal validity $\models \Box p$ is actually symmetric. That is, state formula p is state-valid iff $\Box p$ is temporally valid. Rule GEN allows us to infer $\models \Box p$ from $\Vdash p$. The following rule provides an inference in the other direction. We refer to this rule as *specialization* rule SPEC, since it specializes the universal claim $\Box p$ to individual states.

Rule SPEC (specialization)

For a state formula p,

$$\frac{\models \Box p}{\Vdash p}$$

Unlike most other rules, the conclusion of rule SPEC is a state validity rather than temporal validity. In subsequent discussions we will point out the cases in which an inference of a state validity from a temporal validity is useful.

Instantiation

Having repeatedly emphasized that, due to the presence of sentence symbols, our formulas are actually formula schemes, we give this observation a formal expression by the instantiation rule INST

Rule INST (instantiation)

For a formula scheme p and a replacement α,

$$\frac{p}{p[\alpha]}$$

This rule allows us to infer the instantiated formula $p[\alpha]$ from the more general formula scheme p.

For example, we may extend the proof of the formula $(p \land q) \Rightarrow (q \land p)$ by the additional line

4. $(\Box r \land \Diamond t) \Rightarrow (\Diamond t \land \Box r)$ INST 3

This step formally proves the formula whose validity was claimed earlier.

In many cases, to shorten the presentation of proofs, we may absorb the instantiation step into a preceding step. Consider, for example, the following proof presentation:

1. $\Vdash (p \wedge q) \rightarrow (q \wedge p)$ TAU

2. $\Box[(\Box r \wedge \Diamond t) \rightarrow (\Diamond t \wedge \Box r)]$ GEN+INST $[p \leftarrow \Box r, q \leftarrow \Diamond t]$ 1

3. $(\Box r \wedge \Diamond t) \Rightarrow (\Diamond t \wedge \Box r)$ Definition of $\Rightarrow$

Line 2 of this proof has been derived by applying rule GEN to line 1 and immediately instantiating the result, using rule INST, by the displayed replacement.

If the replacement is obvious from the context, we will use a simpler justification, such as GEN+INST.

Modus Ponens

The most frequently used inference rule is *modus ponens* (MP). It allows the inference of q from p and $p \rightarrow q$. In most cases, $p \rightarrow q$ represents a general property, while p and q represent specific facts, perhaps about a particular program we study. Thus we can view the use of modus ponens as the application of a general rule to one specific fact in order to derive another specific fact. This explains why many of the basic properties already listed have the form of an implication or equivalence, which is a two-way implication.

Rule MP (modus ponens)

$$\frac{(p_1 \wedge \ldots \wedge p_n) \rightarrow q, \quad p_1, \quad \ldots, \quad p_n}{q}$$

Our version of modus ponens allows several premises $p_1, \ldots, p_n$.

Example

We illustrate the use of rule MP by proving the implication

$$\Box p \rightarrow p \, \mathcal{W} \, q.$$

The proof is given by

1. $\Box p \Rightarrow p \, \mathcal{W} \, q$ FX7

2. $\Box(\Box p \rightarrow p \, \mathcal{W} \, q)$ Definition of $\Rightarrow$

3. $\Box(\Box p \rightarrow p \mathcal{W} q) \rightarrow (\Box p \rightarrow p \mathcal{W} q)$ FX0

4. $\Box p \rightarrow p \mathcal{W} q$ MP 3,2 ◢

3.8 Derived Inference Rules

As we have previously discussed, once a formula p has been established as a theorem, i.e., a separate proof whose conclusion is p has been presented, we are allowed to insert p at any step of subsequent proofs. An adequate justification for such a proof line is a reference to the theorem.

If challenged by a formalistic and pedantic proof reader, we can always say that the single proof line containing p is only an abbreviation for the complete proof of p, which we could, in principle, have substituted for the single line.

In an analogous manner, we may find ourselves repeating a certain chain of proof steps that infer a conclusion from premises of a particular form. A similar economy of notation can be obtained if we can encapsulate this repetitive sequence of proof steps in a separate proof labeled by a name, and then conceptually invoke it in a single line referring to that name. Such a capability is provided by the notion of a derived rule.

First we introduce the notion of a conditional proof. A *conditional proof* is a proof constructed as usual, except that some of its lines contain arbitrary statements with the justification "Premise."

For example, the following is a conditional proof:

1. $\models p$ Premise

2. $\Box p$ GEN 1

3. $(\Box p) \rightarrow p$ FX0

4. p MP 3,2

Assume a given conditional proof, with $S_1, \ldots, S_k$ being the proof statements whose justification is "Premise," and Q being the proof statement appearing in the last line of the proof. Then we say that this proof establishes the *derived rule*

$$\frac{S_1, \ldots, S_k}{Q}$$

to which we may assign some appropriate name.

For example, the conditional proof just presented establishes the derived rule

Rule TEMP (temporalization)

For a state formula p,

$$\frac{\Vdash\ p}{\vDash\ p}$$

It is obvious that if we are in the middle of another proof, and have already established the statements $S_1, \ldots, S_k$, we may copy at that point the conditional proof, omitting the premise lines and modifying the references to the premise lines (in the justifications) to refer to the original lines where $S_1, \ldots, S_k$ are established.

For example, assume that we have a proof that contains the line

$\vdots$

5. $\Vdash\ q \vee \neg q$ TAU

Duplicating at this point the conditional proof of the derived rule TEMP with the necessary modifications, we obtain the proof

$\vdots$

5. $\Vdash\ q \vee \neg q$ TAU
6. $\square(q \vee \neg q)$ GEN 5
7. $\square(q \vee \neg q) \rightarrow (q \vee \neg q)$ FX0
8. $q \vee \neg q$ MP 7,6

Instead of copying the full proof, we can apply the derived rule (with the appropriate instantiation) to obtain the conclusion in one step. This would lead to the proof

$\vdots$

5. $\Vdash\ q \vee \neg q$ TAU
6. $q \vee \neg q$ TEMP 5

In this case the economy gained is not impressive. We have saved only two lines. But we can easily envision derived rules with very long proofs, where the gain would be very significant.

Apart from any economy in writing, theorems and derived rules provide a natural way of breaking a long and complex proof into more easily understood small pieces.

In the preceding discussion we considered the simpler case that previous steps in the proof established $S_1, \ldots, S_k$ as they appear in the rule. A more general case is that previous steps established $S_1[\alpha], \ldots, S_k[\alpha]$, i.e., some instantiation of premises $S_1, \ldots, S_k$, where α is some replacement. In this case, similar to the use of a basic rule, we may write $Q[\alpha]$ as a next proof line and quote the rule's name as justification.

Particularization

A useful derived rule is the particularization rule, which infers the validity of p from that of $\Box\, p$.

Rule PAR (particularization)

$$\frac{\Box\, p}{p}$$

For example, we illustrate the use of rule PAR to prove the validity of the implication

$$(\Box\, r \wedge \Diamond\, t) \to \Diamond\, t$$

1.	$\Vdash (p \wedge q) \to q$	TAU
2.	$\Box[(\Box\, r \wedge \Diamond\, t) \to \Diamond\, t]$	GEN+INST 1
3.	$(\Box\, r \wedge \Diamond\, t) \to \Diamond\, t$	PAR 2

Rule PAR can be derived as follows

1.	$\Box\, p$	Premise
2.	$\Box\, p \to p$	FX0
3.	p	MP 2,1

Propositional Reasoning

When we get more experience in the use of the deductive system, we tend to take many abbreviations and short cuts. A very useful short cut can be presented in the form of a rule, to which we refer as *propositional reasoning*, or rule PR.

Rule PR (propositional reasoning)

For propositional state formulas $p_1, \ldots, p_n, q$
such that $(p_1 \wedge \cdots \wedge p_n) \to q$ is a state-valid formula

$$\frac{p_1, \quad \cdots, \quad p_n}{q}$$

At first glance there seems to be only a superficial difference between this rule and rule MP. The difference is that the tautology $(p_1 \wedge \cdots \wedge p_n) \to q$ is not required to appear as an explicit line in the proof but is presented as a textual stipulation to the applicability of the rule.

In spite of the apparent superficiality of this difference, rule PR has proven to be a useful device for removing unnecessary details from the presentation of proofs.

Following is a proof of the property

$$p \mathcal{W} \text{F} \to p,$$

using rule PR. The proof refers to axiom

FX6. $p \mathcal{W} q \Leftrightarrow [q \vee (p \wedge \bigcirc(p \mathcal{W} q))].$

1. $p \mathcal{W} \text{F} \Leftrightarrow \big[\text{F} \vee (p \wedge \bigcirc(p \mathcal{W} \text{F})) \big]$ FX6$[q \leftarrow \text{F}]$

2. $p \mathcal{W} \text{F} \leftrightarrow \big[\text{F} \vee (p \wedge \bigcirc(p \mathcal{W} \text{F})) \big]$ Definition of $\Leftrightarrow$, PAR 1

3. $p \mathcal{W} \text{F} \to p$ PR 2

Note that this proof actually stands for the following longer proof of the same formula that does not use rule PR.

1. $p \mathcal{W} \text{F} \Leftrightarrow \big[\text{F} \vee (p \wedge \bigcirc(p \mathcal{W} \text{F})) \big]$ FX6$[q \leftarrow \text{F}]$

2. $p \mathcal{W} \text{F} \leftrightarrow \big[\text{F} \vee (p \wedge \bigcirc(p \mathcal{W} \text{F})) \big]$ Definition of $\Leftrightarrow$, PAR 1

3. $\Vdash \big[q \leftrightarrow [\text{F} \vee (p \wedge r)] \big] \to [q \to p]$ TAU

4. $\Big[p \mathcal{W} \text{F} \leftrightarrow \big[\text{F} \vee (p \wedge \bigcirc(p \mathcal{W} \text{F})) \big] \Big] \to [p \mathcal{W} \text{F} \to p]$
                                          TEMP+INST$[q \leftarrow p \mathcal{W} \text{F}, \ r \leftarrow \bigcirc(p \mathcal{W} \text{F})]$ 3

5. $p \mathcal{W} \text{F} \to p$ MP 4, 2

The comparison between the shorter and longer proofs in this particular example leads us directly to a conditional proof that establishes the derived rule PR.

1. $\Vdash (p_1 \wedge \cdots \wedge p_n) \rightarrow q$	By rule assumption and TAU
2. $(p_1 \wedge \cdots \wedge p_n) \rightarrow q$	TEMP 1
3. $p_1, \ldots, p_n$	Premises
4. q	MP 2, 3

Entailment Modus Ponens

Rule MP is based on an implication $(p_1 \wedge \cdots \wedge p_n) \rightarrow q$ and establishes that q holds at the first position of every model (q is valid). In many cases, the main premise is an entailment of the form $(p_1 \wedge \cdots \wedge p_n) \Rightarrow q$, and we wish to establish the conclusion $\Box\, q$, which states that q holds at all positions of every model.

The appropriate rule is given by

Rule E-MP (entailment modus ponens)

$$\frac{(p_1 \ \wedge \ \cdots \ \wedge \ p_n) \ \Rightarrow \ q, \qquad \Box\, p_1, \quad \cdots, \quad \Box\, p_n}{\Box\, q}$$

This rule states that if each of $p_1, \ldots, p_n$ holds at all positions of every model, and $(p_1 \wedge \ldots \wedge p_n) \Rightarrow q$ is a valid formula, then q holds at all positions of every model.

Rule E-MP is a derived rule, as can be shown by the conditional proof establishing it for $n = 1$.

1. $\Box(p \rightarrow q) \Rightarrow (\Box\, p \rightarrow \Box\, q)$	FX3
2. $\Box(p \rightarrow q) \rightarrow (\Box\, p \rightarrow \Box\, q)$	PAR 1
3. $p \Rightarrow q$	Premise
4. $\Box(p \rightarrow q)$	Definition of $\Rightarrow$
5. $\Box\, p \rightarrow \Box\, q$	MP 2, 4
6. $\Box\, p$	Premise
7. $\Box\, q$	MP 5, 6

This conditional proof establishes

$$\frac{p \Rightarrow q, \quad \Box\, p}{\Box\, q}$$

Following is an example of the application of rule E-MP in a conditional proof of the derived rule

---

Rule E-TRNS (entailment transitivity)

$$\frac{p \Rightarrow q, \qquad q \Rightarrow r}{p \Rightarrow r}$$

This rule states the transitivity of the entailment operator $\Rightarrow$.

1.	$p \Rightarrow q$	Premise
2.	$\Box(p \rightarrow q)$	Definition of $\Rightarrow$
3.	$q \Rightarrow r$	Premise
4.	$\Box(q \rightarrow r)$	Definition of $\Rightarrow$
5.	$\Vdash \; [(p \rightarrow q) \land (q \rightarrow r)] \; \rightarrow \; (p \rightarrow r)$	TAU
6.	$[(p \rightarrow q) \land (q \rightarrow r)] \; \Rightarrow \; (p \rightarrow r)$	GEN 5
7.	$\Box(p \rightarrow r)$	E-MP 6, 2, 4
8.	$p \Rightarrow r$	Definition of $\Rightarrow$

Entailment Propositional Reasoning

In a similar way that propositional reasoning rule PR provides a more concise way to apply rule MP, we introduce an *entailment propositional reasoning* rule E-PR, which provides a concise representation of rule E-MP.

Rule E-PR (entailment propositional reasoning)

For propositional state formulas $p_1, \ldots, p_n, q$
such that $(p_1 \land \cdots \land p_n) \rightarrow q$ is a state-valid formula

$$\frac{\Box p_1, \quad \cdots, \quad \Box p_n}{\Box q}$$

For example, the proof of rule E-TRNS can be shortened using rule E-PR instead of the E-MP version.

1.	$p \Rightarrow q$	Premise

2. $\Box(p \rightarrow q)$ Definition of $\Rightarrow$

3. $q \Rightarrow r$ Premise

4. $\Box(q \rightarrow r)$ Definition of $\Rightarrow$

5. $\Box(p \rightarrow r)$ E-PR 2, 4

6. $p \Rightarrow r$ Definition of $\Rightarrow$

From Implications to Rules

There is a certain trade-off between representing properties as a single formula and representing them as a rule. Consider, for example, the monotonicity property of operator $\Box$. When listing such properties we expressed this property by the valid implication

$$(p \Rightarrow q) \rightarrow (\Box p \Rightarrow \Box q).$$

An alternative representation of the same property is as a rule,

$$\frac{p \Rightarrow q}{\Box p \Rightarrow \Box q}$$

This rule states that if we have already proven the validity of $p \Rightarrow q$, we may write as the next proof line (infer) the formula $\Box p \Rightarrow \Box q$.

This example illustrates a general principle that is formulated by the following claim.

Claim

If $p \rightarrow q$ is provable, then so is the derived rule $p \vdash q$.

Assume that $p \rightarrow q$ is provable. Then we can provide the following conditional proof for the rule $p \vdash q$, i.e., the rule deriving the validity of q from that of p.

1. p Premise

2. $p \rightarrow q$ By assumption

3. q MP 2, 1

An interesting observation is that the reverse direction is also true. This is expressed by the well-known deduction theorem, claiming that under certain conditions,

if $p \vdash q$ is provable, then so is $p \rightarrow q$.

We will not be using this theorem at all; consequently, we will not discuss it any further.

In **Problem 3.8**, the reader will use the deductive system presented here for the formal derivation of a list of propositional theorems and derived rules.

Example of a Proof

We present an example of a detailed proof in the deductive system. The proof establishes the validity of the formula

$$(\bigcirc p \wedge \boxminus p) \;\Rightarrow\; \bigcirc \boxminus p.$$

Usually, such a proof relies on a sequence of simpler theorems and derived rules that have been established previously. We list the rules and theorems on which the presented proof depends. Their names are taken from Problem 3.8, in which the reader is requested to systematically derive a list of theorems and derived rules.

Rule R1: $p \Leftrightarrow q \;\vdash p \Rightarrow q$

Rule $\bigcirc$M: $p \Rightarrow q \;\vdash\; \bigcirc p \Rightarrow \bigcirc q$

Theorem T1: $\bigcirc(p \wedge q) \;\Leftrightarrow\; (\bigcirc p \wedge \bigcirc q)$

Theorem T19: $\boxminus p \;\Leftrightarrow\; (p \wedge \widetilde{\ominus} \boxminus p).$

The proof proceeds as follows

1.	$\ominus \boxminus p \Rightarrow \widetilde{\ominus} \boxminus p$	PX1
2.	$\bigcirc \ominus \boxminus p \Rightarrow \bigcirc \widetilde{\ominus} \boxminus p$	$\bigcirc$M 1
3.	$\boxminus p \Rightarrow \bigcirc \ominus \boxminus p$	FX8
4.	$\boxminus p \Rightarrow \bigcirc \widetilde{\ominus} \boxminus p$	E-TRNS 3, 2
5.	$(\bigcirc p \wedge \boxminus p) \Rightarrow \bigcirc p$	TAU+GEN+INST
6.	$(\bigcirc p \wedge \boxminus p) \Rightarrow \boxminus p$	TAU+GEN+INST
7.	$(\bigcirc p \wedge \boxminus p) \Rightarrow \bigcirc \widetilde{\ominus} \boxminus p$	E-TRNS 6, 4
8.	$(\bigcirc p \wedge \boxminus p) \Rightarrow (\bigcirc p \wedge \bigcirc \widetilde{\ominus} \boxminus p)$	E-PR 5, 7

Lines 5 and 6 in the proof are based on the state tautologies

$$(\varphi \wedge \psi) \;\rightarrow\; \varphi \quad \text{and} \quad (\varphi \wedge \psi) \;\rightarrow\; \psi.$$

To justify line 8, we begin with the state tautology

$$[(\varphi \rightarrow \psi) \wedge (\varphi \rightarrow \chi)] \;\rightarrow\; (\varphi \rightarrow \psi \wedge \chi).$$

Applying to it rule GEN and the replacement

$$[\varphi \leftarrow (\bigcirc p \wedge \boxminus p), \quad \psi \leftarrow \bigcirc p, \quad \chi \leftarrow \bigcirc \widetilde{\ominus} \boxminus p]$$

we obtain

$$\begin{bmatrix} (\bigcirc p \wedge \boxminus p) \to \bigcirc p \ \wedge \\ (\bigcirc p \wedge \boxminus p) \to \bigcirc \widetilde{\ominus} \boxminus p \end{bmatrix} \Rightarrow [(\bigcirc p \wedge \boxminus p) \to (\bigcirc p \wedge \bigcirc \widetilde{\ominus} \boxminus p)].$$

We now apply rule E-MP to this formula and to lines 5 and 7, which are actually $\Box((\bigcirc p \wedge \boxminus p) \to \bigcirc p)$ and $\Box((\bigcirc p \wedge \boxminus p) \to \bigcirc \widetilde{\ominus} \boxminus p)$, we obtain line 8.

The rest of the proof is

9.	$(p \wedge \widetilde{\ominus} \boxminus p) \Rightarrow \boxminus p$	T19, R1
10.	$\bigcirc(p \wedge \widetilde{\ominus} \boxminus p) \Rightarrow \bigcirc \boxminus p$	$\bigcirc$M 9
11.	$(\bigcirc p \wedge \bigcirc \widetilde{\ominus} \boxminus p) \Rightarrow \bigcirc(p \wedge \widetilde{\ominus} \boxminus p)$	T1, R1
12.	$(\bigcirc p \wedge \bigcirc \widetilde{\ominus} \boxminus p) \Rightarrow \bigcirc \boxminus p$	E-TRNS 11, 10
13.	$(\bigcirc p \wedge \boxminus p) \Rightarrow \bigcirc \boxminus p$	E-TRNS 8, 12

In **Problem 3.9**, the reader will consider a different version of temporal logic, called the *floating version*, in which a formula p is satisfied by a model σ if $(\sigma, i) \models p$ at all positions $i \geq 0$.

3.9 *Equality and Quantifiers*

The axioms and rules we have presented so far deal only with the propositional fragment of the language. It can be shown that the deductive system based on these axioms and rules is complete for proving the validity of any propositional temporal formula, i.e., any valid propositional temporal formula can be proven using the presented deductive system.

In this section, we will extend the deductive system to deal with the first-order elements: variables, equality, and quantification. This extension consists of additional axioms and rules. While the axioms and rules we provide can handle a large number of cases, they do not lead to a complete system.

This is not very surprising since the underlying language assumes variables that range over the integers. We thus find ourselves in a situation shared by everyone who wishes to reason formally about the integers and has to face the fact that no complete deductive system for such reasoning exists.

Parameterized Sentence Symbols

Once we introduce variables into formulas, it is necessary to consider schemes that contain sentence symbols with parameters. For example

$$\Box(x = y) \rightarrow (p(x) \Leftrightarrow p(y))$$

is a formula scheme we would like to consider and claim to be valid. The interpretation of the validity of such a scheme should be such that it implies the validity of any of its instantiations, such as

$$\Box(x = y) \rightarrow (\Diamond(x = 5) \Leftrightarrow \Diamond(y = 5)),$$

which can be obtained using the replacement $p(z) \leftarrow \Diamond(z = 5)$.

A general replacement of a parameterized sentence symbol (assuming for simplicity a single parameter) has the form

$$\alpha: \quad p(z) \leftarrow \varphi(z),$$

where φ is a formula (possibly a formula scheme), that contains one or more occurrences of variable z, which is not quantified in φ. Let ψ be a formula that contains $k \geq 1$ occurrences of the form $p(e_1), \ldots, p(e_k)$, where $e_1, \ldots, e_k$ are expressions. Following the terminology of procedures and functions in programming languages, we refer to variable z appearing in the definition of the replacement as the *parameter*, to each occurrence $p(e_i)$ in ψ as an *invocation* of the sentence symbol p, and to the expression e_i as the *argument* of that invocation.

The instantiation of ψ by α, denoted by $\psi[\alpha]$, is obtained as follows. For each $i = 1, \ldots, k$, replace the invocation $p(e_i)$ by the subformula $\varphi(e_i)$, which is obtained by replacing every occurrence of z within $\varphi(z)$ by e_i. Note that this process involves two substitutions. First, replace parameter z with argument e_i to obtain $\varphi(e_i)$. Then replace the invocation $p(e_i)$ within ψ by the expanded body $\varphi(e_i)$.

Thus, the scheme $\Box(x = y) \rightarrow (p(x) \Leftrightarrow p(y))$ contains two invocations, $p(x)$ and $p(y)$, which are replaced by $\Diamond(x = 5)$ and $\Diamond(y = 5)$, respectively, to form the instantiation

$$\Box(x = y) \rightarrow (\Diamond(x = 5) \Leftrightarrow \Diamond(y = 5)).$$

In the case that the formula ψ contains quantifications, we have to ensure that the process of instantiation does not capture occurrences of variables that are free in the replacing formula. Consequently we define a general replacement

$$p(z_1, \ldots, z_m) \leftarrow \varphi(z_1, \ldots, z_m), \qquad m \geq 0,$$

to be *admissible for instantiation in ψ* (sometimes abbreviated to *admissible for ψ*) if $\varphi(z_1, \ldots, z_m)$ does not contain any variable that is quantified in ψ. Note that by taking $m = 0$, this definition also covers the case of the unparameterized replacement $p \leftarrow \varphi$. If α is a replacement admissible for ψ, we refer to $\psi[\alpha]$ as an *admissible instantiation* of ψ.

Consider, for example, the scheme

$$\psi: \quad p \;\rightarrow\; \exists x: ((x = 0) \wedge p),$$

which we would like to consider as valid. The replacement

$$\alpha: \quad p \;\leftarrow\; (x \neq 0)$$

is an example of a replacement that is not admissible for ψ. This is because α contains variable x, which is quantified in ψ. Indeed, the instantiation $\psi[\alpha]$ given by

$$(x \neq 0) \;\rightarrow\; \exists x: ((x = 0) \wedge (x \neq 0))$$

is an invalid formula.

We are now ready to define the validity of schemes that may contain quantifiers.

A scheme ψ is *valid* if every admissible instantiation $\psi[\alpha]$ is valid.

This definition applies to both the state validity and temporal validity of schemes.

Thus, scheme ψ is valid, even though its instantiation by the inadmissible replacement α yields an invalid formula.

Rule GEN *for Parameterized Schemes*

One of the most powerful rules that we have introduced is rule GEN, which allows us to infer the temporal validity $\vDash \Box\, \psi$ from the state validity $\Vdash \psi$. For the case that ψ is a simple scheme, the conclusion $\vDash \Box\, \psi$ allows instantiation of the (unparameterized) sentence symbols contained in ψ by temporal formulas.

This allows us, for example, to infer the temporal validity of

$$\Box\, [q\,\mathcal{U}\, r \;\vee\; \neg(q\,\mathcal{U}\, r)]$$

by instantiating the scheme

$$\Box\, (p \;\vee\; \neg p),$$

which can be obtained by rule GEN from the tautology $\Vdash (p \vee \neg p)$.

When we extend our consideration to parameterized sentence symbols, additional restrictions have to be imposed on the state scheme ψ we wish to generalize. To see this, we first present a counterexample.

Example

Clearly, the following is a state-valid scheme

$$[(x = y) \;\wedge\; p(x, x)] \;\rightarrow\; p(x, y).$$

That is, any instantiation of the two-parameter sentence symbol $p(u, v)$ by a state formula $\varphi(u, v)$ yields a state-valid formula.

However, if we apply rule GEN to this scheme, we obtain

$$[(x = y) \land p(x, x)] \Rightarrow p(x, y),$$

which is not a valid temporal scheme. That is, it is not the case that any instantiation of $p(u, v)$ yields a valid formula.

To see this, replace $p(u, v)$ by the temporal formula $\Box(u = v)$ to obtain

$$[(x = y) \land \Box(x = x)] \Rightarrow \Box(x = y).$$

This formula is not temporally valid. For example, consider the model

$$\sigma: \quad \langle x{:}0, \; y{:}0 \rangle, \; \langle x{:}1, \; y{:}0 \rangle, \; \langle x{:}2, \; y{:}0 \rangle, \; \ldots .$$

Clearly $\sigma \models (x = y)$ and $\sigma \models \Box(x = x)$, but $\sigma \not\models \Box(x = y)$.

To summarize,

$$\Vdash \; [(x = y) \land p(x, x)] \rightarrow p(x, y)$$

but

$$\not\models \; [(x = y) \land p(x, x)] \Rightarrow p(x, y). \quad \blacksquare$$

The problem can be traced to the fact that flexible variables may be equal at one position but different at another.

To overcome this problem, we restrict the application of rule GEN to formulas in which the expressions occurring as arguments of parameterized sentence symbols are rigid. We define a parameterized occurrence of a sentence symbol $p(e_1, \ldots, e_k)$ to be *rigid* if the expressions $e_1, \ldots, e_k$ are rigid, that is, all variables appearing in $e_1, \ldots, e_k$ are rigid.

Consequently, to make rule GEN, which derives $\models \Box p$ from $\Vdash p$, sound also for the case that p is a parameterized scheme, we add the following stipulation:

All occurrences of parameterized sentence symbols in p must be rigid.

Indeed, we observe that the scheme

$$\psi_1: \quad [(w = t) \land p(w, w)] \Rightarrow p(w, t)$$

is temporally valid for the case that variables w and t are rigid.

Consider, for example, the replacement

$$\alpha: \quad p(u, v) \; \leftarrow \; [\Box(x = u) \land \Box(y = v)],$$

where x and y are flexible variables and u, v are rigid. The formula on the right-hand side of α is satisfied by a model σ only if the values of variable x in the different states of σ all agree and equal the (single) value of u. Similarly, all values of y must equal v.

The instantiated formula $\psi_1[\alpha]$,

$$\big[(w = t) \wedge \big[\Box\,(x = w) \wedge \Box\,(y = w)\big]\big] \;\Rightarrow\; \big[\Box\,(x = w) \wedge \Box\,(y = t)\big],$$

is indeed valid.

Let us consider two more examples of generalization followed by parameterized instantiation.

Example

Consider the state-valid scheme

$$\psi_2: \quad \big[(x \geq v) \to p(v)\big] \;\to\; \big[(x \geq v + 1) \to p(v)\big],$$

for the rigid variable v.

Applying rule GEN followed by the instantiation

$$\alpha: \quad p(u) \leftarrow \Diamond(x = u),$$

to the generalized scheme $\widehat{\psi}_2 = \Box\,\psi_2$, we obtain the valid entailment $\widehat{\psi}_2[\alpha]$

$$\big[(x \geq v) \to \Diamond(x = v)\big] \;\Rightarrow\; \big[(x \geq v + 1) \to \Diamond(x = v)\big]. \quad \blacksquare$$

Example

Consider the state-valid scheme (for a rigid v)

$$\psi_3: \quad \forall v\colon \big[(x \geq v) \to p(v)\big] \;\to\; \forall v\colon \big[(x \geq v + 1) \to p(v + 1)\big].$$

Applying rule GEN followed by the instantiation

$$\alpha: \quad p(u) \leftarrow \Diamond(x = u),$$

we obtain the valid entailment $\Box\,\psi_3[\alpha]$

$$\forall v\colon \big[(x \geq v) \to \Diamond(x = v)\big] \;\Rightarrow\; \forall v\colon \big[(x \geq v + 1) \to \Diamond(x = v + 1)\big]. \quad \blacksquare$$

Rule INST *for Formulas with Quantifiers*

As explained earlier, when we consider instantiations of schemes that may contain quantifiers, the applied replacements must be admissible. We consequently add the following stipulation to rule INST, which makes it applicable also to schemes that contain quantification.

> In the use of rule INST for deriving $p[\alpha]$ from p, replacement α must be admissible for p.

Next, we consider extensions to the deductive system that are necessary to deal with equality and quantification.

Replacement of Variables

In preceding discussions we considered replacements of the form $p \leftarrow \varphi$, which replace a sentence symbol p with a formula φ. Working with variables, we consider here replacements of the form $u \leftarrow e$, which replace a variable u with an expression e.

Recall that an expression e is called *rigid* if it does not refer to any flexible variable. The replacement $u \leftarrow e$ is called *compatible* if either both u and e are rigid or u is flexible.

In the following, when we write $p(u)$, we imply that $p(u)$ has one or more occurrences of the variable u and that there is no quantification over u. The replacement $u \leftarrow e$ is defined to be *admissible* for $p(u)$ if it is compatible and none of the variables appearing in e is quantified in $p(u)$.

This situation is also described by saying that e is *admissible for substitution in $p(u)$* (sometimes abbreviated to *admissible for $p(u)$*) and writing $p(e)$ for the instantiated formula $p(u)[u \leftarrow e]$.

Axioms for Equality

For every expression e, the following axiom states the reflexivity of equality

---

Axiom REFL-E (reflexivity of equality)

$$\Box(e = e)$$

The following axiom states that, whenever two expressions are equal, one can be replaced by the other in a state formula

---

Axiom REPL-E (replacement of equals by equals)

For a state formula $p(u)$ and expressions e_1, e_2, that are admissible for $p(u)$

$$(e_1 = e_2) \;\Rightarrow\; (p(e_1) \leftrightarrow p(e_2))$$

We will show that the two restrictions required by the axiom are essential for its validity.

Consider first the case that $p(u)$ is not a state formula. We may then take $p(u)$ to be $\Box(u = 0)$ and e_1, e_2 to be x, y, respectively, and obtain the invalid formula

$$(x = y) \;\Rightarrow\; \big(\Box(x = 0) \;\leftrightarrow\; \Box(y = 0)\big).$$

To see that this formula is not valid, it is sufficient to consider the sequence

$$\sigma: \quad \langle x{:}\,0,\; y{:}\,0 \rangle,\; \langle x{:}\,0,\; y{:}\,1 \rangle,\; \langle x{:}\,0,\; y{:}\,2 \rangle,\; \ldots.$$

We observe that σ satisfies $x = y$ and $\Box(x = 0)$, but not $\Box(y = 0)$.

Next, consider the case that formula $p(u)$ quantifies over some of the variables of e_1, e_2. For example, take $p(u)$ to be $\exists x{:}\,(x > u)$, and e_1, e_2 to be x, y, respectively. Axiom REPL-E yields for this choice

$$(x = y) \;\Rightarrow\; \big(\exists x{:}\,(x > x) \;\leftrightarrow\; \exists x{:}\,(x > y)\big).$$

Clearly, $\exists x{:}\,(x > x)$ is always false, while if x and y range over the integers, $\exists x{:}\,(x > y)$ is always true.

We can obtain a stronger notion of substitutivity by requiring that $e_1 = e_2$ holds not only at a single position, but throughout the model. Let $p(u)$ be a (temporal) formula with a free variable u and let e_1, e_2 be expressions that are admissible for substitution in $p(u)$. Then the following theorem scheme claims that if $e_1 = e_2$ at all positions of a model, then $p(e_1)$ and $p(e_2)$ are congruent over this model.

SUBS-E (substitutivity of equality) $\Box(e_1 = e_2) \;\rightarrow\; \big(p(e_1) \;\Leftrightarrow\; p(e_2)\big).$

The various instances of this theorem scheme can be proven by induction on the structure of the formula $p(u)$.

The Frame Axiom

The distinction between rigid and flexible variables is that rigid variables are not allowed to change their value from one position to the next in a model. The following axiom, called the *frame axiom*, formally expresses this fact. We call a state formula p *rigid* if it does not refer to any flexible variables.

Axiom FRAME

   For a rigid state formula p

$$p \;\Rightarrow\; \bigcirc p$$

It is not difficult to derive the following consequences from this axiom, all of which refer to a rigid state formula p.

C1. $p \;\Rightarrow\; \widetilde{\ominus}p$

C2. $\ominus p \Rightarrow p$ C3. $\bigcirc p \Rightarrow p$

C4. $p \Leftrightarrow \boxminus p$ C5. $p \Leftrightarrow \Box p$

C6. $p \Leftrightarrow \diamondsuit p$ C7. $p \Leftrightarrow \Diamond p$

Example of a Proof

To illustrate the use of the preceding axioms, we present a proof of theorem C3

$$\bigcirc p \Rightarrow p,$$

for the case that p is a rigid state formula.

In the proof we will use the following derived rule

R1. $p \Leftrightarrow q \vdash p \Rightarrow q$.

The proof proceeds as follows

1. $\neg p \Rightarrow \bigcirc \neg p$ FRAME

2. $\neg \bigcirc \neg p \Rightarrow p$.   E-PR 1

The justification of line 2 is based on the state tautology

$$(\neg \varphi \to \psi) \to (\neg \psi \to \varphi),$$

to which we apply rule GEN and instantiation by the replacement

$$[\varphi \leftarrow p, \ \psi \leftarrow \bigcirc \neg \varphi].$$

3. $\bigcirc \neg p \Rightarrow \neg \bigcirc p$ FX1, R1

4. $\bigcirc p \Rightarrow \neg \bigcirc \neg p$.   E-PR 3

Line 4 can be based on the state tautology

$$(\varphi \to \neg \psi) \to (\psi \to \neg \varphi).$$

5. $\bigcirc p \Rightarrow p$.   E-TRNS 4, 2

Next and Previous Values of Variables

Special axioms characterize the properties of the next and previous values of variables, expressed by the notation x^+ and x^-.

In the following axioms, let u be a rigid variable and x a variable that can be either rigid or flexible. Let $\varphi(u, x)$ denote a state formula in which the only free variables are u or x or both.

Axiom NXTV (next value)

For a rigid variable u and a state formula $\varphi(u, x)$

$$\varphi(u, x^+) \Leftrightarrow \bigcirc \varphi(u, x)$$

A similar version of the axiom exists for the case of state formulas of the form $\varphi(u_1, \ldots, u_m, x_1, \ldots, x_n)$ where $u_1, \ldots, u_m$ are rigid.

For the previous value of a variable, the corresponding axiom considers position 0 as a special case.

Axiom PRVV (previous value)

For a rigid variable u and a state formula $\varphi(u, x)$

$$\varphi(u, x^-) \Leftrightarrow \big(\textit{first} \wedge \varphi(u, x)\big) \vee \ominus \varphi(u, x)$$

A corresponding axiom exists for the case of state formulas of the form $\varphi(u_1, \ldots, u_m, x_1, \ldots, x_n)$ where $u_1, \ldots, u_m$ are rigid.

These axioms can be used to prove, for a rigid variable u, the theorems

$$\Box(u = u^+) \quad \text{and} \quad \Box(u = u^-).$$

Axioms for Quantifiers

To handle quantification we introduce several axioms and rules that describe the basic properties of the quantifiers and their interaction with the other elements of our language. Most of the axioms and rules hold uniformly for quantifications over either rigid or flexible variables. Therefore, we use variables such as x, u, and v in this section to refer to variables of either kind. Wherever there are restrictions on the kind of variables, we will point out such restrictions explicitly.

The first axioms establish the full duality of the two quantifiers.

Axioms Q-DUAL (quantifier duality)

For a variable x and a formula $p(x)$

$$\neg\exists x:\ p(x)\ \Leftrightarrow\ \forall x:\ \neg p(x)$$
$$\neg\forall x:\ p(x)\ \Leftrightarrow\ \exists x:\ \neg p(x)$$

For the next axiom, consider a formula $p(u)$ and an expression e that is admissible for substitution in $p(u)$.

Axiom ∀-INS (quantifier instantiation)

For a variable u, a formula $p(u)$, and an expression e that is admissible for $p(u)$

$$\forall u: p(u)\ \Rightarrow\ p(e)$$

This axiom enables us to infer $p(e)$, for a specific expression e, at any position in which the universal fact $\forall u:\ p(u)$ holds.

It is easy to come up with counterexamples for cases in which the required restrictions are violated.

Example

Consider, for example, the case that u and v are integer variables and formula $p(u)$ has the form $\exists v:\ (v \neq u)$. Clearly, $\forall u:\ p(u)$, i.e., $\forall u \exists v:\ (v \neq u)$ is valid. Taking e to be v, which is not admissible for substitution in $\exists v:\ (v \neq u)$, we obtain for $p(e)$ the contradictory formula $\exists v:\ (v \neq v)$.

To show that the requirement of compatibility (implied by admissibility) is essential, let u be a rigid variable and x a flexible variable. Consider the model

$$\sigma:\quad \langle x{:}0,\ u{:}0\rangle,\ \langle x{:}1,\ u{:}0\rangle,\ \ldots.$$

This model satisfies at position 0 the formula

$$\forall u:\ \Diamond(x \neq u).$$

Note that the actual assignment to u by σ is irrelevant to the evaluation of this formula, since we consider all the u-variants of σ anyway. To see that the preceding formula is satisfied by σ, we have only to consider two cases for the possible values of u in such a u-variant σ'.

- $u = 0$, then $(x \neq u)$ is satisfied at position 1 of σ'.

- $u \neq 0$, then $(x \neq u)$ is satisfied at position 0 of σ'.

Thus we have $(\sigma, 0) \vDash \forall u\colon \Diamond (x \neq u)$. On the other hand, if we take e to be the flexible variable x, which is not compatible with u, we obtain the formula $p(x)\colon \Diamond (x \neq x)$, which is certainly not satisfied by σ.

This situation is rectified if we consider variable u to be flexible. In this case the implication

$$\forall u\colon \Diamond (x \neq u) \;\rightarrow\; \Diamond (x \neq x)$$

is valid. This is because neither $\forall u\colon \Diamond (x \neq u)$ nor $\Diamond (x \neq x)$ can be satisfied by any model. Consider, for example, the model σ. One of its u-variants is

$$\sigma'\colon \quad \langle x\colon 0,\; u\colon 0 \rangle,\; \langle x\colon 1,\; u\colon 1 \rangle,\; \langle x\colon 2,\; u\colon 2 \rangle,\; \dots ,$$

which certainly does not satisfy $\Diamond (x \neq u)$. Consequently σ does not satisfy $\forall u\colon \Diamond (x \neq u)$. ◢

The following theorem can be derived from the axiom ∀-INS:

QT (quantifier abstraction)

$$p(e) \;\Rightarrow\; \exists u\colon p(u),$$

where u is not quantified in $p(u)$ and e is admissible for $p(u)$.

The last axiom concerns the commutation of the universal quantifier and the next operator $\bigcirc$.

Axiom ∀$\bigcirc$-COM (universal commutation)

For a variable x and a formula $p(x)$

$$\forall x\colon \bigcirc p(x) \;\Leftrightarrow\; \bigcirc \forall x\colon p(x)$$

This axiom is known in the literature as one of the Barcan axioms.

Several commutation theorems can be derived from this axiom.

CM1. $\forall x\colon \ominus p(x) \;\Leftrightarrow\; \ominus \forall x\colon p(x)$

CM2. $\exists x\colon \ominus p(x) \;\Leftrightarrow\; \ominus \exists x\colon p(x)$ $\qquad\qquad$ CM3. $\exists x\colon \bigcirc p(x) \;\Leftrightarrow\; \bigcirc \exists x\colon p(x).$

Theorems similar to CM1 and CM2 hold for the weak version $\widetilde{\ominus}$.

Rules for Quantifiers

There is one basic inference rule associated with the quantifiers.

Rule ∀-GEN (universal generalization)

For a variable u and formulas p and $q(u)$
such that u has no free occurrences in p

$$p \;\Rightarrow\; q(u)$$
$$\overline{}$$
$$p \;\Rightarrow\; \forall u\!: q(u)$$

To see the soundness of rule ∀-GEN, assume that the premise $p \Rightarrow q(u)$ is valid. Let σ be an arbitrary model and assume that p holds at position j of σ. We have to show that $\forall u\!: q(u)$ also holds at that position.

Consider any σ', a u-variant of σ. Since p does not depend on u, p also holds at (σ', j). By the validity of $p \Rightarrow q(u)$, $q(u)$ also holds at (σ', j). Thus, $q(u)$ holds at position j of all u-variants of σ. Consequently, $\forall u\!: q(u)$ holds at position j of σ.

Many derived rules can be proved using the preceding axioms and rule. We list several of them here.

Rule E-INST   (expression instantiation)

$$p(u) \;\vdash\; p(e),$$

where e is admissible for $p(u)$.

Rule ∃-INTR   (∃ introduction)

$$p(u) \Rightarrow q \;\;\vdash\;\; \exists u\!: p(u) \;\Rightarrow\; q,$$

where u has no free occurrences in q.

Rules ∀∀-INTR   (∀∀ introduction)

$$p(x) \Rightarrow q(x) \;\;\vdash\;\; \forall x\!: p(x) \Rightarrow \forall x\!: q(x)$$
$$p(x) \Leftrightarrow q(x) \;\;\vdash\;\; \forall x\!: p(x) \Leftrightarrow \forall x\!: q(x).$$

Rules ∃∃-INTR   (∃∃ introduction)

$$p(x) \Rightarrow q(x) \;\;\vdash\;\; \exists x\!: p(x) \Rightarrow \exists x\!: q(x)$$
$$p(x) \Leftrightarrow q(x) \;\;\vdash\;\; \exists x\!: p(x) \Leftrightarrow \exists x\!: q(x).$$

Example of a Proof

To illustrate the use of the deductive system for deriving theorems and rules for quantified formulas, we present a proof of one of the clauses of rule ∀∀-INTR

$$p(x) \Rightarrow q(x) \quad \vdash \quad \forall x\colon p(x) \Rightarrow \forall x\colon q(x).$$

The proof proceeds as follows:

1. $p(x) \Rightarrow q(x)$ Premise
2. $\forall x\colon p(x) \Rightarrow p(x)$ ∀-INS 1
3. $\forall x\colon p(x) \Rightarrow q(x)$ E-TRNS 2, 1
4. $\forall x\colon p(x) \Rightarrow \forall x\colon q(x)$ ∀-GEN 3

Note that the application of ∀-GEN to line 3 is justified because $\forall x\colon p(x)$ has no free occurrences of x.

3.10 From General Validity to Program Validity

The language of temporal logic that we have considered so far was interpreted over general models. In this section we would like to narrow our attention to specific models that correspond to computations of (fair) transition systems.

Models Corresponding to Computations

As defined, computations of a transition system (program) P, are particular sequences of states that obey certain constraints imposed by P.

Each computation of P is an infinite sequence of states over Π, the set of state variables associated with P. As we recall, all the state variables are flexible, i.e., may change from state to state.

Let V be a vocabulary that contains Π. Consider a model over V

$$\sigma\colon s_0, \ s_1, \ \dots.$$

We say that model σ *corresponds* to the computation

$$\sigma'\colon s_0', \ s_1', \ \dots$$

if each state s_j is identical to s_j', when restricted to the subvocabulary Π, that is, $s_j|_\Pi = s_j'$. We refer to a model that corresponds to a computation of transition system P as a P-*model*. Note that while a computation interprets only the variables in Π, a model corresponding to a computation may give interpretation to additional variables.

We denote by $\mathcal{M}_V(P)$ the set of all P-models over V. We define a state to be $\mathcal{M}_V(P)$-*accessible* if it appears at some position in a P-model over V.

Validity and State Validity Over a Program

Let p be a temporal formula and denote by V_p the vocabulary of p, i.e., the set of variables appearing in p. We define p to be *valid over transition system* P (also described as being *P-valid*), if every model in $\mathcal{M}_V(P)$ satisfies p, where $V = V_p \cup \Pi$. It is not difficult to see that this implies that every model in $\mathcal{M}_V(P)$ satisfies p for every vocabulary V that contains $V_p \cup \Pi$.

If the vocabulary V is fixed we refer to $\mathcal{M}_V(P)$ simply as $\mathcal{M}(P)$, and to an $\mathcal{M}_V(P)$-accessible states simply as P-accessible.

We denote by

$$P \vDash p$$

the fact that formula p is P-valid. Clearly, every valid formula is also P-valid, but since $\mathcal{M}(P)$ is only a subset of the universe of all possible models, there are many formulas that are P-valid but not valid in general.

Consider, for example, a transition system P whose initial condition contains the clause $x = 0$. Clearly, the formula $x = 0$ is P-valid, since it holds in the first state of every computation of P. On the other hand, $x = 0$ is obviously not a valid formula, as there are many models whose first state does not satisfy $x = 0$.

A state formula p is *state valid over transition system* P (also described as being *P-state valid*), if $s \Vdash p$ for every P-accessible state s. Intuitively, it means that p holds on every state that can appear in a computation of P. We denote by

$$P \Vdash p$$

the fact that p is state valid over P.

Consider, for example, a program P whose only state variable is x and whose only reduced behavior is given by

$$\langle x : 0 \rangle, \ \langle x : 1 \rangle, \ \langle x : 2 \rangle, \ \ldots.$$

Clearly, the state formula $(x = 0)$ is valid over P, but it is not state valid over P. This is because the state $\langle x : 1 \rangle$ is P-accessible and does not satisfy $(x = 0)$. On the other hand, the state formula $(x \geq 0)$ is both valid and state valid over P.

It is not difficult to see that the following relation holds between the two notions of validity of a state formula p over a program P:

$$P \Vdash p \quad \text{iff} \quad P \vDash \square\, p.$$

We summarize the four notions of validity we have introduced so far.

- For a state formula p:

  $\Vdash p$ — p is state valid. It holds in all states.

  $P \Vdash p$ — p is P-state valid. It holds in all P-accessible states.

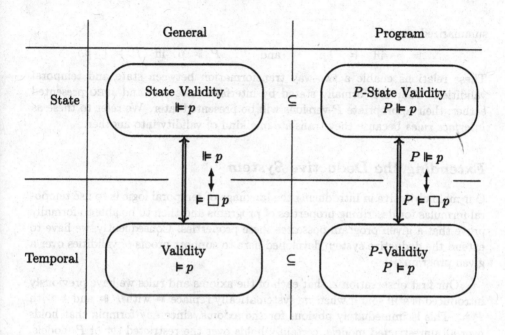

Fig. 3.1. The components of a deductive system.

- For a temporal formula p (which may also be a state formula):

  $\models p$ — p is valid. It holds in the first state of every model.

  $P \models p$ — p is P-valid. It holds in the first state of every P-model.

In Fig. 3.1, we present a diagram that displays the four notions of validity and the interelations between them. Two independent parameters together determine the kind of validity. The first parameter distinguishes between state validity and temporal validity. The second parameter distinguishes between validity over general models and validity over P-models.

The diagram shows two inclusion relations between general and program validities. These relations can be stated as the following:

For each state formula p and program P, if $\Vdash p$ then $P \Vdash p$,

and

For each (temporal) formula p and program P, if $\models p$ then $P \models p$.

Also shown in the diagram are the relations between the state validity of the state formula p and the temporal validity of the formula $\Box p$. These can be summarized as

$$\Vdash p \quad \text{iff} \quad \vDash \Box p \qquad \text{and} \qquad P \Vdash p \quad \text{iff} \quad P \vDash \Box p.$$

These relations enable a two-way transformation between state and temporal validities. They are formally stated by interface rules GEN and SPEC presented earlier; their appropriate P-versions will be presented later. We refer to these as *interface rules* because they translate one kind of validity into another.

Extending the Deductive System

Our main objective in introducing the language of temporal logic is to use temporal formulas for describing properties of programs and then to be able to formally prove that a given program possesses these properties. Consequently, we have to extend the deductive system developed here to support proofs of validities over a given program P.

Our first observation is that each of the axioms and rules we have previously introduced is still sound when we systematically replace $\Vdash$ with $P \Vdash$ and $\vDash$ with $P \vDash$. This is immediately obvious for the axioms, since any formula that holds over all unrestricted models, certainly holds over the restricted set of P-models. For the rules, we can check each one separately and confirm that its soundness is not impaired by the restriction to P-models.

From now on, we consider all the axioms and rules (and consequently the theorems and derived rules) as stated for the validities $P \Vdash$ and $P \vDash$, respectively. We refer to this set of axioms and rules as the *general part* of the deductive system, since it establishes validities that hold over the set of P-models for any program P.

Clearly, to establish properties that are true of only some specific program P, we use additional rules that depend on P. We refer to this component of the deductive system as the *program part*.

Before presenting the program part, we review the general part that deals with state validity over P.

Establishing P-State Validity

The deductive system for P-state validity is very modest. It consists of the P-state versions of axiom TAU, interface rule SPEC, and rule MP.

Even though we previously explained that all these axioms and rules are simply obtained by consistently replacing $\Vdash$ with $P \Vdash$ and $\vDash$ with $P \vDash$, we present them here to illustrate this replacement.

Axiom P-TAU (*P-tautology*)

For every state-valid formula p and program P

$$P \Vdash p$$

Import rule SPEC transforms a validity of the form $P \vDash \Box\, p$, for a state formula p, into the validity $P \Vdash p$. The validity $P \vDash \Box\, p$ claims that p holds at all positions of each computation of P. This is obviously equivalent to p holding on all P-accessible states, as claimed by $P \Vdash p$. We call this rule SPEC (specialization) since it specializes the universal claim $\Box\, p$ to individual P-accessible states.

Rule P-SPEC (*P-specialization*)

For a state formula p and program P

$$\frac{P \vDash \Box\, p}{P \Vdash p}$$

The last rule is modus ponens, applied to P-state validities.

Rule P-SMP (*P-state modus ponens*)

For state formulas $p_1, \ldots, p_n$, q and program P

$$\frac{P \Vdash (p_1 \wedge \cdots \wedge p_n) \rightarrow q, \qquad P \Vdash p_1, \ \ldots, \ P \Vdash p_n}{P \Vdash q}$$

We illustrate how these rules can be used for state reasoning about P-accessible states.

Example

Let P be a transition system with a single state variable x of type integer. In addition to the idling transition τ_I, P has a single transition τ, whose transition relation is

$$\rho_\tau: \quad x' = x + (-1)^x \cdot 2.$$

This transition assigns to x the value $x + 2$ if x is even and the value $x - 2$ if x is odd. The initial condition is Θ: $(x = 0)$, and there are no fairness requirements. P has only one reduced behavior, given by

$$\sigma: \langle 0 \rangle, \langle 2 \rangle, \langle 4 \rangle, \ldots .$$

Assume that by previous reasoning we have established the validity of $P \models \Box\bigl(even(x)\bigr)$. This validity claims that the value of x is even at all states of σ. The next property we would like to establish is that $x \geq 0$ at all P-accessible states. The standard way to establish this fact, as will be amply demonstrated in subsequent chapters, is to prove the P-state validity

$$P \Vdash \bigl[(x \geq 0) \wedge \rho_\tau\bigr] \rightarrow (x' \geq 0),$$

that is,

$$P \Vdash \Bigl[(x \geq 0) \wedge \bigl(x' = x + (-1)^x \cdot 2\bigr)\Bigr] \rightarrow (x' \geq 0).$$

Here, we present a proof of this fact.

1. $P \models \Box\bigl(even(x)\bigr)$ Assumption

2. $P \Vdash even(x)$ P-SPEC 1

3. $P \Vdash even(x) \rightarrow \Bigl\{\bigl[(x \geq 0) \wedge \bigl(x' = x + (-1)^x \cdot 2\bigr)\bigr] \rightarrow (x' \geq 0)\Bigr\}$

                                                                               P-TAU

4. $P \Vdash \Bigl[(x \geq 0) \wedge \bigl(x' = x + (-1)^x \cdot 2\bigr)\Bigr] \rightarrow (x' \geq 0)$ P-SMP 3, 2

This example represents the typical P-state reasoning in which we will engage in the following chapters. It deduces P-state validities p from previously established P-validities $\Box\, p$ and performs state deductions on them, using the P-version of rule MP and any necessary tautologies.

Establishing P-Validity

As indicated in our previous discussion, the ultimate goal of the deductive system is to be able to prove the validity of temporal formulas over programs, i.e., P-validity.

We remind the reader that as axioms of the general part we take FX0–FX8 and PX1–PX8, which are interpreted as stating P-validity. The P-version of axiom TAU has already been presented.

For completeness, we list the P-versions of the basic inference rules.

The P-version of rule GEN is given by

Rule P-GEN (*P-generalization*)

For a program P and a state formula p, in which all the parameterized occurrences of sentence symbols are rigid

$$\frac{P \Vdash p}{P \vDash \Box p}$$

For the case that p contains parameterized sentence symbols, we require all of their occurrences to be rigid.

The P-version of rule INST is given by

Rule P-INST (*P-instantiation*)

For a program P, a formula p, and a replacement α admissible for p

$$\frac{P \vDash p}{P \vDash p[\alpha]}$$

The P-version of the rule MP is given by

Rule P-MP (*P-modus ponens*)

For a program P and formulas $p_1, \ldots, p_n, q$

$$P \vDash (p_1 \wedge \cdots \wedge p_n) \to q, \qquad P \vDash p_1, \ldots, P \vDash p_n$$

$$P \vDash q$$

This concludes the presentation of the general part, which is independent of the particular program P to be analyzed. The program part contains additional rules, all of which refer to the components of the particular program P, such as the initial condition Θ, the transition relations ρ_τ, etc.

The general part also includes the P-versions of the axioms and rules for equality and quantifiers.

Some Program-Dependent Rules

The entire second volume of this book is devoted to the development of special rules for the various classes of properties and to showing how to use these rules for establishing properties of programs. Here, we would like to present only a small sample of these rules.

For the discussion of the program-dependent rules, we fix our attention on a particular transition system (program) P whose components are given by

$$(\Pi, \ \Sigma, \ \mathcal{T}, \ \Theta, \ \mathcal{J}, \ \mathcal{C}).$$

For simplicity, assume that all the transition relations ρ_τ are given in *full form*, i.e., have the form $C_\tau \wedge (\bar{y}' = \bar{e})$, which has a conjunct $y_i' = e_i$ for each state variable $y_i \in \Pi$.

Basic Rules

The first rule we consider allows us to establish a conclusion of the form $P \models p$, for a state formula p. This establishes that p holds at the first state of all the computations of program P.

Rule INIT (initiality)

For a program P and a state formula p

$$\models \Theta \ \rightarrow \ p$$

$$\overline{}$$

$$P \ \models \ p$$

The premise of this rule requires that the implication $\Theta \rightarrow p$ be state-valid. That is, every state that satisfies Θ also satisfies p. It is obvious that if σ: $s_0, s_1, \ldots$ is a computation of P, then its first state s_0 satisfies Θ and, by the premise, it also satisfies p.

To illustrate this rule, consider a simple transition system P_0 given by: $\Pi = \{x\}$, Σ: all assignments of integer values to x, $\mathcal{T} = \{\tau_I, \tau_1\}$ where ρ_{τ_I}: $x' = x$ and ρ_{τ_1}: $x' = x + 1$, Θ: $(x = 0)$, and $\mathcal{J} = \mathcal{C} = \phi$, i.e., no fairness requirements.

Take p: $(x \geq 0)$. Since the formula $(x = 0) \rightarrow (x \geq 0)$ is state-valid, the premise of rule INIT is satisfied, and we may conclude

$$P_0 \ \models \ (x \geq 0).$$

For a state formula q that may refer to variables in Π, we denote by q' the formula obtained by priming any free variable $y \in \Pi$, i.e., replacing y with y'. We refer to q' as the *primed version* of q. For example, $(x \geq 0)'$ is $(x' \geq 0)$.

We introduce the *verification condition*

$$\{p\} \ \tau \ \{q\},$$

as an abbreviation for the implication

$$(p \wedge \rho_\tau) \rightarrow q',$$

for state formulas p and q and a transition $\tau \in \mathcal{T}$. For example, let p: $(x \geq 5)$, q: $(x > 5)$, and ρ_{τ_1}: $(x' = x + 1)$. Then the triplet $\{p\}\tau_1\{q\}$ is given by

$$\big[(x \geq 5) \wedge (x' = x + 1)\big] \rightarrow (x' > 5),$$

which happens to be valid.

For a set of transitions $T \subseteq \mathcal{T}$, we denote

$$\{p\} \ T \ \{q\} \ = \ \bigwedge_{\tau \in T} (\{p\} \ \tau \ \{q\}).$$

The following rule identifies the changes that can occur in one computation step.

Rule STEP (single step)

For a program P and state formulas p, q

$$\Vdash \{p\} \ T \ \{q\}$$

$$\overline{}$$

$$P \vDash (p \Rightarrow \bigcirc q)$$

Assume that $\{p\} \ T \ \{q\}$ is state-valid. Consider a state s_i in a computation of P that satisfies p.

Let us denote by Π_i, Π_{i+1} the values of the state variables in s_i, s_{i+1}, respectively. Since s_i satisfies p, we have $p(\Pi_i) = \text{T}$. Since s_{i+1} is a τ-successor of s_i, we have $\rho_\tau(\Pi_i, \Pi_{i+1}) = \text{T}$. The state validity of $(p \wedge \rho_\tau) \rightarrow q'$ implies in particular $\big[p(\Pi_i) \wedge \rho_\tau(\Pi_i, \Pi_{i+1})\big] \rightarrow q(\Pi_{i+1})$, from which we deduce $q(\Pi_{i+1}) = \text{T}$, i.e., s_{i+1} satisfies q.

This shows that if the premise is true, then the implication $p \rightarrow \bigcirc q$ holds at any position of each computation of P.

Considering the transition system P_0 just defined, let us take

$$p: \ x = u \quad \text{and} \quad q: \ x \geq u,$$

where u is a rigid variable. Since $\mathcal{T} = \{\tau_I, \tau_1\}$, the premise of rule STEP requires showing the implication

$$\big[(x = u) \wedge \rho_\tau\big] \rightarrow (x' \geq u),$$

for each $\tau \in \{\tau_I, \tau_1\}$. This leads to the two implications

$$[(x = u) \wedge (x' = x)] \ \rightarrow \ (x' \geq u)$$
$$[(x = u) \wedge (x' = x + 1)] \ \rightarrow \ (x' \geq u),$$

which are state-valid.

We conclude that the formula

$$(x = u) \ \Rightarrow \ \bigcirc(x \geq u),$$

claiming that x is nondecreasing, is valid over the program P.

Derived Rule

Consider now a state formula p such that both $\Theta \rightarrow p$ and $\{p\}\, T \,\{p\}$ are state-valid. Using the two previous rules, we obtain

1.	$P \models p$	INIT
2.	$P \models (p \Rightarrow \bigcirc p)$	STEP
3.	$P \models (p \Rightarrow \bigcirc p) \ \rightarrow \ (p \Rightarrow \Box p)$	FX5
4.	$P \models p \Rightarrow \Box p$	MP 3,2
5.	$P \models p \rightarrow \Box p$	PAR 4
6.	$P \models \Box p$	MP 5,1

This leads to a derived rule obtained by combining the two previous rules. The new rule establishes conclusions of the form $\Box p$ for a state formula p.

Rule S-INV (simple invariance)

For a program P and a state formula p

$$\frac{\models \ \Theta \ \rightarrow \ p, \qquad \models \ \{p\}\, T \,\{p\}}{P \models \Box p}$$

Consider program P_0 just defined, and take p: $(x \geq 0)$. The two premises of the rule require showing

1. $(x = 0) \ \rightarrow \ (x \geq 0)$

2. $[(x \geq 0) \ \wedge \ (x' = x + 1)] \ \rightarrow \ (x' \geq 0).$

These formulas are state-valid. We therefore conclude

$$P_0 \models \Box(x \geq 0),$$

establishing that x is nonnegative at all states of all computations of P.

The Temporal Semantics Axiom

It is interesting to consider an approach that forms an alternative to the introduction of many individual axioms and rules.

From a theoretical point of view there is a single axiom, denoted by χ_P, that is adequate for proving all the temporal properties of the program P. This axiom consists of several conjuncts, each of which expresses a certain property of the computations of P. We introduce the necessary formulas expressing these properties.

Expressing That a Transition is Enabled

Let τ be a transition with the transition relation $\rho_\tau\colon C_\tau \wedge (\bar{y}' = \bar{e})$. We denote by *enabled*$(\tau)$ the enabling condition C_τ. Clearly, *enabled*(τ) holds at position $i \geq 0$ of a computation iff τ is enabled on s_i.

Expressing that a Transition is Taken

For a transition τ, we define the formula *taken*(τ) by

$$taken(\tau)\colon \quad \rho_\tau(\Pi, \Pi^+).$$

Since we usually present ρ_τ as $\rho_\tau(\Pi, \Pi')$, the meaning of $\rho_\tau(\Pi, \Pi^+)$ is that ρ_τ holds between the current and next state.

For example, for τ such that $\rho_\tau\colon x' = x + 1$, the formula *taken*$(\tau)$ is given by

$$taken(\tau)\colon \quad x^+ = x + 1.$$

Obviously, for a general transition τ, *taken*(τ) holds at position $i \geq 0$ in a computation iff τ is taken at position i, i.e., $\rho_\tau(s_i[\Pi], s_{i+1}[\Pi]) = \text{T}$.

It is not absolutely necessary to use the next value construct x^+ to express the formula *taken*(τ). An alternative formulation is given by

$$taken(\tau)\colon \quad \exists \Pi_0\colon \bigcirc(\Pi = \Pi_0) \wedge \rho_\tau(\Pi, \Pi_0).$$

In this formulation we use the rigid variables Π_0 to represent the values assumed by Π in the next state. The conjunct $\bigcirc(\Pi = \Pi_0)$ ensures that they do.

Expressing Diligence

The formula

$$diligent\colon \quad \bigvee_{\tau \in T_D} enabled(\tau) \; \Rightarrow \; \Diamond \left(\bigvee_{\tau \in T_D} taken(\tau) \right)$$

expresses the requirement of diligence. It requires that any position $j \geq 0$ at which some diligent transition is enabled is followed by a position $k \geq j$ at which some diligent transition is taken.

Expressing Justice

Let τ be a transition. Consider the formula

$$just(\tau): \quad \Diamond \Box \, enabled(\tau) \; \rightarrow \; \Box \Diamond \, taken(\tau).$$

This formula states that if τ is enabled at all but finitely many positions then τ is taken at infinitely many positions. Consequently, any sequence that satisfies $just(\tau)$ is just with respect to τ.

Expressing Compassion

Consider the formula

$$compassionate(\tau): \quad \Box \Diamond \, enabled(\tau) \rightarrow \Box \Diamond \, taken(\tau).$$

This formula states that if τ is enabled at infinitely many positions, then τ is taken at infinitely many positions. It follows that any sequence satisfying formula $compassionate(\tau)$, is compassionate with respect to τ.

The Axiom

For a given program P, we define the formula χ_P, called the *temporal semantics* of program P:

$$\chi_P: \quad \Theta \; \wedge \; \left(\Box \bigvee_{\tau \in \mathcal{T}} taken(\tau) \right) \wedge \; diligent \; \wedge \; \bigwedge_{\tau \in \mathcal{J}} just(\tau) \; \wedge \; \bigwedge_{\tau \in \mathcal{C}} compassionate(\tau).$$

The intended meaning of this formula is that it is satisfied by a model σ iff σ is a P-model.

Let us consider each clause appearing in the formula χ_P:

Θ ensures that the initial state satisfies the initial condition Θ.

$\Box \bigvee_{\tau \in \mathcal{T}} taken(\tau)$ ensures that, for every $i = 0, 1, \dots$, state s_{i+1} is obtained from state s_i by the application of some transition $\tau \in \mathcal{T}$. Note that this allows idling steps performed by $\tau_I \in \mathcal{T}$.

$diligent$ ensures that sequence σ is diligent.

$\bigwedge_{\tau \in \mathcal{J}} just(\tau)$ ensures that sequence σ satisfies all the justice requirements.

$\bigwedge_{\tau \in \mathcal{C}} compassionate(\tau)$ ensures that sequence σ satisfies all the compassion requirements.

The five clauses correspond to and ensure the five requirements a sequence has to satisfy in order to be a computation of program P. This is stated by the following claim.

Claim

A model σ satisfies χ_P iff σ is a P-model.

It is therefore natural to introduce the temporal semantics formula χ_P as an axiom of the program part.

Axiom T-SEM (temporal semantics)

$$P \vDash \chi_P$$

Axiom T-SEM is the only program-dependent element of the deductive system that is necessary for proving the P-validity of any property expressible by a temporal formula. This is a consequence of the following claim.

Claim

For a given program P and a formula p

$$P \vDash p \qquad \text{iff} \qquad \vDash \chi_P \to p.$$

According to this claim, formula p is satisfied by all P-models iff the implication $\chi_P \to p$ is satisfied by all models. Indeed, $\chi_P \to p$ is satisfied by all models iff $\neg \chi_P \vee p$ is satisfied by all models iff each model either does not correspond to a computation of P or satisfies p iff each model corresponding to a computation of P, i.e., each P-model, satisfies p.

Relative Completeness

The strategy suggested by this claim is that in order to prove the P-validity of the formula p, we can instead attempt to prove the general (program-independent) temporal validity of the implication $\chi_P \to p$.

This can be interpreted as a statement of relative completeness of the axiom χ_P for proving P-validities, relative to general temporal validities. This means that if we are equipped with an orable that is guaranteed to provide a proof (or other confirmation) of each valid temporal formula, we can use χ_P to establish the P-validity of any given formula.

This can be made more precise as follows. The omniscient oracle that provides proofs for all valid formulas can be represented by the following single axiom:

Axiom T-TAU (temporal tautology)

For every valid formula p

$$P \vDash p$$

We now claim that axioms T-SEM and T-TAU and (P-version of) rule P-MP form a complete system for proving any P-validity.

The proof of this claim is quite simple. Let p be a formula valid over the program P. According to the previous discussion this means that the implication $\chi_P \to p$ is valid. We may therefore present the following formal proof for $P \vDash p$.

1. $P \vDash \chi_P \to p$ T-TAU

2. $P \vDash \chi_P$ T-SEM

3. $P \vDash p$ MP 1,2

While theoretically conclusive, this approach is far from satisfactory for practical applications. All that has been achieved is a reduction from proving the program validity of p to proving the general validity of $\chi_P \to p$. This reduction has the disadvantage that, even for simple properties such as $\square(x \geq 0)$, the formula $\chi_P \to \square(x \geq 0)$ carries with it the full complexity of χ_P.

Thus, while the use of axiom T-SEM is theoretically adequate, it is not very practical and certainly not the approach we endorse. The approach we do recommend is to introduce additional rules to the program part. The different rules correspond to the particular forms of formulas that express most of the properties we encounter in practice, such as $\square q$ and $p \Rightarrow \Diamond q$ for state formulas p and q. These special rules have the advantage that their premises are state validities and program-state validities rather than general (temporal) validities of the form $\vDash \chi_P \to p$. Thus, the reduction achieved by these rules is from proving (temporal) validity over programs to proving state validity, i.e., using familiar first-order rather than general temporal reasoning.

This approach is extensively developed in Volume 2.

Problems

Problem 3.1 (flexible quantification)   page 192

(a) Write a quantifier-free formula stating that p holds precisely at all even positions, i.e., p is true at positions $0, 2, 4, \ldots$ and false at positions $1, 3, 5, \ldots$.

(b) Using flexible quantification over boolean variables, write a formula stating that p holds at all even positions. The formula should not restrict the value of p at odd positions.

(c) Using flexible quantification over integer variables, write a formula stating that p holds at positions $0, 1, 4, 9, 16, \ldots$, i.e., positions $i_k = k^2$ for $k = 0, 1, \ldots$. Nothing is said about the value of p at other positions.

Problem 3.2 (valid and invalid formulas)   page 201

The following list of temporal congruences and equivalences contains valid and invalid formulas. For each formula, decide if it is valid or not. For formulas claimed to be valid, give an informal (semantic) justification. For formulas φ claimed to be invalid, describe a sequence σ, such that $\sigma \not\models \varphi$. Since each congruence $p \Leftrightarrow q$ consists of two entailments: $p \Rightarrow q$ and $q \Rightarrow p$, consider separately each entailment. That is, identify cases in which one entailment is valid but the other is not. Do the same for each implication for the case of equivalences.

(a) $\Diamond p \wedge \Box q \Leftrightarrow \Diamond(p \wedge \Box q)$

(b) $\Diamond p \wedge \Box q \Leftrightarrow \Box(\Diamond p \wedge q)$

(c) $\Diamond \Box p \wedge \Diamond \Box q \Leftrightarrow \Diamond(\Box p \wedge \Box q)$

(d) $(p \mathcal{U} q) \mathcal{U} q \Leftrightarrow p \mathcal{U} q$

(e) $p \mathcal{U} q \Leftrightarrow [(\neg p) \mathcal{U} q \rightarrow p \mathcal{U} q]$

(f) $p \mathcal{U} q \wedge q \mathcal{U} r \Leftrightarrow p \mathcal{U} r$

(g) $\Diamond p \Leftrightarrow \Box(\Diamond p \vee \ominus p)$

(h) $\Diamond \ominus p \Leftrightarrow \ominus \Diamond p$

(i) $(q \Rightarrow \ominus r) \leftrightarrow (\neg q) \mathcal{W} p$

(j) $(\Box p \vee \Box q) \leftrightarrow \Box(\boxminus p \vee \boxminus q)$

(k) $(p \rightarrow \Box q) \leftrightarrow \Box(\ominus p \rightarrow q)$

(l) $\Diamond(p \wedge \ominus q) \leftrightarrow \Diamond(q \wedge \Diamond p)$

(m) $(\Diamond p \wedge \Diamond q) \leftrightarrow \Diamond(\ominus p \wedge \ominus q)$

(n) $(\Box p \vee \Diamond q) \Leftrightarrow p \mathcal{W} (\Diamond q)$

(o) $(p \Rightarrow \Diamond q) \leftrightarrow \Box \Diamond((\neg p) \mathcal{B} q)$

(p) $(p \Rightarrow \Diamond q) \Leftrightarrow \Box \Diamond((\neg p) \mathcal{B} q)$

(q) $(\Box \Diamond p \wedge \Box \Diamond q) \leftrightarrow \Box \Diamond(q \wedge (\neg q) \widehat{\mathcal{B}} p)$

(r) $\Diamond p \leftrightarrow \Diamond \ominus p$

(s) $(p \Rightarrow \Diamond \Box q) \leftrightarrow \Diamond \Box(\ominus p \rightarrow q)$

(t) $(\Diamond \Box p \vee \Diamond \Box q) \;\leftrightarrow\; \Diamond \Box (q \vee p \,\widehat{\mathcal{B}}\, (p \wedge \neg q))$

(u) $\Diamond \Box (p \rightarrow \Box q) \;\leftrightarrow\; (\Diamond \Box q \vee \Diamond \Box \neg p)$

(v) $\bigcirc \bigcirc p \;\Leftrightarrow\; \Box ((\ominus \ominus \mathit{first}) \rightarrow p)$

(w) $p \,\mathcal{U}\, q \;\leftrightarrow\; \Diamond (q \wedge \widehat{\boxminus} p)$

(x) $(p \Rightarrow (\neg q) \,\mathcal{W}\, r) \;\leftrightarrow\; (q \Rightarrow (\neg p) \,\mathcal{B}\, r).$

Problem 3.3 (derived temporal operators)   page 201

Derived temporal operators can sometimes express properties in a more concise form than the standard operators. We introduce two such operators:

- The *precedence* operator $\mathcal{P}$ can be defined as

$$p \,\mathcal{P}\, q \;=\; (\neg q) \,\mathcal{W}\, (p \wedge \neg q).$$

  (a) Give a semantic definition for $(\sigma, j) \vDash p \,\mathcal{P}\, q$ in the style given for $\mathcal{U}$ in Section 3.2.

  (b) Show how to express $\mathcal{U}$ in terms of $\mathcal{P}$ and the boolean operators.

- The *while* operator W can be defined by

$$(\sigma, j) \;\vDash\; p \,W\, q \quad \text{iff} \quad (\sigma, k) \vDash p \text{ for every } k \geq j, \text{ such that} $$
$$(\sigma, i) \vDash q \text{ for all } i, \; j \leq i \leq k.$$

  (c) Can W be expressed in terms of $\mathcal{U}$ and the boolean operators?

  (d) Can $\mathcal{U}$ be expressed in terms of W and the boolean operators?

*Problem 3.4 (immediate operators and stuttering)   page 201

A *stretching function* is a function $f \colon \mathbb{N} \to \mathbb{N}$ such that $f(0) = 0$ and for every $i < j$, $f(i) < f(j)$.

A sequence $\sigma' \colon s'_0, s'_1, \ldots$ is defined to be a *stretching* of a sequence $\sigma \colon s_0, s_1, \ldots$, denoted by $\sigma \vartriangleleft \sigma'$, if there exists a stretching function f, such that for every $i, i \geq 0$, and every j, $f(i) \leq j < f(i+1)$, $s'_j = s_i$. Thus, the sequence

$$\sigma' \colon s_0, \; s_1, \; \ldots, \; s_k, \; s_k, \; s_k, \; s_{k+1}, \; \ldots$$

is a stretching of the sequence

$$\sigma \colon s_0, \; s_1, \; \ldots, \; s_k, \; s_{k+1}, \; \ldots$$

with the stretching function f defined by

$$f(i) \;=\; \textbf{if } i \leq k \textbf{ then } i \textbf{ else } i + 2.$$

Sequences σ_1 and σ_2 are defined to be *stuttering equivalent* if there exists a sequence $\widehat{\sigma}$ such that both σ_1 and σ_2 stretch $\widehat{\sigma}$.

For example, the sequences

$$\sigma_1: s_0, \ s_1, \ s_1, \ s_1, \ s_2, \ s_3, \ \cdots$$

$$\sigma_2: s_0, \ s_1, \ s_2, \ s_2, \ s_2, \ s_3, \ \cdots$$

are stuttering equivalent since they both stretch

$$\widehat{\sigma}: s_0, \ s_1, \ s_2, \ s_3, \ \cdots.$$

(a) Let φ be a quantifier-free formula with no immediate operators. Prove that validity of φ is robust with respect to stuttering. That is, $\sigma \vDash \varphi$ iff $\widetilde{\sigma} \vDash \varphi$ for every sequence $\widetilde{\sigma}$ stuttering equivalent to σ.

You may consider first a sequence σ and its stretching σ', with stretching function f. Show by induction on the structure of an immediate-free formula φ that $(\sigma, i) \vDash \varphi$ iff $(\sigma', j) \vDash \varphi$ for every i, j, $f(i) \leq j < f(i+1)$. Use this result to derive the required general statement.

(b) Show that the formula

$$p \ \Rightarrow \ \bigcirc q$$

is not equivalent to any quantifier-free formula with no immediate operators.

(c) Show that the formula $p \ \Rightarrow \ \bigcirc q$ is equivalent to a formula that has no immediate operators but uses flexible quantification over boolean variables.

*Problem 3.5 (fixpoints)   page 214

We can define a partial ordering between formulas by

$$p \sqsubseteq q \qquad \text{iff} \qquad p \Rightarrow q \text{ is valid.}$$

This ordering has F as the minimal element and T as the maximal element. Observe that $p \sqsubseteq q$ iff, for each model, the set of positions satisfying p is contained in the set of positions satisfying q.

Consider the congruence

$$(*) \qquad X \ \Leftrightarrow \ q \vee (p \wedge \bigcirc X)$$

which can be viewed as a (fixpoint) equation for the unknown variable X.

(a) Show (formally or informally) that $p \, \mathcal{U} \, q$ is a solution to $(*)$. That is, if we substitute $p \, \mathcal{U} \, q$ for X, we obtain a valid formula.

(b) Show that $p \, \mathcal{U} \, q$ is the minimal solution of $(*)$. That is, if φ is any other solution of $(*)$, then

$$p \, \mathcal{U} \, q \ \sqsubseteq \ \varphi \qquad \text{equivalently} \qquad \vDash p \, \mathcal{U} \, q \ \Rightarrow \ \varphi.$$

Consider an arbitrary sequence σ. We have to show that all positions in σ that satisfy $p \, \mathcal{U} \, q$ also satisfy φ. Consider an arbitrary position j satisfying $p \, \mathcal{U} \, q$. By definition, there exists a position $k \geq j$, such that q holds at k, and p holds at every i, $j \leq i < k$. We show by induction that φ holds at all $i = k, k-1, \ldots, j$.

Start at $i = k$. Equation (*) claims that φ is equivalent to $q \vee (p \wedge \bigcirc \varphi)$ at all positions. Since q holds at k, so does $q \vee (p \wedge \bigcirc \varphi)$ and, consequently, so does φ.

Complete the proof by showing the induction step, inferring $(\sigma, i) \vDash \varphi$ from $(\sigma, i+1) \vDash \varphi$ for all i, $j \leq i < k$.

(c) Show that $p \, \mathcal{W} \, q$ is also a solution of (*).

'(d) Show that $p \, \mathcal{W} \, q$ is the maximal solution of (*). That is, if φ is any other solution of (*) then

$$\varphi \sqsubseteq p \, \mathcal{W} \, q.$$

Consider an arbitrary sequence σ. Show that all positions satisfying φ must also satisfy $p \, \mathcal{W} \, q$.

(e) Consider the equation

$$X \Leftrightarrow (p \wedge \bigcirc X \wedge \widetilde{\ominus} X).$$

Find its minimal and maximal solutions.

(f) Find minimal and maximal solutions to the equation

$$X \Leftrightarrow (p \vee \bigcirc X \vee \ominus X).$$

Problem 3.6 (specification of a sequence)   page 214

Let x be a flexible integer variable. Consider a state sequence σ, which has the general form

$$\langle x \colon 0 \rangle, \ \ldots, \ \langle x \colon 0 \rangle, \ \langle x \colon 2 \rangle, \ \ldots, \ \langle x \colon 2 \rangle, \ \langle x \colon 4 \rangle, \ \ldots, \ \langle x \colon 4 \rangle, \ \langle x \colon 6 \rangle, \ \ldots \, .$$

That is, σ consists of infinitely many finite segments where, in each segment, x assumes the value of an even natural number, and successive segments correspond to successive even numbers.

(a) Write a formula that specifies sequences of this form, using rigid quantification, the boolean operators, and $\bigcirc$, $\square$ as the only temporal operators.

(b) Write a formula specifying such sequences, using $\ominus$, $\square$ as the only temporal operators.

(c) Write a formula specifying such sequences, using all temporal operators, except for $\bigcirc$, $\ominus$, and $\widetilde{\ominus}$.

Problem 3.7 (removing *next* or *previous*)   page 214

The operators $\bigcirc$, $\ominus$, and $\widetilde{\ominus}$ are called the *immediate operators*.

(a) Show that any quantifier-free formula is equivalent to a formula in which the only immediate operators are $\ominus$ and $\widetilde{\ominus}$. We refer to such a formula as a *next-free* formula.

Transformation to next-free form can be done in two stages. The first stage moves all *next* operators to the front of the formula and obtains a formula of the form $\bigcirc^k \varphi$ (i.e., $\underbrace{\bigcirc \cdots \bigcirc}_{k} \varphi$), where φ is next-free. To move the *next* operator across future operators, we may use congruences CN1–CN3 presented in Section 3.4 and additional congruences such as

$$p\,\mathcal{W}(\bigcirc q) \approx \bigcirc((\bigcirc p)\,\mathcal{W}\,q).$$

To move the next operator across past operators, we may use congruences such as

$$\ominus \bigcirc p \approx (\neg\textit{first} \wedge p)$$

$$\boxminus \bigcirc p \approx (\bigcirc p \wedge \boxminus(\textit{first} \vee p)).$$

The second stage transforms the formula $\bigcirc^k \varphi$ into a next-free formula, expressing by means of nonimmediate operators and the operator $\ominus$ the property that φ holds at position k.

Assume that the size of the original formula is n, where the size counts the number of variables and operators in the formula. Give a bound on the size of the transformed next-free formula as a function of n.

(b) Show that any quantifier-free formula is equivalent to a *previous-free* formula, i.e., a formula in which the only immediate operator is $\bigcirc$. The formula may use the special predicate *first*.

Problem 3.8 (formal proofs)   page 232

Consider the following deductive system for propositional temporal logic. As in the text, we take $\bigcirc$, $\mathcal{W}$, $\widetilde{\ominus}$, and $\mathcal{B}$ as basic operators and other operators as derived, using the definitions given in Section 3.6.

- Axioms: FX0–FX8, PX1–PX8 and
  TGI: $\vdash \Box\,\varphi[\alpha]$ for a state-valid formula φ and a replacement α.

  Axiom TGI (tautology-generalization-instantiation) is a combination of axiom TAU and rules GEN and INST.

- Rules: MP.

Use this system for a formal derivation of the rules and theorems listed here.

Rule PAR: $\Box p \vdash p$

Rule E-MP (for $n = 1$): $p \Rightarrow q,\ \Box p \vdash \Box q$

Rule E-MP: $(p_1 \wedge \cdots \wedge p_n) \Rightarrow q,\qquad \Box p_1,\ \ldots,\ \Box p_n \vdash \Box q$

Rule $\Rightarrow$ T ($\Rightarrow$ Transitivity):

$$p \Rightarrow q,\ q \Rightarrow r\ \vdash p \Rightarrow r$$

Rule R1: $p \Leftrightarrow q \vdash p \Rightarrow q$

Rule R2: $p \Rightarrow q, \quad q \Rightarrow p \vdash p \Leftrightarrow q$

Rule $\bigcirc$G ($\bigcirc$ Generalization):
$$\Box p \vdash \Box \bigcirc p$$

Rule $\bigcirc$M ($\bigcirc$ Monotonicity):
(a) $p \Rightarrow q \vdash \bigcirc p \Rightarrow \bigcirc q$

(b) $p \Leftrightarrow q \vdash \bigcirc p \Leftrightarrow \bigcirc q$

Theorem T1: $\bigcirc(p \wedge q) \Leftrightarrow (\bigcirc p \wedge \bigcirc q)$

Theorem T2: $\bigcirc(p \vee q) \Leftrightarrow (\bigcirc p \vee \bigcirc q)$

Rule CI (Computational Induction):
$$p \Rightarrow \bigcirc p \vdash p \Rightarrow \Box p$$

Theorem T3: $\Box p \Leftrightarrow (p \wedge \bigcirc \Box p)$

Theorem T4: $\Box p \Rightarrow p$

Theorem T5: $\Box p \Rightarrow \bigcirc \Box p$

Theorem T6: $\Box p \Rightarrow \bigcirc p$

Theorem T7: $\Box p \Leftrightarrow \Box \Box p$

Rule $\Box$G: $\Box p \vdash \Box \Box p$

Rule $\Box$M: $p \Rightarrow q \vdash \Box p \Rightarrow \Box q$

Rule $\Box$I ($\Box$ Introduction):
$$q \Rightarrow (p \wedge \bigcirc q) \vdash q \Rightarrow \Box p$$

Theorem T8: $\Box p \Rightarrow \Box \bigcirc p$

Theorem T9: $\Box(p \wedge q) \Leftrightarrow (\Box p \wedge \Box q)$

Theorem T10: $p \Rightarrow \Diamond p$

Theorem T11: $\Diamond p \Leftrightarrow \Diamond \Diamond p$

Rule $\Diamond$M: $p \Rightarrow q \vdash \Diamond p \Rightarrow \Diamond q$

Theorem T12: $\Diamond(p \vee q) \Leftrightarrow (\Diamond p \vee \Diamond q)$

Rule $\Diamond$T: $p \Rightarrow \Diamond q, \quad q \Rightarrow \Diamond r \vdash p \Rightarrow \Diamond r$

Rule $\Diamond$C ($\Diamond$ Confluence):
$$p \Rightarrow \Diamond(q \vee r), \quad q \Rightarrow \Diamond t, \quad r \Rightarrow \Diamond t \vdash p \Rightarrow \Diamond t$$

Theorem T13: $\Diamond p \Leftrightarrow p \vee \bigcirc \Diamond p$

Rule $\Diamond$I: $(p \vee \bigcirc q) \Rightarrow q \vdash \Diamond p \Rightarrow q$

Rule $\widetilde{\ominus}$G: $\qquad\qquad \Box p \vdash \Box \widetilde{\ominus} p$

Rule $\widetilde{\ominus}$M: $\qquad\qquad p \Rightarrow q \vdash \widetilde{\ominus} \Rightarrow \widetilde{\ominus} q$

Theorem T14: $\qquad\qquad \widetilde{\ominus}(p \wedge q) \Leftrightarrow (\widetilde{\ominus}p \wedge \widetilde{\ominus}q)$

Theorem T15: $\qquad\qquad \widetilde{\ominus}(p \vee q) \Leftrightarrow (\widetilde{\ominus}p \vee \widetilde{\ominus}q)$

Theorem T16: $\qquad\qquad \neg\widetilde{\ominus}p \Leftrightarrow \ominus \neg p$

Rule $\ominus$M: $\qquad\qquad p \Rightarrow q \vdash \ominus p \Rightarrow \ominus q$

Theorem T17: $\qquad\qquad \ominus(p \wedge q) \Leftrightarrow (\ominus p \wedge \ominus q)$

Theorem T18: $\qquad\qquad \ominus(p \vee q) \Leftrightarrow (\ominus p \vee \ominus q)$

Rule $\boxminus$G: $\qquad\qquad \Box p \vdash \Box \boxminus p$

Rule $\boxminus$M: $\qquad\qquad p \Rightarrow q \vdash \boxminus p \Rightarrow \boxminus q$

Rule RI (Reverse Induction):

$\qquad\qquad\qquad\quad p \Rightarrow \widetilde{\ominus}p \vdash p \Rightarrow \boxminus p$

Theorem T19: $\qquad\qquad \boxminus p \Leftrightarrow p \wedge \widetilde{\ominus}\boxminus p$

Rule $\boxminus$I: $\qquad\qquad q \Rightarrow (p \wedge \widetilde{\ominus}q) \vdash q \Rightarrow \boxminus p$

Theorem T20: $\qquad\qquad \boxminus p \Rightarrow p$

Theorem T21: $\qquad\qquad \boxminus p \Rightarrow \widetilde{\ominus}\boxminus p$

Theorem T22: $\qquad\qquad \boxminus p \Rightarrow \widetilde{\ominus}p$

Theorem T23: $\qquad\qquad \boxminus p \Leftrightarrow \boxminus \boxminus p$

Theorem T24: $\qquad\qquad \boxminus p \Rightarrow \boxminus \widetilde{\ominus}p$

Rule $\boxminus$PG ($\boxminus$ Past Generalization):

$\qquad\qquad\qquad\quad \boxminus p \vdash \boxminus \boxminus p$

Theorem T25: $\qquad\qquad \boxminus(p \wedge q) \Leftrightarrow (\boxminus p \wedge \boxminus q)$

Theorem T26: $\qquad\qquad p \Rightarrow \diamondsuit p$

Theorem T27: $\qquad\qquad \diamondsuit p \Leftrightarrow \diamondsuit \diamondsuit p$

Rule $\diamondsuit$M: $\qquad\qquad p \Rightarrow q \vdash \diamondsuit p \Rightarrow \diamondsuit q$

Theorem T28: $\qquad\qquad \diamondsuit(p \vee q) \Leftrightarrow (\diamondsuit p \vee \diamondsuit q)$

Rule $\diamondsuit$T: $\qquad\qquad p \Rightarrow \diamondsuit q, \quad q \Rightarrow \diamondsuit r \vdash p \Rightarrow \diamondsuit r$

Rule $\diamondsuit$C: $\qquad\qquad p \Rightarrow \diamondsuit(q \vee r), \quad q \Rightarrow \diamondsuit t, \quad r \Rightarrow \diamondsuit t \vdash p \Rightarrow \diamondsuit t$

Theorem T29: $\qquad\qquad \diamondsuit p \Leftrightarrow (p \vee \ominus \diamondsuit p)$

Rule $\diamondsuit$I: $\qquad\qquad (p \vee \ominus q) \Rightarrow q \vdash \diamondsuit p \Rightarrow q$

Rule $\mathcal{W}$I:	$r \Rightarrow (q \vee (p \wedge \bigcirc r)) \vdash r \Rightarrow p\,\mathcal{W}\,q$
Rule $\mathcal{W}$M:	$p \Rightarrow p', \quad q \Rightarrow q' \vdash p\,\mathcal{W}\,q \Rightarrow p'\,\mathcal{W}\,q'$
Theorem T30:	$\square((\neg p)\,\mathcal{W}\,p)$
Theorem T31:	$(p \wedge q)\,\mathcal{W}\,r \Leftrightarrow (p\,\mathcal{W}\,r \wedge q\,\mathcal{W}\,r)$
Theorem T32:	$p\,\mathcal{W}\,(q \vee r) \Leftrightarrow (p\,\mathcal{W}\,q \vee p\,\mathcal{W}\,r)$
Theorem T33:	$(p\,\mathcal{W}\,q)\,\mathcal{W}\,q \Leftrightarrow p\,\mathcal{W}\,q$
Theorem T34:	$p\,\mathcal{W}\,(p\,\mathcal{W}\,q) \Leftrightarrow p\,\mathcal{W}\,q$
Rule $\mathcal{W}$T:	$p \Rightarrow q\,\mathcal{W}\,r, \quad r \Rightarrow q\,\mathcal{W}\,t \vdash p \Rightarrow q\,\mathcal{W}\,t$
Theorem T35:	$(p\,\mathcal{W}\,q \wedge (\neg q)\,\mathcal{W}\,r) \Rightarrow p\,\mathcal{W}\,r$
Theorem T36:	$(p\,\mathcal{W}\,q)\,\mathcal{W}\,r \Rightarrow (p \vee q)\,\mathcal{W}\,r$
Theorem T37:	$p\,\mathcal{W}\,(q\,\mathcal{W}\,r) \Rightarrow (p \vee q)\,\mathcal{W}\,r$
Theorem T38:	$\square((\neg p)\,\mathcal{W}\,q \vee (\neg q)\,\mathcal{W}\,p)$
Theorem T39:	$\square \diamondsuit \widetilde{\ominus} \mathsf{F}$
Theorem T40:	$\boxminus p \Rightarrow p\,\mathcal{B}\,q$
Rule $\mathcal{B}$I:	$r \Rightarrow (q \vee (p \wedge \widetilde{\ominus} r)) \vdash r \Rightarrow p\,\mathcal{B}\,q$
Rule $\mathcal{B}$M:	$p \Rightarrow p', \quad q \Rightarrow q' \vdash p\,\mathcal{B}\,q \Rightarrow p'\,\mathcal{B}\,q'$
Theorem T41:	$\square((\neg p)\,\mathcal{B}\,p)$
Theorem T42:	$(p \wedge q)\,\mathcal{B}\,r \Leftrightarrow (p\,\mathcal{B}\,r \wedge q\,\mathcal{B}\,r)$
Theorem T43:	$p\,\mathcal{B}\,(q \vee r) \Leftrightarrow (p\,\mathcal{B}\,q \vee p\,\mathcal{B}\,r)$
Theorem T44:	$(p\,\mathcal{B}\,q)\,\mathcal{B}\,q \Leftrightarrow p\,\mathcal{B}\,q$
Theorem T45:	$p\,\mathcal{B}\,(p\,\mathcal{B}\,q) \Leftrightarrow p\,\mathcal{B}\,q$
Rule $\mathcal{B}$T:	$p \Rightarrow q\,\mathcal{B}\,r, \quad r \Rightarrow q\,\mathcal{B}\,t \vdash p \Rightarrow q\,\mathcal{B}\,t$
Theorem T46:	$(p\,\mathcal{B}\,q \wedge (\neg q)\,\mathcal{B}\,r) \Rightarrow p\,\mathcal{B}\,r$
Theorem T47:	$(p\,\mathcal{B}\,q)\,\mathcal{B}\,r \Rightarrow (p \vee q)\,\mathcal{B}\,r$
Theorem T48:	$p\,\mathcal{B}\,(q\,\mathcal{B}\,r) \Rightarrow (p \vee q)\,\mathcal{B}\,r$
Theorem T49:	$\square((\neg p)\,\mathcal{B}\,q \vee (\neg q)\,\mathcal{B}\,p).$

Problem 3.9 (the floating version of temporal logic)   page 233

Some of the literature on temporal logics uses a different variant of the logic, to which we refer as the *floating version* of temporal logic. The syntax of the floating version is identical to the one presented here, but the semantics is different.

For a formula p and a model σ, we write

$$\sigma \vDash_{fl} p \qquad \text{iff} \qquad (\sigma, j) \vDash p \text{ for all } j \geq 0$$

and say that p is *universally valid* over σ. The subscript fl affiliates this notion of validity with the floating semantics.

- A formula p is called *universally satisfiable* if $\sigma \vDash_{fl} p$ for some model σ.

- A formula p is called *universally valid*, denoted by $\vDash_{fl} p$, if $\sigma \vDash_{fl} p$ for all models σ. We refer to $\vDash_{fl} p$ also as *floating validity*.

Note that the formula $first = \neg \ominus \text{T}$ is (standardly) satisfiable but is not universally satisfiable. This is because there is no model σ such that $\neg \ominus \text{T}$ holds at all positions of σ.

(a) Show the following relations between standard validity and universal (floating) validity:

$$\vDash p \qquad \text{iff} \qquad \vDash_{fl} first \rightarrow p$$
$$\vDash \Box p \qquad \text{iff} \qquad \vDash_{fl} p.$$

The following deductive system may be used to establish floating validity of propositional temporal formulas. As in the standard case, the operators $\bigcirc$, $\mathcal{W}$, $\ominus$, and $\mathcal{B}$ are taken as basic, and the other operators defined in terms of the basic ones. See Section 3.6 for these definitions. We write $\vdash_{fl} p$ to denote that p is provable by the floating deductive system presented here.

Axioms

FF1. $\bigcirc(\neg p) \leftrightarrow \neg \bigcirc p$	FP1. $\ominus p \rightarrow \widetilde{\ominus} p$
FF2. $\bigcirc(p \rightarrow q) \leftrightarrow (\bigcirc p \rightarrow \bigcirc q)$	FP2. $\widetilde{\ominus}(p \rightarrow q) \leftrightarrow (\widetilde{\ominus} p \rightarrow \widetilde{\ominus} q)$
FF3. $\Box(p \rightarrow q) \rightarrow (\Box p \rightarrow \Box q)$	FP3. $\boxminus(p \rightarrow q) \rightarrow (\boxminus p \rightarrow \boxminus q)$
FF4. $\Box p \rightarrow \bigcirc p$	FP4. $\boxminus p \rightarrow \widetilde{\ominus} p$
FF5. $\Box(p \rightarrow \bigcirc p) \rightarrow (p \rightarrow \Box p)$	FP5. $\boxminus(p \rightarrow \widetilde{\ominus} p) \rightarrow (p \rightarrow \boxminus p)$
FF6. $p \mathcal{W} q \leftrightarrow [q \vee (p \wedge \bigcirc(p \mathcal{W} q))]$	FP6. $p \mathcal{B} q \leftrightarrow [q \vee (p \wedge \widetilde{\ominus}(p \mathcal{B} q))]$
FF7. $\Box p \rightarrow p \mathcal{W} q$	FP7. $\Diamond \widetilde{\ominus} \text{F}$
FF8. $p \rightarrow \bigcirc \ominus p$	FP8. $p \rightarrow \widetilde{\ominus} \bigcirc p$

TAU_{fl}: $\vdash_{fl} p$, for each propositional tautology p.

Rules

INST$_{f\!l}$:   For a formula p and a (possibly temporal) replacement α

$$p \vdash_{f\!l} p[\alpha].$$

MP$_{f\!l}$: $p \to q, p \vdash_{f\!l} q.$

GEN$_{f\!l}$: $p \vdash_{f\!l} \Box p$ and $p \vdash_{f\!l} \boxminus p.$

(b) Show that the same relations holding between standard and floating validity hold between standard and floating provability. That is,

$$\vdash p \qquad \text{iff} \qquad \vdash_{f\!l} \text{ first} \to p$$

$$\vdash \Box p \qquad \text{iff} \qquad \vdash_{f\!l} p.$$

Consider, for example, the claim that if p is provable by the standard deductive system (i.e., $\vdash p$) then *first* $\to p$ is provable using the floating deductive system. To establish this claim, one has to show that every proof of $\vdash p$ can be transformed into a proof of $\vdash_{f\!l} (\text{first} \to p)$. In this case it is enough to show that each axiom φ of the standard system corresponds to a theorem $\vdash_{f\!l} (\text{first} \to \varphi)$ of the floating system, and that each rule $p_1, \ldots, p_m \vdash q$ of the standard system corresponds to a derived rule

$$\text{first} \to p_1, \ \ldots, \ \text{first} \to p_m \ \vdash_{f\!l} \text{first} \to q$$

of the floating system.

As a representative standard deductive system, use the system presented in Problem 3.8.

Bibliographic Notes

Philosophical considerations of time are as old as philosophy itself. Their origins can be attributed to Thales and Zeno as well as to the Bible. There are several views concerning the development of temporal logic and its position with respect to modal logic. Modal logic is concerned with the notions of *necessity* and *possibility* and flourished in medieval times when it served as a tool for theological argumentation. The presently widely accepted possible worlds semantics for modal (and temporal) logics was developed by Kripke [1963]. For modern introductions on modal logic see Hughes and Cresswell [1968] and Chellas [1980].

According to one view, temporal logic evolved from modal logic by interpreting the modal operators in a time-dependent context, or, alternatively, by specializing the logic to *time modalities*. The *Master Argument* of the Stoic logician Diodorus Chronus provides a central classical example of temporalized modal considerations. This view is advocated by Rescher and Urquhart [1971] and Goldblatt [1987].

Another approach and motivation for the study of temporal logic is through the logical analysis of natural languages. It views the development of temporal logic as the formalization of linguistic conventions with regard to tenses into a formal calculus. The fundamental observations of McTaggart that stimulated this approach are surveyed in McTaggart [1927]. This approach is fully applied in the monumental work of Prior summarized in Prior [1967]. Other central works that adopt the linguistic view are Kamp [1968], Gabbay [1976] and van Benthem [1983].

Gabbay [1976]: "In modal logics we are given the syntactical system that formalizes some notions [e.g. S1–S5 tried to formalize necessity and possibility] and we find a convenient class of structures for which the system is complete. In tense logic we are interested in a class of structures and ask, is there a logic X (or a set of axioms) that 'characterizes' this class?"

Temporal Logic in Computer Science: General surveys on the role of temporal logic in computer science include Pnueli [1986a], Goldblatt [1987], and Emerson [1989].

A temporal-like calculus for the specification and reasoning about sequential programs was proposed by Kröger [1977a]. The application of temporal logic to the specification and reasoning about concurrent programs was first proposed by Pnueli [1977], and a temporal semantics for reactive programs was proposed by Pnueli [1981].

Some of the earlier applications of temporal logic for the specification and verification of concurrent programs are reported by Hailpern [1982], Hailpern and Owicki [1980], Owicki and Lamport [1982], and Lamport [1983c].

The literature contains many versions of temporal logic. The basic sets of primitive operators and the rules for the formation of well-defined formulas impose syntactical differences between these versions. On the semantic level, the sets of models on which the temporal formulas are interpreted vary in several respects. Their structure may be either linear or branching. Their sizes may be finite, infinite on one or all directions or mixed. Their density may be discrete or dense, where the density might have the characteristics of the rational numbers, real numbers, etc. A more classical criterion distinguishes between propositional, first-order, or higher-order logics.

Propositional Temporal Logic: The strict *until* and *since* operators were introduced into linear-time temporal logic by Kamp [1968], and shown to be more expressive than $\Box$ and $\Diamond$ alone, regardless of the density of the models. Kamp also proved the expressive completeness (relative to the first-order monadic theory of linear orders) of propositional linear temporal logic with both *until* and *since* operators. The expressive completeness of the future fragment alone was

obtained by Gabbay, Pnueli, Shelah and Stavi [1980a] together with a complete
proof system called DUX and a proof of decidability of the satisfiability problem.
These results apply to both the strict and the reflexive versions of the operators.
Lichtenstein, Pnueli and Zuck [1985] reintroduced the past fragment for the sake
of clear and uniform specifications and accordingly extends DUX to a complete
proof system for the logic that includes both future and past operators. The complexity of deciding the satisfiability problem for several propositional linear-time
logics over discrete models is analyzed by Sistla and Clarke [1985].

Extended Propositional Temporal Logic: An extension with right-linear grammar
operators, called ETL, was suggested by Wolper [1983], showing that it leads to a
greater expressive power, in fact the same as the *second-order* monadic theory of
linear orders. Wolper [1983] also proposes a deductive proof system for ETL, which
was shown to be complete, after some corrections, by Banieqbal and Barringer
[1986]. An alternative approach to ETL is via finite automata on infinite words as
proposed by Wolper, Vardi and Sistla [1983], and elaborated by Sistla, Vardi and
Wolper [1987].

First-Order Temporal Logic: A proof system for first-order temporal logic is given
by Manna and Pnueli [1983c]. Abadi and Manna [1990] consider several proof
systems for first-order temporal logic and prove the inherent incompleteness of
the logic. The notions of program validity and relative completeness are discussed
by Manna and Pnueli [1983a, 1989b].

Quantification: Rigid quantification was introduced in Manna and Pnueli [1981b].
Flexible quantification over propositions is considered by Sistla [1983] and Wolper
[1983], and its complexity is analyzed in Sistla, Vardi and Wolper [1987]. The
general issue of quantification in a modal context is surveyed by Garson [1984]
and motivated in Bacon [1980].

Fixpoints: The connection between temporal logic and fixpoints and the fact that
all temporal operators can be defined in terms of *next* and fixpoints was pointed
out by Emerson and Clarke [1981] and used in the branching-time framework by
Clarke and Emerson [1981] and Clarke, Emerson and Sistla [1986].

   The right-linear grammar operators introduced by Wolper [1983] are in fact
restricted fixpoint operators. Barringer, Kuiper and Pnueli [1984] extends the
temporal language with fixpoint operators that are applied only to positive formulas. Such operators can be shown to be well defined by Tarski's lemma of
Tarski [1955]. Lichtenstein [1990] shows the noncontinuity of these operators and
presents a proof system for a restricted version of the logic. The complexity of
this extended logic is analyzed in Vardi [1988].

   Connections between fixpoints and *dynamic logic*, which is a richer language
than temporal logic, were indicated by Kozen [1983] and Pratt [1981a].

Derived Operators: Some new temporal operators can be derived from the primitive ones. Nevertheless, different systems can be defined with different primitive

operators and other derived ones.

Next: The next operator was introduced as a primitive operator by Manna and Pnueli [1979]. It can be derived from the strict until operator, or alternatively, obtained in terms of the reflexive until and flexible quantification. Lamport [1983d] strongly objects to the use of the next operator in a specification language, claiming that it enables the expression of distinctions between programs that should be considered equivalent. He consistently uses a temporal language with reflexive operators and no *next*.

Precede and Unless: The precede operator is derived from the until operator in Manna and Pnueli [1981b]. The weak until, or unless operator, is introduced in Manna and Pnueli [1983c] where it serves for a uniform representation of precedence properties previously expressed in terms of precede and until.

Leads-to and Entails: The *leads-to* operator, defined in terms of the henceforth and eventually operators, is introduced in Owicki and Lamport [1982] as an essential operator in the specification of program behavior. Modal implication (or entailment), as a stronger concept than logical (or material) implication, is a basic concept of modal logic, and is considered an independent operator in Hughes and Cresswell [1968]. In the context of temporal logic applied to computer science, its importance is stressed in the anchored framework of Manna and Pnueli [1989a].

Past Operators: As already mentioned, classical temporal logic, as defined by Kamp [1968], includes both past and future operators. Gabbay, Pnueli, Shelah and Stavi [1980b] pointed out that restricting the language to its future fragment does not decrease its expressive power and, therefore, recommended using only this fragment for specification and verification. A different opinion is expressed by Lichtenstein, Pnueli and Zuck [1985] (see also Pnueli [1986a]), where it is pointed out that past operators prove helpful in modular reasoning about programs and leads to a more uniform classification of program properties expressible in temporal logic. Past operators were also used by Koymans and de Roever [1983] to specify a buffer.

Branching-Temporal Logic: Different axiomatizations and their corresponding branching-time structures are considered in Rescher and Urquhart [1971]. The logic UB (unified branching) introduced by Ben-Ari, Manna and Pnueli [1981] was the first to use explicit *path operators*. This work contains a complete proof system for UB, whose completeness is proved for the first time using the semantic-tableaux technique. Analogously to the linear-time logics, UB has been extended several times resulting in more expressive logics. The following extensions follow the initial ideas and questions raised by Lamport [1980a]. The computation tree logic CTL was developed by Emerson and Clarke [1981, 1982], and its expressiveness and complexity were analyzed by Emerson and Halpern [1985]. The logic CTL* was developed and analyzed by Emerson and Halpern [1986] and its complexity was established by Emerson and Jutla [1988]. The branching analog of ETL, ECTL*, was defined by Vardi and Wolper [1983]. Lehmann and Shelah [1982] consider a probabilistic branching-time logic. Flexible quantification in a branching framework was considered by Emerson and Sistla [1984]. The full power of branching-time logic was employed by Pnueli and Rosner [1988] in order to express the implementability of linear-time temporal specifications.

Partial-Order Temporal Logic: A temporal logic whose domain of interpretation is a partial order was first proposed by Pinter and Wolper [1984]. An approach that combines syntactical and semantical features from both linear and branching temporal logic, called *interleaving-sets* logic, is presented in Katz and Peled [1987]. It leads to a logic that corresponds to the partial order semantics of programs, traditionally applied in the context of Petri nets. Other partial order temporal logics were proposed by Reisig [1989].

Interval Temporal Logic: Motivated by the will to simplify specifications of concurrent programs, Schwartz, Milliar-Smith and Vogt [1983a] proposes a temporal logic which explicitly refers to finite time intervals. A different approach taken in Moszkowski [1983] extends linear temporal logic with the *chop* operator, analogous to word concatenation in formal language theory, while extending the class of models to both finite and infinite ones. The nonelementary complexity of the propositional level of the resulting logic is established in Halpern, Manna and Moszkowski [1983], and a complete proof system is provided in Rosner and Pnueli [1986].

Continuous Temporal Logic: A proof system for temporal logic over a continuous time domain appears in Burgess [1982]. The decidability of the satisfiability problem for linear temporal logic over continuous linear models is analyzed in Burgess and Gurevich [1985]. Application of continuous-time temporal logics to the specification and reasoning about real-time systems include Barringer,Kuiper and Pnueli [1986], Koymans and de Roever [1983], and Alur, Feder and Henzinger [1991].

Discrete Real Time Logics: A simpler treatment of timing properties by temporal logic assumes that time progresses in discrete units, e.g., can only assume nonnegative integer values. Real time logics based on discrete time steps were presented by Koymans, Vytopyl and de Roever [1983], Ostroff [1989], Alur and Henzinger [1989, 1990], Harel, Lichtenstein and Pnueli [1990], and Henzinger, Manna and Pnueli [1991].

Finite models: Classical temporal logic as defined by Kamp [1968] was interpreted only over infinite sequences of states. To deal with programs that may terminate or deadlock, every finite computation can be extended to an infinite sequence by an idling transition (such as τ_I introduced in Chapter 1), or by stuttering. Some attempts were made, for example, by Pnueli [1986a] and Lichtenstein, Pnueli and Zuck [1985], to consider both finite and infinite sequences as models for temporal formulas. One of the consequences of this attempt is that the *next* operator, as in the case of the *previous* operator, has to be split into a *strong* and a *weak* versions. The strong *next* can hold only at a position which is not the last in the model.

Chandy and Misra [1988] introduce a specification language for the description of properties of *Unity* programs. The basic operators of this language are called *unless, ensures,* and *leads-to.* Even though these operators are closely related to the temporal language and its approach to specification, they cannot be simply expressed in temporal logic.

Anchored Temporal Logic: For temporal logics that do not incorporate past operators, floating and anchored versions coincide. Once past operators are introduced, the two versions differ in their notions of validity and satisfiability. The original logics of Prior and Kamp can be characterized as floating ones. The reintroduction of past in Lichtenstein, Pnueli and Zuck [1985] considers a floating logic too. The introduction of the anchored version of temporal logic, motivated by the search for a uniform syntactical characterization of the hierarchy of temporal properties to be introduced in the next chapter, is first considered by Manna and Pnueli [1989a]. The deductive system presented in this chapter is a variation on the one presented there.

Temporal Logic Based Programming Languages: There are several approaches to the incorporation of temporal logic concepts into programming languages. Two programming languages based on the interval temporal logic of Moszkowski [1983], are TEMPURA, described in Moszkowski [1986], and TOKYO, described in Fujita, Kono, Tanaka and Moto-oka [1986]. Semantic considerations of temporal logic programming appear in Abadi and Manna [1989] and Baudinet [1989].

Applications to Artificial Intelligence: Motivated by the need to formally describe the behavior and knowledge of entities such as robots, AI researchers have developed several temporal formalisms considered to be especially suitable for AI applications. These include the interval-based logic of Ellen [1984], the state-based temporal logic of McDermott [1982] and its interval-based generalization in Shoham [1988].

Chapter 4
Properties of Programs

In this chapter we will illustrate the use of temporal logic for specifying properties of programs. To introduce some structure in the extensive set of program properties, we define a hierarchy of the properties expressible by temporal logic, which is based on the types of formulas used to express the properties. We consider, in turn, each class in the hierarchy of temporal properties and present examples of concrete properties that fall into this class.

Formulas expressing properties of programs consist of *local formulas*, to which we apply the temporal and other logical operators. The local formulas describe properties of individual states and of the transitions leading into states.

First we survey the local language, which is appropriate for expressing these local properties.

4.1   The Local Language

In writing formulas over programs, it is often convenient to use special predicates that refer to specific aspects of the control, such as whether a given statement is ready to be executed or whether a certain value has been communicated along a channel in the last step. Some of these predicates have been introduced in the preceding chapters. Here we review these and introduce some additional predicates. All the predicates considered are local predicates, which depend at most on information contained in a single state and its immediate predecessor.

The *local language* is a first-order language over two types of local predicates: state predicates and transition predicates. State predicates are evaluated over a single state. Transition predicates are evaluated over a pair of states: a state and its immediate predecessor. It follows that every state formula is a *local formula*, i.e., a formula written in the local language.

The constructs that we include in the local language usually depend on the particular concrete model we study. Since most of our examples are taken from the text programming language, we concentrate on the development of a local language suitable for text programs.

Location Predicates

First, we consider state predicates that identify the location of control in a state of a computation.

at$\_\ell$, at$\_S$

For a statement $\ell\colon S$, predicate

$$at\_\ell\colon \quad [\ell] \in \pi$$

holds at a state if control is currently in front of the statement S. Sometimes we refer to S by writing at_S, which has the same meaning as at_ℓ. The definition refers to the control variable π, which ranges over sets of locations, where each location is an equivalence class of labels.

In some cases we want to specify that control is somewhere within a set of locations. We use the notation $at\_\ell_{i_1,\ldots,i_k}$ to denote the disjunction:

$$at\_\ell_{i_1,\ldots,i_k} \;=\; at\_\ell_{i_1} \vee \cdots \vee at\_\ell_{i_k}.$$

In the case that $i_1,\ldots,i_k$ form an interval of consecutive integers we may use an abbreviated interval notation $at\_\ell_{i..j}$, i.e.,

$$at\_\ell_{i..j} \;=\; at\_\ell_i \vee at\_\ell_{i+1} \vee \cdots \vee at\_\ell_j.$$

Similar control predicates exist for two other concrete models: the diagram language and Petri nets.

- *Diagram language*

    In the diagram language, control is represented by the control variables $\pi_1,\ldots,\pi_m$, one for each process. A possible site of control is a location ℓ, which is a node in the diagram for one of the processes, say P_i. Consequently, we define

    $$at\_\ell\colon \quad \pi_i = \ell.$$

- *Petri nets*

    For Petri nets, location predicates that have only two values are not enough. Control in Petri nets is represented by the number of tokens currently located at a place p. Consequently, we need the more detailed control information that is represented by the variable N_p, which specifies the number of tokens currently occupying place p.

We may define

$$at\_p: \quad N_p > 0,$$

denoting the fact that there is at least one token at p.

after_S

Let $\ell: S: \widehat{\ell}$ be a fully labeled statement. The state predicate at_S identifies the location of control in a state of a program as being in front of statement S. In some cases, it is more convenient to identify the location of control as being after statement S. In these cases we use the state predicate $after\_S$ (or equivalently $after\_\ell$). We define

$$after\_S: \quad at\_\widehat{\ell}.$$

In some cases we wish to refer to the state of control at the termination of a program P. We therefore introduce the state predicate

$$after\_P,$$

which holds on termination of P. Assuming that the body of P is

$$\ell_1: S_1: \widehat{\ell}_1 \parallel \cdots \parallel \ell_m: S_m: \widehat{\ell}_m,$$

the predicate $after\_P$ is given by

$$after\_P: \quad at\_\widehat{\ell}_1 \wedge \cdots \wedge at\_\widehat{\ell}_m.$$

in_S

For a statement S, define the predicate in_S to hold if at_S' holds for some S', a substatement of S. That is,

$$in\_S: \quad \bigvee_{S' \preccurlyeq S} at\_S'.$$

Enabledness of Transitions

Given a transition τ, the state predicate $enabled(\tau)$ expresses the fact that τ is ready for activation at a given state. Assuming that the transition relation for τ is given by $\rho_\tau(\Pi, \Pi'): C_\tau \wedge (\bar{y}' = \bar{e})$, we can express

$$enabled(\tau): \quad C_\tau.$$

For a set of transitions $T \subseteq \mathcal{T}$, we define $enabled(T)$ to be the disjunction

$$enabled(T): \quad \bigvee_{\tau \in T} enabled(\tau).$$

Terminality Predicate

An important state predicate is the terminality predicate *terminal*. This predicate is defined by

$$terminal \;=\; \bigwedge_{\tau \in \mathcal{T}_D} \neg enabled(\tau)$$

and states that all diligent transitions in the system are disabled.

Obviously, if s_j satisfies *terminal*, then all states following position j are identical to s_j, and the only transition taken beyond j is the idling transition τ_I.

Transition Predicates

All the predicates considered so far are state predicates, which means that in order to check whether they hold at position j in the model, it is sufficient to examine the state s_j. In addition we may need to refer to properties of transitions, which usually involve the state s_j and its immediate predecessor s_{j-1}. We refer to such properties as *transition predicates*. An example of a transition predicate would be one stating that the last transition taken has written the value m onto channel α.

We define a formula to be a *transition formula* if it has the general form

$$\neg first \;\wedge\; \varphi(\Pi^-, \Pi)$$

for some state formula φ. Thus, a transition formula states that the current position is not the first and that φ holds between the previous and current values of (some of) the state variables.

For example, the transition formula $\neg first \wedge (x = x^- + 1)$ is true at a state iff it has a predecessor and the current value of x is one more than the preceding value of x.

While we prefer to express transition predicates by formulas that use the previous-value notation e^-, they can also be expressed without this notation. For example, an equivalent formulation of the formula $\neg first \wedge (x = x^- + 1)$ is the formula

$$\exists u: \ominus (x = u) \;\wedge\; (x = u + 1),$$

which uses the rigid variable u. Note that the conjunct $\ominus (x = u)$ implies $\neg first$.

We present several useful transition predicates and their definitions in terms of transition formulas.

last-taken(τ)

For a transition τ, we define the predicate

$$last\text{-}taken(\tau): \quad \neg first \;\wedge\; \rho_\tau(\Pi^-, \Pi).$$

Clearly $last\text{-}taken(\tau)$ holds at position j of a computation iff $j > 0$ and s_j is a τ-successor of s_{j-1}, i.e., τ was taken at position $j - 1$.

Communication Predicates

For a language that allows communication statements, we need the ability to observe that a communication has taken place in the transition leading to the current state. We use two transition predicates for that purpose. One of them observes the output of a message on a channel, and the other observes the input of a message from a channel.

We consider separately the cases of asynchronous and synchronous communication.

Asynchronous Communication

In the case of asynchronous communication, we can detect the events of sending and receiving messages off a channel α by the changes to the corresponding state variable α. Consequently, we define

$$[\alpha \Leftarrow v]: \quad \neg first \;\wedge\; (\alpha = \alpha^- \bullet v).$$

This predicate denotes a *sending event*. It holds at position $j > 0$, if the transition leading from s_{j-1} to s_j sent the value v to channel α. We detect this by the fact that α equals α^- with v added to it.

In a similar way, we define the *receiving event*

$$[\alpha \Rightarrow v]: \quad \neg first \;\wedge\; (v \bullet \alpha = \alpha^-).$$

This predicate holds at position j iff $j > 0$ and the current value of α equals the previous value α^- minus its first element, which equals v. Clearly, $[\alpha \Rightarrow v]$ holds precisely at the states in which v has just been read from channel α.

Synchronous Communication

In the case of synchronous communication, there are no state variables that represent the list of pending messages for each channel. Therefore, to observe that a synchronous communication has taken place, we should look for the activation of the joint transitions that perform synchronous communication.

Let $\tau_{\langle \ell,m \rangle}$ be a communication transition associated with the pair of matching statements

$$\ell:\; \alpha \Leftarrow e \text{ provided } c_1 \quad\text{and}\quad m:\; \alpha \Rightarrow u \text{ provided } c_2.$$

We define

$$comm(\ell, m, v): \quad last\text{-}taken(\tau_{\langle \ell,m \rangle}) \;\wedge\; (v = e^-).$$

This formula expresses the fact that the joint transition $\tau_{\langle \ell, m \rangle}$ has just been taken and that the value communicated has been $e^- = v$.

We may now take a disjunction over all matching $\langle \ell, m \rangle$ pairs that refer to channel α and define

$$[\alpha \ll v]: \bigvee_{\langle \ell, m \rangle} comm(\ell, m, v).$$

Thus, the sending event $[\alpha \ll v]$ is defined to have taken place iff the last transition taken is a synchronous communication of value v over channel α.

Note that synchronous communication consists of a receiving event together with a sending event. Consequently, in the specification of such systems we will only use the output predicate $[\alpha \ll v]$.

For both synchronous and asynchronous communication, we sometimes need to specify that an input or output on channel α has taken place, without specifying the value communicated. We define the local predicates

$$[\alpha \gg] \quad \text{and} \quad [\alpha \ll]$$

to hold whenever $[\alpha \gg v]$ and $[\alpha \ll v]$ hold for some v, respectively.

Specification Variables

In many cases it is necessary to use variables in addition to the program variables, in order to express a property of the program.

Consider, for example, a program whose only program variable is x. To specify the property that x never decreases below its initial value, we may use the formula

$$\exists u: (x = u) \wedge \Box(x \geq u).$$

This formula uses a rigid variable u to record the value of x at position 0 and to state that, at all positions, x is never smaller than u. We refer to variable u as a *specification variable*.

The save property can also be specified by the universally quantified formula

$$\psi: \quad \forall u: (x = u) \rightarrow \Box(x \geq u).$$

When writing specifications of properties, we often prefer to omit the explicit representation of outer-level universal quantification over specification variables, and write

$$\varphi: \quad (x = u) \rightarrow \Box(x \geq u).$$

It is important to realize that the formula φ is not equivalent to ψ. On the other hand, if u does not appear in program P then φ is valid over P iff ψ is. This is due to the fact that if a model σ corresponds to a computation of P then all

u-variants of σ also correspond to computations of P. Thus, even though φ and ψ are not equivalent, requiring the validity of φ over P is the same as requiring the validity of ψ over P.

4.2 The Classification of Properties

After introducing the local language that describes properties of single states and transitions, we proceed to study more complex properties that can be expressed by formulas that apply various temporal operators to local formulas. As previously indicated, our study of these properties is based on their organization into a hierarchy of properties.

The hierarchy consists of several classes of properties. Each class is characterized by a canonical temporal formula scheme. The class consists of all properties that can be specified by this formula scheme.

As we will see, each class enjoys certain closure properties. In the second volume of this book, which deals with verification, we will show that each class is also associated with a proof principle for verifying that a given program satisfies a property in the class.

Our main interest in this chapter is in the question of what types of properties are expressible in temporal logic and whether temporal logic is powerful enough to express all the interesting properties of reactive systems.

Formally, we may define a property to be any set of infinite sequences. Let Σ be any set of states and denote by Σ^ω the set of all infinite sequences of states. A *property* $\mathcal{P}$ is any subset of Σ^ω.

Consider, for example, a set Σ that consists of the states assigning integer values to variable x. Let $\mathcal{P}$ be the set of sequences such that

> the value of x always increases from each state to its successor.

Then the sequence

$$\langle x\colon 0 \rangle,\ \langle x\colon 2 \rangle,\ \langle x\colon 3 \rangle \cdots$$

belongs to $\mathcal{P}$, while the sequence

$$\langle x\colon 0 \rangle,\ \langle x\colon 2 \rangle,\ \langle x\colon 1 \rangle \cdots$$

does not.

A property $\mathcal{P}$ is said to be *specified* by the temporal formula φ if

$$\sigma \in \mathcal{P} \qquad \text{iff} \qquad \sigma \vDash \varphi.$$

Thus, the previously considered property is specified by the formula

$$\Box(x^+ > x).$$

Clearly, two properties that are specified by two formulas are equal iff the formulas specifying them are equivalent.

There is a close correspondence between boolean operations on formulas and set operations on the properties they specify. Let the formulas p, q specify the properties $\mathcal{P}, \mathcal{Q} \subseteq \Sigma^\omega$, respectively. Then we observe the following correspondence:

$$p \wedge q \quad \text{specifies} \quad \mathcal{P} \cap \mathcal{Q}$$
$$p \vee q \quad \text{specifies} \quad \mathcal{P} \cup \mathcal{Q}$$
$$\neg p \quad \text{specifies} \quad \overline{\mathcal{P}} = \Sigma^\omega - \mathcal{P}.$$

Safety Properties

We define a *canonical safety formula* to be a formula of the form

$$\Box \, p,$$

for a past formula p. Such a formula states that all positions in a computation satisfy p. A *safety formula* is any formula that is equivalent to a canonical safety formula.

A property that can be specified by a safety formula is called a *safety property*.

Usually, safety formulas express invariance of some state property over all computations, or a precedence constraint of the form: if event e_2 ever happens it is preceded by event e_1.

In the simpler case, p is a state formula, and $\Box p$ specifies the invariance property that all states in the computation satisfy p. An example of such a simple safety property is the formula

$$\Box \, (x \geq 0),$$

which specifies that, in all states of the computation, x is nonnegative.

The following example illustrates the more general case in which formula p actually refers to the past and specifies a precedence property.

Example

Consider a reactive program P with an input variable x and output variable y. Initially $x = y = 0$. Program P is expected to respond to an input $x = 1$ by setting y to 2. A natural property one may want to require of P is that y is not set to 2 unnecessarily, that is, y is not changed to 2 unless x had the value 1 in some previous state.

This property can be expressed by the formula

$$\Box \, [(y = 2) \; \rightarrow \; \Diamond \!\!\!\!\Diamond \, (x = 1)],$$

which claims that any state at which $y = 2$ is weakly preceded by a state at which $x = 1$. This formula is obviously a canonical safety formula. The use of weak precedence allows y to become 2 at the same state that x becomes 1. To express (strict) precedence, we can use the operator $\widehat{\diamondsuit}$ instead of $\diamondsuit$.

One may prefer to express the same property by the equivalent formula

$$(y \neq 2) \; \mathcal{W} \; (x = 1).$$

This unless formula states that $y \neq 2$ as long as $x \neq 1$. This formula does not have the canonical form $\square\, p$ for some past formula p, but is equivalent to such a formula.

Nontermination

As another example of a safety property, consider the property of nontermination of a program. A program is said to be nonterminating if none of its computations contains a terminal state. This property can be expressed by the safety formula

$$\square\,(\neg terminal).$$

Closure of Safety Properties

The class of safety properties is closed under the positive set operations, i.e., intersection and union. As stated before, it suffices to show that if φ and ψ are safety formulas, so are $\varphi \wedge \psi$ and $\varphi \vee \psi$.

To see this, we present the following equivalences for the conjunction and disjunction of safety formulas:

$$[\square\, p \,\wedge\, \square\, q] \;\sim\; \square\,(p \,\wedge\, q)$$

$$[\square\, p \,\vee\, \square\, q] \;\sim\; \square\,(\boxminus\, p \,\vee\, \boxminus\, q).$$

The first equivalence is actually a congruence, but here we need only the equivalence of the two sides.

The left-hand side of the second equivalence states, for a computation σ, that either all positions in σ satisfy p or all positions in σ satisfy q. The right-hand side states that for each position i, either all positions $j \leq i$ satisfy p or all positions $j \leq i$ satisfy q.

To see that the left-hand side implies the right-hand side, observe that $\square\, p$ is equivalent to $\square \boxminus p$ and $\square\, q$ is equivalent to $\square \boxminus q$. By monotonicity we can infer that both $\square\, p$ and $\square\, q$ imply $\square\,(\boxminus\, p \vee \boxminus\, q)$.

To see that the right-hand side implies the left-hand side, consider two cases. If all positions in σ satisfy both p and q then the left-hand side follows. If for some j, $(\sigma, j) \not\models p$, then the only way the right-hand side can hold is by having, for all $i \geq j$, $(\sigma, i) \models \boxminus\, q$, from which $\square\, q$ follows.

Since the right-hand sides of both equivalences are canonical safety formulas (under the assumption that p and q are past formulas), this establishes the closure of safety formulas under conjunction and disjunction.

We may conclude that

the class of safety properties is closed under intersection and union.

This means that if $\mathcal{P}$ and $\mathcal{Q}$ are safety properties then so are $\mathcal{P} \cap \mathcal{Q}$ and $\mathcal{P} \cup \mathcal{Q}$.

Conditional Safety

An important formula is the formula of *conditional safety*, in which a property expressed by $\square\, q$ is conditional on a state formula p holding at the first state of the computation. This formula has the form

$$p \rightarrow \square\, q.$$

While not being a canonical safety formula, this formula is a safety formula. This is due to the equivalence

$$(p \rightarrow \square\, q) \ \sim\ \square\, [\diamondsuit\!\!\!\!-\,(p \wedge \mathit{first}) \rightarrow q].$$

The formula on the right, which is a canonical safety formula, states that, at each position j, if j has been preceded by some position $i \leq j$ that satisfies p and is also first (forcing $i = 0$), then q holds at j.

Guarantee Properties

A *canonical guarantee formula* is a formula of the form

$$\diamondsuit\, p,$$

for some past formula p. Such a formula states that at least one position in a computation satisfies p. A *guarantee formula* is any formula that is equivalent to a canonical guarantee formula. A property that can be specified by a guarantee formula is called a *guarantee property*.

Usually, guarantee formulas ensure that some event eventually happens. They guarantee that the event happens at least once, but do not promise any repetitions of the event. Therefore, they are used mainly to ensure events that happen once in the lifetime of a program execution, such as termination.

An example of the simple case in which p is a state formula is the formula

$$\diamondsuit\, \mathit{terminal},$$

which specifies that some state of the computation is terminal. Clearly if all computations of a given program satisfy this formula, the program is terminating.

The following example illustrates the more general case in which p is a past formula.

Example

Reconsider the example of a reactive program P with an input variable x and output variable y and the requirement that P responds to $x = 1$ by making $y = 2$. The safety property we have already considered claims that y will not be turned to 2 before a preceding change of x to 1. A complementary property is specified by the formula

$$\Diamond [(y = 2) \wedge \Diamondsuit (x = 1)],$$

which guarantees that the computation contains a state at which $y = 2$ and is weakly preceded by a state at which $x = 1$.

The same property can also be specified by the equivalent formula

$$\Diamond [(x = 1) \wedge \Diamond (y = 2)],$$

which is not a canonical guarantee formula but is equivalent to one. It is therefore a guarantee formula.

Duality

The class of guarantee properties is not closed under complementation. On the other hand, the complement of a guarantee property is a safety property. Similarly, the complement of a safety property is a guarantee property.

This is due to the following two equivalences:

$$\neg \Diamond p \sim \Box \neg p$$
$$\neg \Box p \sim \Diamond \neg p.$$

For example, from the first equivalence we can immediately conclude that $\mathcal{P}$ is a guarantee property (specifiable by $\Diamond p$) iff the complementary property $\overline{\mathcal{P}} = \Sigma^\omega - \mathcal{P}$ (i.e., the set of all computations not in $\mathcal{P}$) is a safety property (specifiable by $\Box \neg p$).

We say that the classes of guarantee and safety properties are *dual*. Many properties of the guarantee class can be obtained by complementing properties of the safety class.

Closure of Guarantee Properties

In principle, we can justify the closure properties of the guarantee class by using duality and the corresponding closure properties of the safety class. However, we can also give an independent justification.

As is the case with the safety class, the class of guarantee properties is closed under the positive set operations of union and intersection.

This can be shown using the following equivalences:

$$[\Diamond p \vee \Diamond q] \sim \Diamond (p \vee q)$$

$$[\Diamond p \wedge \Diamond q] \sim \Diamond(\Diamondleft p \wedge \Diamondleft q).$$

The second equivalence claims that a computation σ contains both a p-position (a position satisfying p) and a q-position iff it has a position i such that there exist a q-position $j \leq i$ and a p-position $k \leq i$.

Obligation Properties

Some properties cannot be expressed by either safety or guarantee formulas alone and must be expressed by a boolean combination of such formulas. We therefore consider the class of such properties.

A *canonical simple obligation formula* is a formula of the form

$$\Box p \vee \Diamond q,$$

where p and q are past formulas. This formula states that either p holds at all positions of a computation or q holds at some position. A *simple obligation formula* is any formula that is equivalent to a canonical simple obligation formula.

A property that can be specified by a simple obligation formula is called a *simple obligation property*.

An alternative normal form for simple obligation formulas is

$$\Diamond r \rightarrow \Diamond q,$$

which states that if some position satisfies r then some position (possibly the same or earlier) satisfies q.

Example

Consider our example of a reactive program with input x and output y. The guarantee property stated for this program promises both that x will become 1 and that, sometime later, y will become 2. This is not a very satisfactory specification for a reactive program, since usually the program cannot guarantee that the input will eventually become 1.

A more realistic specification would require that if the input x becomes 1, then y will eventually become 2. This can be described by the simple obligation formula

$$\Diamond(x = 1) \rightarrow \Diamond(y = 2).$$

This formula by itself does not capture the natural expectation that y will become 2 only after x has become 1. For example, it also allows computations in which y becomes 2 first, and only later x becomes 1. This contradicts the intuition that $y = 2$ is a response to $x = 1$. This can be corrected by requiring the considered program to satisfy both the safety property $\Box\,((y = 2) \rightarrow \Diamondleft(x = 1))$, claiming that y cannot become 2 before x became 1, and the simple obligation formula.

Alternately, we can incorporate the considered safety requirement into our obligation specification by writing

$$\Diamond(x = 1) \; \rightarrow \; \Diamond\left[(y = 2) \;\wedge\; \boxminus(y \neq 2) \;\wedge\; \Diamonddownarrow(x = 1)\right].$$

In this form we are guaranteed that the first time y turns 2 is weakly preceded by a position at which $x = 1$. ◼

Another normal form for simple obligation formulas is given by

$$p \; \mathcal{W} \; (\Diamond q),$$

which is equivalent to $\Box p \vee \Diamond q$.

General Obligation Properties

The class of simple obligation properties is closed under union. To see this, we observe the trivial equivalence

$$\left[(\Box p_1 \vee \Diamond q_1) \;\vee\; (\Box p_2 \vee \Diamond q_2)\right] \;\sim\; \left[(\Box p_1 \vee \Box p_2) \;\vee\; (\Diamond q_1 \vee \Diamond q_2)\right].$$

Using the closure of both the safety and guarantee formulas under disjunction, this leads to an equivalent simple obligation formula.

However, the class of simple obligation properties is not closed under intersection. This implies that by taking conjunctions of simple obligation formulas we obtain a more powerful class.

We therefore define a *canonical obligation formula* to be a formula of the form

$$\bigwedge_{i=1}^{n} \left[\Box p_i \vee \Diamond q_i\right].$$

where p_i, q_i, $i = 1, \ldots, n$, are past formulas.

An *obligation formula* is any formula that is equivalent to a canonical obligation formula. Correspondingly, a property specifiable by such a formula is called an *obligation property*.

This class is the largest class that can be obtained by taking finite boolean combinations (i.e., intersections, unions, and complementations) of safety and guarantee properties.

Claim

Every boolean combination of safety and guarantee properties is an obligation property.

To see this, consider an arbitrary boolean combination of safety and guarantee formulas. First push all negations into the past formulas, changing $\wedge$ into $\vee$, $\square$ into $\diamondsuit$, and vice versa. Next bring the formula into a conjunctive normal form:

$$\bigwedge_{i=1}^{n} [\square\, p_1^i \vee \cdots \vee \square\, p_{k_i}^i \vee \diamondsuit\, q_1^i \vee \cdots \vee \diamondsuit\, q_{m_i}^i].$$

Then use the closure properties of the safety and guarantee formulas to collapse all of $\square\, p_1^i \vee \cdots \vee \square\, p_{k_i}^i$ into a single safety formula, and $\diamondsuit\, q_1^i \vee \cdots \vee \diamondsuit\, q_{m_i}^i$ into a single guarantee formula.

This claim also implies that the class of obligation properties is closed under all boolean operations.

Inclusion

The class of simple obligation properties strictly contains the classes of safety and guarantee properties. In fact, the property described by the simple obligation formula $\square\, p \vee \diamondsuit\, q$ for propositions p and q cannot be specified by either safety or guarantee formulas alone.

The class of obligation properties forms an infinite strict hierarchy. The class of properties expressible by a conjunction of $n + 1$ simple obligation formulas strictly contains the class corresponding to a conjunction of only n simple obligation formulas.

Problem 4.9(b) requests a proof that the obligation class strictly includes the safety and guarantee classes.

Response Properties

A *canonical response formula* is a formula of the form

$$\square\, \diamondsuit\, p,$$

for some past formula p. It states that infinitely many positions in the computation satisfy p. A *response formula* is any formula that is equivalent to a canonical response formula.

A property that can be specified by a response formula is called a *response property*. Usually, response properties ensure that some event happens infinitely many times. They can express the property of response of a system, stating that every stimulus has a response.

An alternative normal form for response formulas is

$$p \;\Rightarrow\; \diamondsuit\, q, \qquad \text{i.e.,} \qquad \square(p \to \diamondsuit\, q).$$

This formula states that every p-position is followed by or coincides with a q-position. Thus, we may interpret q as a guaranteed response to p.

To see that this is a response formula we use the equivalence

$$(p \Rightarrow \Diamond q) \sim \Box \Diamond ((\neg p) \mathrel{\mathcal{B}} q).$$

The right-hand side of this formula states that there are infinitely many positions in which all previous requests have been responded to. These are positions such that no new requests (represented by p) have been posted since the last response (represented by q). Note that this covers the case that the last request coincided with the last response and (using the back-to operator $\mathcal{B}$) the case in which no request has been made and consequently no response is necessary.

Example

Consider again the example of a reactive program P with an input variable x and output variable y. This time consider a more elaborate behavior of this program, in which, after setting x to 1, the environment may reset it to 0. Program P is required to respond to $x = 1$ by setting y to 2 and to respond to a reset of x to 0 by resetting y to 0.

The property of response to $x = 1$ is expressed by the formula

$$(x = 1) \;\Rightarrow\; \Diamond(y = 2).$$

This formula states that each position in which $x = 1$ is followed by a position in which $y = 2$.

Similarly, the property of response to resets of $x = 0$ is expressed by

$$(x = 0) \;\Rightarrow\; \Diamond(y = 0). \quad \lrcorner$$

Note that the specification in this example does not require that the response follows the stimulus immediately in the next state, but only requires that eventually some response will occur. This tolerance is essential for the description of realistic systems that cannot guarantee immediate response to every stimulus. This asynchronous style of specification, in which no bounds are put on delays such as the time elapsing between stimulus and response, is characteristic of all the specifications we consider in this chapter.

Observe that the preceding specification does not exclude a sluggish response by the program, in which x alternates between 0 and 1 several times before the program responds to both $x = 1$ and $x = 0$. It also does not guarantee a one-to-one correspondence between stimulus and response.

In **Problem 4.1**, the reader will add a requirement to the specification that will exclude sluggishness.

Closure of Response Properties

The class of response properties is closed under the positive boolean operations.

This is shown by the following equivalences:

$$[\Box \Diamond p \vee \Box \Diamond q] \sim \Box \Diamond (p \vee q)$$

$$[\Box \Diamond p \wedge \Box \Diamond q] \sim \Box \Diamond \big(q \wedge \ominus((\neg q)\, \mathcal{S}\, p)\big)_.$$

The first equivalence states that a sequence contains either infinitely many p-positions or infinitely many q-positions iff it contains infinitely many $(p \vee q)$-positions.

To see the second equivalence we will show that a sequence σ satisfies $\Box \Diamond (q \wedge \ominus((\neg q)\, \mathcal{S}\, p))$ iff σ contains infinitely many p-positions as well as infinitely many q-positions.

Let i be a p-position. We define the *closest q-neighbor* of i to be the smallest position $j > i$ that satisfies q (if there exists such a position). We say that j is a q-*neighbor* position if there exists a p-position i such that j is its closest q-neighbor. By definition, it follows that $i < j$, and for all k, $i < k < j$, position k does not satisfy q.

It is not difficult to see that j is a q-neighbor position iff it satisfies $q \wedge \ominus((\neg q)\, \mathcal{S}\, p)$. Next, we will show that σ contains infinitely many p-positions as well as infinitely many q-positions iff it contains infinitely many q-neighbor positions.

Assume that σ contains infinitely many p-positions and infinitely many q-positions. Let i_1 be the first p-position in σ. Since there are obviously (infinitely many) q-positions beyond i_1, there exists $j_1 > i_1$, the closest q-neighbor of i_1. Let i_2 be the first p-position greater than j_1. Again, there exists $j_2 > i_2$ the closest q-neighbor of i_2. Repeating this construction we identify infinitely many q-neighbors in σ.

In the other direction, let $j_1 < j_2 < \cdots$ be the infinite sequence of q-neighbors in σ. Let $i_1, i_2, \ldots$ be the corresponding p-positions such that j_k is the closest q-neighbor of i_k, for $k = 1, 2, \ldots$. We will show that for every $k > 0$, $j_k \leq i_{k+1} < j_{k+1}$. Assume, to the contrary, that $i_{k+1} < j_k$ for some $k > 0$. In that case j_k, rather than j_{k+1}, would have been the closest q-neighbor of i_{k+1}. We conclude that $i_1 < i_2 < \cdots$ form an infinite sequence of p-positions in addition to the sequence $j_1 < j_2 < \cdots$ of q-positions, showing σ to contain infinitely many positions of both kinds.

Inclusion of the Lower Classes

All safety and guarantee formulas can be shown to be special cases of response formulas. Thus, the class of response properties contains the classes of safety and guarantee properties. This containment is supported by the following two equivalences:

$$\Box p \sim \Box \Diamond (\boxminus p)$$
$$\Diamond p \sim \Box \Diamond (\diamondminus p).$$

The second equivalence, for example, states that a computation σ has a p-position iff there are infinitely many positions in whose past there is a p-position.

The containment of both classes is strict. This means that there is a response property that cannot be expressed by either a safety or a guarantee formula. In fact, the formula $\Box \Diamond p$, for a proposition p, cannot even be expressed by any finite boolean combination of safety and guarantee formulas.

Since each obligation property can be obtained by a positive boolean combination of safety and guarantee properties and the class of response properties is closed under such combinations, it follows that the response class also contains the obligation class. This inclusion is also strict, since the formula $\Box \Diamond p$ is not equivalent to any obligation formula.

In **Problem 4.9(b)**, the reader will show the strictness of these inclusions.

Expressing Justice

One of the important properties belonging to the response class is that of justice. As we recall, a typical justice requirement is associated with a transition τ and requires that either τ is disabled infinitely many times or is taken infinitely many times. This can be expressed by

$$\Box \Diamond [\neg enabled(\tau) \lor last\text{-}taken(\tau)].$$

This formula states the existence of infinitely many positions in which τ is either disabled or taken.

Persistence Properties

A *canonical persistence formula* is a formula of the form

$$\Diamond \Box p,$$

for some past formula p. The formula states that all but finitely many positions in the computation (all positions from a certain point on) satisfy p. A *persistence formula* is any formula that is equivalent to a canonical persistence formula.

A property that can be specified by a persistence formula is called a *persistence property*. Usually, persistence formulas are used to describe the eventual stabilization of some state or past property of the system. They allow an arbitrary delay until the stabilization occurs, but require that once it occurs it is continuously maintained.

In many cases the eventual stabilization is triggered by a preceding event. To cover these cases we may use the formula

$$p \Rightarrow \Diamond \Box q, \quad \text{i.e.,} \quad \Box(p \rightarrow \Diamond \Box q),$$

which specifies the eventual stabilization of q as being caused by p. This formula is a persistence formula due to the equivalence

$$(p \Rightarrow \Diamond \Box q) \sim \Diamond \Box (\Diamond p \to q).$$

The formula on the right states that, from a certain position on, it is continuously true that if p occurred in the past then q holds now.

Example

Reconsider the example of a reactive program P with an input variable x and an output variable y and the requirement that P responds to $x = 1$ by making $y = 2$. Consider a stronger requirement, by which once y is set to 2 in response to $x = 1$, it remains so permanently. This persistence property can be expressed by the formula

$$(x = 1) \Rightarrow \Diamond \Box (y = 2). \quad \lrcorner$$

Closure of Persistence Properties

The class of persistence properties is closed under the positive boolean operations.

This is shown by the following equivalences:

$$[\Diamond \Box p \wedge \Diamond \Box q] \sim \Diamond \Box (p \wedge q)$$

$$[\Diamond \Box p \vee \Diamond \Box q] \sim \Diamond \Box \Big(q \vee \ominus (p \mathcal{S} (p \wedge (\neg q))) \Big).$$

To see the validity of the second equivalence, we first show that the left-hand side implies the right-hand side. Obviously, $\Diamond \Box q$ implies the right-hand side. If $\Diamond \Box p$ is true and $\Diamond \Box q$ is not, let i be the position beyond which p is continuously true and $j > i$ be some position at which q is false (by $\Diamond \Box q$ being false there are infinitely many such positions). It is easy to see that for every position $k > j$, $(\sigma, k) \models \ominus (p \mathcal{S} (p \wedge (\neg q)))$.

Next, we show that the right-hand side implies the left-hand side. Again, we consider two cases. If $\Diamond \Box q$ holds, then obviously the left-hand side follows. In the other case, there are infinitely many $\neg q$-positions. Let i be the position beyond which ψ: $q \vee \ominus (p \mathcal{S} (p \wedge (\neg q)))$ continuously holds. Consider an arbitrary position $j > i$, and let $k > j$ be the smallest $\neg q$-position greater than j. Since ψ holds at k and q does not, it follows that $\ominus (p \mathcal{S} (p \wedge (\neg q)))$ must hold at k. Let m be the largest $\neg q$-position, such that $m < k$. Since there is no $\neg q$-position between j and k, $m \leq j$. As $\ominus (p \mathcal{S} (p \wedge (\neg q)))$ holds at k, it follows that p must hold at all positions ℓ, $m \leq \ell \leq k - 1$. In particular, it must hold at j. Since j is an arbitrarily chosen position greater than i, it follows that $\Box p$ holds at $i + 1$, and hence $\Diamond \Box p$ holds at position 0.

In **Problem 4.2**, the reader will consider additional persistence properties.

Duality

The classes of persistence and response properties are *dual*. This means that the complement of a property in one of the classes belongs to the other. This is supported by the two equivalences:

$$\neg\,\square\,\lozenge\,p \sim \lozenge\,\square\,\neg p$$
$$\neg\,\lozenge\,\square\,p \sim \square\,\lozenge\,\neg p.$$

This duality can be used for easy transfer of results holding for one class into the other class. For example, all the closure and inclusion properties of the persistence class can be derived from the corresponding properties and proofs of the response class.

Inclusion of the Lower Classes

All safety and guarantee formulas are special cases of persistence formulas. Thus, the class of persistence properties contains the classes of safety and guarantee properties. This inclusion is supported by the following two equivalences:

$$\square\,p \sim \lozenge\,\square\,\boxminus\,p$$
$$\lozenge\,p \sim \lozenge\,\square\,\diamondsuit\,p.$$

The second equivalence, for example, states that a computation σ has a p-position iff all positions, from a certain point on, have p in their past.

The inclusion of both classes is strict. This is shown by the property $\lozenge\,\square\,p$ for a proposition p, which cannot be expressed by either a safety or guarantee formula. In fact, it cannot be expressed by any finite boolean combination of safety and guarantee formulas. Consequently, the persistence class also strictly contains the obligation class.

Reactivity Properties

A *canonical simple reactivity formula* is a formula formed by a disjunction of a response formula and a persistence formula

$$\square\,\lozenge\,p \vee \lozenge\,\square\,q.$$

This formula states that either the computation contains infinitely many p-positions or all but finitely many of its positions are q-positions. A *simple reactivity formula* is any formula that is equivalent to a canonical simple reactivity formula. A property that can be specified by a simple reactivity formula is called a *simple reactivity property*.

In many cases we specify such properties by a formula of the form

$$\square\,\lozenge\,r \rightarrow \square\,\lozenge\,p$$

which is obviously equivalent to a canonical simple reactivity formula.

This formula states that if the computation contains infinitely many r-positions it must also contain infinitely many p-positions. It is used to describe a response of a more complicated type, which does not guarantee a response to single stimuli. It is only when we have infinitely many stimuli that we must respond by infinitely many responses. This is a convenient abstraction to a situation in which we want to commit the system to eventually respond to sufficiently many stimuli, but not specify a bound on how many stimuli may happen before the eventual response.

Example

Let us review the different versions of specifying response for our favorite example of a reactive program P with an input x and output y.

The simplest version is a single response (represented by $y = 2$) to a request (represented by $x = 1$) that occurs in the first state of the computation. This property can be specified by the guarantee formula

(1) $(x = 1) \;\rightarrow\; \Diamond(y = 2).$

The next version is the requirement of a single response to a single request that may occur anywhere. This is expressed by the obligation formula

(2) $\Diamond(x = 1) \;\rightarrow\; \Diamond(y = 2).$

A different version of response is the requirement of responses to multiple requests, guaranteeing a response following each request. This property can be expressed by the response formula

(3) $(x = 1) \;\Rightarrow\; \Diamond(y = 2).$

The next version of response is that of infinitely many responses to infinitely many requests. This property is expressed by the simple reactivity formula

(4) $\Box\Diamond(x = 1) \;\rightarrow\; \Box\Diamond(y = 2).$

It is not difficult to see that (3) implies (1), (2), and (4).

The type of response represented by simple reactivity formulas allows the program P to ignore finitely many requests but not infinitely many of them. This description should not be taken too literally, in the sense that no implementation of this requirement can be based on the idea of "let us wait first and see whether there are going to be infinitely many $x = 1$ events or only finitely many of them." Any reasonable implementation of such a requirement must sincerely attempt to respond to all requests, but the liberal specification tolerates failures to respond in the case of only finitely many requests.

The class of properties specifiable by simple reactivity formulas is closed under union. This is due to the trivial equivalence

$$[(\Box \Diamond p_1 \lor \Diamond \Box q_1) \lor (\Box \Diamond p_2 \lor \Diamond \Box q_2)]$$

$$\sim$$

$$[(\Box \Diamond p_1 \lor \Box \Diamond p_2) \lor (\Diamond \Box q_1 \lor \Diamond \Box q_2)]$$

and the closure of the response and persistence classes under union.

However, the simple reactivity class is not, in general, closed under intersections or complementations.

Obviously, the class of simple reactivity properties contains the classes of response and persistence properties and hence the classes of safety, guarantee, and obligation properties. This inclusion is strict since the property specifiable by $\Box \Diamond p \lor \Diamond \Box q$ for propositions p and q cannot be expressed by any formula belonging to a lower class.

Expressing Compassion

Simple reactivity formulas can express the requirements of compassion. Recall that compassion for transition τ requires that if τ is enabled at infinitely many positions of the computation, it is taken at infinitely many positions. This requirement can be specified by the simple reactivity formula

$$\Box \Diamond \, enabled(\tau) \;\rightarrow\; \Box \Diamond \, last\text{-}taken(\tau).$$

General Reactivity Properties

Richer classes of properties can be expressed by conjunctions of simple reactivity formulas of the form

$$\bigwedge_{i=1}^{n} \left[\Box \Diamond p_i \lor \Diamond \Box q_i \right].$$

Since, in general, the conjunction of two simple reactivity formulas is not equivalent to any simple reactivity formula, taking such conjunctions leads to a stronger expressive power.

We call such formulas *canonical reactivity formulas*. A *reactivity formula* is any formula that is equivalent to a canonical reactivity formula. A property that can be specified by a reactivity formula is called a *reactivity property*.

A natural example of a reactivity property is the total statement of fairness for a fair transition system. Since each justice and compassion requirement is expressible by a simple reactivity formula (response formula if it is a justice requirement), the statement that all fairness requirements hold is expressible as the conjunction of several simple reactivity formulas.

Our approach to specification of programs is inherently conjunctive. This means that a specification is presented as a conjunction of requirements, expressed by temporal formulas, all of which should be valid over the program. In verifying

that a specification is valid over a given program, we can verify the validity of
each requirement separately. Therefore, the fact that one of the requirements is
a conjunction by itself, rather than a simple reactivity formula, does not greatly
complicate or simplify the situation. Hence, in the context of a full specification,
which is always a conjunction, we may assume each requirement to be at most a
simple reactivity formula.

The family of reactivity properties forms an infinite hierarchy. Level k of
the hierarchy, for $k > 0$, consists of all the properties that can be specified by a
conjunction

$$\bigwedge_{i=1}^{k} [\Box \Diamond p_i \lor \Diamond \Box q_i].$$

This hierarchy is strict, since the conjunction

$$\bigwedge_{i=1}^{k+1} [\Box \Diamond p_i \lor \Diamond \Box q_i]$$

with propositions p_i, q_i, $i = 1, \ldots, k + 1$, is not equivalent to any conjunction of
k or fewer simple reactivity formulas.

In **Problem 4.9(b)**, the reader will prove that the inclusion of the response
and persistence classes in the reactivity class is strict.

Reactivity is the Maximal Class

The class of reactivity properties is the maximal class we need ever consider. This
is due to the following normal form theorem.

Theorem (normal form)

Every quantifier-free temporal formula is equivalent to a reactivity formula.

The proof of this theorem is based on a translation between future and past
temporal formulas. A full proof of this theorem is beyond the scope of this book,
but Problem 4.12 outlines some of the central steps in such a proof.

We observe that even though the normal form only uses some of the future
operators, namely $\Box$ and $\Diamond$, it covers all the formulas that use the other future
operators.

Examples of normal form representations of some simple formulas are

$$\bigcirc \bigcirc p \sim \Box (\ominus \ominus \textit{first} \rightarrow p)$$

$$p \,\mathcal{U}\, q \sim \Diamond (q \land \widehat{\boxminus} p).$$

The preceding theorem also applies to formulas that contain the previous- and next-value notations x^- and x^+. Recall that a past formula may contain occurrences of x^- but no occurrences of x^+.

Past-Quantifying Formulas

The theorem can be extended to cover some special cases of formulas with quantifiers. We say that a formula is *past-quantifying* if all the temporal operators falling within the scope of a quantification are past operators. In particular, x^- may appear in a scope of a quantification, but x^+ may not.

It is not difficult to see that the normal form theorem also holds for past-quantifying formula. We illustrate the general argument in an example. Consider the past-quantifying formula

$$\varphi: \quad (x = 0) \land (\exists u: \ominus (x = u) \land (x = u + 1)) \, \widehat{\mathcal{U}} \, (x = x^- + 2).$$

This formula describes a sequence in which x is initially 0 and then it keeps increasing by steps of 1 until a position in which it increases by 2. To transform this formula to normal form, consider the formula

$$\psi: \quad p \land q \widehat{\mathcal{U}} r.$$

Clearly, φ can be viewed as an instantiation of ψ, using the replacement

$$\alpha: \quad [p \leftarrow (x = 0), \quad q \leftarrow \exists u: \ominus (x = u) \land (x = u + 1), \quad r \leftarrow (x = x^- + 2)].$$

Observe that this replacement instantiates each sentence symbol by a past formula. We refer to ψ as an *abstraction* of φ.

Since ψ is a propositional quantifier-free formula, it has a normal form equivalent which is the guarantee formula

$$\widehat{\psi}: \quad \Diamond (r \land q \widehat{\mathcal{S}} (p \land \textit{first})).$$

Instantiating $\widehat{\psi}$ by the replacement α, we obtain a normal form equivalent of the past-quantifying formula φ

$$\widehat{\varphi} = \widehat{\psi}[\alpha]: \quad \Diamond \Big(x = x^- + 2 \land$$

$$(\exists u: \ominus (x = u) \land (x = u + 1)) \, \widehat{\mathcal{S}} \, (x = 0 \land \textit{first}) \Big).$$

This sequence of steps can be applied to every past-quantifying formula.

Externally Quantified Formulas

A larger class of quantified formulas for which normal form transformations exist consists of formulas of the form

$$\varphi: \quad \xi_1 x_1 \, \xi_2 x_2 \, \cdots \, \xi_n x_n: \, \psi,$$

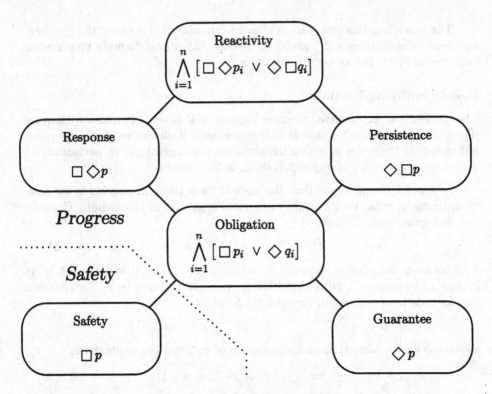

Fig. 4.1.   Classification diagram.

where each ξ_i, $i = 1, \ldots, n$, is a universal or existential quantifier, and ψ is a past-quantifying formula. We refer to such formulas as *externally quantified formulas*. Applying the normal form transformation to ψ, we can claim that every externally quantified formula φ has an equivalent normal form given by

$$\widehat{\varphi}: \quad \xi_1 x_1\ \xi_2 x_2\ \cdots\ \xi_n x_n : \widehat{\psi},$$

where $\widehat{\psi}$ is a reactivity formula.

The Classification

A summary of the classification of properties specifiable by temporal formulas is presented in Fig. 4.1. Nodes in the diagram represent the different classes. The edges in the diagram represent strict inclusion relations holding between the classes.

Safety and Progress

We refer to the classes other than the safety class as the *progress* classes. Syntactically, these classes are distinguished by the operator $\diamondsuit$ that appears in their canonical formulas. As we have seen, the safety class imposes a requirement, represented by a past formula, that must hold at all positions of a computation. The progress classes, on the other hand, specify a requirement that should eventually be fulfilled, and are therefore associated with progress toward fulfillment of the requirement. The progress classes differ from one another in the conditions and frequency at which the requirement is to be fulfilled.

We refer to this classification of properties, which plays a central role in the theory presented in this book, as the *safety-progress* classification.

Many of the features and properties of the classes in the hierarchy are easier to establish when we examine their characterization in a broader context.

In **Problem 4.8**, the reader will consider the hierarchy from a formal language theoretic view. This leads to a hierarchic classification of languages.

In **Problem 4.9**, the reader will relate the classification of languages to the classification of properties. Some inclusion and strict inclusion features of the classification can be transferred from languages to properties.

In **Problem 4.10**, the reader will consider characterization of languages by restrictions on the automata that recognize them.

In **Problem 4.11**, the reader will provide algorithms for identifying the class of a language based on the automaton that recognizes it.

In **Problem 4.12**, the reader will relate the classification by automata to the classification by temporal formulas.

Standard Formulas

The syntactic characterization of the hierarchy of classes we have considered presents for each class a canonical formula. Each of these formulas consists of future operators applied to past formulas. For example, the canonical response formula $\square \diamondsuit p$ applies the future operators $\square$ and $\diamondsuit$ to the past formula p.

While theoretically adequate, we may prefer to use formulas with more elaborate future expressions (using, for example, the operators $\bigcirc$ and $\mathcal{U}$), and still easily identify the class to which the formula belongs. Consequently, we will present for each class a richer set of formulas that all belong to that class. We refer to these formulas as *standard* formulas.

Standard Safety Formulas

We identify the following set of formulas as *standard safety formulas*:

- Any past formula is a standard safety formula.
- If p and q are standard safety formulas, then so are

$$p \wedge q \qquad p \vee q \qquad \bigcirc p \qquad \square p \qquad p \, \mathcal{W} \, q.$$

The second clause of this characterization can be viewed as stating the closure of standard safety formulas under the future operators $\bigcirc$, $\square$, and $\mathcal{W}$. Observe that the canonical safety formula $\square p$ is a standard safety formula.

The restriction to standard formulas in the second clause is essential. To see this, consider the formula *first* $\vee \Diamond p$, which is not a standard safety formula. This formula obviously holds on any sequence since, evaluated at position 0, *first* is always true. Consequently it is equivalent to $\square \top$ and is therefore a safety formula. On the other hand, $\square(first \vee \Diamond p)$ is equivalent to $\square \Diamond p$ and is, therefore, not a safety formula.

The characterization of standard safety formulas enables us to identify as a safety formula

$$p \Rightarrow q_1 \, \mathcal{W} \left(q_2 \, \mathcal{W} \left(\cdots (q_n \, \mathcal{W} \, r)... \right) \right),$$

equivalently,

$$\square \left(\neg p \vee \left(q_1 \, \mathcal{W} \left(q_2 \, \mathcal{W} \cdots (q_n \, \mathcal{W} \, r)... \right) \right) \right),$$

where $p, q_1, \ldots, q_n$, and r are past formulas.

Standard Guarantee Formulas

We identify the following set of formulas as *standard guarantee formulas*:

- Any past formula is a standard guarantee formula.

- If p and q are standard guarantee formulas, then so are

$$p \wedge q \qquad p \vee q \qquad \bigcirc p \qquad \Diamond p \qquad p \, \mathcal{U} \, q.$$

This characterization claims that the class of standard guarantee formulas is closed under the operators $\bigcirc$, $\Diamond$, and $\mathcal{U}$. Observe that the canonical guarantee formula $\Diamond p$ is a standard guarantee formula.

Using the characterization we can identify the following as guarantee formulas:

$$\Diamond[(x = 1) \wedge \Diamond(y = 2)]$$
$$p \rightarrow \Diamond q \qquad \text{equivalently} \qquad \neg p \vee \Diamond q$$
$$p \rightarrow q_1 \, \mathcal{U} \left(q_2 \, \mathcal{U} \left(\cdots (q_n \, \mathcal{U} \, r)... \right) \right),$$

equivalently,

$$\neg p \vee q_1 \, \mathcal{U} \left(q_2 \, \mathcal{U} \left(\cdots (q_n \, \mathcal{U} \, r)... \right) \right),$$

where $p, q, q_1, \ldots, q_n$, and r are past formulas.

Standard Obligation Formulas

The following set of formulas are identified as *standard obligation formulas*:

- Standard safety formulas and standard guarantee formulas are standard obligation formulas.

- If p and q are standard obligation formulas, then so are

$$p \wedge q \qquad p \vee q \qquad \neg p \qquad \bigcirc p.$$

- If p is a standard safety formula, q is a standard obligation formula, and r is a standard guarantee formula, then

$$p \, \mathcal{W} \, q \qquad q \, \mathcal{U} \, r$$

are standard obligation formulas.

Clearly the canonical obligation formula $\Box\, p \vee \Diamond\, q$ is a standard obligation formula.

Standard Response Formulas

We identify the following set of formulas as *standard response formulas*:

- Any standard obligation formula is a standard response formula.

- If p and q are standard response formulas, then so are

$$p \wedge q \qquad p \vee q \qquad \bigcirc p \qquad \Box p.$$

- If p and q are standard response formulas and r is a standard guarantee formula, then

$$p \, \mathcal{W} \, q \qquad p \, \mathcal{U} \, r$$

are standard response formulas.

This characterization claims that the class of standard response formulas is closed under the operators $\bigcirc$ and $\Box$. Observe that the canonical response formula $\Box\,\Diamond\, p$ is a standard response formula.

Using the characterization we can identify the following as response formulas:

$$\begin{aligned}
p \Rightarrow \Diamond\, q \qquad &\text{equivalently} \qquad \Box(\neg p \vee \Diamond\, q) \\
p \Rightarrow q \, \mathcal{U}\, r \qquad &\text{equivalently} \qquad \Box(\neg p \vee q \, \mathcal{U}\, r) \\
(p_1 \wedge \Diamond\, p_2) \Rightarrow \Diamond(q_1 \wedge \Diamond\, q_2)&
\end{aligned}$$

equivalently

$$\Box(\neg(p_1 \wedge \Diamond\, p_2) \vee \Diamond(q_1 \wedge \Diamond\, q_2)),$$

where p, q, p_1, p_2, q_1, q_2, and r are past formulas. In all these cases, the formulas on the right have the general form of $\Box$ applied to a boolean combination of standard guarantee formulas.

Standard Persistence Formulas

We identify the following set of formulas as *standard persistence formulas*:

- Any standard obligation formula is a standard persistence formula.

- If p and q are standard persistence formulas then so are

$$p \land q \qquad p \lor q \qquad \bigcirc p \qquad \diamondsuit p.$$

- If p is a standard safety formulas and q and r are standard persistence formulas, then

$$p \, \mathcal{W} \, q \qquad q \, \mathcal{U} \, r$$

are standard persistence formulas.

This characterization claims that the class of standard persistence formulas is closed under the operators $\bigcirc$ and $\diamondsuit$. Clearly the canonical persistence formula $\diamondsuit \square p$ is a standard persistence formula.

Using the characterization we can identify the following as persistence formulas:

$$p \Rightarrow \diamondsuit \square q \qquad \text{equivalently} \qquad \square \neg p \lor \diamondsuit \square q$$

$$\diamondsuit (p \Rightarrow q \, \mathcal{W} \, r) \qquad \text{equivalently} \qquad \diamondsuit \square (\neg p \lor q \, \mathcal{W} \, r),$$

where p, q, and r are past formulas.

We do not define a class of standard reactivity formulas since all quantifier-free formulas specify reactivity properties.

In **Problem 4.13**, the reader will show, for each class, that standard formulas of this class specify only properties belonging to the class.

The Safety-Liveness Classification

A different classification of the properties identifies two disjoint classes of properties, the class of safety and the class of liveness. We describe this alternative classification for the sake of completeness but will not use it for further developments.

A very informal description of these two classes that has been suggested is

- a *safety* property claims that "something bad" does not happen, and

- a *liveness* property claims that "something good" eventually happens.

It is not difficult to see that the formal definition of safety properties matches very well the informal description.

A natural assumption we can make is that the occurrence of a bad situation can be recognized in a finite time. Indeed, in many cases a bad situation can be described by a state formula. This is the case, for example, with mutual exclusion, whose violation can be characterized by the state formula

$$in\_C_1 \ \wedge \ in\_C_2.$$

In more complex cases we may require, for example, that the first occurrence of q, if any, is preceded by or coincides with an occurrence of p. In this case a bad situation is detected as soon as we observe an occurrence of q with no preceding p. This can be characterized by the past formula

$$q \ \wedge \ \boxminus \neg p.$$

Consequently, if the past formula φ describes a bad situation, then the property claiming that the bad situation never occurs can be specified by the safety formula $\square \neg \varphi$.

If we try to interpret the informal description of liveness in the same way we interpreted safety, then the closest formal definition that is obtained is that of the guarantee class. That is, if we assume that the "good thing" can also be detected in finite time, it can be represented by a past formula φ. The statement that eventually something good happens matches precisely the formula $\diamondsuit \ \varphi$, i.e., eventually we detect a position satisfying φ. However, this is not the accepted interpretation of the liveness class.

Next, we present the formal definitions of the classes of safety and liveness properties. As we will see, the liveness class is different from the guarantee class.

Characterization of Safety and Liveness Properties

Let $\sigma: s_0, s_1, \ldots$ be an infinite sequence of states $s_i \in \Sigma$. For a given $k \geq 0$, we define the finite sequence $\sigma[0..k]: s_0, \ldots, s_k$ to be a *prefix* of the sequence σ. We also say that σ is an (infinite) *extension* of the finite sequence $\sigma[0..k]$.

Let p be a past formula that holds at position k of σ. Clearly, the fact that p holds at position k is completely independent of the states $s_{k+1}, s_{k+2}, \ldots$. In fact p holds at position k of any extension of $\sigma[0..k]$. We can therefore view p as a property of $\sigma[0..k]$.

The classes of safety and liveness formulas can be characterized as follows:

- φ is a safety formula iff

    any sequence σ violating φ (i.e., satisfying $\neg \varphi$) contains a prefix $\sigma[0..k]$ all of whose infinite extensions violate φ.

- φ is a liveness formula iff

    any arbitrary finite sequence $s_0, \ldots, s_k$ can be extended to an infinite sequence satisfying φ.

Let us show that the characterization of safety presented here is consistent with the definition of safety formulas. A safety formula is equivalent to a formula of the form $\square\, p$, for some past formula p. If σ violates $\square\, p$, there exists a position $k \geq 0$, such that $(\sigma, k) \models \neg p$. Obviously, $(\sigma', k) \models \neg p$ for any extension σ' of the prefix $\sigma[0..k]$, and consequently $(\sigma', k) \not\models \varphi$.

In the other direction, any formula that satisfies the safety characterization presented here is equivalent to a canonical safety formula $\square\, p$. This follows from the solution to Problem 4.12(b).

Features of the Classification

One of the important features of the safety-liveness classification is that the classes of safety and liveness properties are (almost) disjoint. This is stated by the following claim.

Claim

The only formulas that are both safety and liveness formulas are equivalent to the trivial formula т.

In comparison, the safety-progress classification is an inclusion hierarchy. For example, any safety formula is also an obligation formula, as well as a response, persistence, and reactivity formula.

The liveness characterization does not provide us with an easy syntactic check to quickly identify whether a given formula is a liveness formula. We do have, though, a useful partial identification.

The canonical formulas for any of the progress classes contain subformulas p (and sometimes q) that are allowed to be arbitrary past formulas. If we restrict these subformulas to be state formulas, we obtain a liveness formula that also belongs to the corresponding class.

Claim

If p, p_i, and q_i are state formulas then

$$\Diamond\, p \qquad \bigwedge_i (\square\, p_i \vee \Diamond\, q_i) \qquad \square \Diamond\, p \qquad \Diamond \square\, p$$

$$\bigwedge_i (\square \Diamond\, p_i \vee \Diamond \square\, q_i)$$

are live-guarantee, live-obligation, live-response, live-persistence, and live-reactivity formulas, respectively.

For example, the formula $\square \Diamond\, p$ is a live-response formula, meaning that it is both a response formula and a liveness formula. On the other hand, it is not difficult to show that each progress class also contains formulas that are not liveness formulas. For example, the formula $\square \Diamond (p \wedge \boxminus q)$, where p and q are state formulas, is a response formula that is definitely not a liveness formula.

Thus, the safety-liveness classification is orthogonal to the safety-progress classification. This means that for any progress class κ (i.e., κ ranges over the five progress classes) there are liveness formulas of class κ as well as formulas of class κ that are not liveness formulas.

Decomposition of Properties into Safety and Liveness

We can strengthen the preceding claim as follows.

Claim

Any formula φ of the progress class κ is equivalent to a conjunction

$$\varphi_S \wedge \varphi_L,$$

where φ_S is a safety formula and φ_L is a liveness formula of class κ.

To illustrate this claim, consider the guarantee formula

$$p \, \mathcal{U} q,$$

for state formulas p and q. To justify its classification we observe that it is equivalent to

$$\Diamond (q \wedge \boxminus p).$$

This formula is not a liveness formula, because the finite sequence

$$\langle p\colon \text{T}, \; q\colon \text{F} \rangle, \; \langle p\colon \text{F}, \; q\colon \text{F} \rangle$$

cannot be extended to an infinite sequence satisfying $p \, \mathcal{U} q$.

On the other hand, this formula is equivalent to the conjunction

$$\square (\neg p \rightarrow \Diamond q) \wedge \Diamond q,$$

where the first conjunct is obviously a safety formula, while the second conjunct is a live-guarantee formula.

It is beyond the scope of this book to give detailed proofs of these claims. However, we will provide some additional information about the structure of these proofs.

Claim

For every temporal formula φ there exists a past formula $Pref(\varphi)$, such that a finite sequence $\widehat{\sigma}\colon s_0, \ldots, s_k$ satisfies $Pref(\varphi)$ at position k iff $\widehat{\sigma}$ can be extended to an infinite sequence satisfying φ.

Thus, $Pref(\varphi)$ characterizes all the finite sequences that can appear as prefixes of a sequence satisfying φ. Using the formula $Pref(\varphi)$ we can give an alternative characterization of safety and liveness formulas.

- φ is a safety formula iff $\square \, Pref(\varphi) \sim \varphi$.

- φ is a liveness formula iff $Pref(\varphi)$ is valid.

We can also give explicit formulations for the conjuncts φ_S and φ_L appearing in the presentation of each formula as the conjunction of safety and liveness formulas.

For an arbitrary formula φ, we define

$$\varphi_S: \quad \Box \, Pref(\varphi)$$

$$\varphi_L: \quad \varphi \vee \Diamond \neg Pref(\varphi).$$

It is simple to show that φ_S is a safety formula, φ_L is a liveness formula, and $\varphi \sim (\varphi_S \wedge \varphi_L)$.

4.3   Examples of Safety: State Invariances

In the following two sections we will consider several typical cases of safety properties that arise naturally in the specification of programs. The canonical form of a safety formula is $\Box \, q$ for some past formula q. In this section we concentrate on two important safety formulas

$$p \rightarrow \Box \, q \quad \text{and} \quad \Box \, q$$

for state formulas p and q.

Global Invariants

Let q be a data assertion, i.e., a state formula referring only to the data variables among the state variables. A general safety property asserts that

> all states in each computation satisfy q, i.e., q remains invariant throughout the computation.

Such a property is expressible by the formula

$$\Box \, q.$$

We refer to such a property as a *global invariant*. Typically, global invariants constrain the range (and sometimes the type) of variables in the program.

Example (binomial coefficient)

In Fig. 4.2 (see also Fig. 1.11) we present program BINOM for computing the binomial coefficient $\binom{n}{k}$. We may assert the following range-constraining global invariant:

$$\Box \left[(n - k \leq y_1 \leq n) \wedge (1 \leq y_2 \leq k + 1) \right]. \quad \blacksquare$$

Some invariants do not hold continuously at all control locations, but become

$$
\begin{array}{l}
\textbf{in} \quad k,\ n \qquad : \textbf{integer where } 0 \le k \le n \\[2pt]
\textbf{local } y_1,\ y_2,\ r: \textbf{integer where } y_1 = n,\ y_2 = 1,\ r = 1 \\[2pt]
\textbf{out} \quad b \qquad\ : \textbf{integer where } b = 1
\end{array}
$$

$$
P_1 ::
\begin{bmatrix}
\textbf{local } t_1: \textbf{integer} \\
\ell_0: \textbf{while } y_1 > (n-k) \textbf{ do} \\
\begin{bmatrix}
\ell_1: \textbf{request}(r) \\
\ell_2: t_1 := b \cdot y_1 \\
\ell_3: b := t_1 \\
\ell_4: \textbf{release}(r) \\
\ell_5: y_1 := y_1 - 1
\end{bmatrix}
\end{bmatrix}
: \widehat{\ell_0}
$$

$$
\|
$$

$$
P_2 ::
\begin{bmatrix}
\textbf{local } t_2: \textbf{integer} \\
m_0: \textbf{while } y_2 \le k \textbf{ do} \\
\begin{bmatrix}
m_1: \textbf{await } (y_1 + y_2) \le n \\
m_2: \textbf{request}(r) \\
m_3: t_2 := b \textbf{ div } y_2 \\
m_4: b := t_2 \\
m_5: \textbf{release}(r) \\
m_6: y_2 := y_2 + 1
\end{bmatrix}
\end{bmatrix}
: \widehat{m_0}
$$

Fig. 4.2. Program BINOM — with protected sections.

true whenever the program visits a particular location or some specific event happens. The general form of such a property is

$$\Box(\lambda \to q),$$

where q is a data assertion and λ is a control assertion, i.e., refers to the location of control. This property states that

whenever λ holds, so does q.

We refer to such properties as *local invariants*.

Partial Correctness

Consider a computational program P that is expected to terminate and whose task is to compute some function. A specification for such a program consists of an assertion q, called the *postcondition*, which refers only to data variables and relates the values of the output variables to the values of the input variables.

Postcondition q characterizes the final state at which the program terminates. For the simple case of a program that has an input variable x, an output variable z, and is expected to compute a function f, a typical postcondition is q: $z = f(x)$. For example, an appropriate postcondition for a program that is expected to compute the square root of its input is $z = \sqrt{x}$.

A typical safety property, which is a local invariant, is *partial correctness* with respect to q:

> every terminating computation of P terminates in a q-state.

Note that partial correctness does not guarantee termination.

Partial correctness with respect to q can be expressed by the safety formula

$$\Box(after\_P \to q).$$

This formula states that if the program ever reaches its terminal location, it satisfies q at that state. This is a safety formula.

In some cases, the specification of such computational programs includes a *precondition* p in addition to postcondition q. The role of the precondition is to characterize the initial states for which the program is expected to behave correctly. For example, for the root-extracting program, the natural precondition is p: $x \geq 0$. However, in our presentation of programs, precondition p is usually asserted in the where part of the declarations for the input variables. This implies that we only consider computations whose first state satisfies p. Consequently, we do not consider p as part of the specification, but rather as part of the initial condition of the program.

For the cases that the precondition p is not a part of the program, we may express partial correctness with respect to the pair $\{p, q\}$ by the safety formula

$$p \to \Box(after\_P \to q).$$

Example (binomial coefficient)

Consider, for example, program BINOM (Fig. 4.2). Its statement of partial correctness can be expressed by the formula

$$\Box\left[(at\_\widehat{\ell}_0 \wedge at\_\widehat{m}_0) \to \left(b = \tbinom{n}{k}\right)\right]$$

Note that the conjunction $at\_\widehat{\ell}_0 \wedge at\_\widehat{m}_0$ characterizes the location of control at the termination of program BINOM. This formula can therefore also be written as $\Box\left(after\_P \to b = \tbinom{n}{k}\right)$. ◢

Deadlock Freedom

An important safety property is deadlock freedom.

We have defined a terminal state to be a state in which all the diligent transitions are disabled (i.e., all transitions except for the idling transition τ_I, which is always enabled). Once such a state appears in a computation at position j, all the states at later positions must be identical to s_j, since τ_I is the only transition that can be taken beyond j. The occurrence of a terminal state represents a situation of termination, i.e., a situation in which the complete program has been executed. It can also represent a *deadlock* situation, in which control is in the middle of the program, yet no part of the program is able to proceed. Such a situation is usually considered a fault in the execution of the program, and we may want to specify that it should never occur.

To guarantee that a program that is expected to terminate never deadlocks, it is sufficient to require the following safety property:

the only terminal state in a computation is that of termination.

This is stated by the following safety formula:

$$\square\,(terminal \;\rightarrow\; after\_P).$$

In the context of nonterminating programs, we need not make exceptions for termination. All terminal states are considered equally harmful. The following formula excludes deadlocks of any kind in all computations of a nonterminating program:

$$\square\;\neg terminal.$$

Local Deadlock Freedom

When we study a specific program and want to establish that it is deadlock free, we can immediately identify locations at which deadlock obviously cannot occur. For example, any unconditional assignment can always be executed and therefore cannot be a statement at which the program deadlocks. We may therefore focus our attention on statements that have a nontrivial enabling condition.

In Section 1.5 we defined, for each statement S, the enabling condition $enabled(S)$, which specifies that one of the transitions associated with S can be taken.

For a specific program P, consider a set of pairwise parallel statements $\ell_1 \colon S_1, \ldots, \ell_m \colon S_m$ that form a candidate for a deadlock site. That is, the set

$$\{[\ell_1], \;\ldots, \;[\ell_m]\}$$

is a possible value of π in a state of some computation. The property of *local deadlock freedom*, relative to a set of locations, states that it is impossible for the program to deadlock at that particular set of locations.

This is specified by the formula

$$\bigwedge_{i=1}^{m} at\_S_i \;\Rightarrow\; \bigvee_{i=1}^{m} enabled(S_i).$$

Example (producer-consumer)

Consider for example program PROD-CONS of Fig. 4.3 (see also Fig. 1.12). It is obvious that a deadlock can occur only when both processes are in front of request statements, since all other statements in the program are always enabled when reached by control. There are only four combinations of pairs of parallel request statements, given by

$$(\ell_2, m_1), \quad (\ell_2, m_2), \quad (\ell_3, m_1), \quad (\ell_3, m_2).$$

The following formula states, for example, that deadlock at (ℓ_2, m_1) is impossible:

$$[at\_\ell_2 \,\wedge\, at\_m_1] \;\Rightarrow\; [(ne > 0) \,\vee\, (nf > 0)].$$

If we list similar requirements for the other three combinations, then the fulfillment of these four requirements guarantees that the program can never deadlock. ◢

Fault Freedom

In many programming languages, certain mishaps are considered to be *faults*, or *exceptions*. Examples of faults are division by zero and out-of-range subscript references. An important property that well-behaved programs should have is the guarantee that

> no faults ever occur during execution.

To formulate this property in our specification language, we have to consider each statement in the program and ensure separately that this statement never causes a fault.

For every statement S in a program, we can formulate a *regularity condition* R_S that guarantees that execution of the transitions associated with the statement generates no faults. Thus, if S contains a division, the regularity condition includes a clause specifying that the divisor is nonzero or not too small (to avoid arithmetic overflow). If the statement contains an array reference, the regularity condition should imply that the subscript expressions are within the declared range.

For example, consider the statement S

$$A[j] \;:=\; \sqrt{x}/B[i],$$

$$\text{local } r, \; ne, \; nf: \textbf{integer where } r = 1, \; ne = N, \; nf = 0$$
$$b \qquad\qquad : \textbf{list of integer where } b = \Lambda$$

$$Prod :: \begin{bmatrix} \textbf{local } x: \textbf{ integer} \\ \ell_0: \textbf{ loop forever do} \\ \begin{bmatrix} \ell_1: \textbf{ compute } x \\ \ell_2: \textbf{ request}(ne) \\ \ell_3: \textbf{ request}(r) \\ \ell_4: \; b := b \bullet x \\ \ell_5: \textbf{ release}(r) \\ \ell_6: \textbf{ release}(nf) \end{bmatrix} \end{bmatrix}$$

$$\|$$

$$Cons :: \begin{bmatrix} \textbf{local } y: \textbf{ integer} \\ m_0: \textbf{ loop forever do} \\ \begin{bmatrix} m_1: \textbf{ request}(nf) \\ m_2: \textbf{ request}(r) \\ m_3: \; (y, \, b) := \big(hd(b), \; tl(b)\big) \\ m_4: \textbf{ release}(r) \\ m_5: \textbf{ release}(ne) \\ m_6: \textbf{ use } y \end{bmatrix} \end{bmatrix}$$

Fig. 4.3. Program PROD-CONS (producer-consumer).

where both A and B are declared as arrays with subscript range 0..10. The regularity condition for S is given by

$$R_S: \quad (0 \leq j \leq 10) \; \wedge \; (0 \leq i \leq 10) \; \wedge \; (x \geq 0) \; \wedge \; \big(B[i] \neq 0\big),$$

where we have ignored faults caused by arithmetic overflow or underflow.

Note that in the case that S is a grouped when statement of the form

$$S: \; \langle \textbf{when } c \textbf{ do } \widetilde{S} \rangle,$$

then

$$R_S: \quad R_c \; \wedge \; (c \to R_{\widetilde{S}}),$$

where R_c is the regularity condition for the evaluation of the boolean expression

c. This is because S may fault while evaluating c, a possibility that the conjunct R_c excludes. If it did not fault and c was found to be false, then $\widetilde{S}$ is not executed. When $\widetilde{S}$ is executed, we may assume that c is true.

Thus, the regularity condition for the statement

$$S: \; \Big\langle \textbf{when } i = 1 \textbf{ do } A[j] := \big(\sqrt{x}/B[i]\big) \Big\rangle$$

is given by

$$(i = 1) \; \rightarrow \; \Big[(0 \leq j \leq 10) \; \wedge \; (x \geq 0) \; \wedge \; \big(B[i] \neq 0\big)\Big].$$

The assertion that statement S never generates a fault is expressed by the formula

$$\Box(at\_S \rightarrow R_S).$$

This local invariant states that

whenever statement S is reached, regularity condition R_S holds.

Example (binomial coefficient)

Consider, for example, program BINOM (Fig. 4.2). To ensure that execution of the statement m_3: $t_2 := b \textbf{ div } y_2$ generates no fault, we may require:

$$\Box\Big[at\_m_3 \; \rightarrow \; \big[(y_2 \neq 0) \; \wedge \; (b \bmod y_2 = 0)\big]\Big].$$

The first conjunct guarantees that division by zero is not attempted. The second conjunct, $b \bmod y_2 = 0$, gives additional information that is not associated with faults but is necessary for the correctness of the program. It indicates that whenever the division is attempted, it is guaranteed to leave no remainder. ⏋

Mutual Exclusion

Consider a program P consisting of two processes P_1 and P_2. Assume that each process contains a critical section, given by C_1 and C_2. The requirement associated with critical sections is mutual exclusion. This means that

P_1 and P_2 never execute their critical sections at the same time.

The property of mutual exclusion for such a program can be expressed by the formula:

$$\Box\neg(in\_C_1 \; \wedge \; in\_C_2).$$

Recall that in_C_i has been defined as being at_S for some S that is a substatement of C_i.

Example (binomial coefficient)

Consider program BINOM of Fig. 4.2. This program uses a semaphore r to ensure that accesses to shared variable b are exclusive. The formula

$$\Box \neg(at\_\ell_{2..4} \wedge at\_m_{3..5})$$

states that the two sections protected by the semaphore are never simultaneously occupied. These critical sections are given by $C_1 = \ell_{2..4}$, $C_2 = m_{3..5}$. Therefore, in_C_1 and in_C_2 are equivalent to $at\_\ell_{2..4}$ and $at\_m_{3..5}$, respectively. Note that while the request statements at ℓ_1 and m_2 do not belong to the critical section, the release statements at ℓ_4 and m_5 do. ◢

Invariances Over Communication Events

Consider a program that computes and prints the sequence of all prime numbers on channel γ. That is, whenever the program has a prime p to print, it performs the operation $\gamma \Leftarrow p$. Such printing statements may appear in different parts of the program. This program is a good example of a nonterminating program, where we cannot use notions such as partial correctness to specify its desired properties.

Temporal logic provides the means by which the required ongoing behavior of such a program can be specified. As a safety property, we can express the requirement that

nothing but primes is ever printed.

This is expressible by the formula

$$\mathcal{P}_1: \quad [\gamma \Leftarrow v] \Rightarrow prime(v).$$

This formula states that, whenever the event $[\gamma \Leftarrow v]$ happens, i.e., a new value v is added to the printed file γ, it must be prime. Note that v is not a program variable, i.e., it does not appear in the program, but is rather an auxiliary specification variable.

We remind the reader that the definition of validity for a formula containing a free variable implies that the formula holds for every value of the variable. Thus, the achieved effect of this specification is equivalent to a formula in which the variable v is universally quantified.

4.4 Examples of Safety: Past Invariances

All the safety properties we have considered in the previous section were expressible by formulas of the general forms

$$p \ \rightarrow \ \Box \, q \quad \text{or} \quad \Box \, q,$$

where p and q are state formulas. This means that they could only state the invariance of a state property.

In this section we consider the more general case that q is a past formula. Typically, safety properties that relate to the past describe some precedence relations between certain events or situations. We consider several such properties.

In discussing precedence properties, we say that position i *(weakly) precedes* position j if $i \leq j$. We say that i *strictly precedes* j if $i < j$.

Monotonicity

Consider again the specification of the nonterminating prime-printing program. So far we have specified that the output contains only primes. This still allows the same prime to appear several times in the output. We can prevent this by requiring that

> The printed primes form a strictly increasing sequence.

One can express this by the safety formula

$$\mathcal{P}_2: \quad ([\gamma \lessdot m] \ \wedge \ \widehat{\diamondsuit} [\gamma \lessdot m']) \ \Rightarrow \ (m' < m).$$

This formula states that, if the prime m is printed at a certain position and the prime m' has been printed at a strictly preceding position, then $m' < m$. Note that we have to use the strict operator $\widehat{\diamondsuit}$ in order not to compare m with itself.

We remind the reader that the validity of formula $\mathcal{P}_2$, containing the rigid specification variables m and m', poses the same requirement as the validity of the quantified formula

$$\forall m, \ m': \quad ([\gamma \lessdot m] \ \wedge \ \widehat{\diamondsuit} [\gamma \lessdot m']) \ \Rightarrow \ (m' < m).$$

Absence of Unsolicited Response

Consider a system that implements a buffer:

It has an input channel α and output channel β. The purpose of this system is to accumulate messages received on α and eventually transmit them on β. For simplicity we assume that all messages arriving on the channel α are distinct. An important safety property of such a system is

> every message transmitted on β must have been previously received on α.

In other words, the system does not invent spurious messages.

This property can be expressed by the safety formula:

$$[\beta \Leftarrow m] \Rightarrow \diamondsuit [\alpha \Rightarrow m].$$

The formula states that any position at which a message m is transmitted on β, is (weakly) preceded by a position at which the same message m is read from α.

To support composition of specifications, it is convenient to express specifications of message-passing systems by using only one type of transmission event, say sending events. When we conform to this convention, the preceding property should be reformulated to state that

> every message transmitted on β was previously transmitted on α.

The temporal formula expressing this version of the absence-of-unsolicited-response property is the following

$$\psi_{aur}: \quad [\beta \Leftarrow m] \Rightarrow \diamondsuit [\alpha \Leftarrow m].$$

This simplification does not cause any major change in the meaning of the specification. In the case that α is a synchronous channel the events $[\alpha \Leftarrow m]$ and $[\alpha \Rightarrow m]$ coincide and the two versions are equivalent. In the case that α is an asynchronous channel, there is an implicit assumption that the program implementing the buffer eventually reads all the messages sent to it on channel α, which is a reasonable assumption. We will therefore follow this convention in most of the cases.

An alternative and equivalent formulation of this property is given by the unless formula

$$\varphi_{aur}: \quad (\neg [\beta \Leftarrow m]) \; \mathcal{W} \; [\alpha \Leftarrow m].$$

This formula expresses the precedence of the appearance of m on α over the appearance of m on β. It states that, scanning the list of events from the beginning of the computation, we cannot encounter an output of m on β before we encounter an output of m on α.

No Output Duplication

Since we assume that all the input messages are distinct, we do not expect to see identical messages on the output channel. This no-output-duplication requirement can be stated by the formula

$$\psi_{nod}: \quad [\beta \Leftarrow m] \Rightarrow \boxminus \neg [\beta \Leftarrow m],$$

which states that no transmission of m on β is strictly preceded by another transmission of m on β.

This property can also be specified by the future formula

$$\varphi_{\text{nod}}: \quad [\beta \leqslant m] \;\Rightarrow\; \widehat{\Box} \neg [\beta \leqslant m].$$

The requirement

$$[\gamma \leqslant m] \;\Rightarrow\; \widehat{\Box} \neg [\gamma \leqslant m]$$

may be used as part of the specification of the prime-printing program. It requires that

> no prime is printed twice.

First-In-First-Out Ordering

Consider again the buffer system. We want to require that

> messages are transmitted over β in the same order that they are transmitted over α.

This property is more complicated than the one considered earlier, since it relates four events, i.e., the transmission of two messages m and m' over β and the transmission of the same two messages over α. One form of expressing such first-in-first-out requirement is by means of the formula

$$\psi_{\text{fifo}}: \quad ([\beta \leqslant m'] \wedge \widehat{\diamondsuit} [\beta \leqslant m]) \;\Rightarrow\; \diamondsuit([\alpha \leqslant m'] \wedge \widehat{\diamondsuit} [\alpha \leqslant m]).$$

This formula states that, if m' is sent on β at t'_β and m is sent on β at t_β, $t_\beta < t'_\beta$, then there exist t_α and t'_α, $t_\alpha < t'_\alpha \leq t'_\beta$, such that m' is sent on α at t'_α and m is sent on α at t_α.

Note that, by taking $m = m'$, this formula states that m can be sent twice on β only if m has been sent twice on α. Since we assume that the input messages are all distinct, this implies the no-output-duplication property, which was independently specified.

An alternative formula, which uses only future operators, is given by

$$\varphi_{\text{fifo}}: \quad \Big((\neg[\beta \leqslant m']) \,\mathcal{U}\, [\beta \leqslant m] \Big) \;\rightarrow\; \Big((\neg[\alpha \leqslant m']) \,\mathcal{W}\, [\alpha \leqslant m] \Big).$$

This formula states that if the transmission of m on β precedes the transmission of m' on β, then the transmission of m on α precedes the transmission of m' on α. The until operator on the left-hand side of the implication ensures that the specified property is a safety property. The use of the unless operator instead of until would have yielded a formula that does not specify a safety property.

The future formula φ_{fifo} is not equivalent to the formula ψ_{fifo}. For example, a computation containing the event $[\beta \leqslant m]$ followed by $[\beta \leqslant m']$, but which does not contain any events over α, satisfies the formula φ_{fifo} but not the formula ψ_{fifo}. This shows that the future formula φ_{fifo} does not imply the absence of unsolicited response, while in some cases ψ_{fifo} does.

However, if we consider complete specifications of the buffer system including a response formula that will be introduced in the next section, then within the context of complete specifications, φ_{fifo} is interchangable with ψ_{fifo}.

In **Problem 4.3**, the reader will compare different styles of specifications of the buffer system and show their equivalence.

Strict Precedence

Let us reconsider a system of two processes that require mutually exclusive access to their critical sections. This system is represented schematically in Fig. 4.4.

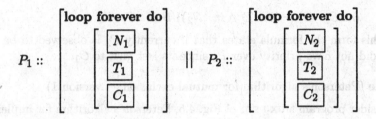

Fig. 4.4. Schematic representation of a mutual exclusion program.

In this schematic representation, the program for each process P_i, $i = 1, 2$, consists of an endless loop. The body of the loop contains three sections, N_i, T_i, and C_i. In the "noncritical" section N_i, the process is engaged in noncritical activity, which does not require coordination with the other process. In the "trying" section T_i, the process is interested in entering the critical section and is engaged in a protocol that coordinates its entry with that of the other process. In the "critical" section C_i, the process is engaged in a critical activity that must be performed exclusively by only one of the processes at any given time.

The trying sections contain the code for coordination between the processes. Entering the trying section signifies the wish of the corresponding process to enter its critical section. In the simple case that the coordination is attained by semaphores, the trying section consists of a single request statement.

We may want to state strict precedence with respect to the order of entries into the critical sections. *Strict precedence* states that

> if P_1 is in the trying section T_1 and has priority over P_2, then P_1 will precede P_2 in entering the critical section.

To be able to use this statement in a meaningful way, we must give a more precise interpretation of the notion of P_1 having priority over P_2.

We can interpret P_1 having priority over P_2 as the situation in which P_1 is already in the trying section T_1, while P_2 is still in N_2. According to this interpretation, strict precedence requires that

> if P_1 is already in T_1 while P_2 is still in N_2,
> then P_1 will precede P_2 in entering the critical section.

This may be expressed by:

$$[in\_T_1 \;\wedge\; in\_N_2] \;\Rightarrow\; (\neg in\_C_2)\,\mathcal{W}\,in\_C_1.$$

A symmetric requirement is stated for P_2.

To show that this unless formula specifies a safety property, observe that it is equivalent to

$$in\_C_2 \;\Rightarrow\; \big(\neg(in\_T_1 \wedge in\_N_2)\big)\;\mathcal{B}\;in\_C_1.$$

In this form the formula states that if currently P_2 is observed to be in C_2 then P_1 did not have priority over P_2 since its last visit to C_1.

Example (Peterson's algorithm for mutual exclusion — version 1)

Consider program MUX-PET1 of Fig. 4.5, Peterson's algorithm for implementing mutual exclusion. Boolean variables y_1 and y_2 are used by each process to signal the other process of active interest in entering the critical section. Thus, on leaving the noncritical section, process P_i sets its own variable y_i, $i = 1, 2$, to T indicating interest in entering the critical section. In a similar way, on exiting the critical section, P_i resets y_i to F. Variable s is used to resolve a tie situation between the two processes, which may arise when both processes are actively interested in entering their critical sections at the same time.

In this program, N_1 and N_2 correspond to $\ell_{1,2}$ and $m_{1,2}$; T_1 and T_2 to ℓ_3 and m_3; and C_1 and C_2 to $\ell_{4,5}$ and $m_{4,5}$. Note that locations ℓ_2 and m_2 are considered as parts of the noncritical sections rather than as parts of the trying sections. This is because, even though being at ℓ_2 reflects an internal decision of P_1 to exit the noncritical section, it has not yet made its intention publicly known. It is only at ℓ_3, after having set y_1 to T (and s to 1), that this decision becomes observable to the other process. In a similar way, we consider locations ℓ_5 and m_5 to be parts of the critical sections. This is because it is only the resetting of y_1 (and y_2) to F performed at ℓ_5 (and m_5) that makes the decision to leave the critical section observable to the other process. Strict precedence is expressed by the formula

$$[at\_\ell_3 \;\wedge\; at\_m_{1,2}] \;\Rightarrow\; (\neg at\_m_{4,5})\,\mathcal{W}\,at\_\ell_{4,5}.$$

A similar formula expresses strict precedence for the case that P_2 is at m_3 while P_1 is at ℓ_1 or ℓ_2. ◢

$$
\begin{aligned}
&\textbf{local } y_1,\ y_2\textbf{: boolean where } y_1 = \text{F},\ y_2 = \text{F} \\
&\qquad s \qquad \textbf{: integer where } s = 1
\end{aligned}
$$

$$
P_1 ::
\begin{bmatrix}
\ell_0: \textbf{loop forever do} \\
\quad
\begin{bmatrix}
\ell_1: \textbf{noncritical} \\
\ell_2: (y_1,\, s) := (\text{T},\, 1) \\
\ell_3: \textbf{await } (\neg y_2) \vee (s \neq 1) \\
\ell_4: \textbf{critical} \\
\ell_5: y_1 := \text{F}
\end{bmatrix}
\end{bmatrix}
$$

$$\|$$

$$
P_2 ::
\begin{bmatrix}
m_0: \textbf{loop forever do} \\
\quad
\begin{bmatrix}
m_1: \textbf{noncritical} \\
m_2: (y_2,\, s) := (\text{T},\, 2) \\
m_3: \textbf{await } (\neg y_1) \vee (s \neq 2) \\
m_4: \textbf{critical} \\
m_5: y_2 := \text{F}
\end{bmatrix}
\end{bmatrix}
$$

Fig. 4.5.   Program MUX-PET1 (Peterson's algorithm
for mutual exclusion) — version 1.

Bounded Overtaking

Strict precedence does not provide us with the answers to all questions. It tells us who will enter first from a situation of $in\_T_1 \wedge in\_N_2$, or from a situation of $in\_N_1 \wedge in\_T_2$. What about a situation of $in\_T_1 \wedge in\_T_2$? Who has the priority then?

In some cases, instead of providing a precise identification of who has the priority in each situation, it is sufficient to provide upper bounds on the amount of overtaking, where overtaking means one process entering the critical section ahead of its rival.

For example, for a general mutual exclusion program, we may prove the property of 1-bounded overtaking, which states that

> from the time P_1 reaches T_1, P_2 may enter the critical section ahead of P_1 (overtake P_1) at most once.

This approach relieves us, in principle, from the need to identify the holder of priority. Essentially, it says that if P_1 is in T_1, then either it already has priority and will be the first to enter the critical section or it will regain priority after the next exit of P_2 from the critical section.

Strict precedence implies a 1-bound on overtaking. This is because if P_1 is waiting at T_1 while P_2 is visiting C_2 then, in order to have a second visit to C_2, P_2 must first pass through N_2. This creates the situation $in\_T_1 \wedge in\_N_2$, at which point P_1 has priority.

In general, the property of k-*bounded overtaking* states that

> from the time P_1 reaches T_1, P_2 may enter its critical section ahead of P_1 at most k times.

To express bounded overtaking, we can use a nested unless formula of the general form

$$p \;\Rightarrow\; q_1 \,\mathcal{W}\, q_2 \,\mathcal{W} \cdots q_n \,\mathcal{W}\, r.$$

The interpretation of this formula is obtained by association to the right

$$p \;\Rightarrow\; q_1 \,\mathcal{W}\, (q_2 \,\mathcal{W}\, (\cdots (q_n \,\mathcal{W}\, r)...)).$$

Such a nested unless formula ensures that every p is followed by an interval of continuous q_1, followed by an interval of continuous $q_2, \ldots$, followed by an interval of continuous q_n, possibly terminated by r. Note, however, that since $p \,\mathcal{W}\, q$ may be satisfied by satisfying q, any of these intervals may be empty. Also, due to the definition of the unless operator, any of the intervals, say the q_m-interval, may extend to infinity, in which case the intervals for $q_{m+1}, \ldots, q_n$ are all empty and r need not occur.

The property of 1-*bounded overtaking* may now be expressed by:

$$in\_T_1 \;\Rightarrow\; (\neg in\_C_2) \,\mathcal{W}\, (in\_C_2) \,\mathcal{W}\, (\neg in\_C_2) \,\mathcal{W}\, (in\_C_1).$$

The formula states that, if P_1 is currently in T_1, then there will be an interval in which P_2 is not in C_2, followed by an interval in which P_2 is in C_2, followed by an interval in which P_2 is not in C_2, followed by an entry of P_1 to C_1. Any of the intervals may be empty, in particular the interval of P_2 being in C_2, which also allows the entry of P_1 to C_1 without P_2 getting to C_2. Also, any of the intervals may be infinite, in which case all the following intervals, as well as the entry of P_1 to C_1, are not guaranteed. Summarizing the meaning of the formula, it states that

> from the time P_1 is in T_1, in the worst case, P_2 precedes P_1 in visiting the critical section at most once.

Note that a continuous stay of a process within a critical section counts as a single visit.

An alternative formulation of this property relies on the fact that once P_1 is in T_1, the only way it can cease being in T_1 is by moving to C_1. With this assumption, we may specify 1-bounded overtaking for P_1 by the formula

$$\text{F1:} \quad in\_T_1 \Rightarrow (\neg in\_C_2)\, \mathcal{W}\, (in\_C_2)\, \mathcal{W}\, (\neg in\_C_2)\, \mathcal{W}\, (\neg in\_T_1).$$

We have already claimed that nested unless formulas are safety formulas. However, it is of special interest to show the direct translation of a nested unless formula into a nested back-to formula.

A nested back-to formula has the general form

$$p \Rightarrow q_1\, \mathcal{B}\, q_2 \cdots q_n\, \mathcal{B}\, r.$$

This formula states that every p-position is preceded by a q_1-interval, which is preceded by a q_2-interval, and so on, until a q_n-interval that may be terminated by an r-position. Any of the intervals may be empty. Also a q_m-interval for some m, $1 \leq m \leq n$, may extend all the way to position 0, in which case the intervals for $q_{m+1}, \ldots, q_n$ are all empty and r need not occur.

The translation between nested unless and nested back-to is provided by the equivalence

$$p_0 \Rightarrow p_1\, \mathcal{W}\, p_2 \cdots p_n\, \mathcal{W}\, r \quad \sim \quad \neg p_n \Rightarrow p_{n-1}\, \mathcal{B}\, p_{n-2} \cdots p_1\, \mathcal{B}\, (\neg p_0)\, \mathcal{B}\, r,$$

which the reader will prove in **Problem 4.4**.

Applying this equivalence to formula F1, we obtain

$$\text{P1:} \quad in\_C_2 \Rightarrow (in\_C_2)\, \mathcal{B}\, (\neg in\_C_2)\, \mathcal{B}\, (\neg in\_T_1)\, \mathcal{B}\, (\neg in\_T_1).$$

This can be further simplified by observing that for any formula q

$$q\, \mathcal{B}\, q \approx q.$$

We thus obtain the expression of 1-bounded overtaking by the following nested back-to formula:

$$in\_C_2 \Rightarrow (in\_C_2)\, \mathcal{B}\, (\neg in\_C_2)\, \mathcal{B}\, (\neg in\_T_1).$$

This formula provides an even clearer intuition of 1-bounded overtaking. It states that if we observe P_2 at C_2, then any previous visit of P_2 to C_2 is separated from the current visit by a point at which P_1 was not waiting in T_1. In other words, P_2 cannot visit C_2 twice in succession while P_1 continuously waits in T_1.

4.5 Examples of Progress Properties: From Guarantee to Reactivity

Next, we consider properties that belong to the progress classes. In a complete specification these properties complement the safety properties and appear as additional requirements. We recall that any formula φ belonging to the progress class κ (i.e., guarantee, ..., reactivity), is equivalent to the conjunction $\varphi_S \wedge \varphi_L$, where φ_S is a safety formula and φ_L is a liveness formula of type κ, to which we refer as a live-κ formula. A good methodology that promotes separation of concerns is to present φ_S separately as a safety requirement and present φ_L as the complementary requirement of class κ. Consequently, most of the progress properties we will specify are going to be liveness properties, and the methodology we follow is to specify as much as we can by safety properties, and to have a minimal progress part in the specification. This strategy is recommended also because safety properties are much easier to verify than properties in the other classes.

As mentioned earlier, progress properties complement safety properties to produce a complete specification. In most cases all the safety properties can be trivially satisfied by a program that does nothing. For example, in the case of the buffer system we considered, all the safety requirements are satisfied by a program that never outputs any messages on the channel β. This is consistent with the observation that "he who does not, errs not."

We may therefore view one of the roles of the progress properties as ensuring that the safety properties are not implemented by a "do-nothing" program.

In this section we illustrate several cases of progress properties, advancing from guarantee to reactivity, and indicate the safety properties that they complement.

Termination and Total Correctness

Let us reconsider a program P that performs a computational task. A typical progress property of such a program is *termination*, which claims that

> all computations properly terminate.

This property is expressible by the (live-) guarantee formula

$$\diamondsuit\; after\_P.$$

When both partial correctness, with respect to a postcondition q, and termination are guaranteed, we obtain *total correctness* with respect to q. This is the property that states

> every computation of P terminates in a q-state.

This property can be expressed as the conjunction of the safety formula

$$\square(after\_P \;\rightarrow\; q)$$

and the guarantee formula

$$\diamondsuit\; after\_P.$$

Alternately, we can express total correctness by the single guarantee formula

$$\Diamond (after\_P \wedge q).$$

As an example, total correctness of the binomial-coefficient program BINOM (Fig. 4.2) is given by the formula:

$$\Diamond \left[(at\_\widehat{\ell}_0 \wedge at\_\widehat{m}_0) \wedge (b = \tbinom{n}{k})) \right].$$

The choice between representing the safety and guarantee properties as two distinct formulas or absorbing the safety part into the guarantee part is possible in many other cases as well. The strategy adopted here recommends keeping the properties separate, since this allows an incremental process of verification, one that does not undertake a proof of too large a formula at each stage.

Guaranteed Events

Reconsider the specification of a program that computes and prints the sequence of all prime numbers. We have already specified two safety properties of this program. The first was that "all printed numbers are prime." The second was that "the sequence of printed numbers is monotonically increasing." Again, it is easy to see that a program that never prints anything trivially satisfies these two properties. Needed, therefore, is a progress requirement that would force the program to print all prime numbers.

This can be expressed by the guarantee formula:

$$\mathcal{P}_3: \quad prime(u) \;\rightarrow\; \Diamond [\gamma \lessgtr u].$$

The formula states that, if u is a prime, then there will be an instant at which u is printed. That is,

> every prime is eventually printed.

Together with the other two properties $\mathcal{P}_1$ and $\mathcal{P}_2$, this presents a complete specification of the prime-printing program.

Intermittent Assertions

In the preceding section, we considered properties expressed by local invariants. A local invariant of the form $\square (at\_\ell \rightarrow q)$, for a data-assertion q and a location ℓ, expresses the property that, when ℓ is visited, q holds. This property does not guarantee that ℓ is ever visited.

The property that we consider here also associates data assertions with locations. For example, it may associate q_1 with ℓ_1 and q_2 with ℓ_2. However, instead of stating an invariance property, it states a property of ensured progress. The general form of such a property is

$$\Diamond (at\_\ell_1 \wedge q_1) \;\rightarrow\; \Diamond (at\_\ell_2 \wedge q_2),$$

which states that

> a computation containing a state in which execution visits ℓ_1 with q_1 holding also contains a state in which execution visits ℓ_2 with q_2 holding.

Since q_2 is not guaranteed to hold at all visits to ℓ_2, this type of property is called an *intermittent assertion property*. Clearly, the formula expressing this property is an obligation formula. Note that the visit to ℓ_2 need not occur later in time than the visit to ℓ_1; it may precede the visit to ℓ_1.

Example (node counting)

To illustrate an application of formulas of this form, consider program NODE-COUNT presented in Fig. 4.6. The program accepts as input a binary tree X and counts the number of nodes that X contains. It uses a variable T that ranges over trees and a variable S ranging over lists of trees. Integer variable C contains the number of nodes that have been so far considered.

---

in X: **tree**
out C: **integer where** $C = 0$
local S : **list of tree where** $S = \langle X \rangle$
          T : **tree**

ℓ_0: **while** $S \neq \Lambda$ **do**
$$\begin{bmatrix} \ell_1\text{:} \ (T,S) := \big(hd(S),\ tl(S)\big) \\ \ell_2\text{:} \ \textbf{if } \neg empty(T) \\ \qquad \textbf{then} \ \begin{bmatrix} \ell_3\text{:} \ C := C + 1 \\ \ell_4\text{:} \ S := left(T) \bullet \big(right(T) \bullet S\big) \end{bmatrix} \end{bmatrix}$$

Fig. 4.6.   Program NODE-COUNT (node counting).

The available operations on trees are functions $left(T)$ and $right(T)$, which respectively yield the left and right subtrees of a tree T. In case tree T is nonempty but does not have a left or a right subtree, the corresponding expressions $left(T)$ or $right(T)$ return the empty tree. Also available is the predicate $empty(T)$, which tests whether T is empty.

The available operations on lists (of trees, in our case) are the functions $hd(S)$ and $tl(S)$ which, respectively, yield the first element of list S, and list S minus its first element. We use the concatenation operation $T \bullet S$, which adds the element T to the head of list S. The empty list is denoted by Λ.

At any iteration of the loop, variable S contains a list of subtrees of X whose nodes have not yet been counted. We may therefore view S as a stack of trees. The initial value of S is a list of a single element, the tree X. The iteration removes one subtree T from the stack S. If T is the empty subtree, we proceed to examine the next subtree on the stack. If T is nonempty, the program increments C by 1 and pushes the left and right subtrees of T onto the stack. When the stack is empty, the program terminates.

If we denote the number of nodes in a tree T by $|T|$, then the total correctness of this program can be specified by:

$$\Diamond \left[after\_P \wedge (C = |X|) \right].$$

It is possible to prove this property by using a local invariant of the form

$$at\_\ell_0 \Rightarrow \left[\left(C + \sum_{t \in S} |t| \right) = |X| \right].$$

This invariant states that, whenever the program is at ℓ_0, the current value of C plus the number of nodes in the trees still contained in S (i.e., nodes in yet uncounted subtrees) equals the number of nodes in the input tree X.

An alternative approach to proving the correctness of the program may be based on the following intermittent-assertion statement:

$$\Diamond \left[at\_\ell_0 \wedge (S = t \bullet s) \wedge (C = c) \right] \rightarrow \Diamond \left[at\_\ell_0 \wedge (S = s) \wedge (C = c + |t|) \right].$$

Here t, s, and c are rigid specification variables, while S and C, being program variables, are flexible. This formula states that being at ℓ_0 with a nonempty list S ensures a corresponding second arrival at ℓ_0. On this second arrival (not necessarily the next visit to ℓ_0) the top element of the stack, represented by t, will have been removed and the value of C incremented by the number of nodes in the tree t. ◾

Freedom from Individual Starvation and Livelocks

We have already observed that freedom from deadlock is a safety property. By definition, a deadlock is a situation in which no component of the program (i.e., no process) can continue. A program may be deadlock free and yet a particular process completely immobilized at a particular location ℓ. We refer to such a situation as *individual starvation* or *livelock* at ℓ.

Let ℓ be a location in a program. To state that the system is free of individual starvation at location ℓ, we may use the response formula

$$\Box \Diamond \neg at\_\ell.$$

This formula states that

the system does not stay forever at ℓ,

and hence a process currently waiting at ℓ must eventually progress.

An equivalent form of this formula is

$$at\_\ell \;\Rightarrow\; \Diamond\, \neg at\_\ell,$$

which states that, whenever execution is at ℓ, it will eventually progress beyond ℓ.

In some cases we are interested in the more general property, claiming that the system does not stay constrained forever within a given range of locations L. We refer to this property as *freedom from livelock* within L.

Consider, for example, a program containing the statement

ℓ_1: **while** c **do** ℓ_2: **skip**.

Clearly, if c is always true, the program may loop forever in the range $\{\ell_1, \ell_2\}$. This is not individual starvation since the program is not stuck at a single location but rather within a range.

The property of not having a livelock within the range of locations L can be expressed by the response formula

$$\Box \Diamond\, \neg in\_L \qquad \text{or equivalently} \qquad in\_L \;\Rightarrow\; \Diamond\, \neg in\_L.$$

Accessibility

Consider again the scheme consisting of two processes that coordinate their entry to critical sections C_1 and C_2 (Fig. 4.4).

We have already specified two safety properties of this program. The first was mutual exclusion, by which the two processes never co-reside in their critical sections. The second was that of 1-bounded overtaking, by which, from the time P_1 enters T_1, P_2 can precede P_1 in entering the critical section at most once. A similar requirement is formulated for the 1-bounded overtaking of P_2 by P_1.

Both these safety properties can be satisfied in a trivial manner by a program that does not allow moving from T_1 to C_1 or from T_2 to C_2 at all. This can be easily done by taking the trying sections to be the statement **await** F. In this trivial protocol no process ever gets to its critical section. It is obvious that in such a case, P_1 and P_2 could never co-reside in their critical sections, since neither of them ever gets to its critical section. It is also clear that neither P_2 nor P_1 can overtake its partner, because neither ever enters its critical section. This illustrates the general principle mentioned earlier, by which a "do-nothing" program usually satisfies all the safety properties.

Only progress requirements can exclude this trivial "do-nothing" implementation. In the case considered here, the natural progress property is that of *accessibility*. This property guarantees that

> any process that wishes to enter its critical section will eventually succeed.

Accessibility may be specified by the response formulas

$$in\_T_1 \Rightarrow \Diamond\, at\_C_1 \quad \text{and} \quad in\_T_2 \Rightarrow \Diamond\, at\_C_2.$$

The first formula, for example, states that whenever P_1 is in T_1, it is guaranteed to eventually reach C_1.

Ensured Response

Let us reconsider the buffer example:

$$\xrightarrow{\quad \alpha \quad} \boxed{\text{Buffer}} \xrightarrow{\quad \beta \quad}$$

We have already expressed several safety properties of this system, including the requirement that every message transmitted must have been previously received and the preservation of ordering between messages.

The main progress property for the buffer system is the guarantee that any message that is placed on input channel α will eventually be transmitted on output channel β. Assuming, as before, that all input messages are distinct, this requirement can be expressed by the response formula

$$\varphi_{\text{res}}: \quad [\alpha \Leftarrow m] \Rightarrow \Diamond[\beta \Leftarrow m].$$

This formula states that every input message m transmitted on channel α must eventually be transmitted on channel β.

Eventual Boundedness

For an example of a persistence property, we may reconsider the prime-printing program. A relevant persistence property states that

> the sequence of printed numbers will eventually be bounded below by any positive integer.

This can be specified by

$$\Diamond\,\Box\,\neg[\gamma \Leftarrow n].$$

The validity of this formula implies that any integer n can be printed at most finitely many times. It is not difficult to see that this property is equivalent to the requirement of eventual boundedness.

Expressing Fairness Requirements

We have already observed that the requirement of justice for a transition τ can be expressed by the response formula

$$\square \diamondsuit \big(\neg enabled(\tau) \vee last\text{-}taken(\tau) \big).$$

The requirement of compassion for a transition τ is expressed by the reactivity formula

$$\square \diamondsuit enabled(\tau) \; \rightarrow \; \square \diamondsuit last\text{-}taken(\tau).$$

Let us consider fair selection. Let

$$[\ell_1 \colon S_1 \; \textbf{fair-or} \; \ell_2 \colon S_2]$$

be a fair-selection statement, introduced in Problem 2.12, and assume that τ_1 is the (only) transition at the front of S_1. The requirement of fair selection with respect to S_1 is

> if ℓ_1 is visited infinitely many times and at all but finitely many of these visits τ_1 is enabled, then τ_1 is taken infinitely many times.

This requirement can be expressed by the reactivity formula

$$\square \diamondsuit \, at\_\ell_1 \; \rightarrow \; \square \diamondsuit \big((at\_\ell_1 \wedge \neg enabled(\tau_1)) \vee last\text{-}taken(\tau_1) \big).$$

The formula states that if at_ℓ_1 holds at infinitely many positions, then there are infinitely many positions at which either at_ℓ_1 holds but τ_1 is disabled or τ_1 is taken.

Eventual Reliability

In modeling and studying unreliable systems, we may often wish to specify an eventually reliable channel. This is a channel that may lose or distort some messages submitted to it for transmission but cannot consistently lose all the submitted messages. If the sender is persistent and keeps resubmitting the same message until its proper transmission is acknowledged, an *eventually reliable* (ER) channel must eventually transmit the message to the receiver. We may model such a channel by the following system:

$$\xrightarrow{\;\alpha\;} \boxed{\text{ER channel}} \xrightarrow{\;\beta\;}$$

The property of eventual reliability states that

> a message that is repeatedly submitted will eventually be transmitted.

This property can be specified by the reactivity formula:

$$\square \diamondsuit [\alpha \preccurlyeq m] \; \Rightarrow \; \diamondsuit [\beta \preccurlyeq m].$$

This formula states that if message m is sent on α the input port to the ER channel infinitely many times, then message m must eventually be sent on channel β, which is the output port of the ER channel. This is stated for all positions in the computation.

This formula is equivalent to

$$\Box \Diamond [\alpha \Leftarrow m] \;\rightarrow\; \Box \Diamond [\beta \Leftarrow m],$$

which states that if m is submitted infinitely many times it is transmitted infinitely many times.

It is interesting to note that such specifications provide nonquantitative representations of probabilistic behavior. A quantitative representation of an eventually reliable channel assigns a fixed probability μ, $0 < \mu < 1$, to the event that the channel loses any individual message. Analyzing, for example, a program that keeps retransmitting a message over such a channel until the intended recipient acknowledges receiving it, we may claim that the message successfully arrives with probability 1. In many cases we can replace the statement of successful arrival with probability 1 over a probabilistically behaving channel, by the claim $\Diamond$ *arr* (*arr* denoting the event of successful arrival) over an eventually reliable channel, i.e., a channel that satisfies the eventual reliability requirement.

In **Problem 4.5**, the reader will show that a simpler version of eventual reliability can be expressed by persistence formulas.

4.6 Example: A Resource Allocator

As a comprehensive example illustrating a complete specification, we consider a system that manages the allocation of a single resource among several competing processes. The system (Fig. 4.7) consists of an allocator (or arbiter) process A and m customer processes $C_1, \ldots, C_m$.

The resource can represent, for example, a shared disk or a printer. In the simple case we consider here, there is only one indivisible resource, but more general cases can be specified as well.

Message-Passing Version

Each customer C_i communicates with allocator A via two asynchronous channels. Channel α_i leads from C_i to A, while channel β_i leads from A to C_i. The expected protocol between C_i and A is the following:

C_i sends the message rq (request) on α_i, signaling a request for the resource.

A sends the message gr (grant) on β_i, signaling that the resource has been

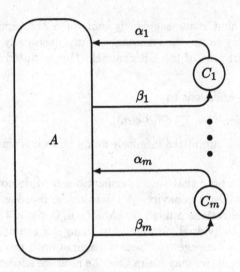

Fig. 4.7.   Resource allocator system.

granted to C_i.

C_i sends the message rl (release) on α_i, signaling a release of the resource.

A sends the message ak (acknowledge) on β_i, acknowledging the release and permitting C_i to submit subsequent requests.

We use the following abbreviations for the events of sending a message on the channels:

$$rq_i = [\alpha_i \lessdot rq] \qquad rl_i = [\alpha_i \lessdot rl]$$
$$gr_i = [\beta_i \lessdot gr] \qquad ak_i = [\beta_i \lessdot ak]$$
$$c_i = rq_i \lor rl_i \lor gr_i \lor ak_i.$$

Event c_i denotes that some message related to C_i is being sent on either α_i or β_i.

Safety

The safety part of the specification consists of the following requirements:

- **Mutual Exclusion**

    This property states that, at any instant, the resource is given to at most one customer.

    We introduce the past formula

    $$granted_i = (\neg ak_i) \, S \, (gr_i).$$

This formula describes a state that has been preceded by a gr_i event, and no ak_i event has occurred since then. This implies that the resource has been given to C_i sometime in the past and has not been withdrawn yet. Formula $granted_i$ characterizes the computation states at which the resource is allocated to C_i.

The property of mutual exclusion is then specified by the formula

$$\square \left(\bigwedge_{i \neq j} \neg(granted_i \wedge granted_j) \right).$$

The formula states, that at most one $granted_i$ can be true at any instant.

• **Conformance with the Protocol**

The next list of requirements ensures that both the allocator and the customers adhere to the protocol. This means that the c_i-events always occur in the cyclic order: rq_i, gr_i, rl_i, ak_i, where the first event is an rq_i.

$$\square \left(rq_i \ \rightarrow \ (\neg c_i) \,\widehat{B}\, ak_i \right).$$

This formula states that the most recent c_i-event preceding rq_i can only be ak_i.

$$\square \left(gr_i \ \rightarrow \ (\neg c_i) \,\widehat{S}\, rq_i \right).$$

This formula states that the most recent c_i-event preceding gr_i can only be rq_i, and that it always happens before gr_i. This formula uses the since operator (unlike the back-to used by the previous formula) to ensure that rq_i actually happens.

$$\square \left(rl_i \ \rightarrow \ (\neg c_i) \,\widehat{S}\, gr_i \right).$$

This formula states that the most recent c_i-event preceding rl_i can only be gr_i, and that it always happens before rl_i.

$$\square \left(ak_i \ \rightarrow \ (\neg c_i) \,\widehat{S}\, rl_i \right).$$

This formula states that the most recent c_i-event preceding ak_i can only be rl_i, and that it always happens before ak_i.

The fact that we have used the back-to for rq_i and since for the other three formulas also identifies rq_i as the first c_i-event in any computation.

An alternative and equivalent expression of these four requirements uses the unless operator:

$$\square \left((ak_i \ \vee \ first) \ \rightarrow \ (\neg c_i) \,\widehat{W}\, rq_i \right)$$

$$\square \left(rq_i \ \rightarrow \ (\neg c_i) \,\widehat{W}\, gr_i \right)$$

$$\square \left(gr_i \ \rightarrow \ (\neg c_i) \,\widehat{W}\, rl_i \right)$$

$$\square \left(rl_i \ \rightarrow \ (\neg c_i) \,\widehat{W}\, ak_i \right).$$

The difference between the past and future formulations of the conformance property is obvious. In the past formulation, we identified for each event its (only) possible predecessor. In the future formulation, we identified for each event its (only) possible successor.

- **Bounded Overtaking**

It is not an essential part of the specification, but we may want to impose the requirement of 1-bounded overtaking. This property states that, from the time C_i makes a request, C_j may be granted the resource ahead of C_i at most once, for any $j \neq i$.

Let $requesting_i$ denote the formula

$$requesting_i = (\neg gr_i) \, \mathcal{S} \, rq_i.$$

The formula $requesting_i$ characterizes situations at which C_i is waiting for service, i.e., it has already requested the resource but has not yet received it.

Then, 1-bounded overtaking of C_j over C_i, for $i \neq j$, can be expressed by:

$$\Box \big[(granted_j \, \wedge \, requesting_i) \; \rightarrow \; (\neg gr_j) \, \widehat{\mathcal{W}} \, gr_i\big].$$

This formula states that, if C_j is granted the resource while C_i is waiting, i.e., C_j has overtaken C_i once, then the next customer among C_i and C_j to get the resource, is C_i. That is, there cannot be two consecutive overtakings of C_i by C_j.

Progress

The progress part of the specification forces both the allocator and the customers to take some vital actions. As usual, all the safety properties can be satisfied by a system in which neither the allocator nor the customers ever send a message. They are also satisfied by a system in which the customers send messages, consistent with the protocol, but the allocator never responds. The role of the progress part is to exclude such trivial solutions.

All the progress requirements are of the response class, ensuring responses to certain events.

- **Response to Requests**

This property ensures that every request for the resource is eventually honored. It is expressed by

$$rq_i \; \Rightarrow \; \Diamond \, gr_i.$$

- **Release of Resource**

The previous requirement is an obligation of the allocator in order to ensure good service. However, some cooperation from the customers is also required. Some of this cooperation was already requested in the safety part, mainly, in the requirement of conformance with the protocol. The progress requirement for the customers is that a customer that has the resource will eventually release it. Clearly, if a customer C_i appropriates the resource and never releases it, the allocator cannot guarantee service to another customer C_j, $j \neq i$, without violating the mutual exclusion requirement. The customer's progress obligation is given by

$$gr_i \Rightarrow \Diamond \, rl_i.$$

- **Response to Releases**

An equally important allocator responsibility is the assurance of response to notification of release. Due to the safety requirements, customer C_i cannot make a next request until its previous release was acknowledged by the ak_i message. Consequently, a devious way for the allocator to withhold service is not to acknowledge a release. The following requirement outlaws such behavior:

$$rl_i \Rightarrow \Diamond \, ak_i.$$

A Single Requirement

The previous three progress properties can be unified into a single requirement. This requirement identifies a state as *quiescent*, relative to C_i, if the last C_i-communication (if any) was an ak_i-event. The requirement states that the computation visits quiescent states infinitely many times, relative to each C_i.

$$\Box \Diamond \left((\neg c_i) \, \mathcal{B} \, ak_i \right).$$

Note that this formula states that either ak_i occurs infinitely many times or eventually ak_i occurs and no further c_i-events take place.

Shared-Variables Version

It is interesting to consider a version of the resource allocator system in which the communication between the allocator and the customers is based on shared variables rather than on message passing. Such a system is schematically represented in Fig. 4.8.

In this version, communication channels α_i and β_i have been replaced by boolean variables r_i ("request") and g_i ("grant"), respectively. Representing them as directed edges implies that C_i may change r_i but may only read g_i, while A may change g_i but only read r_i. We assume that the initial value of all these boolean variables is F.

The four messages participating in the protocol between C_i and A are encoded as follows:

rq_i signaled by C_i setting r_i to T

gr_i signaled by A setting g_i to T

rl_i signaled by C_i resetting r_i to F

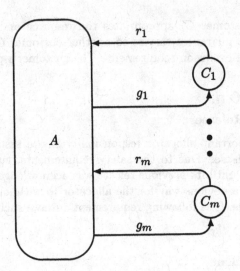

Fig. 4.8.   Shared-variables resource allocator.

ak_i signaled by A resetting g_i to F.

It is possible to define events corresponding to the rising and falling of boolean variables. For a boolean variable b, we define

$$b \uparrow = b \wedge \ominus (\neg b)$$
$$b \downarrow = (\neg b) \wedge \ominus b.$$

The event of b rising occurs in a position $j > 0$, such that $b = $ F at $j - 1$ and $b = $ T at j. Similarly, b falls at position $j > 0$, if $b = $ T at $j - 1$ and $b = $ F at j.

With these definitions we can directly translate the four events rq_i, gr_i, rl_i, and ak_i, considered in the message-passing system, into the events of rise and fall of the two boolean communication variables r_i and g_i:

$$rq_i = r_i \uparrow$$
$$gr_i = g_i \uparrow$$
$$rl_i = r_i \downarrow$$
$$ak_i = g_i \downarrow.$$

Given this translation, it is now straightforward to reinterpret the specification given for the message-passing system in the shared-variables context. However, while it is more natural to use an event-oriented style of specification for message-passing systems, it is more natural to use a state-oriented style of specification for shared-variables systems. We illustrate this point by the following state-oriented specification.

Safety

- **Mutual Exclusion**

  This property is specified by the formula

  $$\Box\left(\sum g_i \leq 1\right).$$

The formula uses arithmetization of boolean values, by which T is interpreted as 1 and F as 0. Consequently, the formula states that at most one g_i can be true (equal 1).

- **Conformance with the Protocol**

  As before, this is given by four formulas.

The expected behavior is presented in Fig. 4.9. The diagram contains four states corresponding to the different possible values of the communication variables r_i and g_i. The transitions drawn between these states represent the possible sequence of changes. We have labeled each transition by the rising or falling event corresponding to the variable that changes.

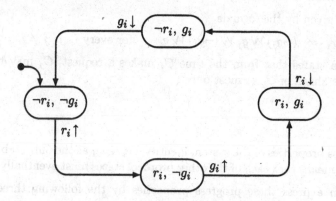

Fig. 4.9.   Expected protocol for C_i.

The following four formulas characterize the changes in the values of the communication variables that are allowed by the protocol. To characterize the next change allowed from a state $(\neg r_i \wedge \neg g_i)$ we can use the formula

$$(\neg r_i \wedge \neg g_i) \Rightarrow (\neg r_i \wedge \neg g_i) \,\mathcal{W}\, (r_i \wedge \neg g_i).$$

However, a shorter equivalent formula is given by

$$\neg g_i \Rightarrow (\neg g_i) \,\mathcal{W}\, (r_i \wedge \neg g_i).$$

This formula states that from the time $g_i = \text{F}$, i.e., the resource is not granted to C_i, g_i will not change to T unless C_i makes a request by turning r_i to T first.

This is another example of an absence of unsolicited response property.

In **Problem 4.6**, the reader will show the equivalence of these two formulas.

Similar formulas complete the specification of the rules of the protocol:

$$r_i \;\Rightarrow\; r_i \,\mathcal{W}\,(r_i \wedge g_i).$$

The formula states that, from the time C_i makes a request, the request is kept up at least until A responds.

$$g_i \;\Rightarrow\; g_i \,\mathcal{W}\,(\neg r_i \wedge g_i).$$

This formula states that the resource will not be prematurely withdrawn, i.e., A will not reset g_i to F until after C_i releases the resource by resetting r_i to F.

$$\neg r_i \;\Rightarrow\; (\neg r_i) \,\mathcal{W}\,(\neg r_i \wedge \neg g_i).$$

The formula states that from the time C_i releases the resource, it will not make another request (by setting r_i to T) until after A acknowledges the release by resetting g_i to F.

- **1-Bounded Overtaking**

  This is given by the formula

  $$r_i \;\Rightarrow\; (\neg g_j) \,\mathcal{W}\, g_j \,\mathcal{W}\, (\neg g_j) \,\mathcal{W}\, g_i \qquad \text{for every } i, \, j, \; j \neq i.$$

  The formula states that from the time C_i makes a request, C_j may be granted the resource ahead of C_i at most once.

Progress

The progress properties of the system identify $\neg r_i \wedge \neg g_i$ as the only stable protocol state. This means that each of the other protocol states must eventually be exited.

We can express these progress properties by the following three response formulas:

$$r_i \;\Rightarrow\; \Diamond g_i.$$

This formula states that every r_i request must be followed by a g_i grant.

$$g_i \;\Rightarrow\; \Diamond \neg r_i.$$

This formula states that once granted the resource, the customer must eventually release it.

$$\neg r_i \;\Rightarrow\; \Diamond \neg g_i.$$

This formula states that once the customer notifies a release, the allocator must respond by resetting g_i to F.

Again, it is possible to group these three requirements into a single requirement, given by

$$\Box \Diamond (\neg r_i \wedge \neg g_i).$$

This specification requires, for each i, that there are infinitely many states in which C_i is quiescent, i.e., there are no pending requests and no grant.

4.7 *Expressivity of the Specification Language*

An important question to be considered is how expressive the specification language we have introduced is. In particular, can it express most of the program properties of interest?

In this section we will show that the expressive power of the propositional fragment of temporal logic, which allows only boolean variables and no quantification, is limited. We will show two examples of properties that cannot be specified in this restricted language. However, once we allow quantification and variables ranging over infinite domains, all of those limitations are removed.

Observing Parity

A well-known example of a property that cannot be specified by propositional temporal logic is the property of parity.

Let p and q be two propositions (flexible boolean variables). A p-position j is defined to be an *even p-occurrence* if the number of (weakly) preceding p-positions is even. A p-position that is not an even occurrence is an *odd p-occurrence*.

Consider the property $\mathcal{P}$ stating that q can hold only at even p-occurrences.

As an example, the following periodic sequence (of period 5) has property $\mathcal{P}$:

$$\langle p{:}\,\text{T},\ q{:}\,\text{F}\rangle,\ \langle p{:}\,\text{T},\ q{:}\,\text{T}\rangle,\ \langle p{:}\,\text{F},\ q{:}\,\text{F}\rangle,\ \langle p{:}\,\text{T},\ q{:}\,\text{F}\rangle,\ \langle p{:}\,\text{T},\ q{:}\,\text{F}\rangle,\ \ldots.$$

Note that q does not hold at every even p-occurrence.

On the other hand, the sequence

$$\langle p{:}\,\text{T},\ q{:}\,\text{T}\rangle,\ \langle p{:}\,\text{T},\ q{:}\,\text{T}\rangle,\ \langle p{:}\,\text{T},\ q{:}\,\text{F}\rangle,\ \ldots$$

does not have property $\mathcal{P}$, since q holds at position 0, which is an odd p-occurrence.

It is known that this property cannot be specified in propositional temporal logic. This can be generalized by observing that what is required in order to express property $\mathcal{P}$ is the ability to count modulo 2 and decide whether the accumulated count is 0 or 1. The more general observation can be stated as the following:

> Propositional temporal logic cannot count modulo any constant greater than 1.

Specifying Parity by Quantified Formulas

If we remove the prohibition to use quantifiers, there is an easy way to specify property $\mathcal{P}$ described earlier. We introduce an auxiliary flexible boolean variable k, whose role is precisely that of counting the number of p-occurrences. The value of k is T at all positions j such that the number of p-positions preceding j is even. Otherwise, k is false.

Consider the formula

$$\exists k \colon (k = \neg p) \;\wedge\; \widehat{\square}(k = k^- +_2 p) \;\wedge\; \square(q \to p \wedge k).$$

The formula states the existence of (a sequence of values for) a flexible variable k that satisfies three clauses. The first clause states that the value of k at position 0 is T iff p is false. If p is true then position 0 is an odd p-occurrence and we expect k to be false at such positions.

The second clause uses the arithmetical interpretation of boolean values to state that the value of k at any position is obtained by adding to its value at the preceding position 1 if p is currently true and 0 otherwise. Addition is performed modulo 2. To emphasize the role of k as a counter modulo 2, we present this clause in an arithmetical notation, where T is represented as 1 and F as 0. A more conventional presentation of this clause is

$$\neg p \;\leftrightarrow\; (k \leftrightarrow \ominus k),$$

by which the value of k at position j equals its value at $j-1$ iff p is false at j.

In both presentations, the clause states that k is equal to $\ominus k$ iff p is currently false.

The last clause states the main claim of the property, namely, that q can be true only at even p-occurrences.

Note the different roles played by the three clauses. The first two clauses make sure that k is indeed a proper counter. They uniquely determine the values assumed by k on any given sequence. The last clause uses the availability of a counter to state a property of q.

We may view the first two clauses as providing an inductive definition of the values assumed by variable k. They specify the initial value of k and give a general rule for computing the new value of k based on the previous value of k and the current value of p.

Using Universal Quantification

In many cases, the introduction of auxiliary variables, such as counter k, can be done in two dual styles. The style presented earlier can be described as an *existential* style. It claims the existence of a variable k that (a) behaves as counter and (b) fulfills $\square(q \to p \wedge k)$.

A dual style of specification, to which we refer as a *universal* style, is presented by the formula

$$\forall k: \; [(k = \neg p) \wedge \widehat{\Box}(k \; = \; k^- +_2 p)] \; \rightarrow \; \Box(q \; \rightarrow \; p \wedge k).$$

The formula states that for every boolean variable k, if k behaves as a counter, then the clause $\Box(q \rightarrow p \wedge k)$ is fulfilled.

This formula has the advantage that the only quantification it contains is universal. According to a general observation made before, this formula is valid iff

$$\varphi: \quad [(k = \neg p) \wedge \widehat{\Box}(k \; = \; k^- +_2 p)] \; \rightarrow \; \Box(q \; \rightarrow \; p \wedge k)$$

is. Thus, to ensure that all computations of a given program have the property $\mathcal{P}$, it is sufficient to show that φ is valid over $\mathcal{P}$.

Note that this does not contradict the statement made earlier, claiming that property $\mathcal{P}$ cannot be specified by quantifier-free formulas. The formula φ does not specify the property $\mathcal{P}$ in the sense that an arbitrary sequence σ has the property $\mathcal{P}$ iff it satisfies φ. In particular, all sequences in which k does not behave like a counter, i.e., $(k = \neg p) \wedge \widehat{\Box}(k = k^- +_2 p)$ is false, trivially satisfy φ.

The only claim made is the weaker one, by which (assuming k does not occur in a program P) if φ is valid over P then all computations of P have the property $\mathcal{P}$.

A Buffer with Duplicate Inputs

Having whetted the tool of auxiliary variables on a simple example, let us confront a more serious case. Consider again the buffer system with the following interface to its environment:

In the previous discussion of this system we made the simplifying assumption that all the input messages are distinct. Under this assumption we can propose a specification consisting of the formulas

$$\psi_{\text{aur}}: \quad [\beta \preccurlyeq m] \; \Rightarrow \; \diamondsuit[\alpha \preccurlyeq m]$$

$$\psi_{\text{fifo}}: \quad ([\beta \preccurlyeq m'] \wedge \widehat{\diamondsuit}[\beta \preccurlyeq m]) \; \Rightarrow \; \diamondsuit([\alpha \preccurlyeq m'] \wedge \widehat{\diamondsuit}[\alpha \preccurlyeq m])$$

$$\varphi_{\text{res}}: \quad [\alpha \preccurlyeq m] \; \Rightarrow \; \diamondsuit[\beta \preccurlyeq m].$$

Formula ψ_{aur} requires that any message transmitted on β was previously transmitted on α. The formula ψ_{fifo} requires that messages are transmitted on β in the same order they are transmitted on α. The formula φ_{res} ensures that every message transmitted on α is eventually transmitted on β.

This specification is adequate under the assumption that all incoming messages are distinct. However, if we consider the more general case, in which identical messages may appear on the input channel, this specification is no longer adequate.

Let us consider a simple case in which there are only two possible values for a message, say, a and b. The input to the system in this case is a (possibly infinite) stream of messages each of which is either a or b. In this case, we do not need the implicit quantification over m and m' that is inherent in the formulas ψ_{aur}, ψ_{fifo}, and φ_{res}, and can consider instead their versions where m and m' are instantiated to a and b. Thus, the instantiated version of ψ_{aur} is given by

$$([\beta \triangleleft a] \;\Rightarrow\; \diamondsuit [\alpha \triangleleft a]) \;\wedge\; ([\beta \triangleleft b] \;\Rightarrow\; \diamondsuit [\alpha \triangleleft b]).$$

The following computation satisfies all the requirements in the specification, yet is not an acceptable behavior of a buffer that outputs messages in the same order it has received them.

$$[\alpha \triangleleft a] \qquad [\alpha \triangleleft b] \qquad [\alpha \triangleleft a] \qquad [\beta \triangleleft b] \qquad [\beta \triangleleft a].$$

The difficulty is not specific to the particular specification we have selected for the distinct-input case. It has been formally proven that a buffer with replicated input messages cannot be specified in unquantified temporal logic. This points to a basic limitation of unquantified temporal logic (similar to the one we have encountered before), namely, its inability to count repeated instances of identical events.

We will discuss several approaches to the solution of this problem.

Specifying a Buffer by Quantified Formulas

We will present two different styles of specification of a general buffer, using quantified temporal logic.

Specification by Abstract Implementation

The first style we consider may be described as *abstract implementation*. In this style we may choose the most straightforward implementation of a buffer and describe its operational behavior by specifying the initial values of the auxiliary variables participating in the implementation and the transitions they may undergo at each step. What makes the implementation abstract is the quantification over the auxiliary variables. This means that we do not require or imply in any way that real implementations of the given specification should contain any of these variables.

The following formula presents a specification of this style for the buffer example. The specification employs several flexible specification variables that are existentially quantified: b ranging over lists (sequences) of messages, and d

ranging over messages.

$$
\varphi: \quad \exists b, d: \left\{
\begin{array}{l}
(b = \Lambda) \\[4pt]
\wedge \; \boxed{\square} \left[
\begin{array}{l}
(\neg[\alpha \ll] \;\wedge\; \neg[\beta \ll] \;\wedge\; (b = b^-)) \;\vee \\[4pt]
([\alpha \ll d] \;\wedge\; (b = b^- \bullet d)) \;\vee \\[4pt]
([\beta \ll d] \;\wedge\; (b^- = d \bullet b))
\end{array}
\right] \\[18pt]
\wedge \; ((b \neq \Lambda) \;\Rightarrow\; \Diamond[\beta \ll])
\end{array}
\right\}
$$

The specification states the existence of a list-valued variable b that is initially empty and a variable d. We may view b as containing the list of pending messages that have been transmitted over α and not yet emitted into β. The messages are kept in the order of their transmission over α. The specification then proceeds to describe what may happen in the transition leading to each state. There are three possible cases:

- There has been no transmission on either α or β and b retains its value.

- There has been a transmission of message d over α and d is appended to the end of b.

- Message d, previously residing at the head of b, i.e., $d = hd(b^-)$, is sent to β and removed from b.

The last clause of the specification contains the response requirement that, as long as there are still pending messages, future outputs on β are guaranteed.

It is most important to realize that, although this specification uses a list-valued variable to express the desired property, this carries no implication that a similar structure must be present in the implementation. This is just a device for a simpler presentation of the specification.

It is not difficult to see that the formula φ implies the absence of unsolicited response and preservation of first-in-first-out ordering without any assumption about distinctness of input messages.

Specification by Unique Identifiers

We now present another style of specification for the buffer example, based on a completely different approach.

Since the main inadequacy of the original specification is due to the fact that input messages may not be distinct, we may use quantified variables to provide unique identifiers to the messages and thus make them distinct. To do so we use the auxiliary flexible variable id, whose domain is immaterial as long as it contains infinitely many distinct values. We introduce the following abbreviations:

$$[\alpha \ll m, i]: \quad [\alpha \ll m] \;\wedge\; (id = i)$$

$$[\beta \prec m, \ i]: \quad [\beta \prec m] \ \wedge \ (id = i).$$

We refer to the value of variable id at a state in which the communication predicate $[\alpha \prec m]$ or $[\beta \prec m]$ holds as the identifier of the events $[\alpha \prec m]$ or $[\beta \prec m]$. We refer to a state at which $[\alpha \prec m]$ holds as an α-*communication* state and to a state satisfying $[\beta \prec m]$ as a β-*communication* state.

The following formula is suggested as a specification for a buffer program:

$\psi: \quad \exists id \ \forall m, \ m', \ i, \ i':$

$$
\left[
\begin{array}{l}
([\alpha \prec m, \ i] \ \Rightarrow \ \widehat{\boxminus} \neg [\alpha \prec m', \ i]) \ \wedge \\[4pt]
([\beta \prec m, \ i] \ \Rightarrow \ \diamondsuit\!\!\!\!\!\diagup\,[\alpha \prec m, \ i]) \ \wedge \\[4pt]
(([\beta \prec m', \ i'] \ \wedge \ \widehat{\diamondsuit}[\beta \prec m, \ i]) \ \Rightarrow \ \diamondsuit\!\!\!\!\!\diagup\,([\alpha \prec m', \ i'] \ \wedge \ \widehat{\diamondsuit}[\alpha \prec m, \ i])) \ \wedge \\[4pt]
[\alpha \prec m, \ i] \ \Rightarrow \ \diamondsuit[\beta \prec m, \ i]
\end{array}
\right]
$$

The body of this formula consists of four clauses:

- The first clause requires that different α-communication states are associated with distinct identifiers. This makes the input messages distinct.

- The second clause represents the requirement of absence of unsolicited response. It requires that any β-communication of the message m with identifier i is preceded by an α-communication of m with the same identifier. Thus, while identifiers are required to be distinct over α-communications, they must be identical between an α-communication and its matching β-communication.

- The third clause requires first-in-first-out ordering between messages, including their identifiers. Note that, since identifiers are distinct over α-messages, this clause implies that they are also distinct over β-messages.

- The last clause provides the response requirement stating that any α-communication of m is followed by a β-communication of m with the same identifier.

Communication History Variables

An interesting approach to the specification of message-passing systems relies on the use of communication history variables.

Let α be a channel. A communication history variable h_α is a list-valued variable that at any state of the computation contains the sequence of all messages that have been transmitted on α in all the preceding transitions, including the one leading to the current state.

The following formula characterizes variable h_α as a communication history variable for channel α:

$$H_\alpha: \quad (h_\alpha = \Lambda) \ \wedge \ \widehat{\Box} \left[\begin{array}{l} (\neg[\alpha \Leftarrow] \ \wedge \ h_\alpha = h_\alpha^-) \ \vee \\ \exists m: ([\alpha \Leftarrow m] \ \wedge \ h_\alpha = h_\alpha^- \bullet m) \end{array} \right].$$

This formula states that the initial value of h_α is the empty list Λ and that ever after, either there is no communication on α (and h_α retains its previous value) or there is communication on α and the communicated value is appended to the end of h_α.

A similar formula H_β characterizes the variable h_β as a communication history variable for channel β. For two list variables x and y, we use the notation $x \prec y$ to denote that the list x is a proper prefix of the list y, and $x \preccurlyeq y$ to denote that x is a prefix of y (possibly $x = y$).

We may now specify a buffer by the formula

$$(H_\alpha \ \wedge \ H_\beta) \ \rightarrow \ \Big(\Box(h_\beta \preccurlyeq h_\alpha) \ \wedge \ ((h_\beta \prec h_\alpha) \ \Rightarrow \ \Diamond[\beta \Leftarrow]) \Big).$$

This succinct specification states that if h_α and h_β behave as communication history variables for α and β then two conjuncts hold. The conjunct $\Box(h_\beta \preccurlyeq h_\alpha)$ claims that the list of messages transmitted on β is a prefix of the list of messages transmitted on α. It covers the properties of absence of unsolicited response and first-in-first-out ordering at the same time. The conjunct $(h_\beta \prec h_\alpha) \Rightarrow \Diamond[\beta \Leftarrow]$ claims that, as long as not every α-message has been transmitted on β, there is still a future β-communication expected.

Data Independence

An interesting different approach to the problem of duplicate messages is provided by the notion of data independence.

Let us reconsider the specification given by the conjunction

$$\varphi: \quad \psi_{\text{aur}} \ \wedge \ \psi_{\text{fifo}} \ \wedge \ \varphi_{\text{res}}.$$

Suppose we have a program that faithfully implements this specification. We know that if the sequence of incoming messages contains no duplicates, the program has no choice but to behave as a good buffer should. On the other hand, if the input sequence contains duplicates, the program may deviate from the behavior of a good buffer.

Notice, however, that in order to display such a behavior, i.e., to satisfy the specification but not be a good buffer for some of the cases, the program has to be able to examine the contents of the input messages, and in particular to be able to compare two messages for equality.

Consider, on the other hand, a program that never examines the contents of a message. It certainly has to be able to read the message into a variable, to copy it from one variable to another, and to output it from some variable. But suppose it never compares it with any other message or constant. We call such a program a *data-independent* program, because its behavior is completely independent of the contents of the messages. An easy syntactic check can determine whether a given program is data-independent. The following claim can be made:

Claim

If P is a data-independent program that satisfies specification φ, then it implements a good buffer.

It is not difficult to see the soundness of the claim. Since program P cannot tell whether the input sequence it currently processes has duplicates, it must always be on its best behavior in outputting each input message precisely once, while respecting the order of arrival.

Thus, while the specification φ does not fully specify the behavior of a good buffer, any data-independent program that satisfies it must behave as a good buffer.

4.8 Specification of Reactive Modules

In the preceding sections, we were concerned with the specification of entire systems. Clearly, a large system is constructed of several components (modules) that are usually developed by different teams. It is therefore of paramount interest to be able to provide a separate specification for each component that serves as the task definition for the implementors of this component.

In this section we introduce the notions necessary for *modular specification*, i.e., specifying the desired behavior of a module within a system.

The Module Statement

We extend our programming syntax by introducing the *module* statement, whose form is

$$M :: \quad [\textbf{module}; \text{ interface specification}; \text{ body}].$$

The key-word **module** identifies this as a module statement.

The *interface specification* is a list of declaration statements, each of the form

$$\text{modes } x_1, \ldots, x_m : \text{ type } \textbf{where } \varphi$$

where *modes* is a list of one or more modes, each of which may be **in**, **out**, or **external**. List $x_1, \ldots, x_m$ consists of names of variables or channels that are declared by this statement. The *type* part specifies the type of the declared variables. The optional assertion φ restricts the initial values of the declared variables. The last component of a module statement is *body* a statement that may contain additional declarations.

Statements within the body B of module M may refer only to variables and channels that are declared either locally within B or within the interface specification of M.

Let x be a variable declared by the interface specification. References to x within statements of B and statements parallel to M are restricted as follows:

- A statement in B may have a reading reference to x only if x is declared to be of the mode **in**.

- A statement in B may have a writing reference to x only if x is declared to be of the mode **out**.

- A statement in a module parallel to M may have a writing reference to x only if x is declared (in M) to be of the mode **external**.

Similar restrictions apply to channels, where a receive statement counts as a reading reference and a send statement counts as a writing reference.

Thus, the purpose of the interface specification is to identify the variables and channels that are used for communication between module M and other modules. It also determines the modes in which these variables may be used, i.e., whether they can be written or only read by the module.

Consider, for example, program PING-PONG presented in Fig. 4.10. In this program, M_2 serves as the environment of M_1 and M_1 as the environment of M_2.

The interface specification of module M_1 declares x and z as writable integer variables, whose initial value is 0. It also forbids these variables (by not declaring them as external) to be written by the environment. Variable y is declared as an integer variable that may be read by M_1 and modified externally. In a complementary way, the interface specification for M_2 identifies x as an integer variable that is read-only for M_2 and writable by the environment. Variable y is identified as writable by M_2 and read-only for the environment of M_2. Note that the bodies of the two modules respect these restrictions.

The program behaves as follows. Initially, the values of x, y, and z are 0. Module M_1 starts a protocol of communication between the two modules by setting x to 1. This is sensed by M_2, which responds by setting y to 1. Module M_1 senses this change and sets z to 1.

Modular Specification

Let M_1 and M_2 be two modules. We say that M_1 and M_2 are *interface compatible* (also that M_1 (respectively M_2) is interface compatible with M_2 (respectively M_1)) if the declarations for any variable x that is declared in both M_1 and M_2

$$
M_1 :: \left[\begin{array}{l} \textbf{module} \\ \textbf{external in } y \quad : \textbf{integer} \\ \textbf{out} \qquad\quad x,\ z \colon \textbf{integer where } x = 0,\ z = 0 \\[4pt] \left[\begin{array}{l} \ell_0\colon\ x := 1 \\ \ell_1\colon\ \textbf{await } (y = 1) \\ \ell_2\colon\ z := 1 \end{array} \right] \end{array} \right]
$$

$$
\|
$$

$$
M_2 :: \left[\begin{array}{l} \textbf{module} \\ \textbf{external in } x \colon \textbf{integer} \\ \textbf{out} \qquad\quad y \colon \textbf{integer where } y = 0 \\[4pt] \left[\begin{array}{l} m_0\colon\ \textbf{await } (x = 1) \\ m_1\colon\ y := 1 \end{array} \right] \end{array} \right]
$$

Fig. 4.10.   Program PING-PONG.

are consistent. By that we mean the following:

- The types specified in both declarations are identical.

- If the two declarations contain where clauses which specify constraints φ_1 and φ_2 on the initial value of the declared variable, then $\varphi_1 \wedge \varphi_2$ is consistent.

- If one of the declarations specifies an out mode, the other specifies an external mode.

If M_1 and M_2 appear as parallel statements in a program, we require that M_1 and M_2 be interface compatible.

To simplify the presentation, we base all our definitions on the case of a program P that has the form

$$P :: \quad [M_1 \| M_2].$$

The transitions associated with a program that contains a module statement are obtained by treating the module statement as a block.

We say that the temporal formula φ_1 is *modularly valid* for module M_1 if

$$[M_1 \| M] \vDash \varphi_1,$$

for every module M that is interface compatible with M_1. Thus, modular validity requires that M_1 satisfies φ_1 independently of the form and behavior of its partner in the program, module M_2, as long as the partner respects the constraints implied by the interface specification of M_1. That is, M_2 may modify variables recognized by M_1 only if they are declared by the interface specification of M_1 to be external.

Consider, for example, program PING-PONG presented in Fig. 4.10. The specification

$$(x = 0) \; W \; \square (x = 1)$$

states that initially $x = 0$ and x will remain 0 unless it changes to 1 and remains 1 forever. We claim that this specification is modularly valid for M_1. It certainly is valid over the given program. However, it is also valid over any program obtained by replacing module M_2 by an arbitrary module that respects the interface specification of M_1. This is because the actions of M_1 maintain the property, and since x is not declared as external in the interface list of M_1, no other module is allowed to modify it.

On the other hand, consider the formula

$$(y = 0) \; W \; \square (y = 1),$$

which states a similar property for variable y. While this formula is valid over program PING-PONG, it is not modularly valid for the module M_1. This is because if we replace module M_2 with the module

$$M_2' :: \quad [\textbf{module; out } y: \textbf{ integer where } y = 0; \; y := 2],$$

the resulting program $M_1 \| M_2'$ does not satisfy $(y = 0) \; W \; \square (y = 1)$.

The formula $(y = 0) \; W \; \square (y = 1)$ is, however, modularly valid for the module M_2. No matter which module M_1' we use to replace M_1, the program $M_1' \| M_2$ satisfies $(y = 0) \; W \; \square (y = 1)$.

The Task of Implementing a Module

Consider the task assigned to an implementing team that is charged with the construction of a module M_1. We may describe the task definition as consisting of two specification elements:

- An interface specification. This part identifies the types of the variables and channels that are used for communication between the module and its environment (module M_2 in our simple case). It also identifies the mode of communication for each of the interface variables and channels, i.e., whether they can be written or only read by the module.

- A behavioral specification. This part consists of a temporal formula, specifying the expected behavior of the module.

Assume that the implementation team for module M_2 is handed an interface specification $inter_2$ and a behavioral specification φ_2. Their task can be described as construct a body B_2 (a statement), such that

$$[M_1' \parallel M_2 :: [\textbf{module}; \; inter_2; \; B_2]] \; \vDash \; \varphi_2,$$

for every module M_1', interface compatible with M_2.

We may conceive, for example, of a programming team receiving the following specification for module M_2:

Interface specification: **external in** x: **integer**

out y: **integer where** $y = 0$.

Behavioral specification: $(y = 0) \, \mathcal{W} \, \square (y = 1) \; \wedge$

$(y = 1) \; \Rightarrow \; \Diamond (x = 1) \; \wedge$

$\square (x = 1) \; \Rightarrow \; \Diamond (y = 1).$

The behavioral specification consists of two safety clauses and one response clause. The first safety clause states that y maintains the value 0 either forever or until it changes to 1 and remains 1 forever. The second clause states that y may change to 1 only in response to x being 1. The response clause states that if from a certain point x continuously equals 1, then eventually y will become 1.

Handed such a specification, the programming team may come up with the following statement as the body B_2 of a module satisfying the given behavioral specification under the constraints implied by the given interface specification:

m_0: **await** $(x = 1)$; m_1: $y := 1$.

The reader may wonder at this point why we use such a strong antecedent, namely, $\square (x = 1)$, in the response formula. Is it not simpler to consider the more natural formulation $(x = 1) \Rightarrow \Diamond (y = 1)$?

The answer to this question is that, while $(x = 1) \Rightarrow \Diamond (y = 1)$ may be simpler to require, it is more difficult, in fact impossible, to implement. To see this, consider the module M_2 appearing in program PING-PONG of Fig. 4.10, whose body is the statement suggested earlier. We claim that $(x = 1) \Rightarrow \Diamond (y = 1)$ is not modularly valid for M_2.

Consider the following replacement candidate for M_1

$M_1' ::$ [**module**; **out** x: **integer where** $x = 0$; $[\ell_0: \; x := 1; \; \ell_1: \; x := 0: \; \widehat{\ell_1}]]$.

We claim that the program $M_1' \parallel M_2$ does not satisfy the formula $(x = 1) \Rightarrow \Diamond (y = 1)$. To see this, consider the computation (listing values of π, x, y):

$$\langle \{\ell_0, \; m_0\}, \; 0, \; 0 \rangle, \; \langle \{\ell_1, \; m_0\}, \; 1, \; 0 \rangle, \; \langle \{\widehat{\ell_1}, \; m_0\}, \; 0, \; 0 \rangle,$$

$$\langle \{\widehat{\ell_1}, \; m_0\}, \; 0, \; 0 \rangle, \; \ldots$$

This computation contains one state in which $x = 1$ but no state in which $y =$

1. Clearly, the problem is that M_2 was not fast enough (technically, was not scheduled at the right moment) to detect the instant at which x equals 1.

While not being a complete proof of the fact that $(x = 1) \Rightarrow \Diamond(y = 1)$ is not implementable under the interface specification **external in** x, the preceding argument certainly indicates that this is the case.

Obstacles to Modular Implementation

The preceding example points to an important question. Having composed a specification that we believe captures our intuition of the desired behavior of a system or a component of a system (a module), how do we check that the specification is implementable?

Imagine that we are professional specifiers whose job is to compose specifications that are later delivered to a programming team. We had better make sure, to the best of our ability, that all specifications we construct are implementable.

When we consider specifications of entire systems, to which we refer as *global specifications*, the major obstacle to implementability is inconsistency of the specification. For example, it is obvious that the specification

$$\Box(x = 0) \ \wedge \ \Diamond(x = 1)$$

cannot be implemented. Checking the consistency of a specification φ is a well-defined problem in logic (albeit not an easy one). We only have to confirm that φ is satisfiable.

However, once we consider modular specifications, we encounter additional obstacles to implementability. In general, a modular specification is unimplementable if it requires the module to maintain a property in a way that is inconsistent with its interface specification. Thus, in some sense, we may still attribute unimplementability to inconsistencies in the specification. In the case of global specifications, inconsistencies can only arise between different parts of the behavioral specification, such as the conjuncts $\Box(x = 0)$ and $\Diamond(x = 1)$. In the case of modular specifications, we may have additional conflicts between the behavioral and interface specifications.

Consider, for example, the combination of the interface specification **external in** x: **integer** with the behavioral specification $\Diamond(x = 1)$. The behavioral part requires that the module causes x to become 1. The interface part requires that the module never modifies x. Clearly, the two requirements are in conflict.

As another example, the interface specification **external out** x: **integer** is in conflict with the behavioral specification $\Box(x = 0)$. This is because, try as it may to keep x at 0, the module may still lose to the environment, which is also allowed to modify x and may manage to set x to a nonzero value.

Computations of a Module

A formula φ has been defined to be modularly valid for a module M_1 if φ is valid over the program $M_1 \| M_2'$ for any module M_2', interface compatible with M_1. This definition seems to imply that, in order to check whether φ is modularly valid for M_1, we somehow should consider all the infinitely many interface compatible modules M_2'.

Here we present a more direct approach to this concept. With a module M we associate a transition system S_M and consider the computations of S_M. We will first consider the case of the shared-variables model.

Computations of a Shared-Variables Module

Let M be a shared-variables module and L_M denote the set of locations in M. The transition system S_M consists of the following components:

- *State variables*: These consist of the control variable π and all data variables Y declared within M. Variable π ranges over sets of locations that may also include locations not in M.

- *States*: All possible interpretations of $\pi \cup Y$ consistent with their types.

- *Transitions*: These consist of the idling transition τ_I, all the transitions associated with statements of M, and the additional environment transition τ_E.

Transition τ_E is intended to represent all the possible interference of the environment with the operation of the module. Let $X \subseteq Y$ be the set of variables declared as external in the interface specification of M. The transition relation for τ_E is given by

$$\rho_{\tau_E}: \quad (\pi' \cap L_M = \pi \cap L_M) \wedge \bigwedge_{y \in Y - X} (y' = y).$$

Thus, transition τ_E pledges to preserve the values of all the nonexternal data variables and the set of M-locations within π. By omission, it may arbitrarily change values of external data variables and modify the set of non-M locations contained in π.

- *Initial condition*: Let φ be the conjunction of all the where parts of declarations in M. For simplicity we assume that M is a single process with initial location ℓ_0. Then the initial condition is

$$\Theta: \quad (\pi \cap L_M = \{\ell_0\}) \wedge \varphi.$$

Note that initially π may contain arbitrary non-M locations but the only M-location it contains is ℓ_0.

- *Justice set*: This consists of all the transitions associated with statements of M, except those associated with an idle statement. Transitions τ_I and τ_E are not contained in the justice set.

• *Compassion set*: This consists of all the transitions associated with synchronization statements of M, such as request or region.

Note that the main differences between S_M and the transition system we would have constructed if M were the entire program are the environment transition τ_E and the domain of π, which is allowed to contain non-M locations.

We define the *computations of module M* to be the computations of system S_M.

Example

Consider the module:

$M_1 ::$ [module; external in out x: integer where $x = 0$; ℓ_0: $x := x + 1$: $\widehat{\ell_0}$].

Based on the construction of the transition system S_{M_1}, this module has the following computation (listing values of π and x and displaying the transitions responsible for each step):

$$\langle \{\ell_0, m_0\},\ 0\rangle \xrightarrow{\tau_E} \langle \{\ell_0, m_1\},\ 5\rangle \xrightarrow{\tau_{\ell_0}} \langle \{\widehat{\ell_0}, m_1\},\ 6\rangle$$
$$\xrightarrow{\tau_E} \langle \{\widehat{\ell_0}, m_2\},\ 0\rangle \to \cdots$$

It is not difficult to see that if M is a shared-variables module, then transition τ_E represents all the interference that can be caused by a parallel interface compatible module M'. This is stated more precisely by the following claim.

Claim

Let $P = M_1 \| M_2$ be a program and σ a sequence of states in which π ranges over subsets of $L_{M_1} \cup L_{M_2}$. Then, σ is a computation of P iff it is a computation of both S_{M_1} and S_{M_2}.

Example

Consider module M_2 defined as

$$M_2 :: \left[\text{module; external in out } x\text{: integer; } \begin{bmatrix} m_0: & x := x + 5 \\ m_1: & x := 0 \\ : m_2 & \end{bmatrix}\right].$$

The following sequence is a computation of $P = M_1 \| M_2$, where M_1 is the module defined earlier:

$$\sigma: \langle \{\ell_0, m_0\},\ 0\rangle,\ \langle \{\ell_0, m_1\},\ 5\rangle,\ \langle \{\widehat{\ell_0}, m_1\},\ 6\rangle,\ \langle \{\widehat{\ell_0}, m_2\},\ 0\rangle,\ \cdots$$

We have seen above that σ is a computation of S_{M_1}. To see that it is also a computation of S_{M_2} we identify the S_{M_2}-transitions leading from each state to its successor

$$\langle \{\ell_0, m_0\},\ 0 \rangle \xrightarrow{m_0} \langle \{\ell_0, m_1\},\ 5 \rangle \xrightarrow{\tau_E} \langle \{\widehat{\ell_0}, m_1\},\ 6 \rangle$$

$$\xrightarrow{m_1} \langle \{\widehat{\ell_0}, m_2\},\ 0 \rangle \longrightarrow \cdots \quad \lrcorner$$

From the preceding claim, it follows that any sequence σ, which is a computation of the program $M \| M'$ for some module M', is also a computation of the module M (i.e., a computation of S_M).

The converse statement also holds. For each σ, a computation of M (i.e., S_M), there exists a module M' and σ', a variant of σ, such that σ' is a computation of $M \| M'$. Sequences σ and σ' may differ at most by the presence or absence of a non-M locations in the interpretation of π.

For simplicity, assume that the programming language contains the multiple random choice statement **choose** $(x_1, \ldots, x_m)$, which assigns arbitrary values of appropriate types to variables $x_1, \ldots, x_m$ in one transition. We have seen in Section 2.10 that, for the case of an integer variable x, **choose** (x) can be emulated by an appropriate cooperation statement.

Using multiple random choice statements, it is possible to construct a single module M_R, such that every computation of M has a π-variant σ', as described earlier, such that σ' is a computation of $M \| M_R$.

It follows that, up to π-differences, σ is a computation of M iff it is a computation of $M \| M'$ for some module M'. Consequently, we conclude the following:

Claim

A formula φ is modularly valid for a module M iff φ holds over all the computations of M.

Computations of an Asynchronously Communicating Module

For the case of asynchronously communicating modules, a single environment transition is not sufficient for representing all possible interferences.

As in the case of shared-variables modules, the transition system S_M is very similar to the transition system that would have been constructed if M were a complete program. For each channel α declared as external-in, S_M has a state variable α and a receiving transition τ_ℓ for each receive statement ℓ: $\alpha \Rightarrow u$. For each channel β declared as out, S_M has a state variable β and a sending transition τ_m for each send statement m: $\beta \Leftarrow e$.

In addition, S_M contains the following environment transitions:

- For each external-in channel α, we define an *environment sending* transition τ_α^{ES}, whose transition relation is

$$\rho_\alpha^{ES}: \quad \exists u: (\alpha' = \alpha \bullet u).$$

This implies that the environment chooses an arbitrary value u to be added to the end of the message buffer α. In the case that α is a bounded channel with the bound N, the relation ρ_α^{ES} also includes the clause $|\alpha| < N$, which restricts the execution of τ_α^{ES} to states in which the buffer has a vacant slot.

- For each out channel β, we define an *environment receiving* transition τ_β^{ER}, whose transition relation is

$$\rho_\beta^{ER}: \quad (|\beta| > 0) \ \wedge \ (\beta' = tl(\beta)).$$

As in the case of shared variables, the initial condition is given by

$$\Theta: \quad (\pi \cap L_M = \{\ell_0\}) \ \wedge \ \varphi,$$

where φ also contains initial settings for the channel variables declared as out. The initial setting is any explicit requirement presented in a where part of a declaration, or the default setting $\alpha = \Lambda$.

No fairness requirements are associated with the environment transitions.

Consider, for example, the asynchronously communicating module presented in Fig. 4.11. The following is a computation associated with this module, listing for each state the values of π, α, x, and y.

$$
M :: \left[
\begin{array}{l}
\textbf{module} \\
\textbf{external in } \alpha \quad : \text{channel of integer} \\
\textbf{local} \qquad\quad x,\ y \text{: } \textbf{where } x = 0,\ y = 0 \\[4pt]
\ell_0 \text{: } \textbf{loop forever do} \\
\quad [\ell_1 \text{: } \alpha \Rightarrow y;\ \ell_2 \text{: } x := x + y]
\end{array}
\right]
$$

Fig. 4.11. A reactive module communicating by asynchronous message passing.

$$\langle \{\ell_0\}, \Lambda, 0, 0 \rangle \xrightarrow{\tau_\alpha^{ES}} \langle \{\ell_0\}, \langle 2 \rangle, 0, 0 \rangle \xrightarrow{\ell_0}$$

$$\langle \{\ell_1\}, \langle 2 \rangle, 0, 0 \rangle \xrightarrow{\tau_\alpha^{ES}} \langle \{\ell_1\}, \langle 2, 3 \rangle, 0, 0 \rangle \xrightarrow{\ell_1}$$

$$\langle \{\ell_2\}, \langle 3 \rangle, 0, 2 \rangle \xrightarrow{\ell_2} \langle \{\ell_0\}, \langle 3 \rangle, 2, 2 \rangle \longrightarrow \cdots \longrightarrow$$

$$\langle \{\ell_0\}, \Lambda, 5, 3 \rangle \longrightarrow \cdots .$$

We define the computations of an asynchronously communicating module M to be the computations of the transition system S_M. It can be shown that the environment transitions included in S_M represent all the possible interactions M may have with its environment.

Consequently, the preceding claim for shared-variables modules is also valid for asynchronously communicating modules.

For the case of synchronously communicating modules, we can no longer model the interaction with the environment by separate environment transitions. Transition system S_M should contain transitions that can perform synchronous communication between the environment and statements of M for each channel declared as external or out. Thus, we need a more elaborate construction of S_M. In **Problem 4.14**, the reader will describe such a construction.

With the appropriately constructed transition system S_M and the resulting notion of computations of a synchronously communicating module, the preceding claim is also true for synchronously communicating modules.

4.9   *Composing Modular Specifications*

Having defined the notions of modules and their specification, we explore the relation between modular validity and validity over the entire program. Consider a program of the form $M_1 \| M_2$.

An immediate consequence of the definitions is the following claim.

Claim

If formulas φ_1 and φ_2 are modularly valid over modules M_1 and M_2, respectively, then $\varphi_1 \wedge \varphi_2$ is valid over the program $M_1 \| M_2$.

This suggests an important methodology for the formal development of reactive systems by top-down decomposition.

Development by Decomposition

To develop a reactive program P satisfying φ,

- design compatible interface specifications $inter_1$ and $inter_2$,

- design behavioral specifications φ_1 and φ_2, such that $(\varphi_1 \wedge \varphi_2) \rightarrow \varphi$,

- develop bodies B_1 and B_2 such that φ_1 and φ_2 are modularly valid for

    $M_1 ::$ [**module**; $inter_1$; B_1]   and

    $M_2 ::$ [**module**; $inter_2$; B_2],   respectively.

The required program is given by $M_1 \| M_2$.

In many cases, the interface specifications $inter_1$ and $inter_2$ or parts of them are already given as part of the problem, and we have only to determine the decomposition of φ into φ_1 and φ_2 and to develop the bodies B_1 and B_2.

In this book we do very little formal development and are much more interested in verification. The same principle underlying the decomposition development strategy can be used for compositional verification.

Compositional Verification

To verify that the program $M_1 \| M_2$ satisfies specification φ, find formulas φ_1 and φ_2 that satisfy

$$(\varphi_1 \wedge \varphi_2) \rightarrow \varphi,$$

and verify that φ_1 and φ_2 are modularly valid for M_1 and M_2, respectively.

A key element common to both the development by decomposition and the compositional verification strategies is the decomposition of a global specification φ into two modular specifications φ_1 and φ_2, such that $(\varphi_1 \wedge \varphi_2) \rightarrow \varphi$. In this section we will illustrate several cases of such decompositions.

Layered Decomposition

Consider again program PING-PONG in Fig. 4.10. As a global specification for this program we take

$$\varphi: \quad \Diamond(z = 1),$$

which states that eventually z will be set to 1. We look for a modular decomposition of this global specification.

In the previous discussion of this program, we presented for module M_2 the modular specification

$$(y = 0)\, \mathcal{W}\, \Box(y = 1) \;\wedge\; (y = 1) \Rightarrow \Diamond(x = 1) \;\wedge\; \Box(x = 1) \Rightarrow \Diamond(y = 1).$$

In our current analysis we try to be more goal-directed, and include in the modular specifications φ_1 and φ_2 only the minimal part necessary to establish the global property $\Diamond(z = 1)$.

As a general methodology for the construction of modular specifications, we often follow a layered process. As the first layer we put into φ_1 and φ_2 some unconditional properties of the modules M_1 and M_2, respectively. These properties are the effects of actions that are performed independently of the behavior of the environment. At the next layer we put into φ_1 and φ_2 conditional properties of the general form "if the environment guarantees p, I will guarantee q." In most cases, such properties can simply be expressed by the implication $p \rightarrow q$, but there are cases where the dependence of q on p is more complicated. In the layered methodology we put into φ_1, say, a property of the form "q depending on p," only if p has already been included in φ_2 (which is the environment of φ_1) as part of a previous layer.

Let us illustrate this methodology with the case we consider. Clearly, the evolution toward the goal $z = 1$ consists of three events: x becomes 1, y becomes 1, and finally z becomes 1. The first event occurs unconditionally. Each of the other two is conditional on the occurrence of its predecessor. Consequently, the layered methodology recommends the following three steps:

Step 1: Put $\diamondsuit \square (x = 1)$ into φ_1. Unconditionally x becomes 1 and stays 1 forever.

Step 2: Put $\diamondsuit \square (x = 1) \rightarrow \diamondsuit \square (y = 1)$ into φ_2. If x eventually becomes permanently 1, then so does y.

Step 3: Put $\diamondsuit \square (y = 1) \rightarrow \diamondsuit (z = 1)$ into φ_1. If y eventually becomes permanently 1, then z eventually becomes 1.

Thus we wind up with the two modular specifications

$$\varphi_1: \quad \diamondsuit \square (x = 1) \wedge (\diamondsuit \square (y = 1) \rightarrow \diamondsuit (z = 1))$$

$$\varphi_2: \quad \diamondsuit \square (x = 1) \rightarrow \diamondsuit \square (y = 1).$$

It is not difficult to see that $\varphi_1 \wedge \varphi_2$ implies $\diamondsuit (z = 1)$.

It is most important to realize that putting a property $p \rightarrow q$ into a modular specification for a module M, when we know that p is guaranteed by the environment, does not contradict our definition that the specification should hold independently of what the environment does. The property $p \rightarrow q$ indeed holds for all environments, even those that do not maintain p. When p is guaranteed we can use this fact to infer q, as we did in the preceding example. It is the validity of q that depends on the behavior of the environment and not the validity of $p \rightarrow q$, which is always guaranteed.

Variables that Change More than Once

The previous example has been particularly easy due to the fact that each variable changed its value at most once. This enabled us to represent the setting of y that is dependent on the setting of x by the implication

$$\diamondsuit \square (x = 1) \rightarrow \diamondsuit \square (y = 1).$$

A more complicated situation is presented in program PING-PONG-PING in Fig. 4.12.

We can describe the behavior of this program by saying that M_1 signals M_2 twice. The first signal is generated by setting x to 1, and the second signal by resetting x once more to 0. Module M_2 signals M_1 once by setting y to 1. Let us

$$
M_1 ::
\begin{bmatrix}
\textbf{module} \\
\textbf{external in } y\text{: } \textbf{integer} \\
\textbf{out} \qquad x\text{: } \textbf{integer where } x = 0 \\[4pt]
\begin{bmatrix}
\ell_0\text{: } x := 1 \\
\ell_1\text{: } \textbf{await } (y = 1) \\
\ell_2\text{: } x := 0
\end{bmatrix}
\end{bmatrix}
$$

$$\|$$

$$
M_2 ::
\begin{bmatrix}
\textbf{module} \\
\textbf{external in } x \quad \text{: } \textbf{integer} \\
\textbf{out} \qquad y,\ z\text{: } \textbf{integer where } y = 0,\ z = 0 \\[4pt]
\begin{bmatrix}
m_0\text{: } \textbf{await } (x = 1) \\
m_1\text{: } y := 1 \\
m_2\text{: } \textbf{await } (x = 0) \\
m_3\text{: } z := 1
\end{bmatrix}
\end{bmatrix}
$$

Fig. 4.12. Program PING-PONG-PING.

consider the incremental construction of the modular specifications.

The first fact we wish to put in φ_1 is that, unconditionally, eventually x becomes 1 and remains 1 long enough to be detected by M_2. In the previous example we simply stated that x becomes 1 and remains 1 forever. Here we can only promise that x remains 1 until y becomes 1, which allows M_1 to go to ℓ_2 and reset x to 0. Consequently, we put into φ_1 the clause

$$\Diamond ((x = 1)\ \mathcal{W}\ (y = 1)).$$

Next, we express in φ_2 the property that, if x becomes 1 and stays 1 long enough, then eventually y will become 1 and stay 1 forever. This property can be expressed by the formula

$$\Diamond ((x = 1)\ \mathcal{W}\ (y = 1))\ \rightarrow\ \Diamond \Box (y = 1).$$

The formula states that if x is sometimes set to 1 and kept at 1 until M_2 responds (by setting y to 1), then indeed M_2 will respond. Furthermore, when y is set to 1 it will remain 1 permanently.

Next, we add to φ_1 the requirement

$$\Diamond \Box (y = 1)\ \rightarrow\ \Diamond \Box (x = 0),$$

which states that if eventually y becomes permanently 1 then x will become permanently 0.

Finally, we should add to φ_2 a requirement stating that if x becomes permanently 0 then z will become eventually 1. A first candidate for expressing this requirement is the formula

$$\Diamond \Box (x = 0) \;\rightarrow\; \Diamond (z = 1).$$

However, this formula is not modularly valid for module M_2. Consider, for example, a variant of M_1, call it M_1', which does nothing, i.e., assigns no values to variables. In the computations of the program $M_1' \| M_2$, x is permanently 0 from the beginning, yet z is never set to 1. This is because if x is always 0, M_2 is not able to go past the await statement m_0.

In view of this, we use the formula

$$[\Diamond \Box (x = 0) \;\wedge\; \Diamond \Box (y = 1)] \;\rightarrow\; \Diamond (z = 1)$$

to capture the intuition that M_2 commits to set z to 1 in response to x staying at 0 sufficiently long, only if M_2 has gone past m_0 and m_1 and has already set y to 1.

Collecting the various clauses, we obtain the two modular specifications:

$$\varphi_1: \quad \Diamond ((x = 1)\, \mathcal{W} \,(y = 1)) \;\wedge\; \left(\Diamond \Box (y = 1) \rightarrow \Diamond \Box (x = 0) \right)$$

$$\varphi_2: \quad \left(\Diamond ((x = 1)\, \mathcal{W} \,(y = 1)) \rightarrow \Diamond \Box (y = 1) \right) \;\wedge$$

$$\left([\Diamond \Box (x = 0) \;\wedge\; \Diamond \Box (y = 1)] \rightarrow \Diamond (z = 1) \right).$$

It can be shown that φ_1 and φ_2 are modularly valid for M_1 and M_2, respectively, and that $\varphi_1 \wedge \varphi_2$ implies $\Diamond (z = 1)$.

Decomposing Safety Specifications

Our previous examples were concerned with the decomposition of global progress specifications of the form $\Diamond (z = 1)$. The decomposition of this global specification showed how this global goal is achieved by M_1 performing some operation (setting x to 1), to which M_2 responded by performing another operation that influences M_1, etc.

Here we consider a global safety property that is an invariant and show how to identify two modular specifications that together ensure the preservation of the invariant.

Consider program KEEPING-UP in Fig. 4.13. Module M_1 in this program repeatedly increments x, provided x does not exceed $y + 1$. Module M_2, similarly, repeatedly increments y, provided y does not exceed $x + 1$. For the combined program we state the global safety property

$$M_1 :: \quad \begin{bmatrix} \textbf{module} \\ \textbf{external in } y\text{: integer} \\ \textbf{out} \qquad x\text{: integer where } x = 0 \\ \ell_0\text{: } \textbf{loop forever do} \\ \quad \begin{bmatrix} \ell_1\text{: } \textbf{await } (x < y + 1) \\ \ell_2\text{: } x := x + 1 \end{bmatrix} \end{bmatrix}$$

$$\|$$

$$M_2 :: \quad \begin{bmatrix} \textbf{module} \\ \textbf{external in } x\text{: integer} \\ \textbf{out} \qquad y\text{: integer where } y = 0 \\ m_0\text{: } \textbf{loop forever do} \\ \quad \begin{bmatrix} m_1\text{: } \textbf{await } (y < x + 1) \\ m_2\text{: } y := y + 1 \end{bmatrix} \end{bmatrix}$$

Fig. 4.13. Program KEEPING-UP.

$$\Box(|x - y| \leq 1),$$

claiming that the difference between x and y never exceeds 1.

To construct appropriate modular specifications that guarantee this property, we again adopt the strategy of layered construction.

At the first step we put into φ_1 and φ_2, respectively, the following two unconditional formulas

$$\Box(x \geq x^-) \quad \text{and} \quad \Box(y \geq y^-).$$

The first formula states that M_1 can only increase the value of x. The second formula states similarly that the value of y can only increase.

Next, we add to φ_1 and φ_2, respectively, the two conditional formulas

$$\Box(y \geq y^-) \rightarrow \Box(x \leq y + 1)$$
$$\Box(x \geq x^-) \rightarrow \Box(y \leq x + 1).$$

The first formula states that if y never decreases, then M_1 can guarantee that x will never exceed $y + 1$. This is because M_1 increases x only at location ℓ_2 to which it gets only if in some previous state $x < y + 1$. Since from that state until now x retained the same value and y did not decrease, we know that when ℓ_2 is performed x is still smaller than $y + 1$.

Thus, the modular specifications we propose are

$$\varphi_1: \quad \Box(x \geq x^-) \,\wedge\, \Big(\Box(y \geq y^-) \to \Box(x \leq y + 1)\Big)$$

$$\varphi_2: \quad \Box(y \geq y^-) \,\wedge\, \Big(\Box(x \geq x^-) \to \Box(y \leq x + 1)\Big)$$

It is easy to see that from the conjunction $\varphi_1 \wedge \varphi_2$ we can infer

$$\Box(x \leq y + 1 \,\wedge\, y \leq x + 1),$$

which implies $\Box(|x - y| \leq 1)$.

Asynchronously Communicating Modules

Program ASYNC-PING-PONG in Fig. 4.14 is a variation of program PING-PONG in Fig. 4.10 where, instead of communicating via shared variables x, y, and z, the modules communicate via asynchronous channels α, β, and γ.

$$
M_1 ::
\begin{bmatrix}
\textbf{module} \\
\textbf{external in } \beta \quad : \textbf{channel } [1..] \textbf{ of integer} \\
\textbf{out} \qquad\quad \alpha,\ \gamma: \textbf{channel } [1..] \textbf{ of integer} \\
\textbf{local} \qquad\quad u \quad : \textbf{integer} \\
\begin{bmatrix}
\ell_0: \alpha \Leftarrow 1 \\
\ell_1: \beta \Rightarrow u \\
\ell_2: \gamma \Leftarrow 1
\end{bmatrix}
\end{bmatrix}
$$

$$\|$$

$$
M_2 ::
\begin{bmatrix}
\textbf{module} \\
\textbf{external in } \alpha: \textbf{channel } [1..] \textbf{ of integer} \\
\textbf{out} \qquad \beta: \textbf{channel } [1..] \textbf{ of integer} \\
\textbf{local} \qquad v: \textbf{integer} \\
\begin{bmatrix}
m_0: \alpha \Rightarrow v \\
m_1: \beta \Leftarrow 1
\end{bmatrix}
\end{bmatrix}
$$

Fig. 4.14. Program ASYNC-PING-PONG.

In addition to these channels, the two modules also use two local variables, u and v, respectively. Apart from the change of the communication medium, the logical structure of this program is identical to that of the program in Fig. 4.10.

Communication starts by M_1 sending a message (the value 1 is unimportant) on channel α. Module M_2 waits for the message to arrive. When the message arrives, M_2 sends a message on channel β. When this message is received by M_1, the module proceeds to send a message on channel γ.

A global property of this program is given by

$$\Diamond[\gamma\Leftarrow],$$

stating that eventually a message will be sent on channel γ.

Let us consider how we can decompose this global specification into two modular specifications. It is not difficult to see how our modular specifications for the shared-variables case can be translated into corresponding communication-based specifications. These are given by:

$$\varphi_1: \quad \Diamond[\alpha\Leftarrow] \,\wedge\, (\Diamond[\beta\Leftarrow]\rightarrow\Diamond[\gamma\Leftarrow])$$

$$\varphi_2: \quad \Diamond[\alpha\Leftarrow] \,\rightarrow\, \Diamond[\beta\Leftarrow].$$

The conjunction $\varphi_1\wedge\varphi_2$ clearly implies $\Diamond[\gamma\Leftarrow]$.

It is interesting to compare the clause $\Diamond[\alpha\Leftarrow]\rightarrow\Diamond[\beta\Leftarrow]$ to its shared-variables counterpart $\Diamond\,\Box\,(x=1)\rightarrow\Diamond\,\Box\,(y=1)$. One may wonder why we need the stronger commitment expressed by the $\Diamond\,\Box$ combination in the case of shared variables and manage with the simpler $\Diamond$ operator in the case of asynchronous communication.

In the case of shared variables, the $\Diamond\,\Box$ is necessary to ensure that the signal generated by M_1 setting x to 1 is not prematurely revoked before it has been sensed by M_2. In the asynchronous message-passing model, signals cannot be revoked, since once a message has been sent by M_1 there is no way for M_1 to change its mind and withdraw or cancel the message.

For this and other reasons that we will see later, of the three models considered in this book (shared-variables, asynchronous, and synchronous communication), asynchronous communication is the most appropriate and easiest model for modular specification and compositional verification.

Synchronously Communicating Modules

Next, we consider the case of synchronously communicating modules. In Fig. 4.15, we present program SYNC-PING-PONG, which is similar to program ASYNC-PING-PONG of Fig. 4.14, except that the channels are synchronous.

Another difference between the two programs is that module M_1 terminates after reading the message from channel β and does not send a message on channel γ. This modification is necessary because in the synchronous communication model the statement $\gamma\Leftarrow 1$ in module M_1 cannot be executed without a matching

$$
\begin{array}{c}
M_1 :: \quad
\left[
\begin{array}{l}
\textbf{module} \\
\textbf{external in } \beta\text{: channel of integer} \\
\textbf{out} \qquad\quad \alpha\text{: channel of integer} \\
\textbf{local} \qquad\quad u\text{: integer} \\[4pt]
\left[
\begin{array}{l}
\ell_0\text{: } \alpha \Leftarrow 1 \\
\ell_1\text{: } \beta \Rightarrow u
\end{array}
\right]
\end{array}
\right]
\\[40pt]
\| \\[30pt]
M_2 :: \quad
\left[
\begin{array}{l}
\textbf{module} \\
\textbf{external in } \alpha\text{: channel of integer} \\
\textbf{out} \qquad\quad \beta\text{: channel of integer} \\
\textbf{local} \qquad\quad v\text{: integer} \\[4pt]
\left[
\begin{array}{l}
m_0\text{: } \alpha \Rightarrow v \\
m_1\text{: } \beta \Leftarrow 1
\end{array}
\right]
\end{array}
\right]
\end{array}
$$

Fig. 4.15.   Program SYNC-PING-PONG.

receiving statement in M_2. Consequently, the global property we consider for this program is

$$\Diamond(u = 1).$$

For simplicity, we assume that all the channels are single-reader single-writer channels.

When we consider synchronous communication, we face a new problem. Consider, for example, the first statement ℓ_0: $\alpha \Leftarrow 1$ in module M_1. In the asynchronous case, seeing such a first statement, we can immediately write down the formula $\Diamond[\alpha \Leftarrow]$ as a modularly valid property for module M_1. This property states that a message will be sent on channel α independently of the behavior of other modules. This is because in the asynchronous case (that assumes channels of unlimited buffering capacity) the operation of sending a message is autonomous and requires no cooperation from the environment.

In the synchronous case, on the other hand, every communication requires cooperation. Module M_1 can send a message on α only if its partner M_2 is ready to participate in a joint transition. To represent this situation we introduce two new state predicates

$$ready([\alpha \Leftarrow]) \qquad \text{and} \qquad ready([\alpha \Rightarrow]).$$

The state predicate $ready([\alpha \Leftarrow])$ (ready to send on α) is true in a state of a computation of a program if control is in front of a statement of the form

$$\alpha \Leftarrow e.$$

Similarly, *ready* $([\alpha >])$ (ready to receive from α) is true in a state if control is in front of a statement

$$\alpha \Rightarrow u.$$

In the case of conditional send or receive statements, e.g., $\alpha \Rightarrow u$ **provided** c, it is also required that condition c holds in this state.

Note that while we have agreed to describe the actual communication events by the single output predicate $[\alpha <]$ (or $[\alpha < v]$), we distinguish between the two ready predicates: *ready* $([\alpha <])$ and *ready* $([\alpha >])$. This is because it is important to know whether the module is waiting for input or output.

With these predicates, the property that corresponds to the statement $\ell_0 \colon \alpha \Leftarrow 1$ in module M_1 can be expressed by

$$\Diamond [\alpha <] \; \vee \; \Box \Big(\mathit{ready}([\alpha <]) \; \wedge \; \neg [\alpha <] \Big).$$

This formula states that either communication on α will take place or M_1 will remain forever ready to send, vainly waiting for a matching communication partner that will agree to receive.

The conjunction of waiting and not communicating is frequently used. Consequently, we define

$$\mathit{yearn}([\alpha <]) \colon \quad \mathit{ready}([\alpha <]) \; \wedge \; \neg [\alpha <]$$

$$\mathit{yearn}([\alpha >]) \colon \quad \mathit{ready}([\alpha >]) \; \wedge \; \neg [\alpha <].$$

Using this abbreviation, we can represent the formula corresponding to the statement $\ell_0 \colon \alpha \Leftarrow 1$ as

$$\Diamond [\alpha <] \; \vee \; \Box \, \mathit{yearn}([\alpha <]).$$

With this understanding, we may proceed to construct modular specifications for M_1 and M_2. A systematic construction of specifications for synchronously communicating modules can be based on the construction of a separate clause for each location in the program. Consequently we have

$$\varphi_1 \colon \quad \varphi_{1.0} \wedge \varphi_{1.1} \qquad \text{and} \qquad \varphi_2 \colon \quad \varphi_{2.0} \wedge \varphi_{2.1},$$

where

$$\varphi_{1.0} \colon \quad \Diamond [\alpha <] \; \vee \; \Box \, \mathit{yearn}([\alpha <])$$

$$\varphi_{1.1} \colon \quad \Big[\Diamond [\alpha <] \; \rightarrow \; \big(\Diamond [\beta <] \; \vee \; \Diamond \Box \, \mathit{yearn}[\beta >]) \big) \Big] \; \wedge$$
$$\big([\beta < 1] \; \Rightarrow \; (u = 1) \big)$$

and

$$\varphi_{2.0}: \quad \Diamond [\alpha \Leftarrow] \lor \Box\, yearn([\alpha \Rightarrow])$$

$$\varphi_{2.1}: \quad \Big[\Diamond [\alpha \Leftarrow] \;\to\; \big(\Diamond [\beta \Leftarrow] \lor \Diamond \Box\, yearn([\beta \Leftarrow])\big)\Big] \land$$

$$([\beta \Leftarrow] \;\Rightarrow\; [\beta \Leftarrow 1]).$$

Clause $\varphi_{1.0}$ claims that either communication over α will occur or some statement (of M_1) will remain ready for output on α forever.

Clause $\varphi_{1.1}$ states two properties. The first is that if there will be an α-communication (after which M_1 must be at ℓ_1), then either there will be a β-communication or M_1 will stay ready for input from β forever. The second property stated by $\varphi_{1.1}$ is a safety property claiming that in every state following a communication of the value 1 over channel β, the value of u equals 1.

Clause $\varphi_{2.0}$ claims that either an α-communication will occur or some statement (of M_2) will remain ready for input from α forever.

Clause $\varphi_{2.1}$ claims that if there will be an α-communication, then either there will be a β-communication of 1, or M_2 will stay ready for output to β forever.

Let us consider the conjunction $\varphi_1 \land \varphi_2$. In the preceding cases we showed that it immediately implied the global property ($\Diamond(u = 1)$ in our case). Here we can only infer from it the weaker disjunction

$$\Box\Big(yearn([\alpha \Leftarrow]) \;\land\; yearn([\alpha \Rightarrow])\Big) \lor$$

$$\Diamond\Box\Big(yearn([\beta \Leftarrow]) \;\land\; yearn([\beta \Rightarrow])\Big) \lor \Diamond(u = 1).$$

This formula states that either M_1 remains ready for α-output and M_2 remains ready for α-input forever, or M_1 remains (from a certain point on) ready for β-input and M_2 remains ready for β-output forever, or $u = 1$ is achieved.

The inference of this disjunction can be based on the following case analysis: If $[\alpha \Leftarrow]$ does not occur then from $\varphi_{1.0}$ and $\varphi_{2.0}$, we obtain $\Box\, yearn([\alpha \Leftarrow]) \land \Box\, yearn([\alpha \Rightarrow])$, which yields the first disjunct. If $[\alpha \Leftarrow]$ does occur, then by $\varphi_{1.1}$ and $\varphi_{2.1}$, we obtain $\Diamond [\beta \Leftarrow] \lor \Diamond \Box\, yearn[\beta \Rightarrow]$ and $\Diamond [\beta \Leftarrow] \lor \Diamond \Box\, yearn[\beta \Leftarrow]$. If $[\beta \Leftarrow]$ does not occur then it follows that $\Diamond \Box\, yearn[\beta \Rightarrow] \land \Diamond \Box\, yearn[\beta \Leftarrow]$ holds, which implies the second disjunct. If $[\beta \Leftarrow]$ does occur, then by $\varphi_{2.1}$, $[\beta \Leftarrow 1]$ occurs, which implies, by $\varphi_{1.1}$, the third disjunct $\Diamond(u = 1)$.

Here we introduce the following *eventual communication axiom*

$$\Box\Diamond\Big(ready([\gamma \Leftarrow]) \;\land\; ready([\gamma \Rightarrow])\Big) \;\to\; \Box\Diamond [\gamma \Leftarrow]$$

stated for each channel γ in the system. This axiom reflects the compassion requirement by which, if a sender to γ and a receiver from γ are simultaneously ready infinitely many times, then there should be infinitely many γ-communications. We can use this axiom to derive the following *matchmaker postulate*

$$\neg \diamondsuit \square \Big(yearn[\gamma \triangleleft] \ \wedge \ yearn[\gamma \triangleright] \Big),$$

which disallows computations in which a sender and receiver continually yearn for one another (but never communicate) from a certain point on. If we apply this axiom with respect to α and β, it rules out the first two disjuncts,

$$\square \Big(yearn([\alpha \triangleleft]) \ \wedge \ yearn([\alpha \triangleright]) \Big) \quad \text{and}$$

$$\diamondsuit \square \Big(yearn([\beta \triangleleft]) \ \wedge \ yearn([\beta \triangleright]) \Big),$$

in the disjunction.

Thus, with the help of the matchmaker postulate, which is always valid, we may infer $\diamondsuit(u = 1)$ from the conjunction $\varphi_1 \wedge \varphi_2$.

Resource Allocation Revisited

As our final example of a decomposition of a global specification into modular ones, we reconsider the problem of the resource allocator. This system was given a global specification in Section 4.6.

We first consider the version communicating by shared variables. We can view the system as consisting of several modules as depicted in Fig. 4.16. Module A represents the allocator, while the array of modules $C[1], \ldots, C[m]$ represents the customers.

$$A :: \begin{bmatrix} \textbf{module} \\ \textbf{external in } r: \textbf{array } [1..m] \textbf{ of boolean} \\ \textbf{out} \qquad g: \textbf{array } [1..m] \textbf{ of boolean where } g = \text{F} \\ \text{Body}_A \end{bmatrix}$$

$$\|$$

$$\overset{m}{\underset{i=1}{\|}} \ C[i] :: \begin{bmatrix} \textbf{module} \\ \textbf{external in } g[i]: \textbf{boolean} \\ \textbf{out} \qquad r[i]: \textbf{boolean where } r[i] = \text{F} \\ \text{Body}_{C[i]} \end{bmatrix}$$

Fig. 4.16. Decomposition of the system into modules.

For completeness and convenience we list here the clauses forming the global specification. To simplify the discussion, we present only some of the originally presented clauses.

$$\text{S1:} \quad \Box\left(\left(\sum_{i=1}^{m} g[i]\right) \le 1\right).$$

This formula states mutual exclusion, i.e., at most one $g[i]$ can be true (equal 1) at each state.

The following four clauses ensure that the changes in the variables $r[i]$ and $g[i]$ follow the cyclic order

$$r[i] \uparrow \qquad g[i] \uparrow \qquad r[i] \downarrow \qquad g[i] \downarrow.$$

$$\text{S2:} \quad \neg g[i] \;\Rightarrow\; (\neg g[i]) \; \mathcal{W} \; (r[i] \wedge \neg g[i])$$

$$\text{S3:} \quad r[i] \;\Rightarrow\; r[i] \; \mathcal{W} \; (r[i] \wedge g[i])$$

$$\text{S4:} \quad g[i] \;\Rightarrow\; g[i] \; \mathcal{W} \; (\neg r[i] \wedge g[i])$$

$$\text{S5:} \quad \neg r[i] \;\Rightarrow\; (\neg r[i]) \; \mathcal{W} \; (\neg r[i] \wedge \neg g[i]).$$

The following three clauses represent the global progress requirements

$$\text{L1:} \quad r[i] \;\Rightarrow\; \Diamond g[i]$$

$$\text{L2:} \quad g[i] \;\Rightarrow\; \Diamond \neg r[i]$$

$$\text{L3:} \quad \neg r[i] \;\Rightarrow\; \Diamond \neg g[i].$$

We proceed to present modular specifications for the customers and allocator that, together, will imply the global specification represented earlier.

Modular Specification for Customer $C[i]$

Let us consider customer $C[i]$. In Fig. 4.17 we present a possible implementation of a customer module $C[i]$. This implementation is not intended as a binding representation but rather as a yardstick against which we can measure the feasibility of the modular specification we are about to develop.

The program contains a noncritical section in which activity that does not need the resource is carried out and a critical section in which activity that needs the resource is performed. The communication protocol involving $r[i]$ and $g[i]$ is self-explanatory and obviously maintains the cyclic order of the events

$$r[i] \uparrow \qquad g[i] \uparrow \qquad \text{Critical-activity} \qquad r[i] \downarrow \qquad g[i] \downarrow.$$

A possible methodology for constructing a modular specification, for a case in which the global specification is given as a list of simple requirements, is to inspect the requirements one by one and try to determine whether the considered module is the one responsible for maintaining this requirement. There is no simple recipe for detecting which module is responsible for maintaining a given property.

A very useful heuristic is available when we can view the property φ as constraining the behavior of a single variable, say, x. In this case the module

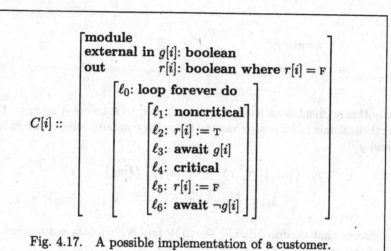

Fig. 4.17. A possible implementation of a customer.

responsible for maintaining φ is the one that can write x (assuming there is only one such module). This heuristic can be generalized to the case that φ constrains the behavior of several variables, all of which can be written only by a single module.

A simple example of this heuristic is to determine that it is the responsibility of the allocator A to maintain the mutual exclusion property $\Box\left(\left(\sum_{i=1}^{m} g[i]\right) \leq 1\right)$. This is because module A is the one that owns (can exclusively write to) the variables $g[1], \ldots, g[m]$.

Once a clause is identified as the responsibility of the module we are considering, we may have to modify it. This modification usually makes explicit the cooperation by the other modules that is necessary in order to maintain the property.

The first global requirement that seems to fall under the responsibility of $C[i]$ is

$$r[i] \;\Rightarrow\; r[i] \; \mathcal{W} \; (r[i] \,\wedge\, g[i]).$$

This property states that if $r[i]$ is true (equals T) at some point, it remains true at least until $g[i]$ is true (if ever). This is obviously a constraint on the execution of statements that set $r[i]$ to F and therefore is one of the liabilities of $C[i]$.

Unfortunately, as stated, the only way to implement this modular specification is never to set $r[i]$ to F. Consider, for example, the following segment of a module that attempts to implement the specification and yet set $r[i]$ to F.

external in $g[i]$**: boolean**

$\vdots$

m_3: **await** $g[i]$

m_4: $r[i] := \text{F}$

m_5:

Clearly this segment does its best not to set $r[i]$ to F before it senses a true $g[i]$. Nevertheless, this module also has the following computation (listing values of π, $r[i]$ and $g[i]$):

$$\cdots \ s_j:\ \langle\{m_3\},\ \text{T},\ \text{T}\rangle \ \xrightarrow{m_3}\ s_{j+1}:\ \langle\{m_4\},\ \text{T},\ \text{T}\rangle \ \xrightarrow{\tau_{\text{E}}}$$

$$s_{j+2}:\ \langle\{m_4\},\ \text{T},\ \text{F}\rangle \ \xrightarrow{m_4}\ s_{j+3}:\ \langle\{m_5\},\ \text{F},\ \text{F}\rangle \ \rightarrow\ \cdots$$

Observe that the formula $r[i] \rightarrow r[i]\,\mathcal{W}\,(r[i] \wedge g[i])$ does not hold at position $j+2$ of the computation.

Obviously, the intended meaning of the property we are discussing is to make sure that once $C[i]$ sets $r[i]$ to T, it maintains the value T at least until module A responds by setting $g[i]$ to T. Thus, it is sufficient to state this property only at the exact points at which $r[i]$ has just changed from F to T.

Consequently, we include in the modular specification of $C[i]$ the weaker requirement

$$\varphi_1[i]: \qquad r[i] \uparrow\ \Rightarrow\ r[i]\,\mathcal{W}\,(r[i] \wedge g[i]).$$

This formula requires the maintainance of $r[i]$ at T at least until $g[i]$ is true only from the points at which $r[i]$ has just changed from F to T.

An alternative formulation of this requirement is given by the nested unless formula

$$\neg r[i]\ \Rightarrow\ (\neg r[i])\,\mathcal{W}\,r[i]\,\mathcal{W}\,(r[i] \wedge g[i]).$$

This formula traces the behavior of $r[i]$ from a position at which it is false. It claims that, following such a position, $r[i]$ will remain false for a while (perhaps forever), but when it changes to true, it will remain true at least until $g[i]$ becomes true. It is not difficult to see that this formula is equivalent to $\varphi_1[i]$.

The next (and last) safety requirement that constrains a variable owned by $C[i]$ is

$$\neg r[i]\ \Rightarrow\ (\neg r[i])\,\mathcal{W}\,(\neg r[i] \wedge \neg g[i]).$$

This property is complementary to the previous one. It requires that if $r[i]$ is currently false, it should remain false at least until $g[i]$ is (becomes) false. As before, the modular version of this property is stated only at points of falling $r[i]$, i.e., points at which $r[i]$ has just changed from T to F

$$\varphi_2[i]: \quad r[i] \downarrow\ \Rightarrow\ (\neg r[i])\,\mathcal{W}\,(\neg r[i] \wedge \neg g[i]).$$

Next we inspect the list of global progress properties looking for properties that constrain variables owned by $C[i]$. The only such property is

$$g[i] \implies \Diamond \neg r[i],$$

claiming that $C[i]$ always releases the resource some time after it has been granted to it.

To make this into a modular specification, we observe that it is impossible to guarantee a response to a true $g[i]$ if it is not held true sufficiently long. Consequently we add to the modular specification of $C[i]$ the clause

$$\varphi_3[i]: \quad g[i] \, \mathcal{W} \, (\neg r[i]) \implies \Diamond \neg r[i].$$

This formula guarantees a response (resetting $r[i]$ to F) to a true $g[i]$ only if $g[i]$ remains true at least until the response is generated.

The complete modular specification for $C[i]$ is given by

$$\varphi[i]: \quad \varphi_1[i] \wedge \varphi_2[i] \wedge \varphi_3[i].$$

Modular Specification for the Allocator

Next we construct a modular specification ψ for the allocator module A. Again we scan the list of global properties and include in ψ modified versions of properties that constrain variables owned by A. It is an encouraging sign if we collect into ψ modified versions of all the properties that have not been collected into $\varphi[i]$.

Clearly, the safety property of mutual exclusion is completely under the responsibility of module A since it refers only to variables owned by A. We therefore include in ψ the clause

$$\psi_1: \quad \Box \left(\left(\sum_{i=1}^{m} g[i] \right) \leq 1 \right).$$

From the remaining safety properties, the relevant ones for A are those that govern the changes of $g[i]$. These are

$$\neg g[i] \implies (\neg g[i]) \, \mathcal{W} \, (r[i] \wedge \neg g[i])$$

$$g[i] \implies g[i] \, \mathcal{W} \, (\neg r[i] \wedge g[i]).$$

As discussed before, the corresponding modular specification should be stated only from the points of change. Consequently, we include in ψ the clauses

$$\psi_2: \quad (first \vee g[i] \downarrow) \implies (\neg g[i]) \, \mathcal{W} \, (r[i] \wedge \neg g[i])$$

$$\psi_3: \quad g[i] \uparrow \implies g[i] \, \mathcal{W} \, (\neg r[i] \wedge g[i]).$$

Note that in ψ_2 we have also included the first position of the computation as a position from which $g[i]$ is required to stay false at least until $r[i]$ becomes true. This represents a requirement of absence of unsolicited response.

Going over to the progress properties, there are two global progress properties that can be viewed as constraining the behavior of $g[i]$. They are

$$\neg r[i] \;\Rightarrow\; \Diamond \neg g[i]$$

$$r[i] \;\Rightarrow\; \Diamond g[i].$$

The first property requires that $g[i]$ is eventually reset to F in response to $r[i]$ being false. Making the usual modification that requires $r[i]$ to stay false long enough, we add to the specification the clause

$$\psi_4: \quad (\neg r[i]) \; \mathcal{W} \; (\neg g[i]) \;\Rightarrow\; \Diamond \neg g[i].$$

The situation is more complex for the second property, requiring that the resource is granted to $C[i]$, i.e., $g[i]$ set to T, in response to a request from $C[i]$, i.e., $r[i] = $ T. Since the modular specification is supposed to also hold for misbehaving customers, consider the following situation. Assume that, some time before a request from $C[i]$, customer $C[j]$, for $j \neq i$, has acquired the resource and not released it yet. Consequently, currently $r[j] = g[j] = $ T. Assume that $C[i]$ has made a request, i.e., $r[i]$ is T, but the rebelious $C[j]$ refuses to release the resource. What can the allocator do? It cannot reset $g[j]$ to F without violating ψ_2. It cannot set $g[i]$ to T without violating ψ_1. It seems that under such a situation we should relieve module A from the obligation to grant the resource to $C[i]$. Consequently, the corresponding clause added to ψ is

$$\psi_5: \quad r[i] \; \mathcal{W} \; g[i] \;\Rightarrow\; \left(\Diamond g[i] \;\vee\; \bigvee_{j \neq i} \Diamond \Box \, g[j] \right).$$

This property states that if $C[i]$ has made a sustained request, then either it will be granted the resource, or we can identify a rebelious $C[j]$ that holds the resource and refuses to release it forever. The latter case can be identified by $g[j]$ remaining true forever. Note that, due to ψ_4, the option of leaving $g[j]$ true forever cannot be misused by the allocator by preferring this option to granting the resource to $C[i]$. This is because, by ψ_4, the allocator can keep $g[j]$ true forever only if $C[j]$ does not reset $r[j]$ to F and holds it at F long enough for the allocator to sense it and respond by resetting $g[j]$ to F.

The complete specification for the allocator module is given by the conjunction

$$\psi: \quad \psi_1 \,\wedge\, \psi_2 \,\wedge\, \psi_3 \,\wedge\, \psi_4 \,\wedge\, \psi_5.$$

It can now be confirmed that the conjunction of the modular specifications

$$\psi \,\wedge\, \bigwedge_{i=1}^{m} \varphi[i]$$

implies each of the global properties that were listed earlier.

Global Properties Should Sometimes be Decomposed

When we considered the global specification of the resource allocator system, we commented that it is possible to replace the three progress requirements L1–L3 with the single requirement

L: $\quad \Box \Diamond (\neg r[i] \ \wedge \ \neg g[i])$.

While this provides a more succinct representation of the global specification it makes the decomposition into modular specifications more difficult. This is because a property such as L constrains at the same time variables owned by $C[i]$ and variables owned by A.

Indeed, if faced with a global specification whose only progress part is given by L, the first recommended step is to break L into the three requirements L1–L3, each of which constrains only one variable. Then we could follow the partitioning policy and decide which of the three should be allocated to $C[i]$ and which to A.

In **Problem 4.7**, the reader will consider a program that manages mutual exclusion by asynchronous message passing and provide a modular specification for its modules.

Problems

Problem 4.1 (prompt response)   page 289

In the text we discussed the example of a program P with an input variable x and output variable y. While discussing response properties, we formulated the requirements that each $x = 1$ is followed by a state at which $y = 2$, and each $x = 0$ is followed by a state at which $y = 0$. However, this specification allows a sluggish response.

Add a requirement that will ensure that a state in which $x = 1$ is followed by a state in which $y = 2$, which happens before x is changed back to 0. Similarly, require that the response to $x = 0$ comes before x is changed to a nonzero value. To which class do these properties belong?

Problem 4.2 (eventual latching)   page 292

Show the equivalence

$$\Diamond \Box (p \to \Box q) \ \sim \ [\Diamond \Box q \ \vee \ \Diamond \Box (\neg p)].$$

The formula on the left states that, from a certain point on, any occurrence of p causes an immediate and permanent locking of q. The formula on the right states that either from a certain point on, q holds permanently or p occurs only finitely many times. The equivalence shows the property specifiable by the formula on the left to be a persistence property.

Problem 4.3 (equivalence of two specification styles)   page 317

Consider two specifications of the safety part of a buffer system. The first specification φ: $\varphi_{\text{aur}} \wedge \varphi_{\text{nod}} \wedge \varphi_{\text{fifo}}$ is a conjunction of three future formulas, given by

$$\varphi_{\text{aur}}: \quad (\neg[\beta \leqslant m])\ \mathcal{W}\ [\alpha \leqslant m]$$

$$\varphi_{\text{nod}}: \quad [\beta \leqslant m]\ \Rightarrow\ \widehat{\Box}(\neg[\beta \leqslant m])$$

$$\varphi_{\text{fifo}}: \quad \left((\neg[\beta \leqslant m'])\ \mathcal{U}\ [\beta \leqslant m]\right)\ \rightarrow\ \left((\neg[\alpha \leqslant m'])\ \mathcal{W}\ [\alpha \leqslant m]\right)$$

The second specification ψ: $\psi_{\text{aur}} \wedge \psi_{\text{nod}} \wedge \psi_{\text{fifo}}$ is a conjunction of three canonical formulas, given by

$$\psi_{\text{aur}}: \quad [\beta \leqslant m]\ \Rightarrow\ \diamondsuit[\alpha \leqslant m]$$

$$\psi_{\text{nod}}: \quad [\beta \leqslant m]\ \Rightarrow\ \widehat{\boxminus}(\neg[\beta \leqslant m])$$

$$\psi_{\text{fifo}}: \quad \left([\beta \leqslant m] \wedge \widehat{\boxminus}(\neg[\beta \leqslant m'])\right)\ \Rightarrow\ \diamondsuit\left([\alpha \leqslant m] \wedge \widehat{\boxminus}(\neg[\alpha \leqslant m'])\right)$$

(a) Show that $\varphi_{\text{aur}} \leftrightarrow \psi_{\text{aur}}$ and $\varphi_{\text{nod}} \leftrightarrow \psi_{\text{nod}}$, but $\varphi_{\text{fifo}} \not\leftrightarrow \psi_{\text{fifo}}$. To show inequivalence of φ_{fifo} and ψ_{fifo}, display a model that satisfies one of the formulas but not the other. Does one of them imply the other?

(b) Show that the conjunctions φ and ψ are equivalent.

(c) Consider another canonical safety formula ψ'_{fifo} that attempts to capture the property of first-in-first-out ordering. This formula is given by

$$\psi'_{\text{fifo}}: \quad \left([\beta \leqslant m'] \wedge \diamondsuit[\beta \leqslant m]\right)\ \Rightarrow\ \diamondsuit\left([\alpha \leqslant m'] \wedge \diamondsuit[\alpha \leqslant m]\right)$$

Show that the conjunction φ is not equivalent to ψ': $\psi_{\text{aur}} \wedge \psi_{\text{nod}} \wedge \psi'_{\text{fifo}}$.

(d) Show the validity of the implication

$$(\chi_{\text{nid}} \wedge \chi_{\text{live}}) \rightarrow (\varphi \leftrightarrow \psi'),$$

where χ_{nid}, defined by

$$\forall m: [\alpha \leqslant m]\ \Rightarrow\ \widehat{\boxminus}(\neg[\alpha \leqslant m]),$$

expresses the restriction that no two input messages are identical and χ_{live}, defined by

$$\forall m: [\alpha \leqslant m]\ \Rightarrow\ \diamondsuit[\beta \leqslant m],$$

expresses the response requirement that every message appearing on α is eventually transmitted on β.

Problem 4.4 (unless and back-to)   page 321

Show the equivalence

$$(p_0 \Rightarrow p_1 \, \mathcal{W} \, p_2 \cdots p_n \, \mathcal{W} \, r) \; \sim \; ((\neg p_n) \Rightarrow p_{n-1} \, \mathcal{B} \, p_{n-2} \cdots p_1 \, \mathcal{B} \, (\neg p_0) \, \mathcal{B} \, r),$$

by establishing

$$(p_0 \Rightarrow p_1 \, \mathcal{W} \, p_2 \cdots p_n \, \mathcal{W} \, r) \; \sim \; \Box ((\neg p_0) \, \mathcal{W} \, p_1 \cdots p_n \, \mathcal{W} \, r)$$

$$(p_0 \Rightarrow p_1 \, \mathcal{B} \, p_2 \cdots p_n \, \mathcal{B} \, r) \; \sim \; \Box ((\neg p_0) \, \mathcal{B} \, p_1 \cdots p_n \, \mathcal{B} \, r)$$

and

$$\Box (q_1 \, \mathcal{W} \, q_2 \cdots q_m \, \mathcal{W} \, r) \; \sim \; \Box (q_m \, \mathcal{B} \, q_{m-1} \cdots q_1 \, \mathcal{B} \, r).$$

The nested unless formula $p_0 \Rightarrow p_1 \, \mathcal{W} \, p_2 \cdots p_n \, \mathcal{W} \, r$, appearing on the left, states that every p_0 is followed by a succession of a p_1 interval, a p_2 interval, and so on, which can be terminated only by an occurrence of r. The equivalence shows that this property is a safety property that also states that every occurrence of $\neg p_n$ is preceded by a succession of p_{n-1} interval, preceded by a p_{n-2} interval, and so on, until a $\neg p_0$ interval. The sequence may be interrupted earlier by an occurrence of r.

Problem 4.5 (eventually reliable channel)   page 329

Consider the formula $\Box \Diamond [\alpha \leqslant m] \rightarrow \Diamond [\beta \leqslant m]$, specifying an eventually reliable channel (from position 0). Show that this formula is actually a persistence formula.

Problem 4.6 (equivalence of specifications)   page 336

Let r_i, g_i be two propositions. Show that the formula

$$(\neg r_i \wedge \neg g_i) \Rightarrow (\neg r_i \wedge \neg g_i) \, \mathcal{W} \, (r_i \wedge \neg g_i)$$

is equivalent to

$$\neg g_i \Rightarrow (\neg g_i) \, \mathcal{W} \, (r_i \wedge \neg g_i).$$

Problem 4.7 (modular specification)   page 371

Consider the program presented in Fig. 4.18.

This program manages mutual exclusion by synchronous message passing, assuming that noncritical sections terminate. In the beginning, M_1 and M_2 synchronize by a message on channel α and then M_1 proceeds to execute its noncritical while M_2 proceeds to execute its critical sections. Eventually, both will terminate and will synchronize by a message on channel β, after which they will switch roles, M_1 executing critically while M_2 executes noncritically. The next interchange of roles requires another synchronization on α.

Write modular specifications φ_1 and φ_2 for M_1 and M_2, respectively, such that $\varphi_1 \wedge \varphi_2$ will imply the property of mutual exclusion: $\Box \neg (at\_\ell_4 \wedge at\_m_2)$. Make sure that the specification for module M_i, $i = 1, 2$, is valid over the computations of all programs that can be formed by taking the parallel composition

$$M_1 ::$$

module
external in β: channel of integer
out α: channel of integer
local u: integer

ℓ_0: loop forever do
ℓ_1: $\alpha \Leftarrow 1$
ℓ_2: Terminating noncritical
ℓ_3: $\beta \Rightarrow u$
ℓ_4: critical

$\|$

$$M_2 ::$$

module
external in α: channel of integer
out β: channel of integer
local v: integer

m_0: loop forever do
m_1: $\alpha \Rightarrow v$
m_2: critical
m_3: $\beta \Leftarrow 1$
m_4: Terminating noncritical

Fig. 4.18.   Mutual exclusion by synchronous message interchange.

of M_i with any other module that is interface compatible with M_i. In particular, the specification of M_i cannot refer to locations in its partner.

*Problem 4.8 (language theoretical view)   page 299

Consider a fixed vocabulary $V = \{p_1, \ldots, p_n\}$ consisting of the propositions $p_1, \ldots, p_n$, for some $n > 0$. Let Σ denote the set of states over V, to which we refer as Σ-*states*. Let Σ^* denote the set of all finite sequences of Σ-states, Σ^+ denote the set of all nonempty finite sequences of Σ-states, and Σ^ω denote the set of all infinite sequences of Σ-states.

We refer to a Σ-state also as a *letter*, and to an infinite sequence of letters as a *word*. In the following we assume that Σ contains at least three letters. We refer to a nonempty finite sequence of letters as a *finite word*. A *language* is a subset of Σ^ω, i.e., a set of words. A *finitary language* is a subset of Σ^+, i.e., a set of finite nonempty words.

For each $k \geq 0$, the finite word $\widehat{\sigma}$: $a_0, \ldots, a_k$ is called a *prefix* of the word σ: $a_0, \ldots, a_k, a_{k+1}, \ldots$, and we write $\widehat{\sigma} \prec \sigma$. The *concatenation* of the finite word σ_1: $a_0, \ldots, a_k$ and the word σ_2: $b_1, b_2 \ldots$, denoted by $\sigma_1 \cdot \sigma_2$, is the word $a_0, \ldots, a_k, b_1, b_2, \ldots$.

Languages and finitary languages may be combined, using the set operations of union and intersection, to form new languages and finitary languages. The *complements* of a language L and a finitary language M, denoted by $\overline{L}$ and $\overline{M}$, are defined as $\overline{L} = \Sigma^\omega - L$ and $\overline{M} = \Sigma^+ - M$.

For a finitary language M and a language L, we define the *language concatenation* $M \cdot L$ as consisting of all the words that can be represented as the concatenation $\sigma_1 \cdot \sigma_2$ for $\sigma_1 \in M$ and $\sigma_2 \in L$.

The *infinite iteration* of L, denoted by L^ω, consists of all the words that can be presented as the infinite concatenation $\sigma_0 \cdot \sigma_1 \cdot \sigma_2 \cdots$, where $\sigma_i \in L$, for $i = 0, 1, \ldots$.

To describe finitary languages and languages, we will use regular expressions and regular expressions extended by the notation e^ω, respectively. The expression e^ω describes the language $(L_e)^\omega$, where L_e is the finitary language described by the regular expression e. The expression e^+ describes the set of all words that can be represented as a finite concatenation $\sigma_1 \cdot \sigma_2 \cdots \sigma_k$, for $k > 0$, where $\sigma_i \in L_e$ for $i = 1, \ldots, k$.

We introduce four operators A, E, R, and P that construct languages out of finitary languages. Let Φ be a finitary language. We define as follows:

- The language $A(\Phi)$ consists of all words σ, such that

    every prefix of σ is in Φ.

For example, if $\Phi = a^+ b^*$, then $A(\Phi) = a^\omega + a^+ b^\omega$.

- The language $E(\Phi)$ consists of all the words σ, such that

    some prefix of σ is in Φ.

For example, $E(a^+ b^*) = a^+ b^* \cdot \Sigma^\omega$. In fact it is true for every finitary language Φ that $E(\Phi) = \Phi \cdot \Sigma^\omega$.

- The language $R(\Phi)$ consists of all words σ, such that

    infinitely many prefixes of σ are in Φ.

For example, $R(\Sigma^* b) = (\Sigma^* b)^\omega$. The words of this language are precisely those that have infinitely many occurrences of b.

- The language $P(\Phi)$ consists of all words σ, such that

    all but finitely many prefixes of σ are in Φ.

For example, $P(\Sigma^* b) = \Sigma^* b^\omega$. The words of this language are precisely those that, from a certain point on, have only the letter b.

Based on these four operators we define four classes of languages.

A language $\Pi \subseteq \Sigma^\omega$ is defined to be

- a *safety* language if $\Pi = A(\Phi)$ for some finitary Φ.

- a *guarantee* language if $\Pi = E(\Phi)$ for some finitary Φ.

- a *response* language if $\Pi = R(\Phi)$ for some finitary Φ.

- a *persistence* language if $\Pi = P(\Phi)$ for some finitary Φ.

It follows, for example, that the languages a^*b^ω, $a^*b \cdot \Sigma^\omega$, $(\Sigma^*b)^\omega$, and Σ^*b^ω are safety, guarantee, response, and persistence languages, respectively.

We refer to these four classes of languages as the *basic* classes.

- A language Π is called a *k-obligation* language, for $k > 0$, if

$$\Pi = \bigcap_{i=1}^{k} \Big(A(\Phi_i) \cup E(\Psi_i) \Big)$$

for some finitary languages Φ_i, Ψ_i, $i = 1, \ldots, k$. A language Π is an *obligation* language if it is a k-obligation language for some $k > 0$.

- A language Π is called a *k-reactivity* language, for $k > 0$, if

$$\Pi = \bigcap_{i=1}^{k} \Big(R(\Phi_i) \cup P(\Psi_i) \Big)$$

for some finitary languages Φ_i, Ψ_i, $i = 1, \ldots, k$. A language Π is a *reactivity* language if it is a k-reactivity language for some $k > 0$.

We refer to the classes of obligation and reactivity languages as the *compound* classes.

(a) (duality of the operators)

The four operators are not completely independent. Show that the operators A and E are dual in the sense that

$$\overline{A(\Phi)} = E(\overline{\Phi}) \quad \text{and} \quad \overline{E(\Phi)} = A(\overline{\Phi}).$$

Show that the operators R and P are also dual

$$\overline{R(\Phi)} = P(\overline{\Phi}) \quad \text{and} \quad \overline{P(\Phi)} = R(\overline{\Phi}).$$

(b) (duality among the basic classes)

Show that

- a language Π is a safety language iff $\overline{\Pi}$ is a guarantee language.

- a language Π is a response language iff $\overline{\Pi}$ is a persistence language.

(c) (closure of the basic classes)

Show that the classes of safety, guarantee, response, and persistence languages are closed under union and intersection.

For example, let us show that the class of guarantee languages is closed under intersection. Let $\Pi_1 = E(\Phi_1)$ and $\Pi_2 = E(\Phi_2)$, where Φ_1 and Φ_2 are finitary languages. Define $\Phi = (\Phi_1 \cdot \Sigma^*) \cap (\Phi_2 \cdot \Sigma^*)$. Clearly a finite word belongs to Φ iff it has a prefix belonging to Φ_1 and a prefix belonging to Φ_2. It follows that $\Pi = E(\Phi)$ is a guarantee language, consisting of all the words that have a prefix in Φ_1 and a prefix in Φ_2, i.e., $\Pi = \Pi_1 \cap \Pi_2$.

(d) (disjunctive forms for obligation and reactivity)

The definitions given for the classes of obligation and reactivity languages use a conjunctive normal form, i.e., represent a language as intersection of unions. A dual disjunctive form also exists. Show that

- Π is an obligation language iff

$$\Pi = \bigcup_{i=1}^{k} \left(A(\Phi_i) \cap E(\Psi_i) \right)$$

  for some finitary languages $\Phi_i, \Psi_i, i = 1, \ldots, k$.

- Π is a reactivity language iff

$$\Pi = \bigcup_{i=1}^{k} \left(R(\Phi_i) \cap P(\Psi_i) \right)$$

  for some finitary languages $\Phi_i, \Psi_i, i = 1, \ldots, k$.

In proving these results, you may use the closure properties of the basic classes.

(e) (closure and duality of the compound classes)

Show that the classes of obligation and reactivity languages are closed under union, intersection, and complementation and that they are self-dual.

(f) (characterization of the safety and guarantee classes)

For a language Π, let $Pref(\Pi)$ denote the set of all prefixes of words in Π. Show that Π is a safety language iff

$$\Pi = A\big(Pref(\Pi)\big).$$

Derive a similar characterization for the class of guarantee languages. Use these characterizations to show that the language $(a + b)^* b^\omega$ is not a safety language and that the language ab^ω is not a guarantee language.

(g) (safety and guarantee strictly included in the obligation class)

Show that the classes of safety and guarantee languages are strictly contained in the class of 1-obligation languages. To show strictness, argue that the 1-obligation language $a^\omega + \Sigma^* b \Sigma^\omega$ is neither a safety nor a guarantee language.

(h) (obligation strictly included in the response and persistence classes)

Show that the class of obligation languages is strictly contained in the classes of response and persistence languages. Strictness is established by showing that neither $L_R \colon (\Sigma^* b)^\omega$ nor $L_P \colon \Sigma^* b^\omega$ are k-obligation properties for any $k > 0$.

We sketch the proof for L_R. Assume to the contrary, that

$$L_R = \bigcap_{i=1}^{k} \left(A(\Phi_i) \cup E(\Psi_i) \right)$$

for some finitary languages $\Phi_i, \Psi_i, i = 1, \ldots, k$.

Let $\sigma_1 = a^\omega$. Since $a^\omega \notin L_R$, there must exist some $i_1 \in \{1..k\}$ and a prefix $b_1 \prec \sigma_1$ such that $b_1 \notin \Phi_{i_1}$. Consider the word $b_1 \cdot b^\omega$. Since this word belongs to $L_R = (\Sigma^* b)^\omega$ but contains a prefix not in Φ_{i_1}, it must contain a prefix $g_1 \in \Psi_{i_1}$. Without loss of generality, we may assume that $b_1 \prec g_1$. Clearly, any word containing g_1 as a prefix, belongs to $A(\Phi_{i_1}) \cup E(\Psi_{i_1})$. Next, consider the word $\sigma_2 = g_1 \cdot a^\omega$. Since $\sigma_2 \notin L_R$, there must exists some $i_2 \in \{1..k\}, i_2 \neq i_1$, and a prefix $b_2 \prec \sigma_2$ such that $b_2 \notin \Phi_{i_2}$. Without loss of generality, we may assume that $g_1 \prec b_2$. In this way we create a sequence of prefixes

$$b_1 \prec g_1 \prec b_2 \prec g_2 \prec \cdots \prec b_k \prec g_k,$$

such that each g_j contains prefixes that are in Ψ_i for j distinct values of i. In particular, g_k contains prefixes of $\Psi_1, \ldots, \Psi_k$. It follows that every word having g_k as a prefix must belong to L_R. However, this is not true for $g_k \cdot a^\omega$, which contradicts the assumption that L_R is an obligation language.

(i) (response and persistence strictly included in the reactivity class)

Show that the classes of response and persistence languages are strictly contained in the class of reactivity languages. To establish strictness, show first that $\Sigma^* (a^* b)^\omega$ is a 2-reactivity language, and prove that this language is neither a response nor a persistence language.

Part of the proof may be based on showing that if $\Sigma^* (a^* b)^\omega = R(\Phi)$, we could construct a word σ, which has an infinite sequence of prefixes

$$g_1 \prec g_1 \cdot c \prec g_2 \prec g_2 \cdot c \prec \cdots,$$

such that $g_1, g_2, \ldots \in \Phi$. This shows that $\sigma \in R(\Phi)$, but having infinitely many c's it does not belong to $\Sigma^* (a^* b)^\omega$.

Problem 4.9 (relating languages to properties)   page 299

We consider temporal formulas over the vocabulary V (introduced in Problem 4.8). Clearly, for each Σ-state (letter) a there exists a state formula χ_a over

V, which is true on a and false on all other states. When there is no danger of ambiguity, we may denote χ_a simply as a.

For a temporal formula p, denote by $sat(p)$ the set of all words (infinite sequences of states) that satisfy p. A language L is said to be *specifiable* (in temporal logic) if there exists a formula p such that $L = sat(p)$. For example, the language $(\Sigma \cdot b)^\omega$ can be specified by the formula $\square \diamond b$.

Let σ: $s_0, s_1, \ldots$ be a sequence of Σ-states and p a past formula. We say that the finite word $\widehat{\sigma}$: $s_0, \ldots, s_k$, which is a prefix of σ, *end-satisfies* p, denoted by $\widehat{\sigma} \dashv p$, if $(\sigma, k) \vDash p$. It is not difficult to see that this definition depends only on the prefix $\sigma[0..k]$ and not on any of the states beyond s_k.

For a past formula p, denote by $esat(p)$, the finitary language consisting of all finite words that end-satisfy p. A finitary language M is said to be *specifiable* (in temporal logic) if there exists a past formula p such that $M = esat(p)$. For example, the finitary language a^*b can be expressed by the past formula $b \wedge \widehat{\boxminus} a$, which claims that b holds now and a holds in all the preceding positions.

Let κ range over the names of the classes safety, guarantee, k-obligation, response, persistence, and k-reactivity.

(a) Show that a language that can be expressed by a κ-formula (i.e., a κ-property) is a κ-language. For example, if $L = sat(\square\, p)$ for some past formula p, then there exists a finitary language Φ such that $L = A(\Phi)$.

(b) Use the correspondence between κ-properties and κ-languages to show the strict inclusion of the safety and guarantee property classes in the class of 1-obligation properties, the strict inclusion of the obligation property class in the response and persistence property classes, and the strict inclusion of the response and persistence property classes in the class of 1-reactivity properties.

*Problem 4.10 (automata view)   page 299

An alternative formalism for specifying temporal properties is by finite-state automata on (infinite) words. A (Streett) *automaton* $\mathcal{A}$ consists of the following components:

- Q — a finite set of *automaton states*.

- $q_0 \in Q$ — an *initial* automaton state.

- $\delta\colon Q \times \Sigma \mapsto Q$ — a *transition function* specifying, for each $q \in Q$ and $s \in \Sigma$, the next state $\delta(q, a)$ to which the automaton moves when reading a while being at state q. For states q and q', we say that there is no transition from q to q' if there is no $a \in \Sigma$ such that $\delta(q, a) = q'$.

- $\mathcal{L}\colon ((R_1, P_1), \ldots, (R_m, P_m))$ — a list of *accepting pairs*. Each pair consists of $R_i \subseteq Q$, the ith set of *recurrent* states, and of $P_i \subseteq Q$ the ith set of *persistent* states.

Let $\sigma: a_0, a_1, \ldots$ be a word. We define the *run* of $\mathcal{A}$ over σ to be the infinite sequence of automaton states $q_0, q_1, \ldots$, each $q_i \in Q$, such that

- the first state of the run, q_0, is the initial state of $\mathcal{A}$.

- for every $i \geq 0$, $q_{i+1} = \delta(q_i, a_i)$.

Note that the automaton always starts at q_0, and a_0 causes it to move from q_0 to some q_1.

For a word σ, we define the *infinite visitation set* of σ, denoted by $vinf(\sigma)$, to be the set of automaton states that are visited infinitely many times by the run of $\mathcal{A}$ over σ. The automaton $\mathcal{A}$ *accepts* a word σ if, for each $i = 1, \ldots, m$, either $vinf(\sigma) \cap R_i \neq \phi$ or $vinf(\sigma) \subset P_i$.

We define the language *recognized* by an automaton $\mathcal{A}$, to be the set of all (infinite) words that are accepted by $\mathcal{A}$. A language L is defined to be *recognizable* if there exists an automaton that recognizes it.

We refer to an automaton with m accepting pairs as an *m-automaton*. For a 1-automaton, which is a also called a *plain automaton*, we refer to R_1 and P_1 as R and P, respectively.

We define the following classes of automata by introducing restrictions on their transition function and accepting pairs.

- A *safety automaton* is a plain automaton such that $R = \phi$ and there is no transition from $q \notin P$ to $q' \in P$. It follows that a run of a safety automaton is accepting iff all the states appearing in the run are in P.

- A *guarantee automaton* is a plain automaton such that $P = \phi$ and there is no transition from $q \in R$ to $q' \notin R$. It follows that a run of a guarantee automaton is accepting iff only finitely many of the states appearing the run are not in R.

- A *k-obligation automaton* is a k-automaton such that, for each $i = 1, \ldots, k$:

  - there is no transition from $q \notin P_i$ to $q' \in P_i$.

  - there is no transition from $q \in R_i$ to $q' \notin R_i$.

This definition implies that once a run of an obligation automaton exits P_i, it can never reenter P_i again, and once it enters R_i, it can never get out. We refer to a 1-obligation automaton also as a *simple obligation* automaton

- A *response automaton* is a plain automaton such that $P = \phi$.

- A *persistence automaton* is a plain automaton such that $R = \phi$.

- A *k-reactivity automaton* is any unrestricted k-automaton. We refer to a 1-reactivity automaton also as a *simple reactivity* automaton.

(a) (example automata)

Assume $\Sigma = \{a, b, c\}$. Construct the following:

1. a safety automaton recognizing the property specifiable by the formula $a \, \mathcal{W} \, b$, i.e., the language $a^\omega + a^* \cdot b \cdot \Sigma^\omega$.

2. a guarantee automaton recognizing the property $a \, \mathcal{U} \, b$.

3. a simple obligation automaton recognizing the property $a \mathcal{W} (\Diamond b)$.

4. a 2-obligation automaton recognizing the property $\Box (a \vee b) \wedge \Diamond b$.

5. a response automaton recognizing the property $\Box \Diamond a \wedge \Box \Diamond b$.

6. a persistence automaton recognizing the property $\Diamond \Box (a \vee c) \vee \Diamond \Box (b \vee c)$.

7. a simple reactivity automaton recognizing the property $\Box \Diamond a \rightarrow \Box \Diamond b$.

8. a 2-reactivity automaton recognizing the property $\Box \Diamond b \wedge \Diamond \Box (a \vee b)$.

(b) (k-ranked automata)

For $k > 0$, we define a *k-ranked* automaton to be a plain automaton, in which each state $q \in Q$ has a rank $\rho(q)$, $1 \le \rho(q) \le k$, such that:

-   there is a transition from q to q' only if $\rho(q) \ge \rho(q')$.
-   there is a transition from $q \notin P$ to $q' \in P$ only if $\rho(q) > \rho(q')$.
-   there is a transition from $q \in R$ to a state $q' \notin R$ only if $\rho(q) > \rho(q')$.

This definition leads to the fact that a run can enter P or exit R at most $k - 1$ times. It is easy to see that the case of $k = 1$ corresponds to the definition of a simple obligation automaton.

Show that a language is recognized by a k-ranked automaton iff it is recognized by a k-obligation automaton. Construct a 2-ranked automaton recognizing the property $\Box (a \vee b) \wedge \Diamond b$.

(c) (a κ-automaton recognizes a κ-language)

Let κ range over safety, guarantee, k-obligation, response, persistence, k-reactivity. Show that the language recognized by a κ-automaton is a κ-language.

We will show this for the case of safety. Consider an automaton $\mathcal{A}$. For each state $q \in Q$, let M_q be the finitary language consisting of all the finite words $\hat{\sigma}$ that cause the automaton to move from q_0 to q while reading $\hat{\sigma}$. Define M_R [respectively, M_P] to be the union of M_q for all $q \in R$ [respectively, $q \in P$].

Let $\mathcal{A}$ be a safety automaton. Clearly, a word σ is accepted by $\mathcal{A}$ iff the run of $\mathcal{A}$ over σ visits only P-states, which means that all prefixes of σ belong to M_P. Thus, the language recognized by $\mathcal{A}$ can be represented as $A(M_P)$ and is, therefore, a safety language. Use similar techniques for the other classes.

(d) (a degenerate case)

Show that any language recognizable by an m-automaton, such that either $R_1 = \cdots = R_m = \phi$ or $P_1 = \cdots = P_m = \phi$ is recognizable by a plain automaton.

**Problem 4.11 (identifying the class of a recognizable language)   page 299

In this problem we will consider the following question: Given an automaton recognizing a language L, find the lowest class to which L belongs.

We start with the safety class. Consider an automaton $\mathcal{A}$. Let L be the language recognized by $\mathcal{A}$. Without loss of generality, we can assume that all states in Q are reachable from q_0. A set of states $S \subseteq Q$ is called *strongly connected* if, for every two states $q, q' \in S$, there exists a directed path (consisting of transitions) from q to q' that only passes through states of S. Clearly, for every strongly connected S there exists a word σ such that $vinf(\sigma) = S$.

A strongly connected set S is called a *strongly connected accepting set* (an SCA for short) if $vinf(\sigma) = S$ for some $\sigma \in L$. It is called a *strongly connected rejecting set* (an SCR for short) if $vinf(\sigma) = S$ for some $\sigma \notin L$.

An automaton state $q \in Q$ is called *hopeful* if it appears in a run over a word in L. Otherwise, q is called *hopeless*. We can check that a state q is hopeful by finding a path in the automaton from q to some state belonging to an SCA. It is not difficult to see that there can be no transition from a hopeless state to a hopeful one.

Let H denote the set of all hopeful states in Q. We claim that L is a safety language iff

For every strongly connected S, S is an SCA iff $S \subseteq H$.

If L is found to be a safety language, we can modify the automaton by redefining $R' = \phi$ and $P' = H$ and obtain a safety automaton $\mathcal{A}'$, which recognizes L.

Extend this result for the other classes. Let κ range over guarantee, k-obligation, response, and 1-reactivity. Prove the following characterizations for automata recognizing a language L of class κ and show that L can also be recognized by a κ-automaton.

(a) A state q is called a *winner* if there exists no path from q to a state in an SCR. Let W denote the set of all winner states. Show that L is a guarantee language iff

for every strongly connected S, S is an SCA iff $S \cap W \neq \phi$.

Show that if L is a guarantee language, there exists a guarantee automaton recognizing it.

(b) Show that L is a response language iff

every strongly connected subset of an SCA is an SCA.

Show that if L is a response language, there exists a response automaton recognizing it.

(c) Show that L is a persistence language iff

> every strongly connected superset of an SCA S (i.e., every S' such that $S' \supseteq S$) is an SCA.

Show that if L is a persistence language, there exists a persistence automaton recognizing it.

(d) Show that L is a 1-reactivity language iff

> for every SCA S, either every strongly connected subset of S is an SCA or every strongly connected superset of S is an SCA.

Show that if L is a 1-reactivity language, there exists a 1-reactivity automaton recognizing it.

(e) Give a similar characterization for the case that L is a k-obligation language. Show that there exists a k-obligation automaton recognizing L.

(f) Give a similar characterization for the case that L is a k-reactivity language. Show that there exists a k-reactivity automaton recognizing L.

For all the cases discussed earlier, assume that the given automaton $\mathcal{A}$ that recognizes L is a Streett automaton. Describe algorithms of time complexity polynomial in the size of Q and the number of pairs R_i, P_i, for determining the (minimal) class of the language recognized by $\mathcal{A}$.

Problem 4.12 (temporally specified automata)   page 299

An automaton is defined to be a *temporally specified automaton* (a *T-automaton* for short) if, for every state $q \in Q$, there exists a propositional past formula φ_q such that the set of finite words that cause the automaton to move from q_0 to q is precisely $esat(\varphi_q)$, the set of finite words that end-satisfy φ_q.

Not every automaton is a T-automaton. Consider an automaton $\mathcal{A}_0$ with states Q: $\{q_0, q_1\}$, and the transition function that yields $\delta(q_0, s) = q_1$ and $\delta(q_1, s) = q_0$, for every $s \in \Sigma$. It is clear that the finite words that lead from q_0 to itself are the words of even length, while the finite words that lead from q_0 to q_1 are the words of odd length. Since these sets of words cannot be specified by propositional temporal formulas, $\mathcal{A}_0$ is not a T-automaton.

Let κ range over safety, guarantee, k-obligation, response, persistence, and k-reactivity.

(a) Show that the language recognized by a κ-automaton is a κ-property.

An important relation holding between temporal formulas and automata is

> for every property Π specifiable by temporal logic, there exists a T-automaton recognizing Π.

(b) Use the preceding claim to show that if a language L of class κ is specifiable by temporal logic, then it is a κ-property, i.e., L can be specified by a κ-canonical formula.

**Problem 4.13 (standard formulas)   page 302

Let κ range over safety, guarantee, obligation, response, and persistence. Show that a property Π specifiable by a κ-standard formulas, as defined in Section 4.2, is a κ-property, i.e., there exists a κ-canonical formula specifying Π.

Problem 4.14 (computations of a synchronously communicating module) page 354

Define the computations of a module that communicates with its environment by synchronous message passing. The definition should be such that a formula φ is modularly valid for a module M iff φ holds over all computations of M.

Base your definition on the construction of a transition system S_M for a given module M. Unlike the cases of shared variables or asynchronous communication, we cannot use separate environment transitions that represent the possible actions of the environment. In the synchronous case, we should have

- a transition $\tau_{\langle \ell, \mathrm{E} \rangle}$ for each statement ℓ: $\alpha \Leftarrow e$ addressing a channel α that is declared as out, and

- a transition $\tau_{\langle \mathrm{E}, \ell \rangle}$ for each statement ℓ: $\alpha \Rightarrow u$ addressing a channel α that is declared as external-in.

Bibliographic Notes

Examples of the use of temporal logic for specifying program properties appear in almost all papers that recommend its use; samples are Pnueli [1977], Manna and Pnueli [1981b], Manna [1982], Hailpern and Owicki [1980], Hailpern [1982], Owicki and Lamport [1982], Koymans and de Roever [1983], Lamport [1983c], Lamport [1983d], Emerson and Clarke [1982], and many others.

In fact, some of these properties have been described in alternative formalisms that predate the use of temporal logic, such as Lamport [1977] and Francez and Pnueli [1978]. Lamport [1977] was the first to classify the properties of reactive systems into the classes of *safety* and *liveness*. As stated by Pnueli [1977], while safety properties can be conveniently expressed as the invariance of a first-order formula, liveness properties are the ones requiring an extended specification language, such as temporal logic.

The safety-progress classification of properties was briefly referred to by Lichtenstein, Pnueli and Zuck [1985] and fully described by Manna and Pnueli

[1990b]. The same hierarchy has many characterizations in various formalisms. It has been studied in the context of ω-automata by Landweber [1969], Wagner [1979], Arnold [1983], Kaminski [1985], Hoogeboom and Rozenberg [1986], and Staiger [1987].

As previously mentioned, the classification of properties into *safety* and *liveness* was proposed by Lamport [1977]. Semantic characterization of the safety class was given by Lamport [1985d]. Semantic characterization of the liveness class was provided by Alpern and Schneider [1985]. Syntactic characterization of the safety and liveness properties recognizable by ω-automata was given by Alpern and Schneider [1987b]. Sistla [1985] provided a full characterization of safety properties specifiable by future propositional temporal logic and a partial characterization of the liveness properties specifiable in that language.

According to Kamp [1968] and Gabbay, Pnueli, Shelah and Stavi [1980a], both propositional temporal logic and its future fragment have the same expressive power as the first-order monadic theory of linear order. McNaughton and Papert [1971] establishes an equivalence between this first-order language and several other formalisms in their ability to define languages of finite words. The most important of these formalisms are star-free regular expressions and counter-free automata. These results were extended to show expressive equivalence over infinitary languages by Ladner [1977], Thomas [1979], Thomas [1981], Perrin [1984], Arnold [1985], Perrin [1985], Perrin and Pin [1986]. For a survey of these topics consult Thomas [1990].

Wolper [1983] pointed out that even simple examples, such as the parity property discussed in the text, cannot be specified by unquantified temporal logic, but can be specified by automata. He proceeded to show that when we add to the temporal language grammar operators (equivalently fixpoints) we obtain a more powerful language which is the same as that of full ω-automata or, as shown by Büchi [1960], has the expressive power of the weak second-order monadic theory of a single successor (S1S).

Assertional specifications methods such as first-order logic Manna [1969a, 1969b], *Hoare's logic* [1969], or the *predicate transformers* of Dijkstra [1975, 1976], were designed for specifying properties of terminating sequential programs. Consequently they provide natural expression of properties such as partial and total correctness.

When the associated proof methods were extended to deal with concurrent programs by Owicki and Gries [1976b] (see also Owicki and Gries [1976a]), it was soon realized that the proof outlines constructed in a verification of a concurrent program provide information about assertions that hold not only on termination of the program but also at intermediate points in the execution. Thus, a proof outline can be interpreted as stating invariance of some assertions throughout the computation.

This fact has been used by Lamport [1980b] and Lamport and Schneider [1984] for deriving proofs of safety properties by assertional methods. Assertional proof methods for message passing were developed by Apt, Francez and de Roever [1980], Levin and Gries [1981], and Sounderarajan [1984] for the synchronous (CSP) case and by Misra and Chandy [1981] for the asynchronous case. Misra and Chandy [1982] proposed an assertional method for specifying and proving both safety and selected liveness properties of message-passing systems.

The interested reader is referred to de Roever [1985] and Hooman and de Roever [1986] for a systemtic examination of assertional approaches to the specification and verification of concurrent programs.

The important role of *auxiliary variables* for specification and verification of concurrent programs was pointed out by Owicki and Gries [1976b]. For message-passing systems, the use of *history variables* that record the list of communication events has been proposed by several researchers. History variables have been used in a temporal framework by Hailpern [1982], Hailpern and Owicki [1980], Schwartz and Melliar-Smith [1982], Nguyen, Gries and Owicki [1985], and Nguyen, Demers, Owicki and Gries [1986], and in an assertional framework by Misra and Chandy [1981], Misra and Chandy [1982], Zwiers, de Bruin and de Roever [1984], and Zwiers, de Roever and van Emde Boas [1985].

Our approach to temporal-logic specifications of message-passing programs is based on Barringer, Kuiper and Pnueli [1985]. The representation of asynchronous message-passing systems has been influenced by Nguyen, Demers, Owicki and Gries [1986] and Nguyen, Gries and Owicki [1985]. In particular, we adopted their recommendation that a specification of a module should refer only to *output* events, even those that occur on input channels.

The observation that a buffer with duplicate messages cannot be specified in temporal logic was first made by Sistla, Clarke, Francez and Gurevich [1982], and further elaborated by Sistla, Clarke, Francez and Meyer [1984]. Some suggestions for extensions of temporal logic that will solve this difficulty are discussed by Koymans [1987]. The notion of *data independence* discussed in Section 4.7, which is one of the possible solutions to message duplication, is taken from Wolper [1986].

The class of precedence properties and their expression by nested *unless* formulas were presented by Manna and Pnueli [1983b]. It has been realized only much later (see Problem 4.4) that precedence properties belong to the safety class. Lamport [1985f] raises the interesting question of the interpretation of precedence for mutual exclusion programs. In some sense, our recommendation to specify bounded overtaking instead of strict precedence, has been influenced by this observation.

The question of modular specification and verification of concurrent programs has been and still is one of the most active areas of research in the field. We mention again the surveys of de Roever [1985] and Hooman and de Roever [1986] covering the field of modular assertional specification and verification. It has long been understood that composition of specifications that consist purely of safety properties is easier than composition of general specifications that may contain some liveness properties. References to composition of specifications that may contain liveness include, among others, Misra, Chandey and Smith [1982], Barringer, Kuiper and Pnueli [1984], Nguyen, Demers, Owicki and Gries [1986], Nguyen, Gries and Owicki [1985], and Jonsson [1987b].

References

Abadi, M. and Z. Manna [1989]. Temporal logic programming. *J. Symb. Comp.*, 8(3):277–295.

Abadi, M. and Z. Manna [1990]. Nonclausal deduction in first-order temporal logic. *J. ACM*, 37(2):279–317.

Allen, J.F. [1984]. Towards a general theory of action and time. *Artificial Intelligence*, 23(2):123–154.

Alpern, B. and F.B. Schneider [1985]. Defining liveness. *Inf. Proc. Letters*, 21(4):181–185.

Alpern, B. and F.B. Schneider [1987]. Recognizing safety and liveness. *Distributed Computing*, 2:117–126.

Alur, R., T. Feder, and T.A. Henzinger [1991]. The benefits of relaxing punctuality. In *Proc. of the 10th Annual ACM Symp. on Princ. of Dist. Comp.*

Alur, R. and T.A. Henzinger [1989]. A really temporal logic. *Proc. 30th IEEE Symp. on Found. of Comp. Sci.*, 164–169, 1989.

Alur, R. and T.A. Henzinger [1990]. Real-time logics: Complexity and expressiveness. *Proc. 5th IEEE Symp. on Logic in Comp. Sci.*, 492–401.

Andrews, G.R. and F.B. Schneider [1983]. Concepts and notations for concurrent programming. *ACM Comp. Surveys*, 15(1):3–43.

Apt, K.R., N. Francez, and S. Katz [1988]. Appraising fairness in languages for distributed programming. *Distributed Computing*, 2:226–241.

Apt, K.R., N. Francez, and W.-P. de Roever [1980]. A proof system for communicating sequential processes. *ACM Trans. on Prog. Lang. and Sys.*, 2:359–385.

Apt, K.R. and E.R. Olderog [1983]. Proof rules and transformation dealing with fairness. *Sci. Comp. Prog.*, 3:65–100.

Apt, K.R. and G.D. Plotkin [1986]. Countable nondeterminism and random assignment. *J. ACM*, 33(4):724–767.

Arnold, A. [1983]. Topological characterizations of infinite behaviors of transition systems. *Proc. 10th Int. Colloq. Lang. Prog.* Lec. Notes in Comp. Sci. 154, Springer-Verlag, Berlin, 28–38.

Arnold, A. [1985]. A syntactic congruence for rational ω-languages. *Theor. Comp. Sci.* 39:333–335.

Bacon, J. [1980].   Substance and first-order quantification over individual-concepts. *J. Symb. Logic*, 45:193–203.

Bandinet, M. [1989]. Temporal logic programming is complete and expressive. *Proc. 16th ACM Symp. on Princ. of Prog. Lang.*, 267–281.

Banieqbal, B. and H. Barringer [1986]. A study of an extended temporal logic and a temporal fixed point calculus. Tech. Report UMCS-86-10-2, Univ. of Manchester.

Barringer, H., R. Kuiper, and A. Pnueli [1984]. Now you may compose temporal logic specifications. *Proc. 16th ACM Symp. on Theory of Comp.*, 51–63.

Barringer, H., R. Kuiper, and A. Pnueli [1985]. A compositional temporal approach to a csp-like language. In *Formal Models of Programming*, E.J. Neuhold and G. Chroust (editors), IFIP, North-Holland, 207–227.

Barringer, H., R. Kuiper, and A. Pnueli [1986]. A really abstract concurrent model and its temporal logic. *Proc. 13th ACM Symp. on Princ. of Prog. Lang.*, 173–183.

Baudinet, M. [1989]. *Logic Programming Semantics: Techniques and Applications*. Ph.D. Thesis, Computer Science Dept., Stanford Univ., Stanford, CA.

Ben-Ari, M. [1990]. *Principles of Concurrent Programming*, Prentice-Hall, London.

Ben-Ari, M., Z. Manna, and A. Pnueli [1981]. The temporal logic of branching time. *Proc. 8th ACM Symp. on Princ. of Prog. Lang.*, Williamsburg, VA, 164–176. Also *Acta Informatica*, 20(3):207–26, 1983.

Bernstein, A.J. [1966]. Analysis of programs for parallel processing. *IEEE Trans. on Electronic Computers*, EC-15(5):757–763.

Best, E. [1984]. Fairness and conspiracies. *Inf. Proc. Letters*, 18:215–220.

Best, E. and C. Lengauer [1989]. Semantic independence. *Sci. Comp. Prog.*, 13(1):23–50.

Büchi, J.R. [1960]. Weak second order arithmetic and finite automata. *Zeitschrift für Math. Log. und Gründl. der Math.*, 6:66–92.

Burgess, J.P. [1982]. Axioms for tense logic II: time periods. *Notre Dame J. of Formal Logic*, 23(4):375–383.

Burgess, J.P. and Y. Gurevich [1985]. The decision problem for linear temporal logic. *Notre Dame J. of Formal Logic*, 26(2):115–128.

Campbell, R.H. and A.N. Habermann [1974]. The specification of process synchronization by path expressions. In *Proc. Int. Symp. on Operating Systems*, Rocquencourt. Lec. Notes in Comp. Sci. 16, Springer-Verlag, Berlin, 89–102.

Chandy, K.M. and J. Misra [1988]. *Parallel Program Design*. Addison-Wesley.

Chellas, B.F. [1980]. *Modal Logic: An Introduction*, Cambridge Univ. Press.

Clarke, E.M. and E.A. Emerson [1981]. Design and synthesis of synchronization skeletons using branching time temporal logic. In *Proc. IBM Workshop on Logics of Programs*. Lec. Notes in Comp. Sci. 131, Springer-Verlag, Berlin, 52–71.

Clarke, E.M., E.A. Emerson, and A.P. Sistla [1986]. Automatic verification of finite state concurrent systems using temporal logic specifications. *ACM Trans. on Prog. Lang. and Sys.*, 8(2):244–263.

Costa, G. and C. Stirling [1984]. A fair calculus of communicationg systems. *Acta Informatica*, 21:417–441.

Courtois, P.J., F. Heymans, and D.L. Parnas [1971]. Concurrent control with "readers" and "writers." *Comm. ACM*, 14(10):667–668.

Darondeau, P. [1985]. About fair asynchrony. *Theor. Comp. Sci.*, 37:305–336.

de Bruijn, N.G. [1967]. Additional comments on a problem in concurrent programming control. *Comm. ACM*, 8(9):137–138.

Dijkstra, E.W. [1965]. Solution of a problem in concurrent programming control. *Comm. ACM* 8(9):569.

Dijkstra, E.W. [1968]. Cooperating sequential processes. In *Programming Languages*, F. Genuys (editor), Academic Press, New York, 43–112.

Dijkstra, E.W. [1971]. Hierarchical ordering of sequential processes. *Acta Informatica*, 1:115–138.

Dijkstra, E.W. [1975]. Guarded commands, nondeterminancy, and formal derivation of programs. *Comm. ACM* 18(8):453–457.

Dijkstra, E.W. [1976]. *A Discipline of Programming*. Prentice-Hall, Engelwood Clifs, NJ.

Emerson, E.A. [1989]. Temporal and modal logic. In *Handbook of Theoretical Computer Science*, J. van Leeuwen (editor), North-Holland, Amsterdam, 995–1072.

Emerson, E.A. and E.M. Clarke [1981]. Characterizing correctness properties of parallel programs as fixpoints. In *Proc. 7th Int. Colloq. Aut. Lang. Prog.* Lec. Notes in Comp. Sci. 85, Springer-Verlag, Berlin, 169–181.

Emerson, E.A. and E.M. Clarke [1982]. Using branching time temporal logic to synthesize synchronization skeletons. *Sci. Comp. Prog.*, 2:241–266.

Emerson, E.A. and J.Y. Halpern [1985]. Decision procedures and expressiveness in the temporal logic of branching time. *J. Comp. Sys. Sci.*, 30(1):1–24.

Emerson, E.A. and J.Y. Halpern [1986]. 'Sometimes' and 'not never' revisited: On branching time versus linear time. *J. ACM*, 33:151–178.

Emerson, E.A. and C.S. Jutla [1988]. The complexity of tree automata and logic of programs. *Proc. 29th IEEE Symp. on Found. of Comp. Sci.*, 328–337.

Emerson, E.A., A.K. Mok, A.P. Sistla, and J. Strinivasan [1991]. Quantitative temporal reasoning. *Computer-Aided Verification 90*, Series in Discrete Mathematics and Theoretical Computer Science, Vol. 3, ACM/AMS, Providence, 136–145.

Emerson, E.A. and A.P. Sistla [1984]. Deciding full branching time logic. *Info. and Cont.*, 61:175–201. '

Francez, N. [1986]. *Fairness*. Springer-Verlag, New York.

Francez, N. and A. Pnueli [1978]. A proof method for cyclic programs. *Acta Informatica*, 9:133–157.

Fujita, M., S. Kono, H. Tanaka, and T. Moto-oka [1986]. Tokio: logic programming language based on temporal logic. In *Proc. 3rd Int. Cong. Logic Prog.*, E. Shapiro (editor). Lec. Notes Comp. Sci. 225, Springer-Verlag, 695–709.

Gabbay, D. [1976]. *Investigations in Modal and Tense Logics with Applications to Problems in Philosophy and Linguistics*. Reidel, Dordrecht, Holland.

Gabbay, D., A. Pnueli, S. Shelah, and J. Stavi [1980a]. On the temporal analysis of fairness. *Proc. 7th ACM Symp. on Princ. of Prog. Lang.*, 163–173.

Gabbay, D., A. Pnueli, S. Shelah, and Y. Stavi [1980b]. Completeness results for the future fragment of temporal logic. Manuscript.

Galton, A. [1987]. Temporal logic and computer science: an overview. In *Temporal Logics and Their Applications*, A. Galton (editor). Academic Press, London, 1–52.

Garson, J.W. [1984]. Quantification in modal logic. In *Handbook of Philosophical Logic*, Vol. II, D. Gabbay and F. Guenthner (editors), Reidel, 249–307.

Goldblatt, R. [1987]. Logics of time and computation. CSLI Lecture Notes 7, CSLI, Stanford Univ., Stanford.

Gries, D. [1981]. *The Science of Programming*. Springer-Verlag, New-York.

Hailpern, B.T. [1982]. *Verifying Concurrent Processes Using Temporal Logic*. Lec. Notes in Comp. Sci. 129., Springer-Verlag, Berlin.

Hailpern, B.T. and S.S. Owicki [1983]. Modular verification of computer communication protocols. *IEEE Trans. on Comm.*, COM-31, 1:56–68.

Halpern, J., Z. Manna, and B. Moszkowski [1983]. A hardware semantics based on temporal intervals. *Proc. 10th Int. Colloq. Aut. Lang. and Prog.* Lec. Notes in Comp. Sci. 154, Springer-Verlag, Berlin, 278–291.

Harel, D. [1986]. Effective transformations on infinite trees, with applications to high undecidability, dominoes, and fairness. *J. ACM*, 33(1):224–248.

Harel, D. [1987]. Statecharts: A visual formalism for complex systems. *Sci. Comp. Prog.*, 8:231–274.

Harel, E., O. Lichtenstein and A. Pnueli [1990]. Explicit clock temporal logic. *Proc. 5th IEEE Symp. on Logic in Comp. Sci.*, 402–413.

Henzinger, T., Z. Manna, and A. Pnueli [1991]. Temporal proof methodologies for real-time systems. *Proc. 18th ACM Symp. on Princ. of Prog. Lang.*, 353–366.

Hoare, C.A.R. [1969]. An axiomatic basis for computer programming. *Comm. ACM*, 12(10):576–580.

Hoare, C.A.R. [1974]. Monitors: An operating system structuring concept. *Comm. ACM*, 17(10):549–557.

Hoare, C.A.R. [1978]. Communicating sequential processes. *Comm. ACM*, 21(8):666–677.

Hoare, C.A.R. [1984]. *Communicating Sequential Processes*, Prentice-Hall, London.

Hoogeboom, H.J. and G. Rozenberg [1986]. Infinitary languages: Basic theory and applications to concurrent systems. In *Current Trends in Concurrency*, J.W. de Bakker, W.-P. de Roever and G. Rozenberg (editors). Lec. Notes in Comp. Sci. 224, Springer-Verlag, Berlin, 266–342.

Hooman, J. and W.-P. de Roever [1986]. The quest goes on: A survey of proof-systems for partial correctness of CSP. In *Current Trends in Concurrency*, J.W. de Bakker, W.-P. de Roever and G. Rozenberg (editors). Lec. Notes in Comp. Sci. 224, Springer-Verlag, Berlin, 343–395.

Hughes, G.E. and M.J. Cresswell [1968]. *An Introduction to Modal Logic*. Methuen, New York.

Jonsson, B. [1987]. Modular verification of asynchronous networks. *Proc. 6th ACM Symp. on Princ. of Dist. Comp.*, 152–166.

Kahn, G. [1974]. The semantics of a simple language for parallel programming. In *Proc. IFIP Congress 74*, North-Holland, Amsterdam, 471–475.

Kaminski, M. [1985]. A classification of ω-regular languages. *Theor. Comp. Sci.*, 36:217–220.

Kamp, J.A.W. [1968]. *Tense Logic and the Theory of Linear Order*. Ph.D. Thesis, Michigan State Univ.

Katz, S. and D. Peled [1987]. Interleaving set temporal logic. *Proc. 6th ACM Symp. on Princ. of Dist. Comp.*, 178–190.

Keller, R.M. [1976]. Formal verification of parallel programs. *Comm. ACM*, 19(7):371–384.

Knuth, D.E. [1966]. Additional commments on a problem in concurrent program control. *Comm. ACM*, 9(5):321.

Koymans, R. [1987]. Specifying mesage buffers requires extending temporal logic. *Proc. 6th ACM Symp. on Princ. of Dist. Comp.*, 191–204.

Koymans, R. and W.-P. de Roever [1983]. Examples of a real-time temporal logic specification. In *The Analysis of Concurrent Systems*, M.I. Jackson and M.J. Wray (editors). Lec. Notes in Comp. Sci. 207, Springer-Verlag, Berlin, 231–252.

Koymans, R., J. Vytopyl, and W.-P. de Roever [1983]. Real-time programming and asynchronous message passing. *Proc. 2nd ACM Symp. on Princ. of Dist. Comp.*, 187–197.

Kozen, D. [1983]. Results on the propositional μ-calculus. *Theor. Comp. Sci.*, 27:333–354.

Kripke, S.A. [1963]. Semantical analysis of modal logic I: normal propositional calculi. *Z. Math. Logik Grund. Math.* 9:67–96.

Kröger, F. [1977]. LAR: A logic of algorithmic reasoning. *Acta Informatica*, 8:243–246.

Kwiatkowska, M.Z. [1989]. Event fairness and noninterleaving concurrency. *Formal Aspects of Computing* 1(3):213–228.

Ladner, R.E. [1977]. Applications of model-theoretic games to discrete linear orders and finite automata. *Inform. and Cont.* 33:281–303.

Lamport, L. [1974]. A new solution of Dijkstra's concurrent programming problem. *Comm. ACM*, 17(8):453–455.

Lamport, L. [1976]. The synchronization of independent processes. *Acta Informatica*, 7(1):15–34.

Lamport, L. [1977]. Proving the correctness of multiprocess programs. *IEEE Trans. on Software Eng.*, SE-3(2):125–143.

Lamport, L. [1980a]. Sometimes is sometimes "not never" — on the temporal logic of programs. *Proc. 7th ACM Symp. on Princ. of Prog. Lang.*, 174–185.

Lamport, L. [1980b]. The 'Hoare logic' of concurrent programs. *Acta Informatica*, 14(1):21–37.

Lamport, L. [1983a]. Specifying concurrent program modules. *ACM Trans. on Prog. Lang. and Sys.*, 5(2):190–222.

Lamport, L. [1983b]. What good is temporal logic. In *Proc. IFIP 9th World Congress*, R.E.A. Mason (editor), North-Holland, 657–668.

Lamport, L. [1985a]. Basic concepts. In *Distributed Systems — Methods and Tools for Specification*. Lec. Notes in Comp. Sci. 190, Springer-Verlag, Berlin, 19–30.

Lamport, L. [1985b]. What it means for a concurrent program to satisfy a specification: Why no one has specified priority. *Proc. 12th ACM Symp. on Princ. of Prog. Lang.*, New Orleans, 79–83.

Lamport, L. and F.B. Schneider [1984]. The "Hoare logic" of CSP, and all that. *ACM Trans. on Prog. Lang. and Sys.*, 6(2):281–296.

Landweber, L.H. [1969]. Decision problems for ω-automata. *Math. Sys. Theory*, 4:376–384.

Lauer, P.E., M.W. Shields, and E. Best [1979]. Formal theory of the basic COSY notation. Computing Lab., Univ. of Newcastle upon Tyne, Tech. Report TR143.

Lehmann, D., A. Pnueli, and J. Stavi [1981]. Impartiality, justice and fairness: The ethics of concurrent termination. In *Proc. 8th Int. Colloq. Aut. Lang. and Prog.* Lec. Notes in Comp. Sci. 115, Springer-Verlag, Berlin, 264–277.

Lehmann, D. and S. Shelah [1982]. Reasoning about time and chance. *Info. and Cont.*, 53(3):165–198.

Levin, G.M. and D. Gries [1981]. A proof technique for communicating sequential processes. *Acta Informatica*, 15:281–302.

Lichtenstein, O. [1990]. *Decidability, Completeness, and Extensions of Linear Time Temporal Logic*. Ph.D. Thesis, Weizmann Institute.

Lichtenstein, O., A. Pnueli, and L. Zuck [1985]. The glory of the past. *Proc. Conf. on Logics of Programs*. Lec. Notes in Comp. Sci. 193, Springer-Verlag, Berlin, 196–218.

Lynch, N.A. and M.R. Tuttle [1987]. Hierarchical correctness proofs for distributed algorithms. *Proc. 6th Symp. on Princ. of Dist. Comp.*, 137–151.

Manna, Z. [1969a]. Properties of programs and the first-order predicate calculus. *J. ACM*, 16(2):244–255.

Manna, Z. [1969b]. The correctness of programs. *J. Comp. Sys. Sci.*, 3(2):119–127.

Manna, Z. [1982]. Verification of sequential programs: Temporal axiomatization. In *Theoretical Foundations of Programming Methodology*, M. Broy and G. Schmidt (editors), NATO Advanced Study Institutes Series, D. Reidel, Dordrecht, Holland, 53–102.

Manna, Z. and A. Pnueli [1979]. The modal logic of programs. *Proc. 6th Int. Colloq. Aut. Lang. Prog.* Lec. Notes in Comp. Sci. 71, Springer-Verlag, Berlin, 385–409.

Manna, Z. and A. Pnueli [1981]. Verification of concurrent programs: The temporal framework. In *The Correctness Problem in Computer Science*, R.S. Boyer and J.S. Moore (editors), Academic Press, London, 215–273.

Manna, Z. and A. Pnueli [1983a]. How to cook a temporal proof system for your pet language. *Proc. 10th ACM Symp. on Princ. of Prog. Lang.*, 141–154.

Manna, Z. and A. Pnueli [1983b]. Proving precedence properties: The temporal way. *Proc. 10th Int. Colloq. Aut. Lang. Prog.* Lec. Notes in Comp. Sci. 154, Springer-Verlag, Berlin, 491–512.

Manna, Z. and A. Pnueli [1983c]. Verification of concurrent programs: A temporal proof system. In *Foundations of Computer Science IV, Distributed Systems: Part 2*, J.W. de Bakker and J. van Leeuwen (editors), Mathematical Centre Tracts 159, Center for Mathematics and Computer Science, Amsterdam, 163–255.

Manna, Z. and A. Pnueli [1989a]. The anchored version of the temporal framework. In *Linear Time, Branching Time and Partial Order in Logics and Models for Concurrency*, J.W. de Bakker, W.-P. de Roever, and G. Rozenberg (editors). Lec. Notes in Comp. Sci. 354, Springer-Verlag, Berlin, 201–284.

Manna, Z. and A. Pnueli [1989b]. Completing the temporal picture. *Proc. 16th Int. Colloq. Aut. Lang. Prog.*, G. Ausiello, M. Dezani-Ciancaglini, and S. Ronchi Della Rocca (editors). Lec. Notes in Comp. Sci. 372, Springer-Verlag, Berlin, 534–558. Also in *Theor. Comp. Sci.*, 1991, 83(1):97–130.

Manna, Z. and A. Pnueli [1990]. A hierarchy of temporal properties. *Proc. 9th ACM Symp. on Princ. of Dist. Comp.*, 377–408.

McDermott, D.V. [1982]. A temporal logic for reasoning about processes and plans. *Cognitive Science*, 6:101-155.

McNaughton, R. and S. Papert [1971]. *Counter Free Automata*. MIT Press, Cambridge, MA.

McTaggart, J.M.E. [1927]. *The Nature of Existence*, Vol. I, Cambridge.

Milner, R. [1980]. *A Calculus of Communicating Systems*. Lec. Notes in Comp. Sci. 92, Springer-Verlag, Berlin.

Milner, R. [1989]. *Communication and Concurrency*. Prentice-Hall, London.

Misra, J. and K.M. Chandy [1981]. Proofs of networks of processes. *IEEE Trans. on Software Eng.*, SE-7(4):417–426.

Misra, J. and K.M. Chandy [1982]. A distributed graph algorithm: Knoth detection. *ACM Trans. on Prog. Lang. and Sys.*, 4(4):678–686.

Misra, J., K.M. Chandy and T. Smith [1982]. Proving safety and liveness of communicating processes with examples. *Proc. ACM Symp. on Princ. of Dist. Comp.*, Ottawa, Canada, 157–164.

Moszkowski, B.C. [1983]. *Reasoning about Digital Circuits*. Ph.D. Thesis, Stanford Univ. Tech. Report STAN-CS-83-970.

Moszkowski, B.C. [1986]. *Executing Temporal Logic Programs*. Cambridge Univ. Press.

Nguyen, V., A. Demers, S. Owicki, and D. Gries [1986]. A modal and temporal proof system for networks of processes. *Distributed Computing*, 1(1):7–25.

Nguyen, B., D. Gries, and S. Owicki [1985]. A model and temporal proof system for network of processes. *Proc. 12th ACM Symp. on Princ. of Prog. Lang.*, 121–131.

Ostroff, J.S. [1989]. *Temporal Logic for Real-Time Systems*. Advanced Software Development Series. Research Studies Press, John Wiley & Sons, Taunton, England.

Owicki, S. and D. Gries [1976a]. An axiomatic proof technique for parallel programs, *Acta Informatica*, 6(4):319–340.

Owicki, S. and D. Gries [1976b]. Verifying properties of parallel programs: An axiomatic approach. *Comm. ACM*, 19(5):279–284.

Owicki, S. and L. Lamport [1982]. Proving liveness properties of concurrent programs. *ACM Trans. on Prog. Lang. and Sys.*, 4(3):455–495.

Park, D. [1980]. On the semantics of fair parallelism. In *Abstract Software Specification*. Lec. Notes in Comp. Sci. 86, Springer-Verlag, Berlin, 504–524.

Park, D. [1981]. A predicate transformer for weak fair interation. *Proc. 6th IBM Symp. on Mathematical Foundations of Computer Science*, Hakone, Japan.

Park, D. [1983]. The fairness problem and nondeterministic computing networks. In *Foundations of Computer Science IV, Distributed Systems*, J.W. de Bakker and J. van Leeuwen (editors), Mathematical Centre Tracts 159, Center for Mathematics and Computer Science, Amsterdam, 133–161.

Perrin, D. [1984]. Recent results on automata and infinite words. *Mathematical Foundations of Comp. Sci.* Lec. Notes in Comp. Sci. 176, Springer-Verlag, Berlin, 134–148.

Perrin, D. [1985]. Variétés de semigroupes et mots infinis. *C.R. Acad. Sci. Paris*, 295:595–598.

Perrin, D. and J.E. Pin [1986]. First order logic and star-free sets. *J. Comp. Syst. Sci.* 32:393–406.

Peterson, G.L. [1983]. A new solution to Lamport's concurrent programming problem. *ACM Trans. on Prog. Lang. and Sys.*, 5(1):56–65.

Peterson, J.L. [1981]. *Petri Net Theory and Modeling of Systems*. Prentice-Hall, Englewood Cliffs, NJ.

Petri, C.A. [1962]. *Kommunikation mit Automaten*. Bonn: Institut für Instrumentelle Mathematik, Schriften des IIm No. 2. Also in English translation: *Communication with Automata*. Tech. Report RADC-TR-65-377, Vol. 1, Suppl 1, Applied Data Research, Princeton, NJ, 1966.

Pinter, S. and P.L. Wolper [1984]. A temporal logic for reasoning about partially ordered computations. *Proc. 3rd ACM Symp. on Princ. of Dist. Comp.*, 28–37.

Pnueli, A. [1977]. The temporal logic of programs. *Proc. 18th IEEE Symp. on Found. of Comp. Sci.*, 46–57.

Pnueli, A. [1981]. The temporal semantics of concurrent programs. *Theor. Comp. Sci.*, 13:1–20.

Pnueli, A. [1983]. On the extremely fair treatment of probabilistic algorithms. *Proc. 15th ACM Symp. on Theory of Comp.*, 278–290.

Pnueli, A. [1986]. Applications of temporal logic to the specification and verification of reactive systems: A survey of current trends. In *Current Trends in Concurrency*, J.W. de Bakker, W.-P. de Roever, and G. Rozenberg (editors). Lec. Notes in Comp. Sci. 224, Springer-Verlag, Berlin, 510–584.

Pnueli, A. and R. Rosner [1988]. A framework for the synthesis of reactive modules. *Proc. Int. Conf. on Concurrency: Concurrency 88*, F.H. Vogt (editor). Lec. Notes in Comp. Sci. 335, Springer-Verlag, Berlin, 4–17.

Pnueli, A. and L. Zuck [1986]. Verification of multiprocess probabilistic protocols. *Distributed Computing*, 1:53–72.

Pratt, V.R. [1981]. A decidable μ-calculus. *Proc. 20th IEEE Symp. on Found. of Comp. Sci.*, 421–427.

Priese, L., R. Rehrmann, and U. Willecke-Klemme [1987]. An introduction to the regular theory of fairness. *Theor. Comp. Sci.*, 53:217–237.

Prior, A. [1967]. *Past, Present, and Future*. Clarendon Press, Oxford.

Queille, J.P. and J. Sifakis [1983]. Fairness and related properties in transition systems — A temporal logic to deal with fairness. *Acta Informatica*, 19:195–220.

Reisig, W. [1985]. *Petri Nets: An Introduction*. EATCS Monographs on Theoretical Computer Science, Vol. 4, Springer-Verlag, Berlin.

Reisig, W. [1989]. Towards a temporal logic for causality and choice in distributed systems. In *Linear Time, Branching Time and Partial Order in Logics and*

Models for Concurrency, J.W. de Bakker, W.-P. de Roever and G. Rozenberg (editors). Lec. Notes in Comp. Sci. 354, Springer-Verlag, Berlin, 1989.

Rescher, N. and A. Urquhart [1971]. *Temporal Logic*. Springer-Verlag, New York.

Reynolds, J.C. [1978]. Syntactic control of interference. *Proc. 5th ACM Symp. on Princ. of Prog. Lang.*, 39–46.

Reynolds, J.C. [1989]. Syntactic control of interference: Part 2. *Proc. 16th Int. Colloq. Aut. Lang. and Prog.* Lec. Notes in Comp. Sci. 372, Springer-Verlag, Berlin, 704–722.

de Roever, W.-P. [1985]. The quest for compositionality — A survey of assertion-based proof systems for concurrent program, Part I: Concurrency based on shared variables. In *The Role of Abstract Models in Computer Science*, E.J. Neuhold (editor), North-Holland, 181–206.

Rosner, R. and A. Pnueli [1986]. A choppy logic. *Proc. 1st IEEE Symp. on Logic in Comp. Sci.*, 306–313.

Schwartz, R.L. and P.M. Melliar-Smith [1982]. From state machines to temporal logic: Specification methods for protocol standards. *IEEE Trans. on Comm.*, 30(12):2486–2496.

Schwartz, R.L., P.M. Melliar-Smith, and F.H. Vogt [1983]. An interval-based temporal logic. *Proc. Workshop on Logics of Programs*, E.M. Clarke and D.C. Kozen (editors). Lec. Notes Comp. Sci. 164, Springer-Verlag, Berlin, 501–512.

Shapiro, E. [1989]. The family of concurrent logic programming languages. *ACM Comp. Surveys*, 21(3):412–510.

Shoham, Y. [1988]. *Reasoning About Change*. MIT Press, Cambridge, MA.

Sistla, A.P. [1983]. *Theoretical Issues in the Design of Distributed and Concurrent Systems*. Ph.D. Thesis, Harvard Univ., Cambridge, MA.

Sistla, A.P. [1985]. On characterization of safety and liveness properties in temporal logic. *Proc. 4th ACM Symp. on Princ. of Dist. Comp.*, 39–48.

Sistla, A.P. and E.M. Clarke [1985]. The complexity of propositional linear temporal logic. *J. ACM*, 32:733–749.

Sistla, A.P., E.M. Clarke, N. Francez and Y. Gurevish [1982]. Can message buffers be characterized in linear temporal logic? *Proc. ACM Symp. on Princ. of Dist. Comp.*, 148–156.

Sistla, A.P., E.M. Clarke, N. Francez, and A.R. Meyer [1984]. Can message buffers be axiomatized in temporal logic? *Info. and Cont.*, 63(1,2):88–112.

Sistla, A.P., M.Y. Vardi, and P. Wolper [1987]. The complementation problem for Büchi automata with application to temporal logic. *Theor. Comp. Sci.*, 49:217–237.

Sounderarajan, N. [1984]. Axiomatic semantics of communicating sequential processes. *ACM Trans. on Prog. Lang. and Sys.*, 6:647–662.

Staiger, L. [1987]. Research in the theory of ω-languages. *J. Inform. Process. Cybernet.* 23:415–439.

Tarski, A. [1955]. A lattice-theoretical fixpoint theorem and its applications. *Pacific J. Math.*, 55:285–309.

Thomas, W. [1979]. Star-free regular sets of ω-sequences. *Info. and Cont.*, 42:148–156.

Thomas, W. [1981]. A combinatorial approach to the theory of ω-automata. *Info. and Cont.*, 48:261–283.

Thomas, W. [1990]. Automata on infinite objects. In *Handbook of Theoretical Computer Science*, J. van Leeuwen (editor), North-Holland, Amsderdam, 134–191.

van Benthem, J.F.A.K. [1983]. *The Logic of Time*. Reidel, Dardrecht.

Vardi, M.Y. [1985]. Automatic verification of probabilistic concurrent finite-state programs. *Proc. 26th IEEE Symp. on Found. of Comp. Sci.*, 327–338.

Vardi, M.Y. [1988]. A temporal fixpoint calculus. *Proc. 15th ACM Symp. on Princ. of Prog. Lang.*, 250–259.

Vardi, M.Y. and P. Wolper [1983]. Yet another process logic. *Proc. Workshop on Logics of Programs*, E.M. Clarke and D.C. Kozen (editors). Lec. Notes Comp. Sci. 164, Springer-Verlag, Berlin, 501–512.

Vardi, M.Y. and P. Wolper [1986]. An automata-theoretic approach to automatic program verification. *Proc. 1st IEEE Symp. on Logic in Comp. Sci.*, 332–344.

Wagner, K. [1979]. On ω-regular sets. *Info. and Cont.*, 43:123–177.

Wolper, P. [1983]. Temporal logic can be more expressive. *Info. and Cont.*, 56:72–99.

Wolper, P. [1986]. Expressing interesting properties of programs in propositional temporal logic. *Proc. 13th ACM Symp. on Princ. of Prog. Lang.*, 184–193.

Wolper, P., M.Y. Vardi, and A.P. Sistla [1983]. Reasoning about infinite computation paths. *Proc. 24th IEEE Symp. on Found. of Comp. Sci.*, 185–194.

Zwiers, J., A. de Bruin, and W.-P. de Roever [1984]. A proof system for partial correctness of dynamic networks. In *Proc. Workshop on Logics of Programs*, E. Clarke and D. Kozen (editors). Lec. Notes in Comp. Sci. 164, Springer-Verlag, Berlin.

Zwiers, J., W.-P. de Roever, and P. van Emde Boas [1985]. Compositionality and concurrent networks: Soundness and completeness of a proofsystem. *Proc. 12th Int. Colloq. Lang. Prog.* Lec. Notes in Comp. Sci. 194, Springer-Verlag, Berlin, 509–519.

Index to Symbols

General Index

priority, 317, 320.
private variable (to statement), 110.
process, 103.
  justice, 132.
  of text program, 43.
  of transition diagram, 12.
  schedule, 20.
process-deterministic (program), 18.
Prod (producer), 64, 82.
PROD-CONS, *see* program PROD-CONS.
producer-consumer problem, 76, 91, 102, *see also* program PROD-CONS.
product (of transitions), 53.
program, 12, 26, *see also* transition diagram, text language.
  ASYNC-PING-PONG, 360.
  BINOM (binomial coefficient), 112.
  BINOM, incorrect version, 56.
  BINOM, LCR version, 113.
  BINOM, text representation, 27.
  BINOM, transition diagram, 16.
  BINOM, with coarser granularity, 123.
  BINOM, with protected sections, 61, 306, 308, 312–313.
  BINOM, with reunited assignments, 122.
  BINOM, with semaphores, 115.
  CONTIG (contiguous communications), 166.
  FAIR-SERVER, using message passing, 85.
  FAIR-SERVER, using shared variables, 83.
  GCD (greatest common divisor), 27.
  IMP-BUF, 166.
  KEEPING-UP, 358.
  MUX-ASYNCH (mutual exclusion by asynchronous communication), 149, 164.
  MUX-PET1 (Peterson's algorithm

for mutual exclusion, Version 1), 318.
  MUX-SEM (mutual exclusion by semaphores), 60, 137.
  MUX-SYNCH (mutual exclusion by synchronous communication), 146.
  NODE-COUNT (node counting), 324.
  OBS-ORD (observing order of arrival), 99.
  PING-PONG, 345.
  PING-PONG-PING, 356.
  PROD-CONS (producer-consumer), 63, 310.
  PROD-CONS, LCR version, 119.
  PROD-CONS, pictorial representation, 78.
  PROD-CONS, using Petri net, 99.
  PROD-CONS, with asynchronous communication, 77.
  PROD-CONS, with bounded buffering, 77.
  PROD-CONS, with multiple producers and consumers, 69.
  PROD-CONS, with region statements, 67.
  PROD-CONS, with synchronous communication, 82.
  PROD-CONS, with two lists, 119.
  PROD-CONS, with unbounded buffering, 77.
  PROD-CONS, without buffering, 81.
  SB (strangely behaving), 94.
  SYNCH-BUF (implementation of buffer by synchronous communication), 165.
  TRY-MUX (mutual exclusion), 96.
  TURN (turn taking), 96.
program
  context, 48.
  dependent rule, 252.
  part (of deductive system), 248.
  validity, 245.